SELECTED CHAPTERS FROM

FILM ART

AN INTRODUCTION

EIGHTH
EDITION

DAVID BORDWELL ▪ KRISTIN THOMPSON
University of Wisconsin

 **Learning Solutions**

Boston Burr Ridge, IL Dubuque, IA New York San Francisco St. Louis
Bangkok Bogotá Caracas Lisbon London Madrid
Mexico City Milan New Delhi Seoul Singapore Sydney Taipei Toronto

Selected Chapters from Film Art: An Introduction, Eighth Edition

3 4 5 6 7 8 9 0   KNG KNG 9

ISBN 13: 978-0-07-729459-5
ISBN-10: 0-07-729459-9

Learning Solutions Specialist: Stephen Tomecek
Production Editor: Nina Meyer
Printer/Binder: King Printing

CONTENTS

PART THREE   Film Style

CHAPTER 4   The Shot: Mise-en-Scene   *112*

CHAPTER 5   The Shot: Cinematography   *162*

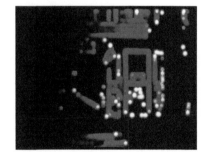

PART TWO

FILM FORM

Chapter 1 outlined some ways in which people, working with technology, make films. Now we can get a little more abstract and ask other questions. By what principles is a film put together? How do the various parts relate to one another to create a whole? Answering these questions will help us understand how we respond to individual movies and how cinema works as an artistic medium.

In the next two chapters, we will start to answer such questions. We assume that a film is not a random collection of elements. If it were, viewers would not care if they missed the beginnings or endings of films or if films were projected out of sequence. But viewers do care. When you describe a book as "hard to put down" or a piece of music as "compelling," you are implying that a pattern exists there, that some overall logic governs the relations among parts and engages your interest. This system of relationships among parts we shall call *form*. Chapter 2 examines form in film to see what makes that concept so important to the understanding of cinema as an art.

Although there are several ways of organizing films into unified formal wholes, the one that we most commonly encounter in films involves telling a story. Chapter 3 examines how *narrative form* can arouse our interest and coax us to follow a series of events from start to finish. Narrative form holds out the expectation that these events are headed toward dramatic changes and a satisfying outcome.

The Significance of Film Form

T he experience that art offers us can be intensely involving. We say that movies *draw us in* or *immerse us.* We get absorbed in a book or lost in a song. When we can't finish a novel, we say, "I couldn't get into it," and we say that music we don't like "doesn't speak to me," as if it were a sluggish conversational partner.

All these ways of talking suggest that artworks involve us by engaging our senses, feelings, and mind in a process. That process sharpens our interest, tightens our involvement, urges us forward. How does this happen? Because the artist has created a pattern. Artworks arouse and gratify our human craving for form. Artists design their works—they give them form—so that we can have a structured experience.

For this reason, form is of central importance in any artwork, regardless of its medium. The idea of artistic form has occupied the thinking of philosophers, artists, and critics for centuries. We can't do justice to it here, but some well-established ideas about form are very helpful for understanding films. This chapter reviews some of them.

The Concept of Form in Film

Form as System

Artistic form is best thought of in relation to the human being who watches the play, reads the novel, listens to the piece of music, or views the film. Perception in all phases of life is an *activity.* As you walk down the street, you scan your surroundings for salient aspects—a friend's face, a familiar landmark, a sign of rain. The mind is never at rest. It is constantly seeking order and significance, testing the world for breaks in the habitual pattern.

Artworks rely on this dynamic, unifying quality of the human mind. They provide organized occasions in which we exercise and develop our ability to pay attention, to anticipate upcoming events, to construct a whole out of parts and to feel an emotional response to that whole. Every novel leaves something to the imagination; every song asks us to expect certain developments in the melody; every film coaxes us to connect sequences into a larger whole. But how does this process work? How does an inert object, the poem on a piece of paper or the sculpture in the park, draw us into such activities?

Some answers to this question are clearly inadequate. Our activity cannot be *in* the artwork itself. A poem is only words on paper; a song, just acoustic vibrations; a film, merely patterns of light and dark on a screen. Objects do nothing. Evidently, then, the artwork and the person experiencing it depend on each other.

The best answer to our question would seem to be that the artwork *cues* us to perform a specific activity. Without the artwork's prompting, we couldn't start the process or keep it going. Without our playing along and picking up the cues, the artwork remains only an artifact. A painting uses color, lines, and other techniques to invite us to imagine the space portrayed, to compare color and texture, to run our eye over the composition in a certain direction. A poem's words may guide us to imagine a scene, to notice a break in rhythm, or to expect a rhyme. In our *Shadow of a Doubt* sequence (pp. 3-7), the dialogue and camerawork during Uncle Charlie's reflection on idle women cued us to see, very starkly, his cold menace, and this created dramatic tension. In general, any work of art presents cues that can elicit our involvement.

We can go further in describing how an artwork cues us to perform activities. These cues are not simply random; they are organized into *systems*. Let us take a system as any set of elements that depend on and affect one another. The human body is one such system; if one component, the heart, ceases to function, all of the other parts will be in danger. Within the body, there are individual, smaller systems, such as the nervous system or the optical system. A single small malfunction in a car's workings may bring the whole machine to a standstill; the other parts may not need repair, but the whole system depends on the operation of each part. More abstract sets of relationships also constitute systems, such as a body of laws governing a country or the ecological balance of the wildlife in a lake.

As with each of these instances, a film is not simply a random batch of elements. Like all artworks, a film has **form**. By film form, in its broadest sense, we mean the overall system of relations that we can perceive among the elements in the whole film. In this part of the book and in Part Three (on film style), we shall be surveying the elements that interact with one another. Since the viewer makes sense of the film by recognizing these elements and reacting to them in various ways, we'll also be considering how form and style participate in the spectator's experience.

This description of form is still very abstract, so let's draw some examples from one movie that many people have seen. In *The Wizard of Oz,* the viewer can notice many particular elements. There is, most obviously, a set of *narrative* elements; these constitute the film's story. Dorothy dreams that a tornado blows her to Oz, where she encounters certain characters. The narrative continues to the point where Dorothy awakens from her dream to find herself home in Kansas. We can also pick out a set of *stylistic* elements: the way the camera moves, the patterns of color in the frame, the use of music, and other devices. Stylistic elements depend on the various film techniques we'll be considering in later chapters.

Because *The Wizard of Oz* is a system and not just a hodgepodge, we actively relate the elements within each set to one another. We link and compare narrative elements. We see the tornado as causing Dorothy's trip to Oz; we identify the characters in Oz as similar to characters in Dorothy's Kansas life. Various stylistic elements can also be connected. For instance, we recognize the "We're Off to See the Wizard" tune whenever Dorothy picks up a new companion. We attribute unity to the film by positing two organizing principles—a narrative one and a stylistic one—within the larger system of the total film.

Moreover, our minds seek to tie these systems to one another. In *The Wizard of Oz,* the narrative development can be linked to the stylistic patterning. Colors

"Screenplays are structure."

— William Goldman, scriptwriter, *Butch Cassidy and the Sundance Kid*

"Because of my character, I have always been interested in the engineering of direction. I loved hearing about how [director] Mark Sandrich would draw charts of Fred Astaire's musicals to work out where to put the dance numbers. What do you want the audience to understand? How do you make things clear? How do you structure sequences within a film? Afterwards—what have you got away with?"

— Stephen Frears, director, *The Grifters*

identify prominent landmarks, such as Kansas (in black and white) and the Yellow Brick Road. Movements of the camera call our attention to story action. And the music serves to describe certain characters and situations. It is the overall pattern of relationships among the various elements that makes up the form of *The Wizard of Oz*.

"Form" Versus "Content"

Very often people think of "form" as the opposite of something called "content." This implies that a poem or a musical piece or a film is like a jug. An external shape, the jug, *contains* something that could just as easily be held in a cup or a pail. Under this assumption, form becomes less important than whatever it's presumed to contain.

Content included in form

We don't accept this assumption. If form is the total system that the viewer attributes to the film, there is no inside or outside. Every component *functions as part of the overall pattern* that engages the viewer. So we'll treat as formal elements many things that some people consider content. From our standpoint, subject matter and abstract ideas all enter into the total system of the artwork. They may cue us to frame certain expectations or draw certain inferences. The viewer relates such elements to one another dynamically. Consequently, subject matter and ideas become somewhat different from what they might be outside the work.

Consider a historical subject, such as the American Civil War. The real Civil War may be studied, its causes and consequences disputed. But in a film such as D. W. Griffith's *The Birth of a Nation,* the Civil War is not neutral content. It enters into relationships with other elements: a story about two families, political ideas about the Reconstruction, and the epic film style of the battle scenes. Griffith's film depicts the Civil War in a way that is coordinated with other elements in the film. A different film by another filmmaker might draw on the same subject matter, the Civil War, but there the subject would play a different role in a different formal system. In *Gone with the Wind,* the Civil War functions as a backdrop for the heroine's romance, but in *The Good, the Bad, and the Ugly,* the war aids three cynical men in their search for gold. Thus subject matter is shaped by the film's formal context and our perceptions of it.

Formal Expectations

We're now in a better position to see how film form guides the audience's activity. Why does an interrupted song or an uncompleted story frustrate us? Because of our urge for form. We realize that the system of relationships within the work has not yet been completed. Something more is needed to make the form whole and satisfying. We have been caught up in the interrelations among elements, and we want to develop and complete the patterns.

One way in which form affects our experience, then, is to create the sense that "everything is there." Why is it satisfying when a character glimpsed early in a film reappears an hour later, or when a shape in the frame is balanced by another shape? Because such relations among parts suggest that the film has its own organizing laws or rules—its own system.

Moreover, an artwork's form creates a special sort of involvement on the part of the spectator. In everyday life, we perceive things around us in a practical way. But in a film, the things that happen on the screen serve no such practical end for us. We can see them differently. In life, if someone fell down on the street, we would probably hurry to help the person up. But in a film, when Buster Keaton or Charlie Chaplin falls, we laugh. We shall see in Chapter 5 how even as basic an act of filmmaking as framing a shot creates a particular way of seeing. We watch a pattern that is no longer just "out there" in the everyday world; it has become a calculated part within a self-contained whole. Film form can even make us perceive things anew, shaking us out of our accustomed habits and suggesting fresh ways of hearing, seeing, feeling, and thinking.

To get a sense of the ways in which purely formal features can involve the audience, try the following experiment. Assume that "A" is the first letter of a series. What follows?

AB

"A" was a cue, and on this basis, you made a formal hypothesis, probably that the letters would run in alphabetical order. Your expectation was confirmed. What follows AB? Most people say "C." But form does not always follow our initial expectation:

ABA

Here form takes us a little by surprise. If we are puzzled by a formal development, we readjust our expectations and try again. What follows ABA?

ABAC

Here the main possibilities were either ABAB or ABAC. (Note that your expectations *limit* possibilities as well as select them.) If you expected ABAC, your expectation was gratified, and you can confidently predict the next letter. If you expected ABAB, you still should be able to make a strong hypothesis about the next letter:

ABACA

Simple as this game is, it illustrates the involving power of form. You as a viewer or listener don't simply let the parts parade past you. You enter into an active participation with them, creating and readjusting expectations as the pattern develops.

2.1 Dorothy pauses while fleeing with Toto at the beginning of *The Wizard of Oz*.

Now consider a story in a film. *The Wizard of Oz* begins with Dorothy running down a road with her dog (**2.1**). Immediately, we form expectations. Perhaps she will meet another character or arrive at her destination. Even such a simple action asks the audience to participate actively in the ongoing process by wondering about what will happen next and readjusting expectations accordingly. Much later in the film, we come to expect that Dorothy will get her wish to return to Kansas. Indeed, the settings of the film give *The Wizard of Oz* a large-scale ABA form: Kansas-Oz-Kansas.

Expectation pervades our experience of art. In reading a mystery, we expect that a solution will be offered at some point, usually the end. In listening to a piece of music, we expect repetition of a melody or a motif. (Songs that alternate verses and refrain follow the ABACA pattern we have just outlined.) In looking at a painting, we search for what we expect to be the most significant features, then scan the less prominent portions. From beginning to end, our involvement with a work of art depends largely on expectations.

This does not mean that the expectations must be immediately satisfied. The satisfaction of our expectations may be delayed. In our alphabet exercise, instead of presenting ABA, we might have presented this:

AB . . .

The ellipsis puts off the revelation of the next letter, and you must wait to find it out. What we normally call *suspense* involves a delay in fulfilling an established expectation. As the term implies, suspense leaves something suspended—not only the next element in a pattern but also our urge for completion.

Expectations may also be cheated, as when we expect ABC but get ABA. In general, *surprise* is a result of an expectation that is revealed to be incorrect. We do not expect that a gangster in 1930s Chicago will find a rocket ship in his garage; if he does, our reaction may require us to readjust our assumptions about what can happen in this story. (This example suggests that comedy often depends on cheating expectations.)

One more pattern of our expectations needs tracing. Sometimes an artwork will cue us to hazard guesses about what has come *before* this point in the work. When

Dorothy runs down the road at the beginning of *The Wizard of Oz,* we wonder not only where she is going but where she's been and what she's fleeing from. Similarly, a painting or photograph may depict a scene that asks the viewer to speculate on some earlier event. Let us call this ability of the spectator to wonder about prior events *curiosity.* As Chapter 3 will show, curiosity is an important factor in narrative form.

Already we have several possible ways in which the artwork can actively engage us. Artistic form may cue us to make expectations and then gratify them, either quickly or eventually. Or form may work to disturb our expectations. We often associate art with peace and serenity, but many artworks offer us conflict, tension, and shock. An artwork's form may even strike us as unpleasant because of its imbalances or contradictions. For example, experimental films may jar rather than soothe us. Viewers frequently feel puzzled or shocked by *Eat, Scorpio Rising,* and other avant-garde works (pp. 357–372). And we'll encounter similar problems when we examine the editing of Eisenstein's *October* (Chapter 6) and the style of Godard's *Breathless* (Chapter 11).

Yet even in disturbing us, such films still arouse and shape formal expectations. For example, on the basis of our experience of most movie stories, we expect that the main characters introduced in the first half of a film will be present in the second half. Yet this does not happen in Wong Kar-wai's *Chungking Express* (pp. 406–409). When our expectations are thwarted, we may feel disoriented, but then we adjust them to look for other, more appropriate, ways of engaging with the film's form.

If we can adjust our expectations to a disorienting work, it may involve us deeply. Our uneasiness may lessen as we get accustomed to a work's unusual formal system. Hollis Frampton's *Zorns Lemma,* for example, slowly trains the viewer to associate a series of images with the letters of the alphabet. Viewers often become quite absorbed in watching the series take shape as a cinematic picture puzzle. As *Chungking Express* and *Zorns Lemma* also suggest, a disturbing work can reveal to us our normal expectations about form. Such films are valuable because they coax us to reflect on our taken-for-granted assumptions about how a movie must behave.

There is no limit to the number of ways in which a film can be organized. Some films will ask us to recast our expectations in drastic ways. Still, our enjoyment of the cinema can increase if we welcome the unfamiliar experiences offered by formally challenging films.

Conventions and Experience

Our ABAC example illustrates still another point. One guide to your hunches was *prior experience.* Your knowledge of the English alphabet makes ABA an unlikely sequence. This fact suggests that aesthetic form is not a pure activity isolated from other experiences.

Precisely because artworks are human creations and because the artist lives in history and society, he or she cannot avoid relating the work, in some way, to other works and to aspects of the world in general. A tradition, a dominant style, a popular form—some such elements will be common to several different artworks. These common traits are usually called *conventions.* We looked briefly at one convention in a shot from *The Shining* (1.12), in which Kubrick prepared the audience for the use of the knife at the film's climax. *Genres,* as we shall see in Chapter 9, depend heavily on conventions. It's a convention of the musical film that characters sing and dance, as in *The Wizard of Oz.* It's one convention of narrative form that the conclusion solves the problems that the characters confront, and *Wizard* likewise accepts this convention by letting Dorothy return to Kansas.

From the spectator's standpoint, the perception of artistic form will arise from cues within the work and from prior experiences—experiences derived from everyday life and from other artworks. You were able to play the ABAC game because you had learned the alphabet. You may have learned it in everyday life (in a classroom or from your parents) or from an artwork (as some children now learn the alphabet from television cartoons). Similarly, we are able to recognize the journey pattern in *The Wizard of Oz*. We've taken trips and we've seen other films organized around this pattern (such as *Stagecoach* or *North by Northwest*), and the pattern is to be found in other artworks, such as Homer's *Odyssey* or J.R.R. Tolkien's *The Lord of the Rings*. Our ability to spot cues, to see them as forming systems, and to create expectations is guided by our real-life experiences and our knowledge of artistic conventions.

In recognizing film form, then, the audience must be prepared to understand formal cues through knowledge of life and of other artworks. But what if the two principles come into conflict? In ordinary life, people don't simply start to sing and dance, as they do in *The Wizard of Oz*. Very often conventions demarcate art from life, saying implicitly, "In artworks of this sort the laws of everyday reality don't operate. By the rules of *this* game, something 'unreal' *can* happen." All stylized art, from opera, ballet, and pantomime to slapstick comedy, depends on the audience's willingness to suspend the laws of ordinary experience and to accept particular conventions. It is simply beside the point to insist that such conventions are unreal or to ask why Tristan sings to Isolde or why Buster Keaton doesn't smile. Very often the most relevant prior experience for perceiving form is not everyday experience but previous encounters with works having similar conventions.

Further, artworks can create new conventions. A highly innovative work can at first seem odd because it refuses to conform to the norms we expect. Cubist painting, the French "New Novel" of the 1950s, and ambient music seemed bizarre initially because of their refusal to adhere to conventions. But a closer look may show that an unusual artwork has its own rules, creating an unorthodox formal system that we can learn to recognize and respond to. Eventually, the new systems offered by such unusual works may themselves furnish conventions and thus create new expectations.

"To a story-teller a journey is a marvelous device. It provides a strong thread on which a multitude of things that he has in mind may be strung to make a new thing, various, unpredictable, and yet coherent. My chief reason for using this form was technical."

— J.R.R. Tolkien

Form and Feeling

Certainly, emotion plays a large role in our experience of form. To understand this role, let's distinguish between *emotions represented in* the artwork and an *emotional response felt by* the spectator. If an actor grimaces in agony, the emotion of pain is represented within the film. If, however, the viewer who sees the painful expression laughs (as the viewer of a comedy might), the emotion of amusement is felt by the spectator. Both types of emotion have formal implications.

Emotions represented within the film interact as parts of the film's total system. For example, that grimace of pain might be consistent with the character's response to bad news. A character's sly expression may prepare us for the later revelation of his or her villainous side. Or a cheerful scene might stand in contrast to a mournful one. A tragic event might be undercut by light-hearted music. All emotions present in a film may be seen as systematically related to one another through that film's form.

The spectator's emotional response to the film is related to form as well. We have just seen how cues in the artwork interact with our prior experience, especially our experience of artistic conventions. Often form in artworks appeals to ready-made reactions to certain images (for example, involving sexuality, race, or social class). But form can create new responses instead of harping on old ones. Just as formal conventions often lead us to suspend our normal sense of real-life experience, so form may lead us to override our everyday emotional responses. People whom we would despise in life may become spellbinding as characters in a film. We can be enthralled by a film about a subject that normally bores us. One cause of these experiences lies in the systematic way we become involved in form. In *The Wizard of Oz*, we might, for example, find the land of Oz far more attractive than Kansas. But because the film's form leads us to sympathize with Dorothy in her desire to go home, we feel great satisfaction when she finally returns to Kansas.

It is first and foremost the dynamic aspect of form that engages our feelings. Expectation, for instance, spurs emotion. To have an expectation about "what happens next" is to invest some emotion in the situation. Delayed fulfillment of an expectation—suspense—may produce anxiety or sympathy. (Will the detective find the criminal? Will boy get girl? Will the melody return?) Gratified expectations may produce a feeling of satisfaction or relief. (The detective solves the mystery; boy does get girl; the melody returns one more time.) Cheated expectations and curiosity about past material may produce puzzlement or keener interest. (So he isn't the detective? This isn't a romance story? Has a second melody replaced the first one?)

Note that all of these possibilities *may* occur. There is no general recipe for concocting a novel or film to produce the "correct" emotional response. It is all a matter of context—that is, of the particular system that is each artwork's overall form. All we can say for certain is that the emotion felt by the spectator will emerge from the totality of formal relationships she or he perceives in the work. This is one reason why we should try to notice as many formal relations as possible in a film; the richer our perception, the deeper and more complex our response may become.

Taken in context, the relations between the feelings represented in the film and those felt by the spectator can be quite complicated. Let's take an example. Many people believe that no more sorrowful event can occur than the death of a child. In most films, this event would be represented so as to summon up the sadness we would also feel in life. But the power of artistic form can alter the emotional tenor of even this event. In Jean Renoir's *The Crime of M. Lange,* the cynical publisher Batala rapes and abandons Estelle, a young laundress. After Batala disappears, Estelle becomes integrated into the neighborhood and returns to her former fiancé. But Estelle is pregnant by Batala and bears his child.

The scene when Estelle's employer, Valentine, announces that the child was born dead is one of the most emotionally complex in cinema. The first reactions represented are solemnity and sorrow; the characters display grief. Suddenly, Batala's cousin remarks, "Too bad. It was a relative." In the film's context, this is taken as a joke, and the other characters break out in smiles and laughter. The shift in the emotion represented in the film catches us off guard. Since these characters are not heartless, we must readjust our reaction to the death and respond as they do—with relief. Estelle's survival is far more important than the death of Batala's child. The film's formal development has rendered appropriate a reaction that might be perverse in ordinary life. This is a daring, extreme example, but it dramatically illustrates how both emotions onscreen and our responses depend on the context created by form.

Form and Meaning

Like emotion, **meaning** is important to our experience of artworks. As an alert perceiver, the spectator is constantly testing the work for larger significance, for what it says or suggests. The sorts of meanings that the spectator attributes to a film may vary considerably. Let's look at four things we might say about the meaning of *The Wizard of Oz.*

1. ***Referential meaning.*** *During the Depression, a tornado takes a girl from her family's Kansas farm to the mythical land of Oz. After a series of adventures, she returns home.*

This is very concrete, close to a bare-bones plot summary. Here the meaning depends on the spectator's ability to identify specific items: the American Depression of the 1930s, the state of Kansas, features of Midwestern climate. A viewer unacquainted with such information would miss some of the meanings cued by the film.

We can call such tangible meanings *referential,* since the film refers to things or places already invested with significance.

A film's subject matter—in *The Wizard of Oz,* American farm life in the 1930s—is often established through referential meaning. And, as you might expect, referential meaning functions within the film's overall form, in the way that we have argued that the subject of the Civil War functions within *The Birth of a Nation.* Suppose that instead of having Dorothy live in flat, spare, rural Kansas, the film made Dorothy a child living in Beverly Hills. When she got to Oz (transported there, perhaps, by a hillside flash flood), the contrast between the crowded opulence of Oz and her home would not be nearly as sharp. Here the referential meanings of Kansas play a definite role in the overall contrast of settings that the film's form creates.

2. ***Explicit meaning.*** *A girl dreams of leaving home to escape her troubles. Only after she leaves does she realize how much she loves her family and friends.*

This assertion is still fairly concrete in the meaning it attributes to the film. If someone were to ask you the *point* of the film—what it seems to be trying to get across—you might answer with something like this. Perhaps you would also mention Dorothy's closing line, "There's no place like home," as a summary of what she learns. Let us call this sort of openly asserted meaning an *explicit meaning.*

Like referential meanings, explicit meanings function within the film's overall form. They are defined by context. For instance, we might want to take "There's no place like home" as a statement of the meaning of the entire film. But, first, *why* do we feel that as a strongly meaningful line? In ordinary conversation, it's a cliché. In context, however, the line gains great force. It's uttered in close-up, it comes at the end of the film (a formally privileged moment), and it refers back to all of Dorothy's desires and ordeals, recalling the film's narrative development toward the achievement of her goal. It is the *form* of the film that gives the homily an unfamiliar weight.

This example suggests that we must examine how explicit meanings in a film interact with other elements of the overall system. If "There's no place like home" adequately and exhaustively summarizes the meaning of *The Wizard of Oz,* no one need ever see the film; the summary would suffice. But like feelings, meanings are born from the dynamics of form. They play a part along with other elements to make up the total system.

Usually, we can't isolate a particularly significant moment and declare it to be *the* meaning of the whole film. Even Dorothy's "There's no place like home," however strong as a summary of *one* meaningful element in *The Wizard of Oz,* must be placed in the context of the film's entire beguiling Oz fantasy. If "There's no place like home" were the whole point of the film, why is there so much that is pleasant in Oz? The explicit meanings of a film arise from the *whole* film and are set in dynamic formal relation to one another.

In trying to see the meaningful moments of a film as parts of a larger whole, it's useful to set individually significant moments against one another. Thus Dorothy's final line could be juxtaposed to the scene of the characters getting spruced up after their arrival at the Emerald City. We can try to see the film as about, not one or the other, but rather the relation of the two—the delight and risk of a fantasy world versus the comfort and stability of home. Thus the film's total system is larger than any one explicit meaning we can find in it. Instead of asking, "What is this film's meaning?" we can ask, "How do *all* the film's meanings relate to one another?"

3. ***Implicit meaning.*** *An adolescent who must soon face the adult world yearns for a return to the simple world of childhood, but she eventually accepts the demands of growing up.*

This is more abstract than the first two statements. It goes beyond what is explicitly stated in the film, suggesting that *The Wizard of Oz* is in some sense about the passage from childhood to adulthood. In this view, the film suggests or implies that, in adolescence, people may desire to return to the apparently uncomplicated world of childhood. Dorothy's frustration with her aunt and uncle and her urge to flee to a place "over the rainbow" become examples of a general conception of adolescence. Unlike the "no place like home" line, this meaning isn't stated directly. We can call this suggestion an *implicit meaning.* When perceivers ascribe implicit meanings to an artwork, they're usually said to be *interpreting* it.

Clearly, **interpretations** vary. One viewer might propose that *The Wizard of Oz* is really about adolescence. Another might suggest that it is really about courage and persistence or that it is a satire on the adult world. One of the appeals of artworks is that they ask us to interpret them, often in several ways at once. Again, the artwork invites us to perform certain activities—here, building up implicit meanings. But once again, the artwork's overall form shapes our sense of implicit meanings.

Some viewers approach a film expecting to learn lessons about life. They may admire a film because it conveys a profound or relevant message. Important as meaning is, though, this attitude often errs by splitting the film into the content portion (the meaning) and the form (the vehicle for the content). The abstract quality of implicit meanings can lead to very broad concepts, often called *themes.* A film may have as its theme courage or the power of faithful love. Such descriptions have some value, but they are very general; hundreds of films fit them. To summarize *The Wizard of Oz* as being simply about the problems of adolescence does not do justice to the specific qualities of the film as an experience. We suggest that the search for implicit meanings should not leave behind the *particular* and *concrete* features of a film.

This is not to say that we should not interpret films. But we should strive to make our interpretations precise by seeing how each film's thematic meanings are suggested by the film's total system. In a film, both explicit and implicit meanings depend closely on the relations between narrative and style. In *The Wizard of Oz,* the Yellow Brick Road has no meaning in and of itself. But if we examine the function it fulfills in relation to the narrative, the music, the colors, and so on, we can argue that the Yellow Brick Road does indeed function meaningfully. Dorothy's strong desire to go home makes the road represent that desire. We want Dorothy to be successful in getting to the end of the road, as well as in getting back to Kansas; thus the road participates in the theme of the desirability of home.

Interpretation need not be an end in itself. It also helps in understanding the overall form of the film. Nor does interpretation exhaust the possibilities of a device. We can say many things about the Yellow Brick Road other than how its meaning relates to the film's thematic material. We could note that the road marks Oz as a fantastical land, since real-world bricks are a brownish-red color. We could analyze how the road becomes the stage for dances and songs along the way. We could see how it is narratively important because her indecision at a crossroads allows Dorothy to meet the Scarecrow. We could work out a color scheme for the film, contrasting the yellow road, the red slippers, the green Emerald City, and so forth. From this standpoint, interpretation may be seen as one kind of formal analysis, one that seeks to reveal a film's implicit meanings. Those meanings should be constantly tested by placing them within the concrete texture of the whole film.

4. *Symptomatic meaning. In a society in which human worth is measured by money, the home and the family may seem to be the last refuge of human values. This belief is especially strong in times of economic crisis, such as that in the United States in the 1930s.*

Like the third statement, this is abstract and general. It situates the film within a trend of thought that is assumed to be characteristic of American society during the 1930s. The claim could apply equally well to many other films, as well as to many novels, plays, poems, paintings, advertisements, radio shows, political speeches, and a host of cultural products of the period.

But there is something else worth noticing about the statement. It treats an explicit meaning in *The Wizard of Oz* ("There's no place like home") as a manifestation of a wider set of values characteristic of a whole society. We could treat implicit meanings the same way. If we say the film implies something about adolescence as a crucial time of transition, we could suggest that emphasis on adolescence as a special period of life is also a recurrent concern of American society. So, it's possible to understand a film's explicit or implicit meanings as bearing traces of a particular set of social values. We can call this *symptomatic meaning,* and the set of values that get revealed can be considered a social **ideology**.

The possibility of noticing symptomatic meanings reminds us that meaning, whether referential, explicit, or implicit, is largely a social phenomenon. Many meanings of films are ultimately ideological; that is, they spring from systems of culturally specific beliefs about the world. Religious beliefs, political opinions, conceptions of race or sex or social class, even our most deeply seated notions of life—all these constitute our ideological frame of reference. Although we may live as if our beliefs were the only true and real explanations of how the world is, we need only compare our own ideology with that of another group or culture or era to see how historically and socially shaped many of those views are. In other times and places, *home* and *adolescence* don't carry the meanings they carry in 21st-century America.

Films, like other artworks, can be examined for their symptomatic meanings. Again, however, the abstract and general quality of such meanings can lead us away from the concrete form of the film. As when analyzing the implicit meanings, the viewer should strive to ground symptomatic meanings in the film's specific aspects. A film *enacts* ideological meanings through its particular and unique formal system. We'll see in Chapter 11 how the narrative and stylistic system of *Meet Me in St. Louis* can be analyzed for ideological implications.

To sum up: Films have meaning because we attribute meanings to them. We cannot therefore regard meaning as a simple content to be extracted from the film. Sometimes the filmmaker guides us toward certain meanings; sometimes we find meanings the filmmaker didn't intend. Our minds will probe an artwork for significance at several levels. One mark of our engagement with the film as an experience is our search for referential, explicit, implicit, and symptomatic meanings. The more abstract and general our attributions of meaning, the more we risk loosening our grasp on the film's specific formal system. In analyzing films, we must balance our concern for that concrete system with our urge to assign it wider significance.

Evaluation

In talking about an artwork, people often *evaluate* it; that is, they make claims about its goodness or badness. Reviews in newspapers and magazines and on the Internet exist almost solely to tell us whether a film is worth seeing; our friends often urge us to go to their latest favorite. But all too often we discover that the film that someone else esteemed appears only mediocre to us. At that point, we may complain that most people evaluate films only on the basis of their own, highly personal, tastes.

How, then, are we to evaluate films with any degree of objectivity? We can start by realizing that there is a difference between *personal taste* and *evaluative judgment.* To say "I liked this film" or "I hated it" is not equal to saying "It's a good film" or "It's wretched." Very few people in the world limit their enjoyment only to the greatest works. Most people can enjoy a film they know is not particularly good. This is perfectly reasonable—unless they start trying to convince people that these pleasant films actually rank among the undying masterpieces. At that point others will probably stop listening to their judgments at all.

So personal preference need not be the sole basis for judging a film's quality. Instead, the critic who wishes to make a relatively objective evaluation will use specific *criteria.* A criterion is a standard that can be applied in the judgment of many works. By using a criterion, the critic gains a basis for comparing films for relative quality.

There are many different criteria. Some people evaluate films on *realistic* criteria, judging a film good if it conforms to their view of reality. Aficionados of military history might judge a film entirely on whether the battle scenes use historically accurate weaponry; the narrative, editing, characterization, sound, and visual style might be of little interest to them.

Other people condemn films because they don't find the action plausible. They dismiss a scene by saying, "Who'd really believe that X would meet Y just at the right moment?" We have already seen, though, that artworks often violate laws of reality and operate by their own conventions and internal rules.

Viewers can also use *moral* criteria to evaluate films. Most narrowly, aspects of the film can be judged outside their context in the film's formal system. Some viewers might feel any film with nudity or profanity or violence is bad, while other viewers might find just these aspects praiseworthy. So some viewers might condemn the death of the newborn baby in *The Crime of M. Lange,* regardless of the scene's context. More broadly, viewers and critics may employ moral criteria to evaluate a film's overall significance, and here the film's complete formal system becomes pertinent. A film might be judged good because of its overall view of life, its willingness to show opposing points of view, or its emotional range.

While realistic and moral criteria are well suited to particular purposes, this book suggests criteria that assess films as artistic wholes. Such criteria should allow us to take each film's form into account as much as possible. *Coherence* is one such criterion. This quality, often referred to as *unity,* has traditionally been held to be a positive feature of artworks. So, too, has *intensity of effect.* If an artwork is vivid, striking, and emotionally engaging, it may be considered more valuable.

Another criterion is *complexity.* We can argue that, all other things being equal, complex films are good. A complex film engages our interest on many levels, creates a multiplicity of relations among many separate formal elements, and tends to create intriguing patterns of feelings and meanings.

Yet another formal criterion is *originality.* Originality for its own sake is pointless, of course. Just because something is different does not mean that it is good. But if an artist takes a familiar convention and uses it in a way that makes it a fresh experience, then (all other things being equal) the resulting work may be considered good from an aesthetic standpoint.

Note that all these criteria are matters of degree. One film may be more complex than another, but the simpler film may be more complex than a third one. Moreover, there is often a give-and-take among the criteria. A film might be very complex but lack coherence or intensity. Ninety minutes of a black screen would make for an original film but not a very complex one. A slasher movie may create great intensity in certain scenes but may be wholly unoriginal, as well as disorganized and simplistic. In applying the criteria, the analyst often must weigh one against another.

Evaluation can serve many useful ends. It can call attention to neglected artworks or make us rethink our attitudes toward accepted classics. But just as the discovery of meanings is not the only purpose of formal analysis, we suggest that evaluation is most fruitful when it is backed up by a close examination of the film. General statements ("*The Wizard of Oz* is a masterpiece") seldom enlighten us very much. Usually, an evaluation is helpful insofar as it points to aspects of the film and shows us relations and qualities we have missed: "*The Wizard of Oz* subtly compares characters in Kansas and Oz, as when Miss Gulch's written order to take Toto is echoed by the Wicked Witch's fiery skywriting to the citizens of the Emerald City, 'Surrender Dorothy.'" Like interpretation, evaluation is most useful when it drives us back to the film itself as a formal system, helping us to understand that system better.

In reading this book, you'll find that we have generally minimized evaluation. We think that most of the films and sequences we analyze are more or less good based on the artistic criteria we mentioned, but the purpose of this book is not to persuade you to accept a list of masterpieces. Rather, we believe that if we show in detail how films may be understood as artistic systems, you will have an informed basis for whatever evaluations you wish to make.

Principles of Film Form

Because film form is a system—that is, a unified set of related, interdependent elements—there must be some principles that help create the relationships among the parts. In disciplines other than the arts, principles may be sets of rules or laws. In the sciences, principles may take the form of physical laws or mathematical propositions. In research and invention, such principles provide firm guidelines as to what is possible. For example, engineers designing an airplane must obey fundamental laws of aerodynamics.

In the arts, however, there are no absolute principles of form that all artists must follow. Artworks are products of culture. Thus many of the principles of artistic form are matters of convention. In Chapter 9, we shall examine how various genres can have very different conventions. A Western is not in error if it does not follow the conventions of classic Westerns. The artist obeys (or disobeys) *norms*—bodies of conventions, not laws.

But within these social conventions, each artwork tends to set up its own specific formal principles. The forms of different films can vary enormously. We can distinguish, however, five general principles that we notice in experiencing a film's formal system: function, similarity and repetition, difference and variation, development, and unity/disunity.

Function

If form in cinema is the overall interrelation among various systems of elements, we can assume that every element has one or more **functions**. That is, every element will be seen as fulfilling roles within the whole system.

Of any element within a film we can ask, What are its functions? In *The Wizard of Oz,* every element in the film fulfills one or more roles. For instance, Miss Gulch, the woman who wants to take Toto from Dorothy, reappears in the Oz section as the Wicked Witch. In the opening portion of the film, Miss Gulch frightens Dorothy into running away from home. In Oz, the Witch prevents Dorothy from returning home by keeping her away from the Emerald City and by trying to seize the ruby slippers.

Even an element as apparently minor as the dog Toto serves many functions. The dispute over Toto causes Dorothy to run away from home and to get back too late to take shelter from the tornado. Later, when Dorothy is about to leave Oz, Toto's pursuit of a cat makes her jump out of the ascending balloon. Toto's gray color, set off against the brightness of Oz, creates a link to the black and white of the Kansas episodes at the film's beginning. Functions, then, are almost always multiple. Both narrative and stylistic elements have functions.

One useful way to grasp the function of an element is to ask what other elements demand that it be present. For instance, the narrative requires that Dorothy run away from home, so Toto functions to trigger this action. Or, to take another example, Dorothy must seem completely different from the Wicked Witch, so costume, age, voice, and other characteristics function to contrast the two. Additionally, the switch from black-and-white to color film functions to signal the arrival in the bright fantasy land of Oz.

Note that the concept of function does not always depend on the filmmaker's intention. Often discussions of films get bogged down in the question of whether the filmmaker really knew what he or she was doing by including a certain element. In asking about function, we do not ask for a production history. From the standpoint of intention, Dorothy may sing "Over the Rainbow" because MGM wanted Judy Garland to launch a hit song. From the standpoint of function, however, we can say that Dorothy's singing that song fulfills certain narrative and stylistic functions. It establishes her desire to leave home, its reference to the rainbow foreshadows her trip through the air to the colorful land of Oz, and so forth. In asking about formal function, therefore, we ask not, "How did this element get there?" but rather, "What is this element *doing* there?" and "How does it cue us to respond?"

One way to notice the functions of an element is to consider the element's **motivation**. Because films are human constructs, we can expect that any one element in a film will have some justification for being there. This justification is the motivation for that element. For example, when Miss Gulch appears as the Witch in Oz, we justify her new incarnation by appealing to the fact that early scenes in Kansas have established her as a threat to Dorothy. When Toto jumps from the balloon to chase a cat, we motivate his action by appealing to notions of how dogs are likely to act when cats are around.

Sometimes people use the word "motivation" to apply only to reasons for characters' actions, as when a murderer acts from certain motives. Here, however, we'll use "motivation" to apply to any element in the film that the viewer justifies on some grounds. A costume, for example, needs motivation. If we see a man in beggar's clothes in the middle of an elegant society ball, we will ask why he is dressed in this way. He could be the victim of practical jokers who have deluded him into believing that this is a masquerade. He could be an eccentric millionaire out to shock his friends. Such a scene does occur in *My Man Godfrey*. The motivation for the beggar's presence at the ball is a scavenger hunt; the young society people have been assigned to bring back, among other things, a beggar. An event, the hunt, *motivates* the presence of an inappropriately dressed character.

Motivation is so common in films that spectators take it for granted. Shadowy, flickering light on a character may be motivated by the presence of a candle in the room. (We might remember that in production the light is provided by offscreen lamps, but the candle purports to be the source and thus motivates the pattern of light.) A character wandering across a room may motivate the moving of the camera to follow the action and keep the character within the frame. When we study principles of narrative form (Chapter 3) and various types of films (Chapters 9 and 10), we will look more closely at how motivation works to give elements specific functions.

Similarity and Repetition

In our example of the ABACA pattern, we saw how we were able to predict the next steps in the series. One reason for this was a regular pattern of repeated elements. Like beats in music or meter in poetry, the repetition of the A's in our pattern established and satisfied formal expectations. Similarity and repetition, then, constitute an important principle of film form.

Repetition is basic to our understanding any film. For instance, we must be able to recall and identify characters and settings each time they reappear. More subtly, throughout any film, we can observe repetitions of everything from lines of dialogue and bits of music to camera positions, characters' behavior, and story action.

It's useful to have a term to describe formal repetitions, and the most common term is **motif**. We shall call *any significant repeated element in a film* a motif. A motif may be an object, a color, a place, a person, a sound, or even a character trait. We may call a pattern of lighting or camera position a motif if it is repeated through the course of a film. The form of *The Wizard of Oz* uses all these kinds of motifs. Even in such a relatively simple film, we can see the pervasive presence of similarity and repetition as formal principles.

Film form uses general similarities as well as exact duplication. To understand *The Wizard of Oz*, we must see the similarities between the three Kansas farmhands

"You can take a movie, for example, like Angels with Dirty Faces, *where James Cagney is a child and says to his pal Pat O'Brien, 'What do you hear, what do you say?'—cocky kid— and then as a young rough on the way up when things are going great for him he says, 'What do you hear, what do you say?' Then when he is about to be executed in the electric chair and Pat O'Brien is there to hear his confession, he says, 'What do you hear, what do you say?' and the simple repetition of the last line of dialogue in three different places with the same characters brings home the dramatically changed circumstances much more than any extensive diatribe would."*

—Robert Towne, screenwriter, *Chinatown*

2.2   The itinerant Kansas fortune-teller, Professor Marvell, bears a striking resemblance to . . .

2.3   . . . the old charlatan known as the Wizard of Oz.

2.4   Miss Gulch's bicycle in the opening section becomes . . .

2.5   . . . the Witch's broom in Oz.

2.6   As the Lion describes his timidity, the characters are lined up to form a mirror reversal of . . .

2.7   . . . the earlier scene in which the others teased Zeke for being afraid of pigs.

and the Scarecrow, the Tin Man, and the Cowardly Lion. We must notice additional echoes between characters in the frame story and in the fantasy (**2.2–2.5**). The duplication isn't perfect, but the similarity is very strong. Such similarities are called *parallelism,* the process whereby the film cues the spectator to compare two or more distinct elements by highlighting some similarity. For example, at one point, Dorothy says she feels that she has known the Scarecrow, the Tin Man, and the Cowardly Lion before. At another point, the staging of a shot reinforces this familiarity (**2.6, 2.7**).

Motifs can assist in creating parallelism. The viewer will notice, and even come to expect, that every time Dorothy meets a character in Oz, the scene will end with the song "We're Off to See the Wizard." Our recognition of parallelism provides part of our pleasure in watching a film, much as the echo of rhymes contributes to the power of poetry.

Difference and Variation

The form of a film could hardly be composed only of repetitions. AAAAAA is rather boring. There must also be some changes, or *variations,* however small. Thus difference is another fundamental principle of film form.

We can readily understand the need for variety, contrast, and change in films. Characters must be differentiated, environments delineated, and different times or activities established. Even within the image, we must distinguish differences in tonality, texture, direction and speed of movement, and so on. Form needs its stable background of similarity and repetition, but it also demands that differences be created.

2.8 Through her crystal ball, the Wicked Witch mocks Dorothy.

2.9 Centered in the upper half of the frame, the Emerald City creates a striking contrast to . . .

2.10 . . . the similar composition showing the castle of the Wicked Witch of the West.

2.11 Dorothy puts her feet on the literal beginning of the Yellow Brick Road, as it widens out from a thin line.

This means that although motifs (scenes, settings, actions, objects, stylistic devices) may be repeated, those motifs will seldom be repeated *exactly*. Variation will appear. In *The Wizard of Oz,* the three Kansas hired hands aren't exactly the same as their "twins" in Oz. Parallelism thus requires a degree of difference as well as striking similarity. When Professor Marvel pretends to read Dorothy's future in a small crystal ball, we see no images in it (2.2). Dorothy's dream transforms the crystal into a large globe in the Witch's castle, where it displays frightening scenes (**2.8**). Similarly, the repeated motif of Toto's disruption of a situation changes its function. In Kansas, it disturbs Miss Gulch and induces Dorothy to take Toto away from home, but in Oz, his disruption prevents Dorothy from returning home.

Differences among the elements may often sharpen into downright opposition among them. We're most familiar with formal oppositions as clashes among characters. In *The Wizard of Oz,* Dorothy's desires are opposed, at various points, by the differing desires of Aunt Em, Miss Gulch, the Wicked Witch, and the Wizard, so that our experience of the film is engaged through dramatic conflict. But character conflict isn't the only way the formal principle of difference may manifest itself. Settings, actions, and other elements may be opposed. *The Wizard of Oz* presents color oppositions: black-and-white Kansas versus colorful Oz, Dorothy in red, white, and blue versus the Witch in black; and so on. Settings are opposed as well—not only Oz versus Kansas but also the various locales within Oz (**2.9, 2.10**). Voice quality, musical tunes, and a host of other elements play off against one another, demonstrating that any motif may be opposed by any other motif.

Not all differences are simple oppositions, of course. Dorothy's three Oz friends—the Scarecrow, the Tin Woodman, and the Lion—are distinguished not only by external features but also by means of a three-term comparison of what they lack (a brain, a heart, courage). Other films may rely on less sharp differences, suggesting a scale of gradations among the characters, as in Jean Renoir's *The Rules of the Game.* At the extreme, an abstract film may create minimal variations among its parts, such as in the slight changes that accompany each return of the same footage in J. J. Murphy's *Print Generation* (p. 359).

Repetition and variation are two sides of the same coin. To notice one is to notice the other. In thinking about films, we ought to look for similarities *and* differences. Shuttling between the two, we can point out motifs and contrast the changes they undergo, recognize parallelisms as repetition, and still spot crucial variations.

Development

One way to keep ourselves aware of how similarity and difference operate in film form is to look for principles of development from part to part. Development constitutes some patterning of similar and differing elements. Our pattern ABACA is based not only on repetition (the recurring motif of A) and difference (the varied insertion of B and C) but also on a principle of *progression* that we could state as a rule: alternate A with successive letters in alphabetical order. Though simple, this is a principle of *development,* governing the form of the whole series.

Think of formal development as *a progression moving from beginning through middle to end.* The story of *The Wizard of Oz* shows development in many ways. It is, for one thing, a *journey:* from Kansas through Oz to Kansas. The good witch Glinda emphasizes this formal pattern by telling Dorothy that "It's always best to start at the beginning" (**2.11**). Many films possess such a journey plot. *The Wizard of Oz* is also a *search,* beginning with an initial separation from home, tracing a series of efforts to find a way home, and ending with home being found. Within the film, there is also a pattern of *mystery,* which usually has the same beginning-middle-end pattern. We begin with a question (Who is the Wizard of Oz?), pass through attempts to answer it, and conclude with the question answered. (The Wizard is a fraud.) Most feature-length films are composed of several developmental patterns.

In order to analyze a film's pattern of development, it is usually a good idea to make a *segmentation.* A segmentation is simply a written outline of the film that breaks it into its major and minor parts, with the parts marked by consecutive numbers or letters. If a narrative film has 40 *scenes,* then we can label each scene with a number running from 1 to 40. It may be useful to divide some parts further (for example, scenes 6a and 6b). Segmenting a film enables us not only to notice similarities and differences among parts but also to plot the overall progression of the form. Following is a segmentation for *The Wizard of Oz.* (In segmenting films, we'll label the opening credits with a "C," the end title with an "E," and all other segments with numbers.)

THE WIZARD OF OZ: PLOT SEGMENTATION

C. Credits
1. Kansas
 a. Dorothy is at home, worried about Miss Gulch's threat to Toto.
 b. Running away, Dorothy meets Professor Marvel, who induces her to return home.
 c. A tornado lifts the house, with Dorothy and Toto, into the sky.
2. Munchkin City
 a. Dorothy meets Glinda, and the Munchkins celebrate the death of the Wicked Witch of the East.
 b. The Wicked Witch of the West threatens Dorothy over the Ruby Slippers.
 c. Glinda sends Dorothy to seek the Wizard's help.
3. The Yellow Brick Road
 a. Dorothy meets the Scarecrow.
 b. Dorothy meets the Tin Man.
 c. Dorothy meets the Cowardly Lion.
4. The Emerald City
 a. The Witch creates a poppy field near the city, but Glinda rescues the travelers.
 b. The group is welcomed by the city's citizens.
 c. As they wait to see the Wizard, the Lion sings of being king.
 d. The terrifying Wizard agrees to help the group if they obtain the Wicked Witch's broomstick.
5. The Witch's castle and nearby woods
 a. In the woods, flying monkeys carry off Dorothy and Toto.
 b. The Witch realizes that she must kill Dorothy to get the ruby slippers.
 c. The Scarecrow, Tin Man, and Lion sneak into the Castle; in the ensuing chase, Dorothy kills the Witch.
6. The Emerald City
 a. Although revealed as a humbug, the Wizard grants the wishes of the Scarecrow, Tin Man, and Lion.
 b. Dorothy fails to leave with the Wizard's hot-air balloon but is transported home by the ruby slippers.
7. Kansas—Dorothy describes Oz to her family and friends
E. End credits

Preparing a segmentation may look a little fussy, but in the course of this book, we'll try to convince you that it sheds a lot of light on films. For now, just consider this comparison. As you walk into a building, your experience develops over time. In many cathedrals, for example, the entryway is fairly narrow. But as you emerge into the open area inside (the nave), space expands outward and upward, your sense of your body seems to shrink, and your attention is directed toward the altar, centrally located in the distance. The somewhat cramped entryway makes you feel a contrast to the broad and soaring space. Your experience has been as carefully planned as any theme park ride. Only by thinking back on it can you realize that the planned progression of the building's different parts shaped your experience. If you could study the builder's blueprints, you'd see the whole layout at a glance. It would be very different from your moment-by-moment experience of it, but it would shed light on how your experience was shaped.

A film isn't that different. As we watch the film, we're in the thick of it. We follow the formal development moment by moment, and we may get more and more involved. If we want to study the overall shape of things, though, we need to stand back a bit. Films don't come with blueprints, but by creating a plot segmentation, we can get a comparable sense of the film's overall design. In a way, we're recovering the basic architecture of the movie. A segmentation lets us see the patterning that we felt intuitively in watching the film. In Chapters 3 and 10, we'll consider how to segment different types of films, and several of our sample analyses in Chapter 11 will use segmentations to show how the films work.

Another way to size up how a film develops formally is to *compare the beginning with the ending.* By looking at the similarities and the differences between the beginning and the ending, we can start to understand the overall pattern of the film. We can test this advice on *The Wizard of Oz.* A comparison of the beginning and the ending reveals that Dorothy's journey ends with her return home; the journey, a search for an ideal place "over the rainbow," has turned into a search for a way back to Kansas. The final scene repeats and develops the narrative elements of the opening. Stylistically, the beginning and ending are the only parts that use black-and-white film stock. This repetition supports the contrast the narrative creates between the dreamland of Oz and the bleak landscape of Kansas.

At the film's end, Professor Marvel comes to visit Dorothy (**2.12**), reversing the situation of her visit to him when she had tried to run away. At the beginning, he had convinced her to return home; then, as the Wizard in the Oz section, he had also represented her hopes of returning home. Finally, when she recognizes Professor Marvel and the farmhands as the basis of the characters in her dream, she remembers how much she had wanted to come home from Oz.

Earlier, we suggested that film form engages our emotions and expectations in a dynamic way. Now we are in a better position to see why. The constant interplay between similarity and difference, and repetition and variation, leads the viewer to an active, developing engagement with the film's formal system. It may be handy to visualize a movie's development in static terms by segmenting it, but we ought not to forget that formal development is a *process.* Form shapes our experience of the film.

2.12   The visits of the final scene.

Unity/Disunity

All of the relationships among elements in a film create the total filmic system. Even if an element seems utterly out of place in relation to the rest of the film, we cannot really say that it isn't part of the film. At most, the unrelated element is enigmatic or incoherent. It may be a flaw in the otherwise integrated system of the film—but it does affect the whole film.

When all the relationships we perceive within a film are clear and economically interwoven, we say that the film has *unity.* We call a unified film tight, because there seem to be no gaps in the formal relationships. Every element present has a specific set of functions, similarities and differences are determinable, the form develops logically, and no element is superfluous. In turn, the film's overall unity gives our experience a sense of completeness and fulfillment.

Unity is, however, a matter of degree. Almost no film is so tight as to leave no ends dangling. For example, at one point in *The Wizard of Oz,* the Witch refers to her having attacked Dorothy and her friends with insects, yet we have never seen them, and the mention becomes puzzling. In fact, a sequence of a bee attack was originally shot but then cut from the finished film. The Witch's line about the insect attack now lacks motivation. More striking is a dangling element at the film's end: we never find out what happens to Miss Gulch. Presumably, she still has her legal order to take Toto away, but no one refers to this in the last scene. The viewer may be inclined to overlook this disunity, however, because Miss Gulch's parallel character, the Witch, has been killed off in the Oz fantasy, and we don't expect to see her alive again. Since perfect unity is scarcely ever achieved, we ought to expect that even a unified film may still contain a few unintegrated elements or unanswered questions.

If we look at unity as a criterion of evaluation, we may judge a film containing several unmotivated elements as a failure. But unity and disunity may be looked at nonevaluatively as well, as the results of particular formal conventions. For example, *Pulp Fiction* lacks a bit of closure in that it never reveals what is inside a briefcase that is at the center of the gangster plot. The contents, however, give off a golden glow, suggesting that they are of very great value (as well as evoking the "whatsit" in *Kiss Me Deadly,* a classical film noir). By not specifying the goods, the film invites us to compare characters' reactions to them—most notably, in the last scene in the diner, when Pumpkin gazes at it lustfully and the newly spiritual hitman Jules calmly insists that he will deliver it to his boss. In such ways, momentary disunities contribute to broader patterns and thematic meanings.

Summary

If one issue has governed our treatment of aesthetic form, it might be said to be *concreteness.* Form is a specific system of patterned relationships that we perceive in an artwork. Such a concept helps us understand how even elements of what is normally considered content—subject matter, or abstract ideas—take on particular functions within any work.

Our experience of an artwork is also a concrete one. Picking up cues in the work, we frame specific expectations that are aroused, guided, delayed, cheated, satisfied, or disturbed. We undergo curiosity, suspense, and surprise. We compare the particular aspects of the artwork with general conventions that we know from life and from art. The concrete context of the artwork expresses and stimulates emotions and enables us to construct many types of meanings. And even when we apply general criteria in evaluating artworks, we ought to use those criteria to help us discriminate more, to penetrate more deeply into the particular aspects of the artwork. The rest of this book is devoted to studying these properties of artistic form in cinema.

We can summarize the principles of film form as a set of questions that you can ask about any film:

1. For any element in the film, what are its functions in the overall form? How is it motivated?

2. Are elements or patterns repeated throughout the film? If so, how and at what points? Are motifs and parallelisms asking us to compare elements?

3. How are elements contrasted and differentiated from one another? How are different elements opposed to one another?

4. What principles of progression or development are at work throughout the form of the film? More specifically, how does a comparison of the beginning and ending reveal the overall form of a film?

5. What degree of unity is present in the film's overall form? Is disunity subordinate to the overall unity, or does disunity dominate?

In this chapter, we examined some major ways in which films as artworks can engage us as spectators. We also reviewed some broad principles of film form. Armed with these general principles, we can press on to distinguish more specific *types* of form that are central to understanding film art.

Where to Go from Here

Form in Film and the Other Arts

Many of the ideas in this chapter are based on ideas of form to be found in other arts. All of the following constitute helpful further reading: Monroe Beardsley, *Aesthetics* (New York: Harcourt Brace & World, 1958), especially chaps. 4 and 5; Rudolf Arnheim, *Art and Visual Perception* (Berkeley: University of California Press, 1974), especially chaps. 2, 3, and 9; Leonard Meyer, *Emotion and Meaning in Music* (Chicago: University of Chicago Press, 1956); and E. H. Gombrich, *Art and Illusion* (Princeton, NJ: Princeton University Press, 1961).

On the relation of form to the audience, see the book by Meyer mentioned above. The ABACA example is borrowed from Barbara Herrnstein Smith's excellent study of literary form, *Poetic Closure* (Chicago: University of Chicago Press, 1968). Compare Kenneth Burke's claim: "Form is the creation of an appetite in the mind of the auditor and the adequate satisfying of that appetite." (See Kenneth Burke, "Psychology and Form," in *Counter-Statement* [Chicago: University of Chicago Press, 1957], pp. 29–44.)

This chapter presupposes that any filmmaker uses basic formal principles. But is the filmmaker fully aware of doing so? Many filmmakers use formal principles intuitively, but others apply them quite deliberately. Spike Lee's cinematographer Ernest Dickerson remarks, "A motif we used throughout *[School Daze]* was two people in profile, 'up in each other's face.' That was a conscious decision" (*Uplift the Race: The Construction of "School Daze"* [New York: Simon & Schuster, 1988], p. 110). Sidney Lumet decided to give *Twelve Angry Men* a strict progression by shooting from different camera positions as the story developed. "As the picture unfolded I wanted the room to seem smaller and smaller. . . . I shot the first third of the movie above eye level, the second third at eye level, and the last third from below eye level. In that way, toward the end, the ceiling began to appear" (Sidney Lumet, *Making Movies* [New York: Knopf, 1995], p. 81).

Form, Meaning, and Feeling

How does cinema evoke emotion? It's actually a bit of a puzzle. If a giant ape were lumbering toward us on the street, we'd run away in fright. But if King Kong is lumbering toward us on the screen, we feel frightened, but we don't flee the theater. Do we feel real fear but somehow block our impulse to run? Or do we feel something that isn't real fear but is a kind of pretend-fear? Similarly, when we say that we *identify* with a character, what does that mean? That we feel exactly the same emotions that the character does? Sometimes, though, we feel some emotions that the character isn't feeling, as when sympathy for her is mixed with pity or anxiety. Can we identify with a character and not have the same feelings she has?

In the 1990s, philosophers and film theorists tried to shed light on these issues. For a sampling, see Carl Plantinga and Greg M. Smith, eds., *Passionate Views: Film, Cognition, and Emotion* (Baltimore: Johns Hopkins University Press, 1999). The essays in this collection grew out of debates around some influential books: Noël Carroll, *The Philosophy of Horror; or, Paradoxes of the Heart* (London: Routledge, 1990); Murray Smith, *Engaging Characters: Fiction, Emotion and the Cinema* (Oxford: Oxford University Press, 1995); Joseph Anderson, *The Reality of Illusion: An Ecological Approach to Cognitive Film Theory* (Carbondale: University of Southern Illinois Press, 1996); and Torben Grodal, *Moving Pictures: A New Theory of Film Genres, Feelings, and Cognition* (Oxford: Oxford University Press, 1997). See also Greg M. Smith, *Film Structure and the Emotion System* (Cambridge: Cambridge University Press, 2003).

An alternative approach to understanding spectators' response to films has been called *reception studies*. For an overview, see Janet Staiger, *Media Reception Studies* (New York: New York University Press, 2005). Often scholars working in this tradition seek to understand how specific social groups, such as ethnic groups or historically located audiences, respond to the films offered to them. Influential examples are Kate Brooks and Martin Barker's *Judge Dredd: Its Friends, Fans, and Foes* (Luton: University of Luton Press, 2003) and Melvin Stokes and Richard Maltby, eds., *American Movie Audiences: From the Turn of the Century to the Early Sound Era* (London: British Film Institute, 1999). In *Perverse Spectators: The Practices of Film Reception* (New York: New York University Press, 2000), Janet Staiger discusses how audiences and critics can respond to films in ways that the filmmakers could not have anticipated.

Many critics concentrate on ascribing implicit and symptomatic meanings to films—that is, interpreting them. A survey of interpretive approaches is offered in R. Barton Palmer, *The Cinematic Text: Methods and Approaches* (New York: AMS Press, 1989). David Bordwell's *Making Meaning: Inference and Rhetoric in the Interpretation of Cinema* (Cambridge, MA: Harvard University Press, 1989) reviews trends in film interpretation.

Linear Segmentation and Diagramming

Dividing a film into sequences in order to analyze its form is usually called *segmentation*. It is usually not difficult to do, though most often we do it intuitively.

Usually, a feature-length film will have no more than 40 sequences and no fewer than 5, so if you find yourself dividing the film into tiny bits or huge chunks, you may want to shift to a different level of generality. Of course, sequences and scenes can also be further subdivided into subsegments. In segmenting any film, use an outline format or a linear diagram to help you visualize formal relations (beginnings and endings, parallels, patterns of development). We employ an outline format in discussing *Citizen Kane* in the next chapter and in discussing modes of filmmaking in Chapter 10.

Websites

www.uca.edu/org/ccsmi/ A site devoted to the Center for Cognitive Studies of the Moving Image, which examines various aspects of psychological and emotional responses to film.

http://en.wikipedia.org/wiki/Art. A helpful introductory essay on the role of form in different art media.

Recommended DVD Supplements

DVD supplements tend to focus on behind-the-scenes production information and on exposing how techniques such as special-effects and music were accomplished. Sometimes, though, such descriptions analyze formal aspects of the film. Despite its title, the supplement "City of Night: The Making of *Collateral*" deals largely with principles of narrative development: the use of chance to bring characters together, character change as a result of the two protagonists' interaction, contrasting types of music, and so on. In "Sweet Sounds," the supplement on the music in *Charlie and the Chocolate Factory,* composer Danny Elfman discusses how the musical numbers that follow the disappearance of each of the obnoxious children created parallels among them and yet achieved variety by being derived from different styles of music.

"Their Production Will Be Second to None," on the *Hard Day's Night* DVD, includes an intelligent interview with director Richard Lester in which he talks about the overall form of the film. He remarks, for example, that in the first third, he deliberately used confined spaces and low ceilings to prepare for the extreme contrast of the open spaces into which the Beatles escape.

Narrative as a Formal System

Principles of Narrative Construction

Stories surround us. In childhood, we learn fairy tales and myths. As we grow up, we read short stories, novels, history, and biography. Religion, philosophy, and science often present their doctrines through parables and tales. Plays tell stories, as do films, television shows, comic books, paintings, dance, and many other cultural phenomena. Much of our conversation is taken up with telling tales—recalling a past event or telling a joke. Even newspaper articles are called stories, and when we ask for an explanation of something, we may say, "What's the story?" We can't escape even by going to sleep, since we often experience our dreams as little narratives. Narrative is a fundamental way that humans make sense of the world.

The prevalence of stories in our lives is one reason that we need to take a close look at how films may embody **narrative form**. When we speak of "going to the movies," we almost always mean that we are going to see a narrative film—a film that tells a story.

Narrative form is most common in fictional films, but it can appear in all other basic types. For instance, documentaries often employ narrative form. *Primary* tells the story of how Hubert Humphrey and John F. Kennedy campaigned in the Wisconsin presidential primary of 1960. Many animated films, such as Disney features and Warner Bros. short cartoons, also tell stories. Some experimental and avant-garde films use narrative form, although the story or the way it is told may be quite unusual, as we shall see in Chapter 10.

Because stories are all around us, spectators approach a narrative film with definite expectations. We may know a great deal about the particular story the film will tell. Perhaps we have read the book on which a film is based, or we have seen the film to which this is a sequel. More generally, though, we have anticipations that are characteristic of narrative form itself. We assume that there will be characters and some action that will involve them with one another. We expect a series of incidents that will be connected in some way. We also probably expect that the problems or conflicts arising in the course of the action will achieve some final state—either they will be resolved or, at least, a new light will be cast on them. A spectator comes prepared to make sense of a narrative film.

As the viewer watches the film, she or he picks up cues, recalls information, anticipates what will follow, and generally participates in the creation of the film's form. The film shapes particular expectations by summoning up curiosity, suspense, and surprise. The ending has the task of satisfying or cheating the expectations prompted by the film as a whole. The ending may also activate memory by cueing the spectator to review earlier events, possibly considering them in a new light. When *The Sixth Sense* was released in 1999, many moviegoers were so intrigued by the surprise twist at the end that they returned to see the film again and trace how their expectations had been manipulated. As we examine narrative form, we consider at various points how it engages the viewer in a dynamic activity.

What Is Narrative?

We can consider a *narrative* to be *a chain of events in cause–effect relationship occurring in time and space.* A narrative is what we usually mean by the term *story,* although we shall be using *story* in a slightly different way later. Typically, a narrative begins with one situation; a series of changes occurs according to a pattern of cause and effect; finally, a new situation arises that brings about the end of the narrative. Our engagement with the story depends on our understanding of the pattern of change and stability, cause and effect, time and space.

All the components of our definition—causality, time, and space—are important to narratives in most media, but causality and time are central. A random string of events is hard to understand as a story. Consider the following actions: "A man tosses and turns, unable to sleep. A mirror breaks. A telephone rings." We have trouble grasping this as a narrative because we are unable to determine the causal or temporal relations among the events.

Consider a new description of these same events: "A man has a fight with his boss; he tosses and turns that night, unable to sleep. In the morning, he is still so angry that he smashes the mirror while shaving. Then his telephone rings; his boss has called to apologize."

We now have a narrative. We can connect the events spatially: The man is in the office, then in his bed; the mirror is in the bathroom; the phone is somewhere else in his home. More important, we can understand that the three events are part of a series of causes and effects. The argument with the boss causes the sleeplessness and the broken mirror. The phone call from the boss resolves the conflict; the narrative ends. In this example, time is important, too. The sleepless night occurs before the breaking of the mirror, which in turn occurs before the phone call; all of the action runs from one day to the following morning. The narrative develops from an initial situation of conflict between employee and boss, through a series of events caused by the conflict, to the resolution of the conflict. Simple and minimal as our example is, it shows how important causality, space, and time are to narrative form.

The fact that a narrative relies on causality, time, and space doesn't mean that other formal principles can't govern the film. For instance, a narrative may make use of parallelism. As Chapter 2 points out (p. 67), parallelism presents a similarity among different elements. Our example was the way that *The Wizard of Oz* made the three Kansas farmhands parallel to Dorothy's three Oz companions. A narrative may cue us to draw parallels among characters, settings, situations, times of day, or any other elements. In Věrá Chytilová's *Something Different,* scenes from the life of a housewife and from the career of a gymnast are presented in alternation. Since the two women never meet and lead entirely separate lives, there is no way that we can connect the two stories causally. Instead, we compare and contrast the two women's actions and situations—that is, we draw parallels.

The documentary *Hoop Dreams* makes even stronger use of parallels. Two high school students from Chicago's black ghetto dream of becoming professional basketball players, and the film follows as each one pursues his athletic

> "Narrative is one of the ways in which knowledge is organized. I have always thought it was the most important way to transmit and receive knowledge. I am less certain of that now—but the craving for narrative has never lessened, and the hunger for it is as keen as it was on Mt. Sinai or Calvary or the middle of the fens."
>
> — Toni Morrison, author, *Beloved*

> "I had actually trapped myself in a story that was very convoluted, and I would have been able to cut more later if I'd simplified it at the script stage, but I'd reached a point where I was up against a wall of story logic. If I had cut too much at that stage, the audience would have felt lost."
>
> — James Cameron, director, on *Aliens*

career. The film's form invites us to compare and contrast their personalities, the obstacles they face, and the choices they make. In addition, the film creates parallels between their high schools, their coaches, their parents, and older male relatives who vicariously live their own dreams of athletic glory. Parallelism allows the film to become richer and more complex than it might have been had it concentrated on only one protagonist.

Yet *Hoop Dreams,* like *Something Different,* is still a narrative film. Each of the two lines of action is organized by time, space, and causality. The film suggests some broad causal forces as well. Both young men have grown up in urban poverty, and because sports is the most visible sign of success for them, they turn their hopes in that direction.

Plot and Story

We make sense of a narrative, then, by identifying its events and linking them by cause and effect, time, and space. As viewers, we do other things as well. We often infer events that are not explicitly presented, and we recognize the presence of material that is extraneous to the story world. In order to describe how we manage to do these things, we can draw a distinction between *story* and *plot* (sometimes called *story* and *discourse*).This isn't a difficult distinction to grasp, but we still need to examine it in a little more detail.

We often make assumptions and inferences about events in a narrative. For instance, at the start of Alfred Hitchcock's *North by Northwest,* we know we are in Manhattan at rush hour. The cues stand out clearly: skyscrapers, bustling pedestrians, congested traffic (**3.1**). Then we watch Roger Thornhill as he leaves an elevator with his secretary, Maggie, and strides through the lobby, dictating memos (**3.2**). On the basis of these cues, we start to draw some conclusions. Thornhill is an executive who leads a busy life. We assume that before we saw Thornhill and Maggie, he was also dictating to her; we have come in on the middle of a string of events in time. We also assume that the dictating began in the office, before they got on the elevator. In other words, we infer causes, a temporal sequence, and another locale even though none of this information has been directly presented. We are probably not aware of having made these inferences, but they are no less firm for going unnoticed.

The set of *all* the events in a narrative, both the ones explicitly presented and those the viewer infers, constitutes the **story**. In our example, the story would consist of at least two depicted events and two inferred ones. We can list them, putting the inferred events in parentheses:

(Roger Thornhill has a busy day at his office.)

Rush hour hits Manhattan.

(While dictating to his secretary, Maggie, Roger leaves the office and they take the elevator.)

Still dictating, Roger gets off the elevator with Maggie and they stride through the lobby.

The total world of the story action is sometimes called the film's *diegesis* (the Greek word for "recounted story"). In the opening of *North by Northwest,* the traffic, streets, skyscrapers, and people we see, as well as the traffic, streets, skyscrapers, and people we assume to be offscreen, are all diegetic because they are assumed to exist in the world that the film depicts.

The term *plot* is used to describe everything visibly and audibly present in the film before us. The plot includes, first, all the story events that are directly depicted. In our *North by Northwest* example, only two story events are explicitly presented in the plot: rush hour and Roger Thornhill's dictating to Maggie as they leave the elevator.

3.1 Hurrying Manhattan pedestrians in *North by Northwest.*

3.2 Maggie takes dictation from Roger Thornhill.

Note, though, that the film's plot may contain material that is extraneous to the story world. For example, while the opening of *North by Northwest* is portraying rush hour in Manhattan, we also see the film's credits and hear orchestral music. Neither of these elements is diegetic, since they are brought in from *outside* the story world. (The characters can't read the credits or hear the music.) Credits and such extraneous music are thus *nondiegetic* elements. In Chapters 6 and 7, we'll consider how editing and sound can function nondiegetically. At this point, we need only notice that the film's plot—the totality of the film—can bring in nondiegetic material.

Nondiegetic material may occur elsewhere than in credit sequences. In *The Band Wagon,* we see the premiere of a hopelessly pretentious musical play. Eager patrons file into the theater **(3.3)**, and the camera moves closer to a poster above the door **(3.4)**. There then appear three black-and-white images **(3.5–3.7)** accompanied by a brooding chorus. These images and sounds are clearly nondiegetic, inserted from outside the story world in order to signal that the production was catastrophic and laid an egg. The plot has added material to the story for comic effect.

In sum, story and plot overlap in one respect and diverge in others. The plot explicitly presents certain story events, so these events are common to both domains. The story goes beyond the plot in suggesting some diegetic events that we never witness. The plot goes beyond the story world by presenting nondiegetic images and sounds that may affect our understanding of the action. A diagram of the situation would look like this:

Story

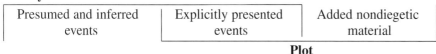

Presumed and inferred events	Explicitly presented events	Added nondiegetic material

Plot

We can think about these differences between story and plot from two perspectives. From the standpoint of the storyteller—the filmmaker—the story is the sum total of all the events in the narrative. The storyteller can present some of these events directly (that is, make them part of the plot), can hint at events that are not presented, and can simply ignore other events. For instance, though we learn later in *North by Northwest* that Roger's mother is still close to him, we never learn what happened to his father. The filmmaker can also add nondiegetic material, as in the example from *The Band Wagon.* In a sense, then, the filmmaker makes a story into a plot.

From the perceiver's standpoint, things look somewhat different. All we have before us is the plot—the arrangement ozf material in the film as it stands. We create the story in our minds on the basis of cues in the plot. We also recognize when the plot presents nondiegetic material.

The story–plot distinction suggests that if you want to give someone a synopsis of a narrative film, you can do it in two ways. You can summarize the story, starting from the very earliest incident that the plot cues you to assume or infer and running straight through to the end. Or you can tell the plot, starting with the first incident you encountered in watching the film.

Our initial definition and the distinction between plot and story constitute a set of tools for analyzing how narrative works. We shall see that the story–plot distinction affects all three aspects of narrative: causality, time, and space.

Cause and Effect

If narrative depends so heavily on cause and effect, what kinds of things can function as causes in a narrative? Usually, the agents of cause and effect are *characters.* By triggering and reacting to events, characters play roles within the film's formal system.

3.3   A hopeful investor in the play enters the theater . . .

3.4   . . . and the camera moves in on a poster predicting success for the musical . . .

3.5   . . . but three comic nondiegetic images reveal it to be a flop: ghostly figures on a boat . . .

3.6   . . . a skull in a desert . . .

3.7   . . . and an egg.

Most often, characters are persons, or at least entities like persons—Bugs Bunny or E.T. the extraterrestrial or even the singing teapot in *Beauty and the Beast.* For our purposes here, Michael Moore is a character in *Roger and Me* no less than Roger Thornhill is in *North by Northwest,* even though Moore is a real person and Thornhill is fictional. In any narrative film, either fictional or documentary, characters create causes and register effects. Within the film's formal system, they make things happen and respond to events. Their actions and reactions contribute strongly to our engagement with the film.

Unlike characters in novels, film characters typically have a visible body. This is such a basic convention that we take it for granted, but it can be contested. Occasionally, a character is only a voice, as when the dead Obi-Wan Kenobi urges the Jedi master Yoda to train Luke Skywalker in *The Empire Strikes Back.* More disturbingly, in Luis Buñuel's *That Obscure Object of Desire,* one woman is portrayed by two actresses, and the physical differences between them may suggest different sides of her character. Todd Solondz takes this innovation further in *Palindromes,* in which a 13-year-old girl is portrayed by male and female performers of different ages and races.

Along with a body, a character has *traits.* Traits are attitudes, skills, habits, tastes, psychological drives, and any other qualities that distinguish the character. Some characters, such as Mickey Mouse, may have only a few traits. When we say a character possesses several varying traits, some at odds with one another, we tend to call that character complex, or three-dimensional, or well developed. A memorable character such as Sherlock Holmes is a mass of traits. Some bear on his habits, such as his love of music or his addiction to cocaine, while other traits reflect his basic nature: his penetrating intelligence, his disdain for stupidity, his professional pride, his occasional gallantry.

As our love of gossip shows, we're curious about other humans, and we bring our people-watching skills to narratives. We're quick to assign traits to the characters onscreen, and often the movie helps us out. Most characters wear their traits far more openly than people do in real life, and the plot presents situations that swiftly reveal them to us. The opening scene of *Raiders of the Lost Ark* throws Indiana Jones's personality into high relief. We see immediately that he's bold and resourceful. He's courageous, but he can feel fear. By unearthing ancient treasures for museums, he shows an admirable devotion to scientific knowledge. In a few minutes, his essential traits are presented straightforwardly, and we come to know and sympathize with him.

It's not accidental that all of the traits that Indiana Jones displays in the opening scene are relevant to later scenes in *Raiders.* In general, a character is given traits that will play causal roles in the overall story action. The second scene of Alfred Hitchcock's *The Man Who Knew Too Much* (1934) shows that the heroine, Jill, is an excellent shot with a rifle. For much of the film, this trait seems irrelevant to the action, but in the last scene, Jill is able to shoot one of the villains when a police marksman cannot do it. This skill with a rifle is not a natural part of a person named Jill; it is a trait that helps make up a character named Jill, and it serves a particular narrative function.

Not all causes and effects in narratives originate with characters. In the so-called disaster movies, an earthquake or tidal wave may precipitate a series of actions on the parts of the characters. The same principle holds when the shark in *Jaws* terrorizes a community. Still, once these natural occurrences set the situation up, human desires and goals usually enter the action to develop the narrative. A man escaping from a flood may be placed in the situation of having to decide whether to rescue his worst enemy. In *Jaws,* the townspeople pursue a variety of strategies to deal with the shark, propelling the plot as they do so.

In general, the spectator actively seeks to connect events by means of cause and effect. Given an incident, we tend to imagine what might have caused it or what it might in turn cause. That is, we look for causal motivation. We have mentioned an instance of this in Chapter 2: In the scene from *My Man Godfrey,* a scavenger hunt serves as a cause that justifies the presence of a beggar at a society ball (see p. 66).

Causal motivation often involves the planting of information in advance of a scene, as we saw in the kitchen scene of *The Shining* (1.12, 1.13). In *L.A. Confidential,* the idealistic detective Exley confides in his cynical colleague Vincennes that the murder of his father had driven him to enter law enforcement. He had privately named the unknown killer "Rollo Tomasi," a name that he has turned into an emblem of all unpunished evil. This conversation initially seems like a simple bit of psychological insight. Yet later, when the corrupt police chief Smith shoots Vincennes, the latter mutters "Rollo Tomasi" with his last breath. When the puzzled Smith asks Exley who Rollo Tomasi is, Exley's earlier conversation with Vincennes motivates his shocked realization that the dead Vincennes has given him a clue identifying his killer. Near the end, when Exley is about to shoot Smith, he says that the chief is Rollo Tomasi. Thus an apparently minor detail returns as a major causal and thematic motif. And perhaps the unusual name, Rollo Tomasi, functions to help the audience remember this important motif across several scenes.

Most of what we have said about causality pertains to the plot's direct presentation of causes and effects. In *The Man Who Knew Too Much,* Jill is shown to be a good shot, and because of this, she can save her daughter. But the plot can also lead us to *infer* causes and effects, and thus build up a total story. The detective film furnishes the best example of how we actively construct the story.

A murder has been committed. That is, we know an effect but not the causes— the killer, the motive, and perhaps also the method. The mystery tale thus depends strongly on curiosity—on our desire to know events that have occurred before the events that the plot presents to us. It's the detective's job to disclose, at the end, the missing causes—to name the killer, explain the motive, and reveal the method. That is, in the detective film, the climax of the plot (the action we see) is a revelation of prior incidents in the story (events we did not see). We can diagram this:

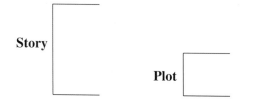

Story | **Plot** |
a. Crime conceived
b. Crime planned
c. Crime committed
d. Crime discovered
e. Detective investigates
f. Detective reveals a, b, and c

Although this pattern is most common in detective narratives, any film's plot can withhold causes and thus arouse our curiosity. Horror and science fiction films often leave us temporarily in the dark about what forces lurk behind certain events. Not until three-quarters of the way through *Alien* do we learn that the science officer Ash is a robot conspiring to protect the alien. In *Caché,* a married couple receive an anonymous videotape recording their daily lives. The film's plot shows them trying to discover who made it and why it was made. In general, whenever any film creates a mystery, it suppresses certain story causes and presents only effects in the plot.

The plot may also present causes but withhold story *effects,* prompting suspense and uncertainty in the viewer. After Hannibal Lecter's attack on his guards in the Tennessee prison in *The Silence of the Lambs,* the police search of the building raises the possibility that a body lying on top of an elevator is the wounded Lecter. After an extended suspense scene, we learn that he has switched clothes with a dead guard and escaped.

A plot's withholding of effects is perhaps most disruptive at the end of a film. A famous example occurs in the final moments of François Truffaut's *The 400 Blows.* The boy Antoine Doinel, having escaped from a reformatory, runs along the

3.8   The final image of *The 400 Blows* leaves Antoine's future uncertain.

seashore. The camera zooms in on his face, and the frame freezes **(3.8)**. The plot does not reveal whether he is captured and brought back, leaving us to speculate on what might happen in Antoine's future.

Time

Causes and their effects are basic to narrative, but they take place in time. Here again our story–plot distinction helps clarify how time shapes our understanding of narrative action.

As we watch a film, we construct story time on the basis of what the plot presents. For example, the plot may present events out of chronological order. In *Citizen Kane,* we see a man's death before we see his youth, and we must build up a chronological version of his life. Even if events are shown in chronological order, most plots don't show every detail from beginning to end. We assume that the characters spend uneventful time sleeping, traveling from place to place, eating, and the like, but the story duration containing irrelevant action has simply been skipped over. Another possibility is to have the plot present the same story event more than once, as when a character recalls a traumatic incident. In John Woo's *The Killer,* an accident in the opening scene blinds a singer, and later we see the same event again and again as the protagonist regretfully thinks back to it.

Such options mean that in constructing the film's story out of its plot, the viewer is engaged in trying to put events in chronological *order* and to assign them some *duration* and *frequency*. We can look at each of these temporal factors separately.

Temporal Order   We are quite accustomed to films that present events out of story **order**. A flashback is simply a portion of a story that the plot presents out of chronological order. In *Edward Scissorhands,* we first see the Winona Ryder character as an old woman telling her granddaughter a bedtime story. Most of the film then shows events that occurred when she was a high school girl. Such reordering doesn't confuse us because we mentally rearrange the events into the order in which they would logically have to occur: childhood comes before adulthood. From the plot order, we infer the story order. If story events can be thought of as ABCD, then the plot that uses a flashback presents something like BACD. Similarly, a flash-forward—that is, moving from present to future then back to the present—would also be an instance of how plot can shuffle story order. A flash-forward could be represented as ABDC.

One common pattern for reordering story events is an alternation of past and present in the plot. In the first half of Terence Davies' *Distant Voices, Still Lives,* we see scenes set in the present during a young woman's wedding day. These alternate with flashbacks to a time when her family lived under the sway of an abusive, mentally disturbed father. Interestingly, the flashback scenes are arranged out of chronological story order: Childhood episodes are mixed with scenes of adolescence, further cueing the spectator to assemble the story.

Sometimes a fairly simple reordering of scenes can create complicated effects. The plot of Quentin Tarantino's *Pulp Fiction* begins with a couple deciding to rob the diner in which they're eating breakfast. This scene takes place somewhat late in the story, but the viewer doesn't learn this until near the end of the film, when the robbery interrupts a dialogue involving other, more central, characters eating breakfast in the same diner. Just by pulling a scene out of order and placing it at the start, Tarantino creates a surprise. Later in *Pulp Fiction,* a hired killer is shot to death. But he reappears alive in subsequent scenes, which show him and his partner trying to dispose of a dead body. Tarantino has shifted a block of scenes from the middle of the story (before the man was killed) to the end of the plot. By coming at the film's conclusion, these portions receive an emphasis they wouldn't have if they had remained in their chronological story order.

Temporal Duration   The plot of *North by Northwest* presents four crowded days and nights in the life of Roger Thornhill. But the story stretches back far before that, since information about the past is revealed in the course of the plot. The story events include Roger's past marriages, the U.S. Intelligence Agency's plot to create a false agent named George Kaplan, and the villain Van Damm's series of smuggling activities.

In general, a film's plot selects certain stretches of story **duration**. This could involve concentrating on a short, relatively cohesive time span, as *North by Northwest* does. Or it could involve highlighting significant stretches of time from a period of many years, as *Citizen Kane* does when it shows us the protagonist in his youth, skips over some time to show him as a young man, skips over more time to show him middle-aged, and so forth. The sum of all these slices of *story* duration yields an overall *plot* duration.

But we need one more distinction. Watching a movie takes time—20 minutes or two hours or eight hours (as in Hans Jürgen Syberberg's *Our Hitler: A Film from Germany*). There is thus a third duration involved in a narrative film, which we can call *screen* duration. The relationships among story duration, plot duration, and screen duration are complex (see "Where to Go from Here" for further discussion), but for our purposes, we can say this: the filmmaker can manipulate screen duration independently of the overall story duration and plot duration. For example, *North by Northwest* has an overall story duration of several years (including all relevant prior events), an overall plot duration of four days and nights, and a screen duration of about 136 minutes.

Just as plot duration selects from story duration, so screen duration selects from overall plot duration. In *North by Northwest,* only portions of the film's four days and nights are shown to us. An interesting counterexample is *Twelve Angry Men,* the story of a jury deliberating a murder case. The 95 minutes of the movie approximate the same stretch of time in its characters' lives.

At a more specific level, the plot can use screen duration to override story time. For example, screen duration can *expand* story duration. A famous instance is that of the raising of the bridges in Sergei Eisenstein's *October.* Here an event that takes only a few moments in the story is stretched out to several minutes of screen time by means of the technique of film editing. As a result, this action gains a tremendous emphasis. The plot can also use screen duration to compress story time, as when a lengthy process is condensed into a rapid series of shots. These examples suggest that film techniques play a central role in creating screen duration. We shall consider this in more detail in Chapters 5 and 6.

Temporal Frequency   Most commonly, a story event is presented only once in the plot. Occasionally, however, a single story event may appear twice or even more in the plot treatment. If we see an event early in a film and then there is a flashback to that event later on, we see that same event twice. Some films use multiple narrators, each of whom describes the same event; again, we see it occur several times. This increased **frequency** may allow us to see the same action in several ways. The plot may also provide us with more information, so that we understand the event in a new context when it reappears. This occurs in *Pulp Fiction,* when the robbery of the diner, triggered at the start of the film, takes on its full significance only when it is repeated at the climax. In *Run Lola Run,* a single event is repeated many times after it first occurs: Lola's boyfriend reports by phone that he has lost a bag (*Tasche*) full of drug money, and we hear him and Lola shouting "Tasche" several times, even though we realize that they really say it only once or twice each. The repetition of their shouts underlines their terror in a way characteristic of this hyperkinetic movie. In our examination of *Citizen Kane,* we shall see another example of how repetition can recontextualize old information.

The various ways that a film's plot may manipulate story order, duration, and frequency illustrate how we actively participate in making sense of the narrative film. The plot supplies cues about chronological sequence, the time span of the actions, and the number of times an event occurs, and it's up to the viewer to make assumptions and inferences and to form expectations. In some cases, understanding of temporal relations can get quite complicated. In *The Usual Suspects,* a seemingly petty criminal spins an elaborate tale of his gang's activities to an FBI agent. His recounting unfolds in many flashbacks, some of which repeat events we witnessed in the opening scene. Yet a surprise final twist reveals that some of the flashbacks must have contained lies, and we must piece together both the chronology of events and the story's real cause–effect chain. Such time scrambling has become more common in recent decades. (See "A Closer Look", p. 83.)

Often we must motivate manipulations of time by the all-important principle of cause and effect. For instance, a flashback will often be caused by some incident that triggers a character's recalling some event in the past. The plot may skip over years of story duration if they contain nothing important to the chains of cause and effect. The repetition of actions may also be motivated by the plot's need to communicate certain key causes very clearly to the spectator.

Space

In some media, a narrative might emphasize only causality and time. Many of the anecdotes we tell each other don't specify where the action takes place. In film narrative, however, **space** is usually an important factor. Events occur in well-defined locales, such as Kansas or Oz; the Flint, Michigan, of *Roger and Me;* or the Manhattan of *North by Northwest.* We shall consider setting in more detail when we examine mise-en-scene in Chapter 4, but we ought briefly to note how plot and story can manipulate space.

Normally, the place of the story action is also that of the plot, but sometimes the plot leads us to infer other locales as part of the story. We never see Roger Thornhill's office or the colleges that kicked Kane out. Thus the narrative may ask us to imagine spaces and actions that are never shown. In Otto Preminger's *Exodus,* one scene is devoted to Dov Landau's interrogation by a terrorist organization he wants to join. Dov reluctantly tells his questioners of life in a Nazi concentration camp (**3.13**). Although the film never shows this locale through a flashback, much of the scene's emotional power depends on our using our imagination to fill in Dov's sketchy description of the camp.

Further, we can introduce an idea akin to the concept of screen duration. Besides story space and plot space, cinema employs screen space: the visible space

PLAYING GAMES WITH STORY TIME

For a spectator, reconstructing story order from the plot might be seen as a sort of game. Most Hollywood films make this game fairly simple. Still, just as we enjoy learning the rules of new games rather than playing the same one over and over, in unusual films, we can enjoy the challenge of unpredictable presentations of story events.

Since the 1980s, occasional films have exploited that enjoyment by using techniques other than straightforward flashbacks and flash-forwards to tell their stories. For instance, the story events might be reordered in novel ways. *Pulp Fiction* (1994) begins and ends with stages of a restaurant holdup—seemingly a conventional frame story. Yet in fact the final event to occur in the story—the Bruce Willis character and his girlfriend fleeing Los Angeles—happens well *after* the last scene. The reordering of events is startling and confusing at first, but it is dramatically effective in the way the conclusion forces us to rethink events we have seen earlier.

The success of *Pulp Fiction* made such a play with story order more acceptable in American filmmaking. *GO* (Doug Liman, 1999) presents the actions of a single night three times, each time from a different character's point of view. We cannot fully figure out what happened until the end, since various events are withheld from the first version and shown in the second and third.

Pulp Fiction and *GO* were independent films, but more mainstream Hollywood movies have also played with the temporal relations of story and plot. Steven Soderbergh's *Out of Sight* (1998) begins with the story of an inept bank robber who falls in love with the FBI agent who pursues him despite her obvious attraction to him. As their oddball romance proceeds, there is a string of flashbacks not motivated by any character's memory. These seem to involve a quite separate plotline, and their purpose is puzzling until the film's second half, when the final flashback, perhaps a character's recollection, loops back to the action that had begun the film and thus helps explain the main plot events.

Mainstream films may also use science fiction or fantasy premises to present alternative futures, often called "what if?" narratives. (The film industry website Box Office Mojo even lists "What If" as a separate genre and defines it as "Comedies About Metaphystical Questions That Come to Pass by Fantastical Means but in Realistic Settings.") Such films typically present a situation at the beginning, then show how it might proceed along different cause–effect chains if one factor were to be changed. *Sliding Doors* (Peter Howitt, 1998), for example, shows the heroine, Helen, fired from her job and heading home to her apartment, where her boyfriend is in bed with another woman. We see Helen entering the subway and catching her train, but then the action runs backward and she enters again, this time bumping into a child on the stairs and missing the train. The rest of the film's plot moves between two alternative futures for Helen. By catching the train, Helen arrives in time to discover the affair and moves out. By missing the train, she arrives after the other woman has left and hence she stays with her faithless boyfriend. The plot moves back and forth between these mutually exclusive cause–effect chains before neatly dovetailing them at the end.

Groundhog Day (Harold Ramis, 1993) helped to popularize "what if?" plots. On February 1, an obnoxious weatherman, Phil, travels to Punxsutawney to cover the famous Groundhog Day ceremonies. He then finds himself trapped in February 2, which repeats over and over, with variants depending on how Phil acts each day, sometimes frivolously, sometimes breaking laws (**3.9, 3.10**), and later trying to improve his life. Only after many such days does he become an admirable character, and the repetitions mysteriously stop.

Neither *Sliding Doors* nor *Groundhog Day* provides any explanation for the forking of its protagonist's life into various paths. We simply must assume that some higher power has intervened in order to improve his or her situation. Other films may provide some

3.9 During one repetition of February 2 in *Groundhog Day*, Phil tests whether he can get away with crimes, getting himself tossed in jail in the evening . . .

3.10 . . . only to find himself waking up, as on other Groundhog Days, back in bed at the bed-and-breakfast inn.

again travel back to 1955 to stop Biff from changing events. By the end of Part II, he becomes trapped there, while Doc is accidentally sent back to 1885. Marty joins him there in Part III for another set of threatened changes to the future. If all this sounds complicated, it is. Although the narrative maintains a remarkably unified series of cause–effect chains, it becomes so convoluted that at one point Doc diagrams events for Marty (and us) on a blackboard!

Not surprisingly, such narrative games were influenced by a similar trend in European films. In 1981, Polish director Krzysztof Kieslowski made *Blind Chance,* which showed three sets of consequences depending on whether the protagonist caught a train at the beginning or not. Unlike *Sliding Doors,* however, *Blind Chance* presents these alternative futures as self-contained stories, one after the other. The same approach appears in *Run Lola Run* (Tom Tykwer, 1998, Germany), where the heroine's desperate attempts to replace a large sum that her inept boyfriend owes to drug dealers are shown as three stories that end very differently after small changes of action on Lola's part. Alternative versions of events based on characters' conflicting recollections had already been used, most famously in Akira Kurosawa's *Rashomon* (1950) and Alain Resnais's *Last Year at Marienbad* (1961).

Although temporal scrambling and "what if?" premises make it more difficult for us to piece story events together, filmmakers usually give us enough clues along the way to keep us from frustration. Usually, the film does not provide a huge number of alternative futures—perhaps only two or three. Within these futures, the cause–effect chain remains linear, so that we can piece it together. The characters and settings tend to remain quite consistent for all the alternative story lines—though often small differences of appearance are introduced to help us keep track of events **(3.11, 3.12)**. The individual story lines tend to parallel one another. In all three presentations of events in *Run Lola Run,* the goal is the same, even though the progression and outcomes are different. The final presentation of

motivation for the changes, such as a time machine. The three *Back to the Future* films (Robert Zemekis, 1985, 1989, 1990) posit that Marty's friend Doc has invented such a machine, and in the first film, it accidentally transports Marty back to 1955, a time just before his parents fell in love. By accidentally changing the circumstances that caused their romance, Marty endangers his own existence in 1985. Despite being comedies aimed primarily at teenagers and despite providing the time machine motivation for the changes, the three films, and particularly Parts I and II, created complex crisscrossings of cause and effect. Marty induces his parents to fall in love and returns safely to 1985 (where his life has been improved as a result of his first time trip). But events that take place in his life in 2015 have effects in 1955, as the villain Biff uses the time machine to travel back and change what happened then in yet another way—one that ends with terrible consequences for Doc and for Marty's whole family. Marty must

3.11 In one story line of *Sliding Doors*, Helen helpfully gets her hair cut short so that we can distinguish her from . . .

3.12 . . . the Helen of the other story line, who keeps her hair long. (A bandage on her forehead was a crucial clue before the haircut, when the two Helens were otherwise identical.)

events tends to give us the impression of being the real, final one, and so "what if?" films usually achieve a sense of closure. Characters sometimes even talk about the events that have changed their lives, as with Doc's blackboard explanation in *Back to the Future II*. In *Sliding Doors*, Helen remarks, "If only I had just caught that bloody train, it'd never have happened."

These films appeal to the way we think in ordinary life. We sometimes speculate about how our lives would change if a single event had been different. We easily understand the sort of game that these films present, and we're willing to play it.

More and more, however, *puzzle films* have denied us this degree of unity and clarity. Here filmmakers create perplexing patterns of story time or causality, trusting that viewers will search for clues by rewatching the movie. An early example was Christopher Nolan's *Memento* (1998), which presents the hero's investigation along two time tracks.

Brief black-and-white scenes show an ongoing present, with story action moving forward chronologically. The more expanded scenes, which are in color, move *backward* through time, so the first plot event we see is the final story event, the second plot event is the next-to-last story event, and so on. This tactic reflects the hero's loss of short-term memory, but it also challenges viewers to piece everything together. At the same time, there are enough uncertainties about the hero's memories to lead viewers to speculate that some mysteries remain unresolved at the close.

The DVD format, which allows random access to scenes, encouraged filmmakers along this path, as did the Internet. Websites and chatrooms buzzed with speculations about what really happened in *Donnie Darko* (2001), *Identity* (2003), *Primer* (2004), and *The Butterfly Effect* (2004). Like other films that twist or break up story time, puzzle movies try to engross us in the dynamics of narrative form.

3.13   In *Exodus,* Dov Landau recounts his traumatic stay in a concentration camp. Instead of presenting this through a flashback, the narration dwells on his face, leaving us to visualize his ordeal.

within the frame. We'll consider screen space and offscreen space in detail in Chapter 5, when we analyze framing as a cinematographic technique. For now, it's enough to say that, just as screen duration selects certain plot spans for presentation, so screen space selects portions of plot space.

Openings, Closings, and Patterns of Development

In Chapter 2, our discussion of formal development in general within the film suggested that it's often useful to compare beginnings and endings. A narrative's use of causality, time, and space usually involves a change from an initial situation to a final situation.

A film does not just start, it *begins.* The opening provides a basis for what is to come and initiates us into the narrative. In some cases, the plot will seek to arouse curiosity by bringing us into a series of actions that has already started. (This is called opening *in medias res,* a Latin phrase meaning "in the middle of things.") The viewer speculates on possible causes of the events presented. *The Usual Suspects* begins with a mysterious man named Keyser Söze killing one of the main characters and setting fire to a ship. Much of the rest of the film deals with how these events came to pass. In other cases, the film begins by telling us about the characters and their situations before any major actions occur.

Either way, some of the actions that took place before the plot started will be stated or suggested so that we can start to connect up the whole story. The portion of the plot that lays out important story events and character traits in the opening situation is called the *exposition.* In general, the opening raises our expectations by setting up a specific range of possible causes for and effects of what we see. Indeed, the first quarter or so of a film's plot is often referred to as the *setup.*

As the plot proceeds, the causes and effects will define narrower patterns of development. There is no exhaustive list of possible plot patterns, but several kinds crop up frequently enough to be worth mentioning.

Most patterns of plot development depend heavily on the ways that causes and effects create a change in a character's situation. The most common general pattern is a *change in knowledge.* Very often, a character learns something in the course of the action, with the most crucial knowledge coming at the final turning point of the plot. In *Witness,* when John Book, hiding out on an Amish farm, learns that his partner has been killed, his rage soon leads to a climactic shoot-out.

A very common pattern of development is the *goal-oriented* plot, in which a character takes steps to achieve a desired object or state of affairs. Plots based on *searches* would be instances of the goal plot. In *Raiders of the Lost Ark,* the protagonists try to find the Ark of the Covenant; in *Le Million,* characters search for a missing lottery ticket; in *North by Northwest,* Roger Thornhill looks for George Kaplan. A variation on the goal-oriented plot pattern is the *investigation,* so typical of detective films, in which the protagonist's goal is not an object, but information, usually about mysterious causes. In more strongly psychological films, such as Fellini's *8¹/₂,* the search and the investigation become internalized when the protagonist, a noted film director, attempts to discover the source of his creative problems.

Time or space may also provide plot patterns. A framing situation in the present may initiate a series of flashbacks showing how events led up to the present situation, as in *The Usual Suspects'* flashbacks. *Hoop Dreams* is organized around the two main characters' high school careers, with each part of the film devoted to a year of their lives. The plot may also create a specific duration for the action, a *deadline.* In *Back to the Future,* the hero must synchronize his time machine with a bolt of lightning at a specific moment in order to return to the present. This creates a goal toward which he must struggle. Or the plot may create patterns of repeated action via cycles of events: the familiar "here we go again" pattern. Such a pattern occurs in Woody Allen's *Zelig,* in which the chameleon-like hero repeatedly loses his own identity by imitating the people around him.

Space can also become the basis for a plot pattern. This usually happens when the action is confined to a single locale, such as a train (Anthony Mann's *The Tall Target*) or a home (Sidney Lumet's *Long Day's Journey into Night*).

A given plot can, of course, combine these patterns. Many films built around a journey, such as *The Wizard of Oz* or *North by Northwest,* involve deadlines. *The Usual Suspects* puts its flashbacks at the service of an investigation. Jacques Tati's *Mr. Hulot's Holiday* uses both spatial and temporal patterns to structure its comic plot. The plot confines itself to a beachside resort and its neighboring areas, and it consumes one week of a summer vacation. Each day certain routines recur: morning exercise, lunch, afternoon outings, dinner, evening entertainment. Much of the film's humor relies on the way that Mr. Hulot alienates the other guests and the townspeople by disrupting their conventional habits **(3.14).** Although cause and effect still operate in *Mr. Hulot's Holiday,* time and space are central to the plot's formal patterning.

For any pattern of development, the spectator will create specific expectations. As the film trains the viewer in its particular form, these expectations become more and more precise. Once we comprehend Dorothy's desire to go home, we see her every action as furthering or delaying her progress toward her goal. Thus her trip through Oz is hardly a sightseeing tour. Each step of her journey (to the Emerald City, to the Witch's castle, to the Emerald City again) is governed by the same principle—her desire to go home.

In any film, the pattern of development in the middle portion may delay an expected outcome. When Dorothy at last reaches the Wizard, he sets up a new

3.14 In *Mr. Hulot's Holiday,* Hulot's aged, noisy car has a flat tire that breaks up a funeral.

obstacle for her by demanding the Witch's broom. Similarly, in *North by Northwest,* Hitchcock's journey plot constantly postpones Roger Thornhill's discovery of the Kaplan hoax, and this, too, creates suspense. The pattern of development may also create surprise, the cheating of an expectation, as when Dorothy discovers that the Wizard is a fraud or when Thornhill sees the minion Leonard fire point-blank at his boss Van Damm. Patterns of development encourage the spectator to form long-term expectations that can be delayed, cheated, or gratified.

A film doesn't simply stop; it *ends.* The narrative will typically resolve its causal issues by bringing the development to a high point, or *climax.* In the climax, the action is presented as having a narrow range of possible outcomes. At the climax of *North by Northwest,* Roger and Eve are dangling off Mount Rushmore, and there are only two possibilities: They will fall, or they will be saved.

Because the climax focuses possible outcomes so narrowly, it typically serves to settle the causal issues that have run through the film. In the documentary *Primary,* the climax takes place on election night; both Kennedy and Humphrey await the voters' verdict and finally learn the winner. In *Jaws,* several battles with the shark climax in the destruction of the boat, the death of Captain Quint, the apparent death of Hooper, and Brody's final victory. In such films, the ending resolves, or closes off, the chains of cause and effect.

Emotionally, the climax aims to lift the viewer to a high degree of tension or suspense. Since the viewer knows that there are relatively few ways the action can develop, she or he can hope for a fairly specific outcome. In the climax of many films, formal resolution coincides with an emotional satisfaction.

A few narratives, however, are deliberately anticlimactic. Having created expectations about how the cause–effect chain will be resolved, the film scotches them by refusing to settle things definitely. One famous example is the last shot of *The 400 Blows* (p. 80). In Michelangelo Antonioni's *L'Eclisse* ("The Eclipse"), the two lovers vow to meet for a final reconciliation but aren't shown doing so.

In such films, the ending remains relatively open. That is, the plot leaves us uncertain about the final consequences of the story events. Our response becomes less firm than it does when a film has a clear-cut climax and resolution. The form may encourage us to imagine what might happen next or to reflect on other ways in which our expectations might have been fulfilled.

Narration: The Flow of Story Information

A plot presents or implies story information. The opening of *North by Northwest* shows Manhattan at rush hour and introduces Roger Thornhill as an advertising executive; it also suggests that he has been busily dictating before we see him. Filmmakers have long realized that the spectator's interest can be aroused and manipulated by carefully divulging story information at various points. In general, when we go to a film, we know relatively little about the story; by the end, we know a lot more, usually the whole story. What happens in between?

The plot may arrange cues in ways that withhold information for the sake of curiosity or surprise. Or the plot may supply information in such a way as to create expectations or increase suspense. All these processes constitute **narration**, the plot's way of distributing story information in order to achieve specific effects. Narration is the moment-by-moment process that guides us in building the story out of the plot. Many factors enter into narration, but the most important ones for our purposes involve the *range* and the *depth* of story information that the plot presents.

Range of Story Information

The plot of D. W. Griffith's *The Birth of a Nation* begins by recounting how slaves were brought to America and how people debated the need to free them. The plot then shows two families, the northern Stoneman family and the southern Camerons. The plot also dwells on political matters, including Lincoln's hope of averting civil war. From the start, then, our range of knowledge is very broad. The plot takes us across historical periods, regions of the country, and various groups of characters. This breadth of story information continues throughout the film. When Ben Cameron founds the Ku Klux Klan, we know about it at the moment the idea strikes him, long before the other characters learn of it. At the climax, we know that the Klan is riding to rescue several characters besieged in a cabin, but the besieged people do not know this. On the whole, in *The Birth of a Nation,* the narration is very *unrestricted:* We know more, we see and hear more, than any of the characters can. Such extremely knowledgeable narration is often called *omniscient narration.*

Now consider the plot of Howard Hawks's *The Big Sleep.* The film begins with the detective Philip Marlowe visiting General Sternwood, who wants to hire him. We learn about the case as he does. Throughout the rest of the film, Marlowe is present in every scene. With hardly any exceptions, we don't see or hear anything that he can't see and hear. The narration is thus *restricted* to what Marlowe knows.

Each alternative offers certain advantages. *The Birth of a Nation* seeks to present a panoramic vision of a period in American history (seen through peculiarly racist spectacles). Omniscient narration is thus essential to creating the sense of many destinies intertwined with the fate of the country. Had Griffith restricted narration the way *The Big Sleep* does, we would have learned story information solely through one character—say, Ben Cameron. We could not witness the prologue scene, or the scenes in Lincoln's office, or most of the battle episodes, or the scene of Lincoln's assassination, since Ben is present at none of these events. The plot would now concentrate on one man's experience of the Civil War and Reconstruction.

Similarly, *The Big Sleep* derives functional advantages from its restricted narration. By limiting us to Marlowe's range of knowledge, the film can create curiosity and surprise. Restricted narration is important to mystery films, since the films engage our interest by hiding certain important causes. Confining the plot to an investigator's range of knowledge plausibly motivates concealing other story information. *The Big Sleep* could have been less restricted by, say, alternating scenes of Marlowe's investigation with scenes that show the gambling boss, Eddie Mars, planning his crimes, but this would have given away some of the mystery. In each of the two films, the narration's range of knowledge functions to elicit particular reactions from the viewer.

Unrestricted and restricted narration aren't watertight categories but rather are two ends of a continuum. Range is a matter of degree. A film may present a broader range of knowledge than does *The Big Sleep* and still not attain the omniscience of *The Birth of a Nation.* In *North by Northwest,* for instance, the early scenes confine us pretty much to what Roger Thornhill sees and knows. After he flees from the United Nations building, however, the plot moves to Washington, where the members of the U.S. Intelligence Agency discuss the situation. Here the viewer learns something that Roger Thornhill will not learn for some time: the man he seeks, George Kaplan, does not exist. Thereafter, we have a greater range of knowledge than Roger does. In at least one important respect, we also know more than the Agency's staff: we know exactly how the mix-up took place. But we still do not know many other things that the narration could have divulged in the scene in Washington. For instance, the Agency's staff do not identify the real agent they have working under Van Damm's nose. In this way, any film may oscillate between restricted and unrestricted presentation of story information. (For more on narration in *North by Northwest,* see pp. 81–82.)

In fact, across a whole film, narration is never completely unrestricted. There is always something we are not told, even if it is only how the story will end. Usually, therefore, we think of a typical unrestricted narration as operating in the way that it does in *The Birth of a Nation:* The plot shifts constantly from character to character to change our source of information.

"In the first section [of Reservoir Dogs], up until Mr. Orange shoots Mr. Blonde, the characters have far more information about what's going on than you have—and they have conflicting information. Then the Mr. Orange sequence happens and that's a great leveller. You start getting caught up with exactly what's going on, and in the third part, when you go back into the warehouse for the climax you are totally ahead of everybody—you know far more than any one of the characters."

— Quentin Tarantino, director

Similarly, a completely restricted narration is not common. Even if the plot is built around a single character, the narration usually includes a few scenes that the character is not present to witness. Though *Tootsie*'s narration remains almost entirely attached to actor Michael Dorsey, a few shots show his acquaintances shopping or watching him on television.

The plot's range of story information creates a *hierarchy of knowledge*. At any given moment, we can ask if the viewer knows more than, less than, or as much as the characters do. For instance, here's how hierarchies would look for the three films we have been discussing. The higher someone is on the scale, the greater his or her range of knowledge:

The Birth of a Nation	*The Big Sleep*	*North by Northwest*
(unrestricted narration)	(restricted)	(mixed and fluctuating)
viewer	viewer—Marlowe	the Agency
all characters		viewer
		Thornhill

An easy way to analyze the range of narration is to ask, *Who knows what when?* The spectator must be included among the "whos," not only because we may get more knowledge than any one character but also because we may get knowledge that *no* character possesses. We shall see this happen at the end of *Citizen Kane*.

Our examples suggest the powerful effects that narration can achieve by manipulating the range of story information. Restricted narration tends to create greater curiosity and surprise for the viewer. For instance, if a character is exploring a sinister house, and we see and hear no more than the character does, a sudden revelation of a hand thrusting out from a doorway will startle us. In contrast, as Hitchcock pointed out, a degree of unrestricted narration helps build suspense. He explained it this way to François Truffaut:

> We are now having a very innocent little chat. Let us suppose that there is a bomb underneath this table between us. Nothing happens, and then all of a sudden, "Boom!" There is an explosion. The public is surprised, but prior to this surprise, it has seen an absolutely ordinary scene, of no special consequence. Now, let us take a suspense situation. The bomb is underneath the table and the public knows it, probably because they have seen the anarchist place it there. The public is aware that the bomb is going to explode at one o'clock and there is a clock in the decor. The public can see that it is a quarter to one. In these conditions this innocuous conversation becomes fascinating because the public is participating in the scene. The audience is longing to warn the characters on the screen: "You shouldn't be talking about such trivial matters. There's a bomb beneath you and it's about to explode!"
>
> In the first case we have given the public fifteen seconds of surprise at the moment of the explosion. In the second case we have provided them with fifteen minutes of suspense. The conclusion is that whenever possible the public must be informed. (François Truffaut, *Hitchcock* [New York: Simon & Schuster, 1967], p. 52)

Hitchcock put his theory into practice. In *Psycho*, Lila Crane explores the Bates mansion in much the same way as our hypothetical character is doing above. There are isolated moments of surprise as she discovers odd information about Norman and his mother. But the overall effect of the sequence is built on suspense because we know, as Lila does not, that Mrs. Bates is in the house. (Actually, as in *North by Northwest*, our knowledge isn't completely accurate, but during Lila's investigation, we believe it to be.) As in Hitchcock's anecdote, our superior range of knowledge creates suspense because we can anticipate events that the character cannot.

Depth of Story Information

A film's narration not only manipulates the range of knowledge but also manipulates the depth of our knowledge. Here we are referring to how deeply the plot plunges into a character's psychological states. Just as there is a spectrum between restricted and unrestricted narration, there is a continuum between objectivity and subjectivity.

A plot might confine us wholly to information about what characters say and do: their external behavior. Here the narration is relatively *objective*. Or a film's plot may give us access to what characters see and hear. We might see shots taken from a character's optical standpoint, the **point-of-view shot**, as we saw in our very first example from *Shadow of a Doubt* (pp. 3–7). Or we might hear sounds as the character would hear them, what sound recordists call *sound perspective*. Visual or auditory point of view offers a degree of subjectivity, one we might call *perceptual subjectivity*.

There is the possibility of still greater depth if the plot plunges into the character's mind. We might hear an internal voice reporting the character's thoughts, or we might see the character's inner images, representing memory, fantasy, dreams, or hallucinations. This can be termed *mental subjectivity*. In such ways, narrative films can present story information at various depths of the character's psychological life.

Does a restricted range of knowledge create a greater subjective depth? Not necessarily. *The Big Sleep* is quite restricted in its range of knowledge, as we've seen. Still, we very seldom see or hear things from Marlowe's perceptual vantage point, and we never get direct access to his mind. *The Big Sleep* uses almost completely objective narration. The omniscient narration of *The Birth of a Nation*, however, plunges to considerable depth with optical point-of-view shots, flashbacks, and the hero's final fantasy vision of a world without war. Hitchcock delights in giving us greater knowledge than his characters have, but at certain moments, he confines us to their perceptual subjectivity (as we've seen, relying on point-of-view shots). Range and depth of knowledge are independent variables.

Incidentally, this is one reason why the term *point of view* is ambiguous. It can refer to range of knowledge (as when a critic speaks of an "omniscient point of view") or to depth (as when speaking of "subjective point of view"). In the rest of this book, we will use point of view only to refer to perceptual subjectivity, as in the phrase "optical point-of-view shot."

Manipulating the depth of knowledge can achieve many purposes. Plunging to the depths of mental subjectivity can increase our sympathy for a character and can cue stable expectations about what the characters will later say or do. The memory sequences in Alain Resnais's *Hiroshima mon amour* and the fantasy sequences in Fellini's *8 1/2* yield information about the protagonists' traits and possible future actions that would be less vivid if presented objectively. A subjectively motivated flashback can create parallels among characters, as does the flashback shared by mother and son in Kenji Mizoguchi's *Sansho the Bailiff* (**3.15–3.18**). A plot can create curiosity about a character's motives and then use some degree of subjectivity— for example, inner commentary or subjective flashback—to explain the cause of the behavior. In *The Sixth Sense,* the child psychologist's odd estrangement from his wife begins to make sense when we hear his inner recollection of something his young patient had told him much earlier.

On the other hand, objectivity can be an effective way of withholding information. One reason that *The Big Sleep* does not treat Marlowe subjectively is that the detective genre demands that the detective's reasoning be concealed from the viewer. The mystery is more mysterious if we do not know his hunches and conclusions before he reveals them at the end. At any moment in a film, we can ask, "How deeply do I know the characters' perceptions, feelings, and thoughts?" The answer will point directly to how the narration is presenting or withholding story information in order to achieve a formal function or a specific effect on the viewer.

One final point about the depth of knowledge that the narration presents: Most films insert *subjective* moments into an overall framework of *objectivity*. For instance, in *North by Northwest,* point-of-view editing is used as we see Roger

3.15   One of the early flashbacks in *Sansho the Bailiff* starts with the mother, now living in exile with her children, kneeling by a stream.

3.16   Her image is replaced by a shot of her husband in the past, about to summon his son Zushio.

3.17   At the climax of the scene in the past, the father gives Zushio an image of the goddess of mercy and admonishes him always to show kindness to others.

3.18   Normal procedure would come out of the flashback showing the mother again, emphasizing it as her memory. Instead, we return to the present with a shot of Zushio, bearing the goddess's image. It is as if he and his mother have shared the memory of the father's gift.

3.19   In *North by Northwest,* Roger Thornhill looks in Van Damm's window (objective narration).

3.20   A shot from Roger's point of view follows (perceptual subjectivity).

3.21   This is followed by another shot of Roger looking (objectivity again).

Thornhill crawl up to Van Damm's window (**3.19–3.21**). Similarly, a dream sequence will often be bracketed by shots of the sleeper in bed.

Flashbacks offer a fascinating instance of the overarching power of objective narration. They are usually motivated as mental subjectivity, since the events we see are triggered by a character's recalling the past. Yet, once we are inside the flashback, events will typically be presented from a wholly objective standpoint. They will usually be presented in an unrestricted fashion, too, and may even include action that the remembering character could have no way of knowing.

In other words, most films take objective narration as a baseline from which we may depart in search of subjective depth but to which we will return. There are, however, other films that refuse this convention. Fellini's *8¹/₂,* Buñuel's *Belle de jour* and Haneke's *Caché,* Resnais's *Last Year at Marienbad,* and Nolan's *Memento* mix objectivity and subjectivity in ambiguous ways. Here, as elsewhere, the manipulation of story information is not just a matter of what action takes place in the film. Any choice about range or depth affects how the spectator thinks and feels about the film as it progresses.

The Narrator

Narration, then, is the process by which the plot presents story information to the spectator. This process may shift between restricted and unrestricted ranges of knowledge and varying degrees of objectivity and subjectivity. Narration may also use a *narrator,* some specific agent who purports to be telling us the story.

The narrator may be a *character* in the story. We are familiar with this convention from literature, as when Huck Finn or Jane Eyre recounts a novel's action. In Edward Dmytryk's film *Murder, My Sweet,* the detective tells his story in flashbacks, addressing the information to inquiring policemen. In the documentary *Roger and Me,* Michael Moore frankly acknowledges his role as a character narrator. He starts the film with his reminiscences of growing up in Flint, Michigan, and he appears on camera in interviews with workers and in confrontations with General Motors security staff.

A film can also use a *noncharacter narrator.* Noncharacter narrators are common in documentaries. We never learn who belongs to the anonymous "voice of God" we hear in *The River, Primary,* or *Hoop Dreams.* A fictional film may employ this device as well. *Jules and Jim* uses a dry, matter-of-fact commentator to lend a flavor of objectivity, while other films might call on this device to lend a sense of realism, as in the urgent voice-over we hear during *The Naked City.*

A film may play on the character/noncharacter distinction by making the source of a narrating voice uncertain. In *Film About a Woman Who . . . ,* we might assume that a character is the narrator, but we cannot be sure because we cannot tell which character the voice belongs to. In fact, it may be coming from an external commentator.

Note that either sort of narrator may present various sorts of narration. A character narrator is not necessarily restricted and may tell of events that she or he did not witness, as the relatively minor figure of the village priest does in John Ford's *The Quiet Man.* A noncharacter narrator need not be omniscient and could confine the commentary to what a single character knows. A character narrator might be highly subjective, telling us details of his or her inner life, or might be objective, confining his or her recounting strictly to externals. A noncharacter narrator might give us access to subjective depths, as in *Jules and Jim,* or might stick simply to surface events, as does the impersonal voice-over commentator in *The Killing.* In any case, the viewer's process of picking up cues, developing expectations, and constructing an ongoing story out of the plot will be partially shaped by what the narrator tells or doesn't tell.

Summing Up Narration

We can summarize the shaping power of narration by considering George Miller's *The Road Warrior* (also known as *Mad Max II*). The film's plot opens with a voice-over commentary by an elderly male narrator who recalls "the warrior Max." After presenting exposition that tells of the worldwide wars that led society to degenerate into gangs of scavengers, the narrator falls silent. The question of his identity is left unanswered.

The rest of the plot is organized around Max's encounter with a group of peaceful desert people. They want to flee to the coast with the gasoline they have refined, but they're under siege by a gang of vicious marauders. The plot action involves Max's agreement to work for the settlers in exchange for gasoline. Later, after a brush with the gang leaves him wounded, his dog dead, and his car demolished, Max commits himself to helping the people escape their compound. The struggle against the encircling gang comes to its climax in an attempt to escape with a tanker truck, with Max at the wheel.

Max is at the center of the plot's causal chain; his goals and conflicts propel the developing action. Moreover, after the anonymous narrator's prologue, most of the film is restricted to Max's range of knowledge. Like Philip Marlowe in *The Big Sleep,* Max is present in every scene, and almost everything we learn gets funneled through him. The depth of story information is also consistent. The narration provides optical point-of-view shots as Max drives his car (**3.22**) or watches a skirmish through a telescope. When he is rescued after his car crash, his delirium is rendered as mental subjectivity, using the conventional cues of slow motion, superimposed imagery, and slowed-down sound (**3.23**). All of these narrational devices encourage us to sympathize with Max.

3.22   A point-of-view shot as Max drives up to an apparently abandoned gyro in *The Road Warrior.*

3.23   The injured Max's dizzy view of his rescuer uses double exposure.

3.24   As the camera tracks away from Max, we hear the narrator's voice: "And the Road Warrior? That was the last we ever saw of him. He lives now only in my memories."

At certain points, however, the narration becomes more unrestricted. This occurs principally during chases and battle scenes, when we witness events Max probably does not know about. In such scenes, unrestricted narration functions to build up suspense by showing both pursuers and pursued or different aspects of the battle. At the climax, Max's truck successfully draws the gang away from the desert people, who escape to the south. But when his truck overturns, Max—and we—learn that the truck holds only sand. It has been a decoy. Thus our restriction to Max's range of knowledge creates a surprise.

There is still more to learn, however. At the very end, the elderly narrator's voice returns to tell us that he was the feral child whom Max had befriended. The desert people drive off, and Max is left alone in the middle of the highway. The film's final image—a shot of the solitary Max receding into the distance as we pull back **(3.24)**—suggests both a perceptual subjectivity (the boy's point of view as he rides away from Max) and a mental subjectivity (the memory of Max dimming for the narrator).

In *The Road Warrior,* then, the plot's form is achieved not only by causality, time, and space but also by a coherent use of narration. The middle portion of the film channels our expectations through an attachment to Max, alternating with more unrestricted portions. And this middle section is framed by the mysterious narrator who puts all the events into the distant past. The narrator's presence at the opening leads us to expect him to return at the end, perhaps explaining who he is. Thus both the cause–effect organization and the narrational patterning help the film give us a unified experience.

The Classical Hollywood Cinema

The number of possible narratives is unlimited. Historically, however, fictional filmmaking has tended to be dominated by a single tradition of narrative form. We'll refer to this dominant mode as the "classical Hollywood cinema." This mode is "classical" because of its lengthy, stable, and influential history, and "Hollywood" because the mode assumed its most elaborate shape in American studio films. The same mode, however, governs many narrative films made in other countries. For example, *The Road Warrior,* though an Australian film, is constructed along classical Hollywood lines. And many documentaries, such as *Primary,* rely on conventions derived from Hollywood's fictional narratives.

This conception of narrative depends on the assumption that the action will spring primarily from *individual characters as causal agents.* Natural causes (floods, earthquakes) or societal causes (institutions, wars, economic depressions) may affect the action, but the narrative centers on personal psychological causes: decisions, choices, and traits of character.

Often an important trait that functions to get the narrative moving is a *desire.* The character wants something. The desire sets up a *goal,* and the course of the narrative's development will most likely involve the process of achieving that goal. In *The Wizard of Oz,* Dorothy has a series of goals, as we've seen: first to save Toto from Miss Gulch, then to get home from Oz. The latter goal creates short-term goals along the way: getting to the Emerald City and then killing the Witch.

If this desire to reach a goal were the only element present, there would be nothing to stop the character from moving quickly to achieve it. But there is a counterforce in the classical narrative: an opposition that creates conflict. The protagonist comes up against a character whose traits and goals are opposed to his or hers. As a result, the protagonist must seek to change the situation so that he or she can achieve the goal. Dorothy's desire to return to Kansas is opposed by the Wicked Witch, whose goal is to obtain the Ruby Slippers. Dorothy must eventually eliminate the Witch before she is able to use the slippers to go home. We shall see in *His Girl Friday* how the two main characters' goals conflict until the final resolution (pp. 401–402).

Cause and effect imply *change.* If the characters didn't desire something to be different from the way it is at the beginning of the narrative, change wouldn't occur. Therefore characters' traits and wants are a strong source of causes and effects.

But don't all narratives have protagonists of this sort? Actually, no. In 1920s Soviet films, such as Sergei Eisenstein's *Potemkin, October,* and *Strike,* no *individual* serves as protagonist. In films by Eisenstein and Yasujiro Ozu, many events are seen as caused not by characters but by larger forces (social dynamics in the former, an overarching nature in the latter). In narrative films such as Michelangelo Antonioni's *L'Avventura,* the protagonist is not active but passive. So the active, goal-oriented protagonist, though common, doesn't appear in every narrative film.

In the classical Hollywood narrative, the chain of actions that results from predominantly psychological causes tends to motivate most other narrative events. Time is subordinated to the cause–effect chain in a host of ways. The plot will omit significant durations in order to show only events of causal importance. (The hours Dorothy and her entourage spend walking on the Yellow Brick Road are omitted, but the plot dwells on the moments during which she meets a new character.) The plot will arrange story chronology so as to present the cause–effect chain most strikingly. For instance, in one scene of *Hannah and Her Sisters,* Mickey (played by Woody Allen) is in a suicidal depression. When we next see him several scenes later, he is bubbly and cheerful. Our curiosity about this abrupt change enhances his comic explanation to a friend, via a flashback, that he achieved a serene attitude toward life while watching a Marx Brothers film.

Specific devices make plot time depend on the story's cause–effect chain. The *appointment* motivates characters' encountering each other at a specific moment. The *deadline* makes plot duration dependent on the cause–effect chain. Throughout, motivation in the classical narrative film strives to be as clear and complete as possible—even in the fanciful genre of the musical, in which song-and-dance numbers become motivated as either expressions of the characters' emotions or stage shows mounted by the characters.

Narration in the classical Hollywood cinema exploits a variety of options, but there's a strong tendency for it to be objective in the way discussed on pages 90–92. It presents a basically objective story reality, against which various degrees of perceptual or mental subjectivity can be measured. Classical cinema also tends toward fairly unrestricted narration. Even if we follow a single character, there are portions of the film giving us access to things the character does not see, hear, or know. *North by Northwest* and *The Road Warrior* remain good examples of this tendency. This weighting is overridden only in genres that depend heavily on mystery, such as the detective film, with its reliance on the sort of restrictiveness we saw at work in *The Big Sleep.*

Finally, most classical narrative films display a strong degree of *closure* at the end. Leaving few loose ends unresolved, these films seek to complete their causal

"Movies to me are about wanting something, a character wanting something that you as the audience desperately want him to have. You, the writer, keep him from getting it for as long as possible, and then, through whatever effort he makes, he gets it."

— Bruce Joel Rubin, screenwriter, *Ghost*

chains with a final effect. We usually learn the fate of each character, the answer to each mystery, and the outcome of each conflict.

Again, none of these features is necessary to narrative form in general. There is nothing to prevent a filmmaker from presenting the dead time, or narratively unmotivated intervals between more significant events. (François Truffaut, Jean-Luc Godard, Carl Dreyer, and Andy Warhol do this frequently, in different ways.) The filmmaker's plot can also reorder story chronology to make the causal chain *more* perplexing. For example, Jean-Marie Straub and Danièle Huillet's *Not Reconciled* moves back and forth among three widely different time periods without clearly signaling the shifts. Dušan Makavejev's *Love Affair, or the Case of the Missing Switchboard Operator* uses flash-forwards interspersed with the main plot action; only gradually do we come to understand the causal relations of these flash-forwards to the present-time events. More recently, puzzle films tease the audience to find clues to enigmatic narration or story events.

The filmmaker can also include material that is unmotivated by narrative cause and effect, such as the chance meetings in Truffaut's films, the political monologues and interviews in Godard's films, the intellectual montage sequences in Eisenstein's films, and the transitional shots in Ozu's work. Narration may be completely subjective, as in *The Cabinet of Dr. Caligari,* or it may hover ambiguously between objectivity and subjectivity, as in *Last Year at Marienbad.* Finally, the filmmaker need not resolve all of the action at the close; films made outside the classical tradition sometimes have quite open endings.

We'll see in Chapter 6 how the classical Hollywood mode also makes cinematic space serve causality by means of continuity editing. For now we can simply note that the classical mode tends to treat narrative elements and narrational processes in specific and distinctive ways. For all of its effectiveness, the classical Hollywood mode remains only one system among many that can be used for constructing narrative films.

Narrative Form in *Citizen Kane*

With its unusual organizational style, *Citizen Kane* invites us to analyze how principles of narrative form operate across an entire film. *Kane*'s investigation plot carries us toward analyzing how causality and goal-oriented characters may operate in narratives. The film's manipulations of our knowledge shed light on the story–plot distinction. *Kane* also shows how ambiguity may arise when certain elements aren't clearly motivated. Furthermore, the comparison of *Kane*'s beginning with its ending indicates how a film may deviate from the patterns of classical Hollywood narrative construction. Finally, *Kane* clearly shows how our experience can be shaped by the way that narration governs the flow of story information.

Overall Narrative Expectations in *Citizen Kane*

We saw in Chapter 2 that our experience of a film depends heavily on the expectations we bring to it and the extent to which the film confirms them. Before you saw *Citizen Kane,* you may have known only that it is regarded as a film classic. Such an evaluation would not give you a very specific set of expectations. A 1941 audience would have had a keener sense of anticipation. For one thing, the film was rumored to be a disguised version of the life of the newspaper publisher William Randolph Hearst. Spectators would thus be looking for events and references keyed to Hearst's life.

Several minutes into the film itself, the viewer can form more specific expectations about pertinent genre conventions. The early "News on the March" sequence suggests that this film may be a fictional biography, and this hint is confirmed once the reporter, Thompson, begins his inquiry into Kane's life. The film does indeed follow the conventional outline of the fictional biography, which typically covers an individual's whole life and dramatizes certain episodes in the period. Examples of this genre would be *Anthony Adverse* (1936) and *The Power and the Glory* (1933). (The latter film is often cited as an influence on *Citizen Kane* because of its complex use of flashbacks.)

The viewer can also quickly identify the film's use of conventions of the newspaper reporter genre. Thompson's colleagues resemble the wisecracking reporters in *Five Star Final* (1931), *Picture Snatcher* (1933), and *His Girl Friday* (1940). In this genre, the action usually depends on a reporter's dogged pursuit of a story against great odds. We are therefore prepared to expect not only Thompson's investigation but also his triumphant discovery of the truth. In the scenes devoted to Susan, there are also some conventions typical of the musical film: frantic rehearsals, backstage preparations, and, most specifically, the montage of her opera career, which parodies the conventional montage of singing success in films like *Maytime* (1937). More broadly, the film evidently owes something to the detective genre, since Thompson is aiming to solve a mystery (What is Rosebud?), and his interviews resemble those of a detective questioning suspects in search of clues.

Note, however, that *Kane*'s use of genre conventions is somewhat equivocal. Unlike many biographical films, *Kane* is more concerned with psychological states and relationships than with the hero's public deeds or adventures. As a newspaper film, *Kane* is unusual in that the reporter fails to get his story. And *Kane* is not exactly a standard mystery, since it answers some questions but leaves others unanswered. *Citizen Kane* is a good example of a film that relies on genre conventions but often thwarts the expectations they arouse.

The same sort of equivocal qualities can be found in *Kane*'s relation to the classical Hollywood cinema. Even without specific prior knowledge about this film, we expect that, as an American studio product of 1941, it will obey norms and rules of that tradition. In most ways, it does. We'll see that desire propels the narrative, causality is defined around traits and goals, conflicts lead to consequences, time is motivated by plot necessity, and narration is objective, mixing restricted and unrestricted passages. We'll also see some ways in which *Citizen Kane* is more ambiguous than most films in this tradition. Desires, traits, and goals are not always spelled out; the conflicts sometimes have an uncertain outcome; at the end, the narration's omniscience is emphasized to a rare degree. The ending in particular doesn't provide the degree of closure we would expect in a classical film. Our analysis will show how *Citizen Kane* draws on Hollywood narrative conventions but also violates some of the expectations that we bring to a Hollywood film.

Plot and Story in *Citizen Kane*

In analyzing a film, it's helpful to begin by segmenting it into sequences. Sequences are often demarcated by cinematic devices (fades, dissolves, cuts, black screens, and so on). In a narrative film, the sequences constitute the parts of the plot.

Most sequences in a narrative film are called *scenes.* The term is used in its theatrical sense, to refer to distinct phases of the action occurring within a relatively unified space and time. Our segmentation of *Citizen Kane* appears below. In this outline, numerals refer to major parts, some of which are only one scene long. In most cases, however, the major parts consist of several scenes, and each of these is identified by a lower-case letter. Many of these segments could be further divided, but this segmentation suits our immediate purposes.

Our segmentation lets us see at a glance the major divisions of the plot and how scenes are organized within them. The outline also helps us notice how the plot organizes story causality and story time. Let's look at these factors more closely.

CITIZEN KANE: PLOT SEGMENTATION

C. Credit title
1. Xanadu: Kane dies
2. Projection room:
        a. "News on the March"
        b. Reporters discuss "Rosebud"
3. El Rancho nightclub: Thompson tries to interview Susan
4. Thatcher library:
        a. Thompson enters and reads Thatcher's manuscript
        b. Kane's mother sends the boy off with Thatcher
First flashback   **c.** Kane grows up and buys the *Inquirer*
        d. Kane launches the *Inquirer's* attack on big business
        e. The Depression: Kane sells Thatcher his newspaper chain
        f. Thompson leaves the library
5. Bernstein's office:
        a. Thompson visits Bernstein
        b. Kane takes over the *Inquirer*
        c. Montage: the *Inquirer's* growth
Second flashback   **d.** Party: the *Inquirer* celebrates getting the *Chronicle* staff
        e. Leland and Bernstein discuss Kane's trip abroad
        f. Kane returns with his fiancée Emily
        g. Bernstein concludes his reminiscence
6. Nursing home:
        a. Thompson talks with Leland
Third flashback   **b.** Breakfast table montage: Kane's marriage deteriorates
        c. Leland continues his recollections
        d. Kane meets Susan and goes to her room
        e. Kane's political campaign culminates in his speech
Third flashback (cont.)   **f.** Kane confronts Gettys, Emily, and Susan
        g. Kane loses the election, and Leland asks to be transferred
        h. Kane marries Susan
        i. Susan has her opera premiere
        j. Because Leland is drunk, Kane finishes Leland's review
        k. Leland concludes his reminiscence
7. El Rancho nightclub:
        a. Thompson talks with Susan
        b. Susan rehearses her singing
        c. Susan has her opera premiere
        d. Kane insists that Susan go on singing
        e. Montage: Susan's opera career
Fourth flashback   **f.** Susan attempts suicide and Kane promises she can quit singing
        g. Xanadu: Susan is bored
        h. Montage: Susan plays with jigsaw puzzles
        i. Xanadu: Kane proposes a picnic
        j. Picnic: Kane slaps Susan
        k. Xanadu: Susan leaves Kane
        l. Susan concludes her reminiscence
8. Xanadu:
        a. Thompson talks with Raymond
Fifth flashback   **b.** Kane destroys Susan's room and picks up a paperweight, murmuring "Rosebud"
        c. Raymond concludes his reminiscence; Thompson talks with the other reporters; all leave
        d. Survey of Kane's possessions leads to a revelation of Rosebud; exterior of gate and of castle; the end
E. End credits

Citizen Kane's Causality

In *Citizen Kane,* two distinct sets of characters cause events to happen. On the one hand, a group of reporters seeks information about Kane. On the other hand, Kane and the characters who know him provide the subject of the reporters' investigations.

The initial causal connection between the two groups is Kane's death, which leads the reporters to make a newsreel summing up his career. But the newsreel is already finished when the plot introduces the reporters. The boss, Rawlston, supplies the cause that initiates the investigation of Kane's life. Thompson's newsreel fails to satisfy him. Rawlston's desire for an angle for the newsreel gets the search for Rosebud under way. Thompson thus gains a goal, which sets him delving into Kane's past. His investigation constitutes one main line of the plot.

Another line of action, Kane's life, has already taken place in the past. There, too, a group of characters has caused actions to occur. Many years before, a poverty-stricken boarder at Kane's mother's boardinghouse has paid her with a deed to a silver mine. The wealth provided by this mine causes Mrs. Kane to appoint Thatcher as young Charles's guardian. Thatcher's guardianship results (in somewhat unspecified ways) in Kane's growing up into a spoiled, rebellious young man.

Citizen Kane is an unusual film in that the object of the investigator's search is not an object but a set of character traits. Thompson seeks to know what aspects of Kane's personality led him to say "Rosebud" on his deathbed. This mystery motivates Thompson's detective-like investigation. Kane, a very complex character, has many traits that influence the other characters' actions. As we shall see, however, *Citizen Kane*'s narrative does not ultimately define all of Kane's character traits.

Kane himself has a goal; he, too, seems to be searching for something related to Rosebud. At several points, characters speculate that Rosebud was something that Kane lost or was never able to get. Again, the fact that Kane's goal remains so vague makes this an unusual narrative.

Other characters in Kane's life provide causal material for the narrative. The presence of several characters who knew Kane well makes Thompson's investigation possible, even though Kane has died. Significantly, the characters provide a range of information that spans Kane's entire life. This is important if we are to be able to reconstruct the progression of story events in the film. Thatcher knew Kane as a child; Bernstein, his manager, knew his business dealings; his best friend, Leland, knew of his personal life (his first marriage in particular); Susan Alexander, his second wife, knew him in middle age; and the butler, Raymond, managed Kane's affairs during his last years. Each of these characters has a causal role in Kane's life, as well as in Thompson's investigation. Note that Kane's wife Emily does not tell a story, since Emily's story would largely duplicate Leland's and would contribute no additional information to the present-day part of the narrative, the investigation. Hence the plot simply eliminates her (via a car accident).

Time in *Citizen Kane*

The order, duration, and frequency of events in the story differ greatly from the way the plot of *Citizen Kane* presents those events. Much of the film's power to engage our interest arises from the complex ways in which the plot cues us to construct the story.

To understand this story in its chronological order and assumed duration and frequency, the spectator must follow an intricate tapestry of plot events. For example, in the first flashback, Thatcher's diary tells of a scene in which Kane loses control of his newspapers during the Depression (4e). By this time, Kane is a middle-aged man. Yet in the second flashback, Bernstein describes young Kane's arrival at the *Inquirer* and his engagement to Emily (5b, 5f). We mentally sort these plot events into a correct chronological story order, then continue to rearrange other events as we learn of them.

Similarly, the earliest *story* event about which we learn is Mrs. Kane's acquisition of a deed to a valuable mine. We get this information during the newsreel, in the second sequence. But the first event in the *plot* is Kane's death. Just to illustrate the maneuvers we must execute to construct the film's story, let's assume that Kane's life consists of these phases:

Boyhood

Youthful newspaper editing

Life as a newlywed

Middle age

Old age

Significantly, the early portions of the plot tend to roam over many phases of Kane's life, while later portions tend to concentrate more on particular periods. The "News on the March" sequence (2a) gives us glimpses of all periods, and Thatcher's manuscript (4) shows us Kane in boyhood, youth, and middle age. Then the flashbacks become primarily chronological. Bernstein's recounting (5) concentrates on episodes showing Kane as newspaper editor and fiancé of Emily. Leland's recollections (6) run from newlywed life to middle age. Susan (7) tells of Kane as a middle-aged and an old man. Raymond's perfunctory anecdote (8b) concentrates on Kane in old age.

The plot becomes more linear in its ordering as it goes along, and this aids the viewer's effort to understand the story. If every character's flashback skipped around Kane's life as much as the newsreel and Thatcher's account do, the story would be much harder to reconstruct. As it is, the early portions of the plot show us the results of events we have not seen, while the later portions confirm or modify the expectations that we formed earlier.

By arranging story events out of order, the plot cues us to form specific anticipations. In the beginning, with Kane's death and the newsreel version of his life, the plot creates strong curiosity about two issues. What does "Rosebud" mean? And what could have happened to make so powerful a man so solitary at the end of his life?

There is also a degree of suspense. When the plot goes back to the past, we already have quite firm knowledge. We know that neither of Kane's marriages will last and that his friends will drift away. The plot encourages us to focus our interest on *how and when* a particular thing will happen. Thus many scenes function to delay an outcome that we already know is certain. For example, we know that Susan will abandon Kane at some point, so we are constantly expecting her to do so each time he bullies her. For several scenes (7b–7j), she comes close to leaving him, though after her suicide attempt he mollifies her. The plot could have shown her walking out (7k) much earlier, but then the ups and downs of their relations would have been less vivid, and there would have been no suspense.

This process of mentally rearranging plot events into story order might be quite difficult in *Citizen Kane* were it not for the presence of the "News on the March" newsreel. The very first sequence in Xanadu disorients us, for it shows the death of a character about whom we so far know almost nothing. But the newsreel gives us a great deal of information quickly. Moreover, the newsreel's own structure uses parallels with the main film to supply a miniature introduction to the film's overall plot:

A. Shots of Xanadu

B. Funeral; headlines announcing Kane's death

C. Growth of financial empire

D. Silver mine and Mrs. Kane's boardinghouse

E. Thatcher testimony at congressional committee

F. Political career

G. Private life; weddings, divorces

H. Opera house and Xanadu

I. Political campaign

J. The Depression

K. 1935: Kane's old age

L. Isolation of Xanadu

M. Death announced

A comparison of this outline with the one for the whole film shows some striking similarities. "News on the March" begins by emphasizing Kane as "Xanadu's Landlord"; a short segment (A) presents shots of the house, its grounds, and its contents. This is a variation on the opening of the whole film (1), which consisted of a series of shots of the grounds, moving progressively closer to the house. That opening sequence had ended with Kane's death; now the newsreel follows the shots of the house with Kane's funeral (B). Next comes a series of newspaper headlines announcing Kane's death. In a comparison with the plot diagram of *Citizen Kane,* these headlines occupy the approximate formal position of the whole newsreel itself (2a). Even the title card that follows the headlines ("To forty-four million U.S. news buyers, more newsworthy than the names in his own headlines was Kane himself. . . .") is a brief parallel to the scene in the projection room, in which the reporters decide that Thompson should continue to investigate Kane's "newsworthy" life.

The order of the newsreel's presentation of Kane's life roughly parallels the order of scenes in the flashbacks related to Thompson. "News on the March" moves from Kane's death to a summary of the building of Kane's newspaper empire (C), with a description of the boardinghouse deed and the silver mine (including an old photograph of Charles with his mother, as well as the first mention of the sled). Similarly, the first flashback (4) tells how Thatcher took over the young Kane's guardianship from his mother and how Kane first attempted to run the *Inquirer.* The rough parallels continue: The newsreel tells of Kane's political ambitions (F), his marriages (G), his building of the opera house (H), his political campaign (I), and so on. In the main plot, Thatcher's flashback describes his own clashes with Kane on political matters. Leland's flashback (6) covers the first marriage, the affair with Susan, the political campaign, and the premiere of the opera *Salammbo.*

These are not all of the similarities between the newsreel and the overall film. You can tease out many more by comparing the two closely. The crucial point is that the newsreel provides us with a map for the investigation of Kane's life. As we see the various scenes of the flashbacks, we already expect certain events and have a rough chronological basis for fitting them into our story reconstruction.

Kane's many flashbacks allow us to see past events directly, and in these portions story and plot duration are close to the same. We know that Kane is 75 years old at his death, and the earliest scene shows him at perhaps 10. Thus the plot covers roughly 65 years of his life, plus the week of Thompson's investigation. The single earlier story event of which we only hear is Mrs. Kane's acquisition of the mine deed, which we can infer took place a short time before she turned her son over to Thatcher. So the story runs a bit longer than the plot—perhaps closer to 70 years. This time span is presented in a screen duration of almost 120 minutes.

Like most films, *Citizen Kane* uses ellipses. The plot skips over years of story time, as well as many hours of Thompson's week of investigations. But plot duration also compresses time through montage sequences, such as those showing the *Inquirer*'s campaign against big business (4d), the growth of the paper's circulation (5c), Susan's opera career (7e), and Susan's bored playing with jigsaw puzzles (7h). Here long passages of story time are condensed into brief summaries quite different from ordinary narrative scenes. We will discuss montage sequences in more detail in Chapter 8, but we can already see the value of such segments in condensing story duration in a comprehensible way.

Citizen Kane also provides a clear demonstration of how events that occur only once in the story may appear several times in the plot. In their respective flashbacks, both Leland and Susan describe the latter's debut in the Chicago premiere of *Salammbo.* Watching Leland's account (6i), we see the performance from the front; we witness the audience reacting with distaste. Susan's version (7c) shows us the performance from behind and on the stage, to suggest her humiliation. This repeated presentation of Susan's debut in the plot doesn't confuse us, for we understand the two scenes as depicting the same story event. ("News on the March" has also referred to Susan's opera career, in parts G and H.) By repeating scenes of her embarrassment, the plot makes vivid the pain that Kane forces her to undergo.

Overall, *Citizen Kane*'s narrative dramatizes Thompson's search by means of flashbacks that encourage us to seek the sources of Kane's failure and to try to identify "Rosebud." As in a detective film, we must locate missing causes and arrange events into a coherent story pattern. Through manipulations of order, duration, and frequency, the plot both assists our search and complicates it in order to provoke curiosity and suspense.

Motivation in *Citizen Kane*

Some critics have argued that Welles's use of the search for "Rosebud" is a flaw in *Citizen Kane,* because the identification of the word proves it to be a trivial gimmick. If indeed we assume that the whole point of *Citizen Kane* is really to identify Rosebud, this charge might be valid. But in fact, Rosebud serves a very important motivating function in the film. It creates Thompson's goal and thus focuses our attention on his delving into the lives of Kane and his associates. *Citizen Kane* becomes a mystery story; but instead of investigating a crime, the reporter investigates a character. So the Rosebud clues provide the basic motivation necessary for the plot to progress. (Of course, the Rosebud device serves other functions as well; for instance, the little sled provides a transition from the boardinghouse scene to the cheerless Christmas when Thatcher gives Charles a new sled.)

Citizen Kane's narrative revolves around an investigation into traits of character. As a result, these traits provide many of the motivations for events. (In this respect, the film obeys principles of the classical Hollywood narrative.) Kane's desire to prove that Susan is really a singer and not just his mistress motivates his manipulation of her opera career. His mother's overly protective desire to remove her son from what she considers to be a bad environment motivates her appointment of Thatcher as the boy's guardian. Dozens of actions are motivated by character traits and goals.

At the end of the film, Thompson gives up his search for the meaning of Rosebud, saying he doesn't think "any word can explain a man's life." Up to a point Thompson's statement motivates his acceptance of his failure. But if we as spectators are to accept this idea that no key can unlock the secrets of a life, we need further motivation. The film provides it. In the scene in the newsreel projection room, Rawlston suggests that "maybe he told us all about himself on his deathbed." Immediately, one of the reporters says, "Yeah, and maybe he didn't." Already the suggestion is planted that Rosebud may not provide any adequate answers about Kane. Later Leland scornfully dismisses the Rosebud issue and goes on to talk of other things. These brief references to Rosebud help justify Thompson's pessimistic attitude in the final sequence.

The presence of the scene in which Thompson first visits Susan at the El Rancho nightclub (3) might seem puzzling at first. Unlike the other scenes in which he visits people, no flashback occurs here. Thompson learns from the waiter that Susan knows nothing about Rosebud; he could easily learn this on his later visit to her. So why should the plot include the scene at all? One reason is that it evokes curiosity and deepens the mystery around Kane. Moreover, Susan's story, when she does tell it, covers events relatively late in Kane's career. As we've seen, the flashbacks go through Kane's life roughly in order. If Susan had told her story first, we would not have all of the material necessary to understand it. But it is plausible that Thompson should start his search with Kane's ex-wife, presumably the surviving person closest to him. In Thompson's first visit, Susan's drunken refusal to speak to him motivates the fact that her flashback comes later. By that point, Bernstein and Leland have filled in enough of Kane's personal life to prepare the way for Susan's flashback. This first scene functions partly to justify postponing Susan's flashback until a later part of the plot.

Motivation makes us take things for granted in narratives. Mrs. Kane's desire for her son to be rich and successful motivates her decision to entrust him to Thatcher, a powerful banker, as his guardian. We may just take it for granted that Thatcher is a rich businessman. Yet on closer inspection, this feature is necessary to motivate other events. It motivates Thatcher's presence in the newsreel; he is powerful enough to have been asked to testify at a congressional hearing. More important, Thatcher's success motivates the fact that he has kept a journal now on deposit at a memorial library that Thompson visits. This, in turn, justifies the fact that Thompson can uncover information from a source who knew Kane as a child.

Despite its reliance on psychological motivation, *Citizen Kane* also departs somewhat from the usual practice of the classical Hollywood narrative by leaving some motivations ambiguous. The ambiguities relate primarily to Kane's character. The other characters who tell Thompson their stories all have definite opinions of Kane, but these do not always tally. Bernstein still looks on Kane with sympathy and affection, whereas Leland is cynical about his own relationship with Kane. The reasons for some of Kane's actions remain unclear. Does he send Leland the $25,000 check in firing him because of a lingering sentiment over their old friendship or from a proud desire to prove himself more generous than Leland? Why does he insist on stuffing Xanadu with hundreds of artworks that he never even unpacks? By leaving these questions open, the film invites us to speculate on various facets of Kane's personality.

Citizen Kane's Parallelism

Parallelism doesn't provide a major principle of development in *Citizen Kane*'s narrative form, but it crops up more locally. We've already seen important formal parallels between the newsreel and the film's plot as a whole. We've also noticed a parallel between the two major lines of action: Kane's life and Thompson's search. In different sense, both men are searching for Rosebud. Rosebud serves as a summary of the things Kane strives for through his adult life. We see him repeatedly fail to find love and friendship, living alone at Xanadu in the end. His inability to find happiness parallels Thompson's failure to locate the significance of the word "Rosebud." This parallel doesn't imply that Kane and Thompson share similar character traits. Rather, it allows both lines of action to develop simultaneously in similar directions.

Another narrative parallel juxtaposes Kane's campaign for the governorship with his attempt to build up Susan's career as an opera star. In each case, he seeks to inflate his reputation by influencing public opinion. In trying to achieve success for Susan, Kane forces his newspaper employees to write favorable reviews of her performances. This parallels the moment when he loses the election and the *Inquirer* automatically proclaims a fraud at the polls. In both cases, Kane fails to realize that his power over the public is not great enough to hide the flaws in his projects: first his affair with Susan, which ruins his campaign, then her lack of singing ability, which Kane refuses to admit. The parallels show that Kane continues to make the same kinds of mistakes throughout his life.

Patterns of Plot Development in *Citizen Kane*

The order of Thompson's visits to Kane's acquaintances allows the series of flashbacks to have a clear pattern of progression. Thompson moves from people who knew

Kane early in his life to those who knew him as an old man. Moreover, each flash-back contains a distinct type of information about Kane. Thatcher establishes Kane's political stance; Bernstein gives an account of the business dealings of the newspaper. These provide the background to Kane's early success and lead into Leland's stories of Kane's personal life, where we get the first real indications of Kane's failure. Susan continues the description of his decline with her account of how he manipulated her life. Finally, in Raymond's flashback, Kane becomes a pitiable old man.

Thus, even though the order of events in the story varies greatly from that given in the plot, *Citizen Kane* presents Kane's life through a steady pattern of development. The present-day portions of the narrative—Thompson's scenes—also follow their own pattern of a search. By the ending, this search has failed, as Kane's own search for happiness or personal success had also failed.

Because of Thompson's failure, the ending of *Citizen Kane* remains somewhat more open than was the rule in Hollywood in 1941. True, Thompson does resolve the question of Rosebud for himself by saying that it would not have explained Kane's life. To this extent, we have the common pattern of action leading to greater knowledge. Thompson has come to understand that a life cannot be summed up in one word. Still, in most classical narrative films, the main character reaches his or her initial goal, and Thompson is the main character of this line of action.

The line of action involving Kane himself has even less closure. Not only does Kane apparently not reach his goal, but the film never specifies what that goal is to start with. Most classical narratives create a situation of conflict. The character must struggle with a problem and solve it by the ending. Kane begins his adult life in a highly successful position (happily running the *Inquirer*), then gradually falls into a barren solitude. We are invited to speculate about exactly what, if anything, would make Kane happy. *Citizen Kane*'s lack of closure in this line of action made it a very unusual narrative for its day.

The search for Rosebud does lead to a certain resolution at the end. We the audience discover what Rosebud was. The ending of the film, which follows this discovery, strongly echoes the beginning. The beginning moved past fences toward the mansion. Now a series of shots takes us away from the house and back outside the fences, with the "No Trespassing" sign and large K insignia.

"Kane, we are told, loved only his mother—only his newspaper—only his second wife—only himself. Maybe he loved all of these, or none. It is for the audience to judge. Kane was selfish and selfless, an idealist, a scoundrel, a very big man and a very little one. It depends on who's talking about him. He is never judged with the objectivity of an author, and the point of the picture is not so much the solution of the problem as its presentation."

— Orson Welles, director

But even at this point, when we learn the answer to Thompson's question, a degree of uncertainty remains. Just because we have learned what Kane's dying word referred to, do we now have the key to his entire character? Or is Thompson's final statement *correct*—that no one word can explain a person's life? Perhaps the "No Trespassing" sign hints that neither Thompson nor we should have expected to explore Kane's mind. It is tempting to declare that all of Kane's problems arose from the loss of his sled and his childhood home life, but the film also suggests that this is too easy a solution. It is the kind of solution that the slick editor Rawlston would pounce on as an angle for his newsreel.

For years critics have debated whether the Rosebud solution does give us a key that resolves the entire narrative. This debate itself suggests the ambiguity at work in *Citizen Kane*. The film provides much evidence for both views and hence avoids complete closure. You might contrast this slightly open ending with the tightly closed narratives of *His Girl Friday* and *North by Northwest* in Chapter 11. You might also compare *Citizen Kane*'s narrative with that of another somewhat open-ended film, *Do The Right Thing*, also discussed in Chapter 11.

Narration in *Citizen Kane*

In analyzing how *Kane*'s plot manipulates the flow of story information, it's useful to consider a remarkable fact: The only time we see Kane directly and in the present is when he dies. On all other occasions, he is presented at one remove—in the newsreel or in various characters' memories. This unusual treatment makes the film something of a portrait, a study of a man seen from different perspectives.

The film employs five narrators, the people whom Thompson tracks down: Thatcher (whose account is in writing), Bernstein, Leland, Susan, and the butler, Raymond. The plot thus motivates a series of views of Kane that are more or less restricted in their range of knowledge. In Thatcher's account (4b–4e), we see only scenes at which he is present. Even Kane's newspaper crusade is rendered as Thatcher learns of it, through buying copies of the *Inquirer*. In Bernstein's flashback (5b–5f), there is some deviation from what Bernstein witnesses, but in general his range of knowledge is respected. At the *Inquirer* party, for example, we follow Bernstein and Leland's conversation while Kane dances in the background. Similarly, we never see Kane in Europe; we merely hear the contents of Kane's telegram, which Bernstein delivers to Leland.

Leland's flashbacks (6b, 6d–6j) deviate most markedly from the narrator's range of knowledge. Here we see Kane and Emily at a series of morning breakfasts, Kane's meeting with Susan, and the confrontation of Kane with Boss Gettys at Susan's apartment. In scene 6j, Leland is present but in a drunken stupor most of the time. (The plot motivates Leland's knowledge of Kane's affair with Susan by having Leland suggest that Kane told him about it, but the scenes present detailed knowledge that Leland is unlikely to possess.) By the time we get to Susan's flashback (7b–7k), however, the range of knowledge again fits the character more snugly. (There remains one scene, 7f, in which Susan is unconscious for part of the action.) The last flashback (8b) is recounted by Raymond and plausibly accords with his range of knowledge; he is standing in the hallway as Kane wrecks Susan's room.

Using different narrators to transmit story information fulfills several functions. It offers itself as a plausible depiction of the process of investigation, since we expect any reporter to hunt down information through a series of inquiries. More deeply, the plot's portrayal of Kane himself becomes more complex by showing somewhat different sides of him, depending on who's talking about him. Moreover, the use of multiple narrators makes the film like one of Susan's jigsaw puzzles. We must put things together piece by piece. The pattern of gradual revelation enhances curiosity—what is it in Kane's past that he associates with Rosebud?—and suspense—how will he lose his friends and his wives?

This strategy has important implications for film form. While Thompson uses the various narrators to gather data, the plot uses them both to furnish us with story information and to *conceal* information. The narration can motivate gaps in knowledge about Kane by appealing to the fact that no informant can know everything about anyone. If we were able to enter Kane's consciousness, we might discover the meaning of Rosebud much sooner—but Kane is dead. The multiple-narrator format appeals to expectations we derive from real life in order to motivate the bit-by-bit transmission of story information, the withholding of key pieces of information, and the arousing of curiosity and suspense.

Although each narrator's account is mostly restricted to his or her range of knowledge, the plot doesn't treat each flashback in much subjective depth. Most of the flashbacks are rendered objectively. Some transitions from the framing episodes use a voice-over commentary to lead us into the flashbacks, but these don't represent the narrators' subjective states. Only in Susan's flashbacks are there some attempts to render subjectivity. In scene 7c, we see Leland as if from her optical point of view on stage, and the phantasmagoric montage of her career (7e) suggests some mental subjectivity that renders her fatigue and frustration.

Against the five character narrators, the film's plot sets another purveyor of knowledge, the "News on the March" short. We've already seen the crucial function of the newsreel in introducing us both to *Kane*'s story and to its plot construction, with the newsreel's sections previewing the parts of the film as a whole. The newsreel also gives us a broad sketch of Kane's life and death that will be filled in by the more restricted behind-the-scenes accounts offered by the narrators. The newsreel is also highly objective, even more so than the rest of the film; it reveals nothing about Kane's inner life. Rawlston acknowledges this: "It isn't enough to tell us what a man did, you've got to tell us who he was." In effect, Thompson's aim is to add depth to the newsreel's superficial version of Kane's life.

Yet we still aren't through with the narrational manipulations in this complex and daring film. For one thing, all the localized sources of knowledge—"News on the March" and the five narrators—are linked together by the shadowy reporter Thompson. To some extent, he is our surrogate in the film, gathering and assembling the puzzle pieces.

Note, too, that Thompson is barely characterized; we can't even identify his face. This, as usual, has a function. If we saw him clearly, if the plot gave him more traits or a background or a past, he would become the protagonist. But *Citizen Kane* is less about Thompson than about his *search*. The plot's handling of Thompson makes him a neutral conduit for the story information that he gathers (though his conclusion at the end—"I don't think any word can explain a man's life"—suggests that he has been changed by his investigation).

Thompson is not, however, a perfect surrogate for us because the film's narration inserts the newsreel, the narrators, and Thompson within a still broader range of knowledge. The flashback portions are predominantly restricted, but there are other passages that reveal an overall narrational omniscience.

From the very start, we are given a god's-eye-view of the action. We move into a mysterious setting that we will later learn is Kane's estate, Xanadu. We might have learned about this locale through a character's journey, the way we acquaint ourselves with Oz by means of Dorothy's adventures there. Here, however, an omniscient narration conducts the tour. Eventually, we enter a darkened bedroom. A hand holds a paperweight, and over this is superimposed a flurry of snow **(3.25)**.

3.25   The elusive image of the paperweight in *Citizen Kane.*

The image teases us. Is the narration making a lyrical comment, or is the image subjective, a glimpse into the dying man's mind or vision? In either case, the narration reveals its ability to command a great deal of story information. Our sense of omniscience is enhanced when, after the man dies, a nurse strides into the room. Apparently, no character knows what we know.

At other points in the film, the omniscient narration calls attention to itself, as when, during Susan's opera debut in Leland's flashback (6i), we see stagehands high above reacting to her performance. (Such omniscient asides tend to be associated with camera movements, as we shall see in Chapter 8.) Most vivid, however, is the omniscient narration at the end of the film. Thompson and the other reporters leave, never having learned the meaning of Rosebud. But we linger in the vast storeroom of Xanadu. And, thanks to the narration, we learn that Rosebud is the name of Kane's childhood sled (see 8.13). We can now associate the opening's emphasis on the paperweight with the closing scene's revelation of the sled.

This narration is truly omniscient. It withheld a key piece of story information at the outset, teased us with hints (the snow, the tiny cottage in the paperweight), and finally revealed at least part of the answer to the question posed at the outset. A return to the "No Trespassing" sign reminds us of our point of entry into the film. Like *The Road Warrior,* then, the film derives its unity not only from principles of causality and time but also from a patterned narration that arouses curiosity and suspense and yields a surprise at the very end.

Summary

Not every narrative analysis runs through the categories of cause–effect, story–plot differences, motivations, parallelism, progression from opening to closing, and narrational range and depth in that exact order, as we have done here. Our purpose in this examination of *Citizen Kane* has been as much to illustrate these concepts as to analyze the film's narrative. With practice, the critic becomes more familiar with these analytical tools and can use them flexibly, suiting his or her approach to the specific film at hand.

In looking at any narrative film, such questions as these may help in understanding its formal structures:

1. Which story events are directly presented to us in the plot, and which must we assume or infer? Is there any nondiegetic material given in the plot?

2. What is the earliest story event of which we learn? How does it relate to later events through a series of causes and effects?

3. What is the temporal relationship of story events? Has temporal order, frequency, or duration been manipulated in the plot to affect our understanding of events?

4. Does the closing reflect a clear-cut pattern of development that relates it to the opening? Do all narrative lines achieve closure, or are some left open?

5. How does the narration present story information to us? Is it restricted to one or a few characters' knowledge, or does it range freely among the characters in different spaces? Does it give us considerable depth of story information by exploring the characters' mental states?

6. How closely does the film follow the conventions of the classical Hollywood cinema? If it departs significantly from those conventions, what formal principle does it use instead?

Most films that we see employ narrative form, and the great majority of theatrical movies stick to the premises of Hollywood storytelling. Still, there are other formal possibilities. We'll consider aspects of non-narrative form in Chapter 11.

In the meantime, other matters will occupy us. In discussing form, we've been examining how we as viewers engage with the film's overall shape. The film, however, also presents a complex blend of images and sounds. Art designers, actors, camera operators, editors, sound recordists, and other specialists contribute to the cues that guide our understanding and stimulate our pleasure. In Part Three, we'll examine the technical components of cinematic art.

Where to Go from Here

Narrative Form

The best introduction to the study of narrative is H. Porter Abbott's *Cambridge Introduction to Narrative* (Cambridge: Cambridge University Press, 2002). For an overview of narrative in history and culture, see Robert Scholes and Robert Kellogg, *The Nature of Narrative* (New York: Oxford University Press, 1966).

Most conceptions of narrative are drawn from literary theory. Umberto Eco's *Six Walks in the Fictional Woods* (Cambridge, MA: Harvard University Press, 1994) provides an entertaining tour. A more systematic introduction is offered by Seymour Chatman in *Story and Discourse: Narrative Structure in Fiction and Film* (Ithaca, NY: Cornell University Press, 1978). See also the journal *Narrative* and the anthology edited by Marie-Laure Ryan, *Narrative Across Media: The Languages of Storytelling* (Lincoln: University of Nebraska Press, 2004).

The Spectator

What does the spectator *do* in making sense of a narrative? Richard J. Gerrig proposes what he calls a "side-participant" model in *Experiencing Narrative Worlds: On the Psychological Activities of Reading* (New Haven, CT: Yale University Press, 1993). Meir Sternberg emphasizes expectation, hypotheses, and inference in his *Expositional Modes and Temporal Ordering in Fiction* (Baltimore: Johns Hopkins University Press, 1978). David Bordwell proposes a model of the spectator's story-comprehending activities in chap. 3 of *Narration in the Fiction Film* (Madison: University of Wisconsin Press, 1985). Compare Edward Branigan, *Narrative Comprehension in Film* (New York: Routledge, 1992).

Narrative Time

Most theorists agree that both cause–effect relations and chronology are central to narrative. The books by Chatman and Sternberg cited above provide useful analyses of causation and time. For specifically cinematic discussions, see Brian Henderson, "Tense, Mood, and Voice in Film (Notes After Genette)," *Film Quarterly* 26, 4 (Summer 1983): 4–17; and Maureen Turim, *Flashbacks in Film: Memory and History* (New York: Routledge, 1989).

Our discussion of the differences between plot duration, story duration, and screen duration is necessarily simplified. The distinctions hold good at a theoretical level, but the differences may vanish in particular cases. Story duration and plot duration differ most drastically at the level of the *whole* film, as when two years of action (story duration) are shown or told about in scenes that occur across a week (plot duration) and then that week is itself rendered in two hours (screen duration). At the level of a smaller *part* of the film—say, a shot or a scene—we usually assume story and plot duration to be equal, and screen—duration may or may not be equal to them. These nuances are discussed in chap. 5 of Bordwell, *Narration in the Fictional Film* (cited above).

Narration

One approach to narration has been to draw analogies between film and literature. Novels have first-person narration ("Call me Ishmael") and third-person narration ("Maigret puffed his pipe as he walked along slowly, hands clasped behind his back"). Does film have first-person or third-person narration, too? The argument for applying the linguistic category of "person" to cinema is discussed most fully in Bruce F. Kawin, *Mindscreen: Bergman, Godard, and First-Person Film* (Princeton, NJ: Princeton University Press, 1978).

Another literary analogy is that of point of view. The best survey in English is Susan Snaider Lanser, *The Narrative Act: Point of View in Prose Fiction* (Princeton, NJ: Princeton University Press, 1981). The applicability of point of view to film is discussed in detail in Edward Branigan, *Point of View in the Cinema: A Theory of Narration and Subjectivity in Classical Film* (New York: Mouton, 1984).

As we'd expect, filmmakers are particularly interested in narration. They must decide what the audience should know at various points and how to present that information in the most striking way. Just as important, the filmmakers must decide how to keep information back and let the audience's curiosity ripen. Gus van Sant's *Elephant,* whose story traces events leading up to a high school shooting, has a plot that shifts backward and forward in time, as scenes are attached to what different characters know. "The multiple points of view replaced the linear story," van Sant explains. "Watching a repeated action or an intersection happen again and again . . . they hold the audience in the story. It's like watching a puzzle unfold."

Is the Classical Hollywood Cinema Dead?

Since the early 1990s, some film historians have claimed that the classical approach to Hollywood narrative faded away during the 1970s, replaced by something variously termed postclassical, postmodern, or post-Hollywood cinema. Contemporary films are thought to be characterized by extremely simple, high-concept premises, with the cause–effect chain weakened by a concentration on high-pitch action at the expense of character psychology. Tie-in merchandising and distribution through other media have also supposedly fragmented the filmic narrative. Other historians argue that the changes are superficial and that in many ways underlying classical principles endure.

For important early texts arguing for postclassicism, see Thomas Schatz, "The New Hollywood," in *Film Theory Goes to the Movies,* ed. Jim Collins, Hilary Radner, and Ava Preacher Collins (New York: Routledge, 1993), pp. 8–36, and Justin Wyatt, *High Concept: Movies and Marketing in Hollywood* (Austin: University of Texas Press, 1994). *Contemporary Hollywood Cinema,* ed. Steven Neale and Murray Smith (New York: Routledge, 1998), contains essays supporting (by Thomas Elsaesser, James Schamus, and Richard Maltby) and opposing (Murray Smith, Warren Buckland, and Peter Krämer) this notion. For arguments that Hollywood cinema still adheres to its traditions, see Kristin Thompson, *Storytelling in the New Hollywood: Understanding Classical Narrative Technique* (Cambridge, MA: Harvard University Press, 1999), and David Bordwell, *The Way Hollywood Tells It: Story and Style in Modern Movies* (Berkeley: University of California Press, 2006).

Screenwriting teachers have also argued that the best modern moviemaking continues the classic studios' approach to structure. The two most influential script gurus are Syd Field, *Screenplay: The Foundations of Screenwriting* (New York: Delta, 2005), and Robert McKee, *Story: Substance, Structure, Style, and the Principles of Screenwriting* (New York: HarperCollins, 1997).

"Rosebud"

Critics have scrutinized *Citizen Kane* very closely. For a sampling, see Joseph McBride, *Orson Welles* (New York: Viking, 1972); Charles Higham, *The Films of Orson Welles* (Berkeley: University of California Press, 1970); Robert Carringer, "Rosebud, Dead or Alive: Narrative and Symbolic Structure in *Citizen Kane*," *PMLA* (March 1976): 185–93; James Naremore, *The Magic World of Orson Welles* (New York: Oxford University Press, 1978); and Laura Mulvey, *Citizen Kane* (London: British Film Institute, 1993).

Pauline Kael, in a famous essay on the making of the film, finds Rosebud a naïve gimmick. Interestingly, her discussion emphasizes *Citizen Kane* as part of the journalist film genre and emphasizes the detective story aspect. See *The "Citizen Kane" Book* (Boston: Little, Brown, 1971), pp. 1–84. In contrast, other critics find Rosebud an incomplete answer to Thompson's search; compare particularly the Naremore and Carringer analyses above. In "Interpreting *Citizen Kane*," in *Interpreting the Moving Image* (Cambridge: Cambridge University Press, 1998), pp. 155–65, Noël Carroll argues that the film stages a debate between the Rosebud interpretation and the enigma interpretation. Robert Carringer's *Making of "Citizen Kane,"* rev. ed. (Berkeley: University of California Press, 1996), offers the most extensive account of the film's production.

Websites

www.screenwritersutopia.com/ Contains discussion of screenwriting problems, including debates about classic screenplay structure.

www.wga.org/writtenby/writtenby.aspx/ The official site of the magazine *Written By,* published by Writers Guild West, the professional organization of American screenwriters. Includes informative articles about trends in screenwriting.

www.creativescreenwriting.com/index.html/ Another magazine, *Creative Screenwriting,* that publishes selected articles and interviews online.

Recommended DVD Supplements

Discussions of narrative form are rare in DVD supplements. In "Making of *Titus*," director Julie Taymor talks about such narrative elements as motifs, point of view, tone, and emotional impact, as well as the functions of film techniques such as music, setting, editing, cinematography, and lighting. In an unusual supplement for *The Godfather,* "Francis Coppola's Notebook," the director shows how he worked by making detailed annotations in his copy of Mario Puzo's original novel. Coppola discusses rhythm, emphasis, and the narrative functions of various techniques. The "Star Beast: Developing the Story" section of *Alien*'s supplements traces the story as it went through a series of very different versions.

PART THREE

FILM STYLE

We are still seeking to understand the principles by which a film is put together. Chapter 2 showed that the concept of film form offers a way to do this. Chapter 3 examined how films can be organized by narrative form, and later we'll see that other types of form are often used in documentaries and experimental films.

When we see a film, though, we do not engage only with its form. We experience a *film*— not a painting or a novel. Analyzing a painting demands a knowledge of color, shape, and composition; analyzing a novel demands knowledge of language. To understand form in any art, we must be familiar with the medium that art utilizes. Consequently, our understanding of a film must also include features of the *film medium*. Part Three of this book investigates just this area. We shall look at four sets of cinematic techniques: two techniques of the shot, mise-en-scene and cinematography; the technique that relates shot to shot, editing; and the relation of sound to film images.

Each chapter will introduce a single technique, surveying the choices it offers to the filmmaker. We'll suggest how you can recognize the technique and its uses. Most important, we'll concentrate on the formal functions of each technique. We'll try to answer such questions as these: How may a technique guide expectations or furnish motifs for the film? How may it develop across a film? How may it direct our attention, clarify or emphasize meanings, and shape our emotional response?

In Part Three, we will also discover that in any film, certain techniques tend to create a formal system of their own. Every film develops specific techniques in patterned ways. This unified, developed, and significant use of particular technical choices we will call *style*. In our study of certain films, we'll see how each filmmaker creates a distinctive stylistic system.

The use a film makes of the medium—the film's style—cannot be studied apart from the film's overall form. We will find that film style interacts with the formal system. In a narrative film, techniques can function to advance the cause–effect chain, create parallels, manipulate story–plot relations, or sustain the narration's flow of information. But some uses of film technique can call attention to patterns of style. In either event, the chapters that follow will continually return to the problem of relations between a film's overall form and its style.

The Shot: Mise-en-Scene

Of all the techniques of cinema, **mise-en-scene** is the one with which we are most familiar. After seeing a film, we may not recall the cutting or the camera movements, the dissolves or the offscreen sound. But we do remember the costumes in *Gone with the Wind* and the bleak, chilly lighting in Charles Foster Kane's Xanadu. We retain vivid impressions of the misty streets in *The Big Sleep* and the labyrinthine, fluorescent-lit lair of Buffalo Bill in *The Silence of the Lambs.* We recall Harpo Marx clambering over Edgar Kennedy's peanut wagon (*Duck Soup*), Katharine Hepburn defiantly splintering Cary Grant's golf clubs (*The Philadelphia Story*), and Michael J. Fox escaping high-school bullies on an improvised skateboard (*Back to the Future*). In short, many of our most sharply etched memories of the cinema turn out to center on mise-en-scene.

What Is Mise-en-Scene?

In the original French, *mise en scène* (pronounced meez-ahn-sen) means "putting into the scene," and it was first applied to the practice of directing plays. Film scholars, extending the term to film direction, use the term to signify the director's control over what appears in the film frame. As you would expect, mise-en-scene includes those aspects of film that overlap with the art of the theater: setting, lighting, costume, and the behavior of the figures. In controlling the mise-en-scene, the director *stages the event* for the camera.

Mise-en-scene usually involves some planning, but the filmmaker may be open to unplanned events as well. An actor may add a line on the set, or an unexpected change in lighting may enhance a dramatic effect. While filming a cavalry procession through Monument Valley for *She Wore a Yellow Ribbon,* John Ford took advantage of an approaching lightning storm to create a dramatic backdrop for the action **(4.1)**. The storm remains part of the film's mise-en-scene even though Ford neither planned it nor controlled it; it was a lucky accident that helped create one of the film's most affecting passages. Jean Renoir, Robert Altman, and other directors have allowed their actors to improvise their performances, making the films' mise-en-scene more spontaneous and unpredictable.

4.1 *She Wore a Yellow Ribbon:* a thunderstorm in Monument Valley.

Realism

Before we analyze mise-en-scene in detail, one preconception must be brought to light. Just as viewers often remember this or that bit of mise-en-scene from a film, so they often judge mise-en-scene by standards of realism. A car may seem to be realistic for the period the film depicts, or a gesture may not seem realistic because "real people don't act that way."

Realism as a standard of value, however, raises several problems. Notions of realism vary across cultures, over time, and even among individuals. Marlon Brando's acclaimed realist performance in the 1954 film *On the Waterfront* looks stylized today. American critics of the 1910s praised William S. Hart's Westerns for being realistic, but equally enthusiastic French critics of the 1920s considered the same films to be as artificial as a medieval epic. Most important, to insist rigidly on realism for all films can blind us to the vast range of mise-en-scene possibilities.

Look, for instance, at the frame from *The Cabinet of Dr. Caligari* (**4.2**). Such a depiction of rooftops certainly does not accord with our conception of normal reality. Yet to condemn the film for lacking realism would be inappropriate, because the film uses stylization to present a madman's fantasy. *The Cabinet of Dr. Caligari* borrows conventions of Expressionist painting and theater, and then assigns them the function of suggesting the madman's delusion.

It is best, then, to examine the *functions* of mise-en-scene in the films we see. While one film might use mise-en-scene to create an impression of realism, others might seek very different effects: comic exaggeration, supernatural terror, understated beauty, and any number of other functions. We should analyze mise-en-scene's function in the total film—how it is motivated, how it varies or develops, how it works in relation to other film techniques.

4.2 An Expressionist rooftop scene created from jagged peaks and slanted chimneys in *The Cabinet of Dr. Caligari.*

The Power of Mise-en-Scene

Confining the cinema to some notion of realism would impoverish mise-en-scene. This technique has the power to transcend normal conceptions of reality, as we can see from a glance at the cinema's first master of the technique, Georges Méliès. Méliès's mise-en-scene enabled him to create a totally imaginary world on film.

A caricaturist and magician, Méliès became fascinated by the Lumière brothers' demonstration of their short films in 1895. (For more on the Lumières, see pp. 182–183.) After building a camera based on an English projector, Méliès began filming unstaged street scenes and moments of passing daily life. One day, the story goes, he was filming at the Place de l'Opéra, and his camera jammed as a bus was passing. After some tinkering, he was able to resume filming, but by this time, the bus had gone and a hearse was passing in front of his lens. When Méliès screened the film, he discovered something unexpected: a moving bus seemed to transform instantly into a hearse. Whether or not the anecdote is true, it at least illustrates Méliès's recognition of the magical powers of mise-en-scene. He would devote most of his efforts to cinematic conjuring.

To do so would require preparation, since Méliès could not count on lucky accidents like the bus–hearse transformation. He would have to plan and stage action for the camera. Drawing on his experience in theater, Méliès built one of the first film studios—a small, crammed affair bristling with theatrical machinery, balconies, trapdoors, and sliding backdrops. He sketched shots beforehand and designed sets and costumes. The correspondence between his detailed drawings and the finished shots is illustrated in **4.3** and **4.4**. As if this were not enough, Méliès starred in his own films (often in several roles per film). His desire to create magical effects led Méliès to control every aspect of his films' mise-en-scene.

Such control was necessary to create the fantasy world he envisioned. Only in a studio could Méliès produce *The Mermaid* (**4.5**). He could also surround himself (playing an astronomer) with a gigantic array of cartoonish cut-outs in *La Lune à un mètre* (**4.6**).

"When Buñuel was preparing The Discreet Charm of the Bourgeoisie, *he chose a tree-lined avenue for the recurring shot of his characters traipsing endlessly down it. The avenue was strangely stranded in open country and it perfectly suggested the idea of these people coming from nowhere and going nowhere. Buñuel's assistant said, 'You can't use that road. It's been used in at least ten other movies.' 'Ten other movies?' said Buñuel, impressed. 'Then it must be good.'"*

4.3   Georges Méliès's design for the rocket-launching scene in *A Trip to the Moon* and . . .

4.4   . . . the scene in the film.

4.5   *The Mermaid* created an undersea world by placing a fish tank between the camera and an actress, some backdrops, and "carts for monsters."

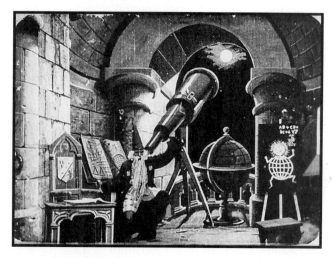

4.6   The telescope, globe, and blackboard are all flat, painted cut-outs in *La Lune á une mètre.*

Méliès's "Star-Film" studio made hundreds of short fantasy and trick films based on such a control over every element in the frame, and the first master of mise-en-scene demonstrated the great range of technical possibilities it offers. The legacy of Méliès's magic is a delightfully unreal world wholly obedient to the whims of the imagination.

Aspects of Mise-en-Scene

What possibilities for selection and control does mise-en-scene offer the filmmaker? We can mark out four general areas: setting, costumes and makeup, lighting, and staging.

Setting

Since the earliest days of cinema, critics and audiences have understood that setting plays a more active role in cinema than it usually does in the theater. André Bazin writes,

> The human being is all-important in the theatre. The drama on the screen can exist without actors. A banging door, a leaf in the wind, waves beating on the shore can heighten the dramatic effect. Some film masterpieces use man only as an accessory, like an extra, or in counterpoint to nature, which is the true leading character.

Cinema setting can come to the forefront; it need not be only a container for human events but can dynamically enter the narrative action. (See 4.124, 4.127, 6.114, 6.124, 6.125, 8.135, and 8.136 for examples of settings without characters.)

The filmmaker may control setting in many ways. One way is to select an already existing locale in which to stage the action, a practice stretching back to the earliest films. Louis Lumière shot his short comedy *L'Arroseur arrosé* ("The Waterer Watered," **4.7**) in a garden, and Jean-Luc Godard filmed the exteriors for *Contempt* on the resort island of Capri, off the coast of Italy (**4.8**). At the close of World War II, Roberto Rossellini shot *Germany Year Zero* in the rubble of Berlin (**4.9**). Today filmmakers often go on location to shoot.

Alternatively, the filmmaker may construct the setting. Méliès understood that shooting in a studio increased his control, and many filmmakers followed his lead. In France, Germany, and especially the United States, the possibility of creating a wholly artificial world on film led to several approaches to setting.

Some directors have emphasized authenticity. For example, Erich von Stroheim prided himself on meticulous research into details of locale for *Greed* (**4.10**). *All the President's Men* (1976) took a similar tack, seeking to duplicate the *Washington Post* office on a soundstage (**4.11**). Even wastepaper from the actual office

4.7 *L'Arroseur arrosé.*

4.8 The filmmakers constructed none of the setting in this shot from *Contempt,* but control of character placement and framing turn it into a nearly abstract composition.

4.9 *Germany Year Zero.*

4.10   Details like hanging flypaper and posters create a tavern scene in *Greed.*

4.11   Replicating an actual newsroom in *All the President's Men.*

4.12   The Babylonian sequences of *Intolerance* combined influences from Assyrian history, 19th-century biblical illustration, and modern dance.

4.13   In *Ivan the Terrible,* Part 2, the decor makes the characters seem to wriggle from one space to another.

4.14   In *Wings of Desire,* busy, colorful graffiti on a wall draw attention away from the man lying on the ground.

4.15   In *Bram Stoker's Dracula,* apart from the candles, the setting of this scene has been obliterated by darkness.

was scattered around the set. Other films have been less committed to historical accuracy. Though D. W. Griffith studied the various historical periods presented in *Intolerance,* his Babylon constitutes a personal image of that city (**4.12**). Similarly, in *Ivan the Terrible,* Sergei Eisenstein freely stylized the decor of the czar's palace to harmonize with the lighting, costume, and figure movement, so that characters crawl through doorways that resemble mouseholes and stand frozen before allegorical murals (**4.13**).

Setting can overwhelm the actors, as in Wim Wender's *Wings of Desire* (**4.14**), or it can be reduced to nothing, as in Francis Ford Coppola's *Bram Stoker's Dracula* (**4.15**).

The overall design of a setting can shape how we understand story action. In Louis Feuillade's silent crime serial *The Vampires,* a criminal gang has killed a courier on his way to a bank. The gang's confederate, Irma Vep, is also a bank employee, and just as she tells her superior that the courier has vanished, an imposter, in beard and bowler hat, strolls in behind them (**4.16**). They turn away from us in surprise as he comes forward (**4.17**). Working in a period when cutting to closer shots was rare in a French film, Feuillade draws our attention to the man by centering him in the doorway.

Something similar happens in a more crowded setting in Juzo Itami's *Tampopo.* The plot revolves around a widow who is trying to improve the food and service she offers in her restaurant. In one scene, a truck driver (in a cowboy hat) helps her by taking her to another noodle shop to study technique. Itami has staged the scene so that the kitchen and the counter serve as two arenas for the action. At first, the widow watches the noodle-man take orders, sitting by her mentor on the edge of the kitchen (**4.18**). Quickly, the counter fills with customers calling out orders. The truck driver challenges her to match the orders with the customers, and she steps closer to the center of the kitchen (**4.19**). After she calls out the orders correctly, she turns her back to us, and our interest shifts to the customers at the counter, who applaud her (**4.20**).

As the *Tampopo* example shows, color can be an important component of settings. The dark colors of the kitchen surfaces make the widow's red dress stand out. Robert Bresson's *L'Argent* creates parallels among its various settings by the recurrence of drab green backgrounds and cold blue props and costumes (**4.21–4.23**). In contrast, Jacques Tati's *Play Time* displays sharply changing color schemes. In the first portion of *Play Time,* the settings and costumes are mostly gray, brown, and black—cold, steely colors. Later in the film, however, beginning in the restaurant scene, the settings start to sport cheery reds, pinks, and greens. This change in the settings' colors supports a narrative development that shows an inhuman city landscape that is transformed by vitality and spontaneity.

A full-size setting need not always be built. Through much of the history of the cinema, filmmakers used miniature buildings to create fantasy scenes or simply to economize. Parts of settings could also be rendered as paintings and combined photographically with full-sized sections of the space. Now, digital special effects are used to fill in portions of the setting, such as cities in *The Phantom Menace* and *The Fifth Element* (**4.24**). Since such special effects also involve cinematography, we look at them in the next chapter.

In manipulating a shot's setting, the filmmaker may create *props*—short for *property*. This is another term borrowed from theatrical mise-en-scene. When an object in the setting has a function within the ongoing action, we can call it a prop. Films teem with examples: the snowstorm paperweight that shatters at the beginning of *Citizen Kane,* the little girl's balloon in *M,* the cactus rose in *The Man Who Shot Liberty Valance,* Sarah Connor's hospital bed turned exercise machine in *Terminator 2: Judgment Day.* Comedies teem with props used for humorous purposes (**4.25**).

In the course of a narrative, a prop may become a motif. The shower curtain in *Psycho* is at first an innocuous part of the setting, but when the killer enters the bathroom, the curtain screens her from our sight. Later, after the murder, Norman Bates uses the curtain to wrap up the victim's body.

Alexander Payne created a story motif by repeating one type of prop in *Election.* The fussy, frustrated high-school teacher begins his day by cleaning out the

4.16 In *Les Vampires,* a background frame created by a large doorway . . .

4.17 . . . emphasizes the importance of an entering character.

"The best sets are the simplest, most 'decent' ones; everything should contribute to the feeling of the story and anything that does not do this has no place. Reality is usually too complicated. Real locations contain too much that is extreme or contradictory and always require some simplifying: taking things away, unifying colors, etc. This strength through simplicity is much easier to achieve on a built set than in an existing location."

— Stuart Craig, art director, *Notting Hill*

4.18   In *Tampopo,* at the start of the scene, the noodle counter, with only two customers, occupies the center of the action. The widow and her truck driver mentor stand inconspicuously at the left.

4.19   After the counter is full, the dramatic emphasis shifts to the kitchen when the widow rises and takes the challenge to name the customers' orders. Her red dress helps draw attention to her.

4.20   When she has triumphantly matched the orders, she gets a round of applause. By turning her away from us, Itami once more emphasizes the counter area, now filled with customers.

4.21   Color links the home in *L'Argent* . . .

4.22   . . . to the school . . .

4.23   . . . and later to the prison.

faculty refrigerator (**4.26**). Soon afterward, he picks up hallway litter (**4.27**). At a major turning point in the plot, he decides to conceal a decisive ballot, which he crumples and secretly drops into a wastebasket (**4.28**). Payne calls this the motif of trash, "of throwing things away, since that's in fact the climax of the film. . . . So we establish it early on."

When the filmmaker uses color to create parallels among elements of setting, a color motif may become associated with several props, as in Souleymane Cissé's

4.24 *The Fifth Element* creates a collagelike city using computer graphics to join images from various sources.

4.25 The irresponsible protagonist of *Groundhog Day* eats an enormous breakfast made up of props that dominate the foreground of the diner setting.

Finye (*The Wind,* **4.29–4.31**). In these and other scenes, the recurrent use of orange creates a cluster of nature motifs within the narrative. Later in this chapter, we shall examine in more detail how elements of setting can weave through a film to form motifs within the narrative.

Costume and Makeup

Like setting, costume can have specific functions in the total film, and the range of possibilities is huge. Erich von Stroheim, for instance, was as passionately committed to authenticity of dress as of setting, and he was said to have created underwear that would instill the proper mood in his actors even though it was never to be seen in the film. In Griffith's *The Birth of a Nation,* a poignant moment occurs when the Little Sister decorates her dress with "ermine" made of cotton dotted with spots of soot (**4.32**). The costume displays the poverty of the defeated Southerners at the end of the Civil War.

In other films, costumes may be quite stylized, calling attention to their purely graphic qualities. Throughout *Ivan the Terrible,* costumes are carefully orchestrated with one another in their colors, their textures, and even their movements. One shot of Ivan and his adversary gives their robes a plastic sweep and dynamism (**4.33**). In *Freak Orlando,* Ulrike Ottinger (herself a costume designer) boldly

4.26   In *Election,* as he discards spoiled leftovers, the teacher is suspiciously watched by the custodian—who will play an important role in his downfall.

4.27   He tosses a scrap of paper into the corridor trash bin.

4.28   A close-up of the teacher's hand discarding the crucial vote for student council president.

4.29   *Finye* begins with a woman carrying an orange calabash as the wind rustles through weeds.

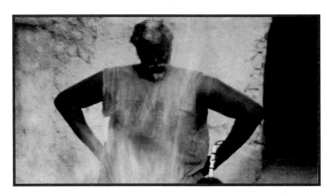

4.30   Later, the vengeful grandfather prepares to stalk his grandson's persecutor by dressing in orange and making magic before a fire.

4.31   At the end, the little boy passes his bowl to someone offscreen—possibly the couple seen earlier.

4.32   In *The Birth of a Nation,* the Little Sister realizes how shabby her dress remains despite her attempts to add festive trimming.

4.33   The sweeping folds of a priest's lightweight black robe contrast with the heavy cloak and train of the czar's finery in *Ivan the Terrible.*

4.34   Stylized costumes in *Freak Orlando.*

4.35   In *8½*, sunglasses shield Marcello from the world.

uses costumes to display the spectrum's primary colors in maximum intensity (**4.34**).

Costumes can play important motivic and causal roles in narratives. The film director Guido in Fellini's *8½* persistently uses his dark glasses to shield himself from the world (**4.35**). To think of Dracula is to recall how his billowing cape enwraps his victims. When Hildy Johnson, in *His Girl Friday,* switches from her role of aspiring housewife to that of reporter, her hats change as well (**4.36, 4.37**). In the runaway bus section of *Speed,* during a phone conversation with Jack, the villain Howard refers to Annie as a "Wildcat"; Jack sees Annie's University of Arizona sweater and realizes that Howard has hidden a video camera aboard the bus. A costume provides the clue that allows Jack to outwit Howard.

As we have already seen in *Tampopo* and *L'Argent* (p. 118), costume is often coordinated with setting. Since the filmmaker usually wants to emphasize the human figures, setting may provide a more or less neutral background, while costume helps pick out the characters. Color design is particularly important here. The *Freak Orlando* costumes (4.34) stand out boldly against the neutral gray background of an artificial lake. In *The Night of the Shooting Stars,* luminous wheat fields set off the hard black-and-blue costumes of the fascists and the peasants (**4.38**). The director may instead choose to match the color values of setting and costume more closely. One shot in Fellini's *Casanova* creates a color gradation that runs from bright red costumes to paler red walls, the whole composition capped by a small white accent (**4.39**). This "bleeding" of the costume into the setting is carried to a kind of limit in the prison scene of *THX 1138,* in which George Lucas strips both locale and clothing to stark white on white (**4.40**).

Ken Russell's *Women in Love* affords a clear example of how costume and setting can contribute to a film's overall narrative progression. The opening scenes portray the characters' shallow middle-class life by means of saturated primary and complementary colors in costume and setting (**4.41**). In the middle portions of the film, as the characters discover love on a country estate, pale pastels predominate (**4.42**). The last section of *Women in Love* takes place around the Matterhorn, and the characters' ardor has cooled. Now the colors have become even paler, dominated by pure black and white (**4.43**). By integrating with setting, costume may function to reinforce narrative and thematic patterns.

Many of these points about costume apply equally to a closely related area of mise-en-scene, the actors' makeup. Makeup was originally necessary because actors' faces would not register well on early film stocks. Up to the present, it has been used in various ways to enhance the appearance of actors on the screen. Over

4.36   Hildy's stylish hat with a low-dipping brim worn early in *His Girl Friday* . . .

4.37   . . . is replaced by a "masculine" hat with its brim pushed up, journalist-style, when she returns to work.

4.38   The climactic skirmish of *The Night of the Shooting Stars.*

4.39   *Casanova:* subtle color gradations and a dramatic accent in the distance.

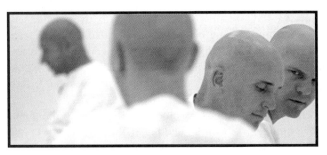

4.40   Heads seem to float in space as white costumes and settings blend in *THX 1138.*

4.41   Bright colors in an early scene of *Women in Love* give way . . .

4.42   . . . to the softer hues of trees and fields . . .

4.43   . . . and finally to a predominantly white-and-black scheme.

4.44   Light, blank backgrounds focus attention on the actors' faces in many shots of *La Passion de Jeanne d'Arc.*

4.45   In *Ivan the Terrible,* Part 1, makeup shapes the eyebrows and hollows the eye sockets to emphasize Ivan's piercing gaze.

the course of film history, a wide range of possibilities has emerged. Dreyer's *La Passion de Jeanne d'Arc* was famous for its complete avoidance of makeup (**4.44**). This film relied on close-ups and tiny facial changes to create an intense religious drama. On the other hand, Nikolai Cherkasov did not look particularly like Eisenstein's conception of Czar Ivan IV, so he wore a wig and false beard, nose, and eyebrows for *Ivan the Terrible* (**4.45**). Changing actors to look like historical personages has been one common function of makeup.

Today makeup usually tries to pass unnoticed, but it also accentuates expressive qualities of the actor's face. Since the camera may record cruel details that would pass unnoticed in ordinary life, any unsuitable blemishes, wrinkles, and sagging skin will have to be hidden. The makeup artist can sculpt the face, making it seem narrower or broader by applying blush and shadow. Viewers expect that female performers will wear lipstick and other cosmetics, but the male actors are often wearing makeup, too (**4.46, 4.47**).

Film actors rely on their eyes to a very great extent (see box, p. 134), and makeup artists can often enhance eye behavior. Eyeliner and mascara can draw attention to the eyes and emphasize the direction of a glance. Nearly every actor will also have expressively shaped eyebrows. Lengthened eyebrows can enlarge the face, while shorter brows make it seem more compact. Eyebrows plucked in a slightly rising curve add gaiety to the face, while slightly sloping ones hint at sadness. Thick, straight brows, commonly applied to men, reinforce the impression of a hard, serious gaze. Thus eye makeup can assist the actor's performance (**4.48, 4.49**).

In recent decades, the craft of makeup has developed in response to the popularity of horror and science fiction genres. Rubber and plasticine compounds create bumps, bulges, extra organs, and layers of artificial skin in such films as David Cronenberg's *The Fly* (**4.50**). In such contexts, makeup, like costume, becomes important in creating character traits or motivating plot action.

Lighting

Much of the impact of an image comes from its manipulation of lighting. In cinema, lighting is more than just illumination that permits us to see the action. Lighter and darker areas within the frame help create the overall composition of each shot and thus guide our attention to certain objects and actions. A brightly illuminated patch may draw our eye to a key gesture, while a shadow may conceal a detail or build up suspense about what may be present. Lighting can also articulate textures: the curve of a face, the grain of a piece of wood, the tracery of a spider's web, the sheen of glass, the sparkle of a gem.

4.46   In *Heat,* Al Pacino's makeup gives him slightly rounded eyebrows and, with the help of the lighting, minimizes the bags under his eyes.

4.47   In *The Godfather Part III,* made five years before *Heat,* Pacino looks older. Not only has his hair been whitened, but the makeup, again assisted by the lighting, gives him more sunken and baggy eyes, more hollow cheeks, and a longer, flatter chin.

4.48   In *Speed,* Sandra Bullock's eyeliner, shadow, and arched brows make her eyes vivid and give her an alert expression.

4.49   For the same scene, the eyeliner on Keanu Reeves makes the upper edges of his eyes stand out. Note also the somewhat fierce curve of the eyebrows, accentuating his slight frown.

4.50   Jeff Goldblum, nearly unrecognizable under grotesque makeup, during his transformation into *The Fly.*

4.51   In *The Cheat,* Cecil B. DeMille suggested a jail cell by casting a bright light on a man's face and body through unseen bars.

4.52   Robert Bresson's *Pickpocket.*

Lighting shapes objects by creating highlights and shadows. A highlight is a patch of relative brightness on a surface. The man's face in **4.51** and the edge of the fingers in **4.52** display highlights. Highlights provide important cues to the texture of the surface. If the surface is smooth, like glass or chrome, the highlights tend to gleam or sparkle; a rougher surface, like a coarse stone facing, yields more diffuse highlights.

There are two basic types of shadows, each of which is important in film composition: *attached* shadows, or *shading,* and *cast* shadows. An attached shadow occurs when light fails to illuminate part of an object because of the object's shape or surface features. If a person sits by a candle in a darkened room, patches of the face and body will fall into darkness. Most obviously, the nose often creates a patch of darkness on an adjoining cheek. This phenomenon is shading, or attached shadow. But the candle also projects a shadow on the wall behind. This is a cast shadow, because the body blocks out the light. The shadows in 4.51, for example, are cast shadows, made by bars between the actor and the light source. But in 4.52, the small, dark patches on the hand are attached shadows, for they are caused by the three-dimensional curves and ridges of the hand itself.

"Light is everything. It expresses ideology, emotion, colour, depth, style. It can efface, narrate, describe. With the right lighting, the ugliest face, the most idiotic expression can radiate with beauty or intelligence."

— Frederico Fellini, director

4.53   Attached shadows on faces create a dramatic composition in John Huston's *Asphalt Jungle*.

As these examples suggest, highlights and shadows help create our sense of a scene's space. In 4.51, a few shadows imply an entire prison cell. Lighting also shapes a shot's overall composition. One shot from John Huston's *Asphalt Jungle* welds the gang members into a unit by the pool of light cast by a hanging lamp (**4.53**). At the same time, it sets up a scale of importance, emphasizing the protagonist by making him the most frontal and clearly lit figure.

A shot's lighting affects our sense of the shape and texture of the objects depicted. If a ball is lit straight on from the front, it appears round. If the same ball is lit from the side, we see it as a half-circle. Hollis Frampton's short film *Lemon* consists primarily of light moving around a lemon, and the shifting shadows create dramatically changing patterns of yellow and black. This film almost seems designed to prove the truth of a remark made by Josef von Sternberg, one of the cinema's masters of film lighting: "The proper use of light can embellish and dramatize every object."

For our purposes, we can isolate four major features of film lighting: its quality, direction, source, and color.

Lighting *quality* refers to the relative intensity of the illumination. *Hard* lighting creates clearly defined shadows, crisp textures, and sharp edges, whereas *soft* lighting creates a diffused illumination. In nature, the noonday sun creates hard light, while an overcast sky creates soft light. The terms are relative, and many lighting situations will fall between the extremes, but we can usually recognize the differences (**4.54, 4.55**).

The *direction* of lighting in a shot refers to the path of light from its source or sources to the object lit. "Every light," wrote von Sternberg, "has a point where it is brightest and a point toward which it wanders to lose itself completely. . . . The journey of rays from that central core to the outposts of blackness is the adventure and drama of light." For convenience we can distinguish among frontal lighting, sidelighting, backlighting, underlighting, and top lighting.

Frontal lighting can be recognized by its tendency to eliminate shadows. In **4.56**, from Jean-Luc Godard's *La Chinoise*, the result of such frontal lighting is a fairly flat-looking image. Contrast **4.57**, from *Touch of Evil*, in which Orson Welles uses a hard **sidelight** (also called a *crosslight*) to sculpt the character's features.

Backlighting, as the name suggests, comes from behind the subject filmed. It can be positioned at many angles: high above the figure, at various angles off to the side, pointing straight at the camera, or from below. Used with no other sources of light, backlighting tends to create silhouettes, as in **4.58**. Combined with more frontal sources of light, the technique can create an unobtrusively illuminated contour. This use of backlighting is called *edge lighting* or *rim lighting* (**4.59**).

As its name implies, **underlighting** suggests that the light comes from below the subject. In **4.60**, the underlighting suggests an offscreen flashlight. Since

4.54   In this shot from Satyajit Ray's *Aparajito*, Apu's mother and the globe she holds are emphasized by hard lighting, while . . .

4.55   . . . in another shot from the same film, softer lighting blurs contours and textures and makes for more diffusion and gentler contrasts between light and shade.

4.56   In *La Chinoise*, frontal lighting makes the actress's shadow fall directly behind her, where we cannot see it.

4.57 In *Touch of Evil,* sidelight creates sharp attached shadows by the character's nose, cheek, and lips, while long cast shadows appear on the file cabinets at the left.

4.58 In Godard's *Passion,* the lamp and window provide backlighting that presents the woman almost entirely in silhouette.

4.59 In *Wings,* a narrow line of light makes each actor's body stand out from the background.

4.60 In *The Sixth Sense,* a flashlight lights the boy's face from below, enhancing our empathy with his fright as he feels the presence of a ghost.

4.61 Top lighting in Josef von Sternberg's *Shanghai Express.*

4.62 Apparent and hidden light sources in *The Miracle Worker.*

underlighting tends to distort features, it is often used to create dramatic horror effects, but it may also simply indicate a realistic light source, such as a fireplace. As usual, a particular technique can function differently according to context.

Top lighting is exemplified by **4.61**, where the spotlight shines down from almost directly above Marlene Dietrich's face. Von Sternberg frequently used such a high frontal light to bring out the line of his star's cheekbones. (Our earlier example from *Asphalt Jungle* in Figure 4.53 provides a less glamorous instance of top lighting.)

Lighting can also be characterized by its *source.* In making a documentary, the filmmaker may be obliged to shoot with the light available in the actual surroundings. Most fictional films, however, use extra light sources to obtain greater control of the image's look. In most fictional films, the table lamps and streetlights you see in the mise-en-scene are not the principal sources of illumination for the filming. But these visible sources of light will motivate the lighting decisions made in production. The filmmaker will usually strive to create a lighting design that is consistent with the sources in the setting. In **4.62**, from *The Miracle Worker,* the window in the rear and the lantern in the right foreground are purportedly the sources of illumination, but you can see the many studio lights used in this shot reflected as tiny white dots in the glass lantern.

Directors and cinematographers manipulating the lighting of the scene will start from the assumption that any subject normally requires two light sources:

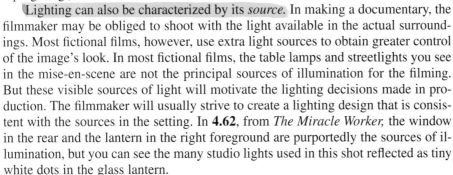

4.63   Strong key and soft fill light combined in *The Bodyguard*.

4.64   *Bezhin Meadow.*

"When taking close-ups in a colour picture, there is too much visual information in the background, which tends to draw attention away from the face. That is why the faces of the actresses in the old black and white pictures are so vividly remembered. Even now, movie fans nostalgically recall Dietrich . . . Garbo . . . Lamarr . . . Why? Filmed in black and white, those figures looked as if they were lit from within. When a face appeared on the screen over-exposed—the high-key technique, which also erased imperfections—it was as if a bright object was emerging from the screen."

— Nestor Almendros, cinematographer

a **key light** and a **fill light**. The key light is the primary source, providing the dominant illumination and casting the strongest shadows. The key light is the most directional light, and it usually corresponds to the motivating light source in the setting. A fill is a less intense illumination that "fills in," softening or eliminating shadows cast by the key light. By combining key and fill, and by adding other sources, lighting can be controlled quite exactly.

The key lighting source may be aimed at the subject from any angle, as our examples of lighting direction have indicated. As one shot from *Ivan the Terrible* shows (4.77), underlighting may be the key source, while a softer and dimmer fill falls on the setting behind the figure.

Lights from various directions can be combined in any way. A shot may use key and fill lights without backlighting. In the frame from *The Bodyguard* (**4.63**), a strong key light from offscreen left throws a dramatic shadow on the wall at the right. The dim fill light inconspicuously shows the back wall and ceiling of the set, but leaves the right side of the actor's head dark.

In **4.64**, from *Bezhin Meadow*, Eisenstein uses a number of light sources and directions. The key light falling on the figures comes from the left side, but it is hard on the face of the old woman in the foreground and softened on the face of the man because a fill light comes in from the right. This fill light falls on the woman's forehead and nose.

Classical Hollywood filmmaking developed the custom of using at least three light sources per shot: key light, fill light, and backlight. The most basic arrangement of these lights on a single figure is shown in **4.65**. The *backlight* comes from behind and above the figure, the *key light* comes diagonally from the front, and a *fill light* comes from a position near the camera. The key will usually be closer to the figure or brighter than the fill. Typically, each major character in a scene will have his or her own key, fill, and backlight. If another actor is added (as in the dotted figure in 4.65), the key light for one can be altered slightly to form the backlight for the other, and vice versa, with a fill light on either side of the camera.

In **4.66**, the Bette Davis character in *Jezebel* is the most important figure, and the **three-point lighting** centers attention on her: a bright backlight from the rear upper right highlights her hair and edge-lights her left arm. The key light is off left, making her right arm brightly illuminated. A fill light comes from just to the right of the camera. It is less bright than the key. This balanced lighting creates mild shading, modeling Davis's face to suggest volume rather than flatness. (Note the slight shadow cast by her nose.) Davis's backlight and key light serve to illuminate the woman behind her at the right, but less prominently. Other fill lights, called *background* or *set lighting*, fall on the setting and on the crowd at the left rear. Three-point lighting emerged during the studio era of Hollywood filmmaking, and it is still widely used, as in **4.67**, from Steven Spielberg's *Catch Me If You Can*.

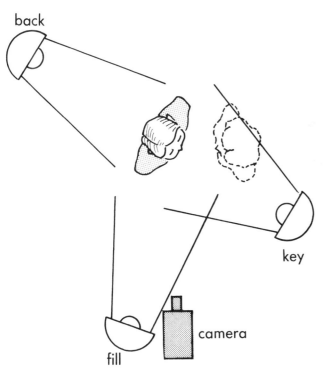

4.66   The three-point system's effect as it looks on the screen in *Jezebel.*

4.65   Three-point lighting, one of the basic techniques of Hollywood cinema.

4.67   In *Catch Me If You Can,* the ne'er-do-well father can't suppress a grin at his son's impersonation, and the high-key lighting accentuates the upbeat tone of the scene.

4.68   *Back to the Future:* day . . .

You may have already noticed that this three-point lighting system demands that the lamps be rearranged virtually every time the camera shifts to a new framing of the scene. In spite of the great cost involved, most Hollywood films have a different lighting arrangement for each camera position. Such variations in the light sources do not conform to reality, but they do enable filmmakers to create clear compositions for each shot.

Three-point lighting was particularly well suited for the high-key lighting used in classical Hollywood cinema and other filmmaking traditions. **High-key lighting** refers to an overall lighting design that uses fill light and backlight to create low contrast between brighter and darker areas. Usually, the light quality is soft, making shadow areas fairly transparent. The frames from *Jezebel* (4.66) and from *Catch Me If You Can* (4.67) exemplify high-key lighting. Hollywood directors and cinematographers have relied on this for comedies, adventure films, and most dramas.

4.69   . . . versus night.

4.70 In *Kanal*, low-key lighting creates a harsh highlight on one side of the woman's face, a deep shadow on the other.

"When I started watching films in the 1940s and 1950s, Indian cinematography was completely under the influence of Hollywood aesthetics, which mostly insisted on the 'ideal light' for the face, using heavy diffusion and strong backlight. I came to resent the complete disregard of the actual source of light and the clichéd use of backlight. Using backlight all the time is like using chili powder in whatever you cook."

— Subrata Mitra, cinematographer

High-key lighting is not used simply to render a brightly lit situation, such as a dazzling ballroom or a sunny afternoon. High-key lighting is an overall approach to illumination that can suggest different lighting conditions or times of day. Consider, for example, two frames from *Back to the Future*. The first shot (**4.68**) uses high-key illumination matched to daylight and a brightly lit malt shop. The second frame (**4.69**) is from a scene set in a room at night, but it still uses the high-key approach, as can be seen from the lighting's softness, its low contrast, and its detail in shadow areas.

Low-key illumination creates stronger contrasts and sharper, darker shadows. Often the lighting is hard, and fill light is lessened or eliminated altogether. The effect is of *chiaroscuro,* or extremely dark and light regions within the image. An example is **4.70**, from Andrzej Wajda's *Kanal*. Here the fill light and background light are significantly less intense than in high-key technique. As a result, shadow areas on the left third of the screen remain hard and opaque. In **4.71**, a low-key shot from Leos Carax's *Mauvais sang*, the key light is hard and comes from the side. Carax eliminates both fill and background illumination, creating very sharp shadows and a dark void around the characters.

As our examples indicate, low-key lighting has usually been applied to somber or mysterious scenes. It was common in horror films of the 1930s and films noirs (dark films) of the 1940s and 1950s. The low-key approach was revived in the 1980s in such films as *Blade Runner* and *Rumble Fish* and continued in the 1990s in films noirs like *Se7en* and *The Usual Suspects*. In *El Sur* (**4.72**), Victor Erice's low-key lighting yields dramatic chiaroscuro effects that portray the adult world as a child imagines it.

When the actors move, the director must decide whether to alter the lighting. By overlapping several different key lights, the filmmaker can maintain a constant intensity as actors move around the set. Although constant lighting is not particularly realistic, it has advantages, the main one being that distracting shadows and highlights do not move across actors. At the end of Fellini's *Nights of Cabiria,* for example, the heroine moves diagonally toward us, accompanied by a band of singing young people (**4.73, 4.74**). Alternatively, the filmmaker may have his or her figures move through patches of light and shadow. The sword fight in *Rashomon* is intensified by the contrast between the ferocious combat and the cheerfully dappled lighting pouring into the glade (**4.75**).

We tend to think of film lighting as limited to two colors—the white of sunlight or the soft yellow of incandescent interior lamps. In practice, filmmakers who choose to control lighting typically work with as purely white a light as they can. By use of filters placed in front of the light source, the filmmaker can color the onscreen illumination in any fashion. There may be a realistic source in the scene

4.71 In *Mauvais sang*, a single key light without any fill on the actress's face leaves her expression nearly invisible.

4.72 Low-key lighting in *El Sur* suggests a child's view of the adult world as full of mystery and danger.

4.73   In *Nights of Cabiria,* the heroine is surounded by a band young street musicians.

4.74   As she walks, the lighting on her face does not change, enabling us to notice slight changes in her expression.

4.75   Dappled lighting in *Rashomon.*

4.76   An orange filter suggests that all the light in this scene from *The Green Room* comes from candles.

4.77   In *Ivan the Terrible,* a character's fear registers on his face . . .

4.78   . . . but a blue light also suddenly and briefly shines on it until it disappears and the scene continues.

to motivate the hue of the light. For example, cinematographers often use filters over lighting equipment to suggest the orange tint of candlelight, as in François Truffaut's *The Green Room* (**4.76**). But colored light can also be unrealistic in its motivation. Eisenstein's *Ivan the Terrible,* Part 2, uses a blue light suddenly cast on an actor, nondiegetically, to suggest the character's terror and uncertainty (**4.77, 4.78**). Such a shift in stylistic function—using colored light to perform a function usually confined to acting—is all the more effective because it is so unexpected.

Most film lighting is applied during shooting, but computer-generated imagery allows filmmakers to create virtual lighting designs. Powerful 3D programs enable filmmakers to add broad overall illumination or strongly directional effects. Spotlights can sprinkle highlights on shiny metal, while "shader" tools model objects with attached shadows. In normal filming, filmmakers must reduce the vast amount of visual information in front of the camera, using lighting to clarify and simplify the space. In contrast, digital lighting is built up little by little from simple elements. For this reason, it is very time-consuming; a program may need a day and a night to render moving cast shadows in a single shot. Still, new software and faster computers are likely to accelerate the work process.

We are used to ignoring the illumination of our everyday surroundings, so film lighting is also easy to take for granted. Yet the look of a shot is centrally controlled by light quality, direction, source, and color. The filmmaker can manipulate and combine these factors to shape the viewer's experience in a great many ways. No component of mise-en-scene is more important than "the drama and adventure of light."

4.79   In *The Hudsucker Proxy,* when the mailboy Norville proposes his new toy idea, the clicking balls on his boss's desktop suddenly and inexplicably stop.

4.80   The abstract film *Parabola* uses lighting and a pure background to emphasize sculptural forms.

4.81   The actors strike weary poses in *Seven Samurai.*

4.82   In *White Heat,* Cody Jarrett (James Cagney) bursts up from the prison mess table after learning of his mother's death.

Staging: Movement and Performance

The director may also control the behavior of various figures in the mise-en-scene. Here the word *figures* covers a wide range of possibilities, since the figure may represent a person but could also be an animal (Lassie, the donkey Balthasar, Donald Duck), a robot (R2D2 and C3PO in the *Star Wars* series), an object (**4.79**), or even a pure shape (**4.80**). Mise-en-scene allows such figures to express feelings and thoughts; it can also dynamize them to create various kinetic patterns.

In **4.81**, from *Seven Samurai,* the samurai have won the battle with the bandits. Virtually the only movement in the frame is the driving rain, but the slouching postures of the men leaning on their spears express their tense weariness. In contrast, in *White Heat,* explosive movement and ferocious facial expression present an image of psychotic rage (**4.82**).

In cinema, facial expression and movement are not restricted to human figures. Chapter 10 will discuss animation's flexibility in combining abstract drawings or three-dimensional objects with highly dynamic movement. For example, in science fiction and fantasy films, monsters and robots may be given expressions and gestures through the technique of *stop-action* (also called *stop-motion*). Typically, a small-scale model is made with articulated parts. In filming, it is posed as desired, and a frame or two is shot. Then the figure is adjusted slightly and another frame or two is exposed, and so on. The result on screen is a continuous, if sometimes jerky, movement. The horrendous onslaught of ED-209, the crime-fighting robot in *Robocop,* was created by means of a 12-inch miniature filmed in stop-action (**4.83**). (A full-scale but unmoving model was also built for long shots.) Stop-action can also be used for more abstract and unrealistic purposes, as in Jan Švankmajer's *Dimensions of Dialogue* (**4.84**).

The filmmaker can stage action without three-dimensional objects moving in real space. Drawings of characters who never existed, like Aladdin or Daffy Duck, can be used in animated films. Dinosaurs and fabulous monsters created only as models can be scanned and made to move in a lifelike fashion through computer-generated imagery (see 1.29).

Acting and Actuality   Although abstract shapes and animated figures can become important in the mise-en-scene, the most intuitively familiar cases of figure expression and movement are actors playing roles. Like other aspects of mise-en-scene, the performance is created in order to be filmed. An actor's performance

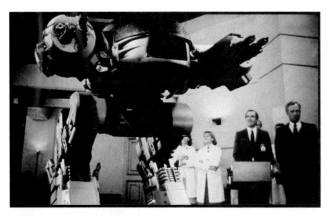

4.83   A miniature used in *Robocop*.

4.84   A conversation between clay figures degenerates as they begin to claw each other to bits in *Dimensions of Dialogue.*

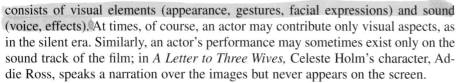

consists of visual elements (appearance, gestures, facial expressions) and sound (voice, effects). At times, of course, an actor may contribute only visual aspects, as in the silent era. Similarly, an actor's performance may sometimes exist only on the sound track of the film; in *A Letter to Three Wives,* Celeste Holm's character, Addie Ross, speaks a narration over the images but never appears on the screen.

Acting is often approached as a question of realism. But concepts of realistic acting have changed over film history. Today we may think that the performances of Russell Crowe and Renee Zellweger in *Cinderella Man* or those given by Heath Ledger and Jake Gyllenhaal in *Brokeback Mountain* are reasonably close to people's real-life behavior. Yet in the early 1950s, the New York Actors Studio style, as exemplified by Marlon Brando's performances in *On the Waterfront* and *A Streetcar Named Desire,* was also thought to be extremely realistic. Fine though we may still find Brando's work in these films, it seems deliberate, heightened, and quite unrealistic. The same might be said of the performances, by professional and amateur actors alike, in post–World War II Italian neorealist films. These were hailed when they first appeared as almost documentary depictions of Italian life, but many of them now seem to us to contain polished performances suitable to Hollywood films. Already, major naturalistic performances of the 1970s, such as Robert De Niro's protagonist in *Taxi Driver,* seem quite stylized. Who can say what the acting in *The Insider, In the Bedroom,* and other recent films will look like in a few decades?

Changing views of realism are not the only reason to be wary of this as a concept for analyzing acting. Often, when people call a performance unrealistic, they are evaluating it as bad. But not all films try to achieve realism. Since the performance an actor creates is part of the overall mise-en-scene, films contain a wide variety of acting styles. Instead of assuming that acting must be realistic, we should try to understand what kind of acting style the film is aiming at. If the functions of acting in the film are best served by a nonrealistic performance, that is the kind that the skillful actor will strive to present. Obvious examples of nonrealistic acting style can be found in *The Wizard of Oz,* for fantasy purposes. (How would a real Wicked Witch behave?) Moreover, realistic performance will always be only one option in film acting. In mass-production filmmaking from Hollywood, India, Hong Kong, and other traditions, overblown performances are a crucial source of the audience's pleasure. Viewers do not expect narrowly realistic acting from Jim Carrey or from martial-arts stars such as Jet Li or Jackie Chan.

Finally, when we watch any fictional film, we are to some degree aware that the performances on the screen are the result of the actors' skills and decisions. (See "A Closer Look.") When we use the phrase "larger than life" to describe an effective performance, we seem to be tacitly acknowledging the actor's deliberate craft. In analyzing a particular film, it is usually necessary to go beyond assumptions about realism and consider the functions and purposes that the actor's craft serves.

"I get impatient with many Hollywood films because there's this assumption that meaning or emotion is contained in those few square inches of an actor's face and I just don't see it that way at all. I think there's a power in withholding information, revealing things gradually. Letting the audience discover things within the frame in time, in the way they stand."

— Alison Maclean, director, *Crush*

THE FILM ACTOR'S TOOLKIT

We might think that the most important task facing an actor is reading dialogue in a convincing and stirring way. Certainly, voice and delivery are very important in cinema, but considered in terms of mise-en-scene, the actor is always part of the overall visual design. Many film scenes contain little or no dialogue, but at every moment onscreen, the actor must be in character. The actor and director shape the performance pictorially.

At all times, film actors use their faces. This was most evident before movies had sound, and theorists of the silent film were full of praise for the subtle facial acting of Charlie Chaplin, Greta Garbo, and Lillian Gish. Since some basic facial expressions (happiness, fear, anger) are understood easily across cultures, it's not surprising that silent film could become popular around the world. Today, with mainstream fiction films using many close-ups (see pp. 43–44), actor's faces are hugely enlarged, and the performers must control their expressions minutely.

The most expressive parts of the face are the brows, mouth, and eyes. All work together to signal how the character is responding to the dramatic situation. In *Jerry Maguire,* the accountant Dorothy Boyd accidentally meets Jerry at an airport baggage conveyor. She has a crush on him, partly because she admires the courageous mission statement he has issued to the sports agency they work for. As he starts to back off from the statement, she eagerly quotes it from memory; Renee Zellwegger's earnest smile and steady gaze suggest that she takes the issues more seriously than Jerry does **(4.85)**. This impression is confirmed when Jerry says, "Uh-huh," and studies her skeptically, his fixed smile signaling social politeness rather than genuine pride **(4.86)**. This encounter sets up one premise of the film—that Jerry's idealistic impulses will need constant shoring up, for he might at any moment slip back into being "a shark in a suit."

The eyes hold a special place in film. In any scene, crucial story information is conveyed by the direction of a character's glance, the use of eyelids, and the shape of the eyebrows. One of Chaplin's most heartrending moments comes in *City Lights,* when the blind flower girl, now sighted, suddenly realizes that he's her benefactor. Chaplin twirls a flower in his teeth, so we can't see the shape of his mouth; we must read yearning in his brows and rapt, dark gaze **(4.87)**.

4.85 Perky and sincere, Dorothy pledges allegiance to Jerry Maguire's idealistic memo.

4.86 Jerry smiles politely, but his sideways glance and brows suggest that he is a bit put off by her earnestness.

Normally, we don't stare intently at the people we talk with. We glance away about half the time to gather our thoughts, and we blink 10–12 times a minute. But actors must learn to look directly at each other, locking eyes and seldom blinking. If an actor glances away from the partner in the conversation, it suggests distraction or evasion. If an actor blinks, it suggests a reaction to what is happening in the scene (surprise, or anxiety). Actors playing forceful characters often stare fixedly. Anthony Hopkins said this of playing Hannibal Lecter: "If you don't blink you can keep the audience mesmerized." (See 10.1, 10.3.) In our *Jerry Maguire* scene, the protagonists watch each other fixedly. When Jerry does close his eyes in response to Dorothy's praise, it indicates his nervousness about confronting the issues that his mission statement raised.

Actors act with their bodies as well. How a character walks, stands, or sits conveys a great deal about personality and attitude. In fact, during the 18th and 19th centuries, *attitude* was used to refer to the way a person stood. Stage acting gave early film a repertoire of postures that could express a character's state of mind. In the 1916 Italian film *Tigre Reale* (*The Royal Tigress*), the diva Pina Menichelli plays a countess with a shady past. At one point, she confesses this in a florid attitude that expresses noble suffering (**4.88**). While few actors today would resort to this stylized posture, early film audiences would have accepted it as vividly expressive, like a movement in dance. Menichelli plays the rest of the scene more quietly, but she still employs expressive attitudes (**4.89, 4.90**).

Chaplin's and Menichelli's gestures show that hands are important tools of the film actor. Hands are to the body what eyes are to the face: They focus our attention and evoke the character's thoughts and feelings. Actress Maureen O'Hara said of Henry Fonda, "All he had to do was wag his little finger and he could steal a scene from anybody." A good example can be seen in the doomsday thriller *Fail-Safe*. Henry Fonda plays the U.S. president, who has learned that an American warplane has been accidentally sent to bomb the Soviet Union. Fonda stands erect at the phone as he hears distressing news about the plane's progress, and he hangs up with his left hand (**4.91–4.94**). By keeping most of the shot still and bare, director Sidney Lumet has given Fonda's fingers the main role, letting them express the president's measured prudence but also suggesting the strain of the crisis.

4.87 In the climax of *City Lights*, by concealing his mouth with the flower he twirls nervously, Chaplin obliges us to find his hope expressed in the upper part of his face.

4.88 In *Tigre Reale*, Menichelli's right hand seizes her hair, as if pulling her head back in agony; but her body still expresses defiance, thrust forward and standing firm as the left hand grips her waist.

4.89 As Menichelli begins to feel shame, she retreats toward the fireplace, turning from us and slumping in a way that suggests regret.

4.90 She keeps her back to the camera as she withdraws, now a pathetic figure.

4.91 In *Fail-Safe,* the president stands erect at the phone as he hears distressing news about the plane's progress, and he hangs up with his left hand.

4.92 The president pauses and rubs his fingers together thoughtfully . . .

4.93 . . . then he taps into the intercom with his right hand.

4.94 As he waits, for a brief moment his left fingers waggle anxiously.

Acting: Functions and Motivation In 1985, Hollywood observers were surprised that Steve Martin wasn't nominated for an Academy Award for *All of Me.* In that film, Martin portrays a man whose body is suddenly inhabited on the right side by the soul of a woman who has just died. Martin used sudden changes of voice, along with acrobatic pantomime, to suggest a split body. In 1999, a similar outcry occurred when Jim Carrey was not nominated for an Oscar for *The Truman Show,* a comedy about a man who is unaware that his entire life has been broadcast as a sitcom on television. Neither Martin nor Carrey could be expected to perform realistically in the narrow sense of the word, since the situations they portray could not exist in the real world. Yet in the context of each of these fantasy-comedies, the performance is completely appropriate.

In films like *All of Me* and *The Truman Show,* a more muted and superficially realistic performance would clearly be inappropriate to the context established by the genre, the film's narrative, and the overall mise-en-scene. This suggests that a performance, realistic or not, should be examined according to its *function* in the context of the film.

We can consider performance along two dimensions. A performance will be more or less *individualized,* and it will be more or less *stylized.* Often we have both in mind when we think of a realistic performance: it creates a unique character, and it does not seem too exaggerated or too underplayed. Marlon Brando's portrayal of Don Vito Corleone in *The Godfather* is quite individualized. Brando gives the Godfather a complex psychology, a distinctive appearance and voice, and a string of facial expressions and gestures that make him significantly different from the standard image of a gang boss. As for stylization, Brando keeps Don Vito in the middle range. His performance is neither flat nor flamboyant; he isn't impassive, but he doesn't chew the scenery either.

But this middle range, which we often identify with realistic performance, isn't the only option. On the individuality scale, films may create broader, more anonymous *types*. Classical Hollywood narrative was built on ideologically stereotyped roles: the Irish cop on the beat, the black servant, the Jewish pawnbroker, the wisecracking waitress or showgirl. Through *typecasting*, actors were selected and directed to conform to type. Often, however, skillful performers gave these conventions a freshness and vividness. In the Soviet cinema of the 1920s, several directors used a similar principle, called *typage*. Here the actor was expected to portray a typical representative of a social class or historical movement (**4.95, 4.96**).

Whether more or less typed, the performance can also be located on a continuum of stylization. A long tradition of film acting strives for a resemblance to what is thought of as realistic behavior. This sense of realism may be created by giving the actors small bits of business to perform while they speak their lines. Frequent gestures and movements by the actors add plausibility to the humor of Woody Allen's films (**4.97**). More intense and explicit emotions dominate *Winchester 73*, in which James Stewart plays a man driven by a desire for revenge (**4.98**).

Psychological motivation is less important in a film like *Trouble in Paradise*, a sophisticated comedy of manners in which the main concern is with more stereotypical characters in a comic situation. In **4.99**, two women competing for the same man pretend to be friendly. Again, the performances are perfectly appropriate to the genre, narrative, and overall style of the film.

4.95 The opening of Sergei Eisenstein's *Strike* presents the cartoonish cliché of the top-hatted capitalist . . .

4.96 . . . while in contrast the workers are later presented as earnest and resolute.

4.97 Verisimilitude in acting: Mia Farrow as Hannah, Diane Wiest as her sister Holly, and Carrie Fisher as their friend April set a table, chatting about the other guests in *Hannah and Her Sisters*.

4.98 In *Winchester 73*, Jimmy Stewart's mild manner occasionally erupts into explosions of anger, revealing him as on the brink of psychosis.

4.99 The exaggerated smiles and gestures in *Trouble in Paradise* are amusing because we know that each woman is trying to deceive the other.

4.100 Nikolai Cherkasov's dramatically raised arm and thrown-back head are appropriate to the heightened style of *Ivan the Terrible*.

Comedy doesn't provide the only motivation for greater stylization. *Ivan the Terrible* is a film that heightens every element—music, costume, setting—to create a larger-than-life portrait of its hero. Nikolai Cherkasov's broad, abrupt gestures fit in perfectly with all of these other elements to create an overall unity of composition (**4.100**).

Some films may combine different degrees of stylization. *Amadeus* contrasts a grotesque, giggling performance by Tom Hulce as Mozart with Murray Abraham's suave Salieri. Here the acting sharpens the contrast between the older composer's decorous but dull music and the young man's irrepressible but offensive genius.

Films like *Caligari, Ivan the Terrible,* and *Amadeus* create stylized performances through extroversion and exaggeration. The director can also explore the possibilities of very muted performances. Compared to normal practice, highly restrained acting can seem quite stylized. Robert Bresson is noted for such restrained performances. Using nonprofessional actors and drilling them in the details of the characters' physical actions, Bresson makes his actors quite inexpressive by conventional standards (**4.101, 4.102**). Although these performances may upset our expectations, we soon realize that such restraint focuses our attention on details of action we never notice in most movies.

Acting in the Context of Other Techniques   By examining how an actor's performance functions in the context of the overall film, we can also notice how acting cooperates with other film techniques. For instance, the actor is always a

4.101   Playing the heroine of *Au Hasard Balthasar,* Anna Wiazemsky looks without expression at her would-be seducer, who wants her to get in his car . . .

4.102   . . . and glances downward, still without registering her thoughts, before getting into the car.

4.103   In *The Cabinet of Dr. Caligari,* Cesare's body echoes the tilted tree trunks, his arms and hands their branches and leaves.

4.104   Jean Seberg in *Breathless,* an inexpressive performance or an enigmatic one?

graphic element in the film, but some films underline this fact. In *The Cabinet of Dr. Caligari,* Conrad Veidt's dancelike portrayal of the somnambulist Cesare makes him blend in with the graphic elements of the setting (**4.103**). As we shall see in our examination of the history of film styles, the graphic design of this scene in *Caligari* typifies the systematic distortion characteristic of German Expressionism.

In *Breathless,* director Jean-Luc Godard juxtaposes Jean Seberg's face with a print of a Renoir painting (**4.104**). We might think that Seberg is giving a wooden performance, for she simply poses in the frame and turns her head. Indeed, her acting in the entire film may seem flat and inexpressive. Yet her face and general demeanor are visually appropriate for her role, a capricious American woman unfathomable to her Parisian boyfriend.

The context of a performance may also be shaped by the technique of film editing. Because a film is shot over a period of time, actors perform in bits. This can work to the filmmaker's advantage, since these bits can be selected and combined to build up a performance in ways that could never be accomplished on the stage. If a scene has been filmed in several shots, with alternate takes of each shot, the editor may select the best gestures and expressions and create a composite performance better than any one sustained performance could be. Through the addition of sound and the combination with other shots, the performance can be built up still further. The director may simply tell an actor to widen his or her eyes and stare off-screen. If the next shot shows a hand with a gun, we are likely to think the actor is depicting fear.

Camera techniques also create a controlling context for acting. Film acting, as most viewers know, differs from theatrical acting. At first glance, that suggests that cinema always call for more underplaying, since the camera can closely approach the actor. But cinema actually calls for a stronger interplay between restraint and emphasis.

In a theater, we are usually at a considerable distance from the actor on the stage. We certainly can never get as close to the theater actor as the camera can put us in a film. But recall that the camera can be at *any* distance from the figure. Filmed from very far away, the actor is a dot on the screen—much smaller than an actor on stage seen from the back of the balcony. Filmed from very close, the actor's tiniest eye movement may be revealed.

Thus the film actor must behave differently than the stage actor does, but not always by being more restrained. Rather, she or he must be able to *adjust to each type of camera distance.* If the actor is far from the camera, he or she will have to gesture broadly or move around to be seen as acting at all. But if the camera and actor are inches apart, a twitch of a mouth muscle will come across clearly. Between these extremes, there is a whole range of adjustments to be made.

Basically, a scene can concentrate on either the actor's facial expression or on pantomimic gestures of the body. Clearly, the closer the actor is to the camera, the more the facial expression will be visible and the more important it will be (although the filmmaker may choose to concentrate on another part of the body, excluding the face and emphasizing gesture). But if the actor is far away from the camera, or turned to conceal the face, his or her gestures become the center of the performance.

Thus both the staging of the action and the camera's distance from it determine how we will see the actors' performances. Many shots in Bernardo Bertolucci's *The Spider's Stratagem* show the two main characters from a distance, so that their manner of walking constitutes the actors' performances in the scene (**4.105**). In conversation scenes, however, we see their faces clearly, as in **4.106.**

Such factors of context are particularly important when the performers are not actors, or even human beings. Framing, editing, and other film techniques can make trained animals give appropriate performances. Jonesy, the cat in *Aliens,* seems threatening because his hissing movement has been emphasized by lighting, framing, editing, and the sound track (**4.107**). In animated films, the

4.105   In this long shot from *The Spider's Stratagem,* the stiff, upright way in which the heroine holds her parasol is one of the main facets of the actress's performance . . .

4.106   . . . while in a conversation scene we can see details of her eye and lip movements.

"You can ask a bear to do something like, let's say, 'Stand up,' and the bear stands up. But you cannot say to a bear, 'Look astonished.' So you have him standing up, but then you have to astonish him. I would bang two saucepans, or get a chicken from a cage, then shake it so it squawked, and the bear would think, 'What was that?' and 'click' I'd have that expression."

— Jean-Jacques Annaud, director, *The Bear*

4.107   A cat "acting" in *Aliens.*

4.108   Devil and thief puppets in *The Mascot.*

filmmaker's manipulation must go further, as in Ladislav Starevich's *The Mascot.* There a conversation between a devil and a thief includes subtle facial expressions and gestures, all created through the frame-by-frame manipulation of puppets (**4.108**).

As with every element of a film, acting offers an unlimited range of distinct possibilities. It cannot be judged on a universal scale that is separate from the concrete context of the entire film's form.

Putting It All Together: Mise-en-Scene in Space and Time

Sandro and Claudia are searching for Anna, who has mysteriously vanished. Anna is Claudia's friend and Sandro's lover, but during their search, they've begun to drift from their goal of finding her. They've also begun a love affair. In the town of Noto, they stand on a church rooftop near the bells, and Sandro says he regrets giving up architectural design. Claudia is encouraging him to return to his art when suddenly he asks her to marry him.

She's startled and confused, and Sandro comes toward her. She is turned away from us. At first, only Sandro's expression is visible as he reacts to her plea "Why can't things be simpler?" (**4.109**). Claudia twists her arms around the bell rope, then turns away from him, toward us, grasping the rope and fluttering her hand. Now we can see that she's quite distraught. Sandro, a bit uneasy, turns away as she says anxiously, "I'd like to see things clearly" (**4.110**).

Brief though it is, this exchange in Michelangelo Antonioni's *L'Avventura* ("The Adventure") shows how the tools of mise-en-scene—setting, costume, lighting, performance, and staging—can work together smoothly. We've considered them separately in order to examine the contribution each one makes, but in any shot, they mesh. They unfold on the screen in space and time, fulfilling several functions.

Most basically, the filmmaker has to guide the audience's attention to the most important areas of the image. We need to spot the items important for the ongoing action. The filmmaker also wants to build up our interest by arousing curiosity and suspense. And the filmmaker tries to add expressive qualities, giving the shot an emotional coloration. Mise-en-scene helps the filmmaker achieve all these purposes.

How did Antonioni guide our attention in the Claudia–Sandro exchange? First, we're watching the figures, not the railing behind them. Based on the story so far, we expect Sandro and Claudia to be the objects of interest. At other points in the film, Antonioni makes his couple tiny figures in massive urban or seaside landscapes. Here, however, his mise-en-scene keeps their intimate interchange foremost in our minds.

4.109   A striking instance of frontality in *L'Avventura:* The characters alternate . . .

4.110   . . . turning their backs on the camera.

Consider the first image merely as a two-dimensional picture. Both Sandro and Claudia stand out against the pale sky and the darker railing. They're also mostly curved shapes—heads and shoulders—and so they contrast with the geometrical regularity of the rails. In the first frame, light strikes Sandro's face and suit from the right, picking him out against the rails. His dark hair is well positioned to make his head stand out against the sky. Claudia, a blonde, stands out against the railing and sky less vividly, but her polka-dot blouse creates a distinctive pattern. And considered only as a picture, the shot roughly balances the two figures, Sandro in the left half and Claudia in the right.

It's hard to think of the shot as simply two-dimensional, though. We instinctively see it as portraying a space that we could move around in. Claudia seems closer to us because her body masks things farther away, a spatial cue called *overlap*. She's also somewhat larger in the frame than Sandro, which reinforces our sense that she's closer. The rope slices across the bottom third of the frame, separating her from him (overlap again). Sandro himself overlaps the railing, which in turn overlaps the sky and the town. We get a sense of distinct planes of space, layers lying closer to or farther from us. Elements of mise-en-scene like costume, lighting, setting, and figure placement create this sense of a three-dimensional arena for the action.

Antonioni has used mise-en-scene to emphasize his characters and their interaction. But that interaction unfolds in time, and it gives him an opportunity to guide our attention while building up suspense and expressing emotion. Claudia is turned away from us when Sandro presses her to marry him, and the rope is taut between them (4.109). How will she respond?

Antonioni starts by giving Claudia a bit of business. She twists the rope around her arms and slips it over her back. This could be a hint that she's drawn to Sandro's proposal. At the same time, she hesitates. For as soon as he presses her, she turns away from him (4.110).

We know that faces give us access to characters' thoughts and emotions. Another filmmaker might have had Claudia already facing us when Sandro asked, so we'd see her response immediately. Antonioni instead makes things uncertain for a moment. He has concealed Claudia's reaction and then lets her turn toward us. To make sure that we watch her and not Sandro at this moment, Antonioni has him turn away when she gestures and speaks ("I'd like to see things clearly"). Our attention is riveted on her.

Soon enough, Sandro turns back toward the camera, so we can see his reaction, but already Claudia's anxiety has flashed out at us. Her complex relation to Sandro—attraction (sliding under the bell rope) and uncertainty (turning away tensely)—has been presented to us concretely.

This is only one moment in a complex scene and complex film, but it shows how various elements of mise-en-scene can cooperate to create a specific effect—

4.111   Narrative expectations guide our eye to the main characters in *Tootsie*.

4.112   A limited palette emphasizes this symmetrical composition in *Life on a String*.

the delayed revelation of a character's emotion. That revelation couldn't have occurred without the director's choices about what to show us at particular points. When we look at an image, we look purposefully. What we notice is guided by our expectations about what might be significant.

Often the form of the whole film sets up our expectations. If a shot shows a crowd, we will tend to scan it looking for a character we recognize from earlier scenes. In **4.111**, although there are several people in the foreground of this shot from *Tootsie,* we will likely notice Julie (Jessica Lange) and Dorothy Michaels (Dustin Hoffman) quickly, since they are our main characters. Similarly, we notice Les, seen here for the first time, because he and Dorothy are exchanging smiles. Similarly, sound can become an important factor controlling our attention, as we shall see in Chapter 7. In addition to the film's story context, there are several ways directors can guide our expectations about what to notice. In the spirit of trying to grasp all the options on the mise-en-scene menu, let's look in more detail at the spatial and temporal possibilities.

Space

Screen Space   In many respects, a film shot resembles a painting. It presents a flat array of colors and shapes. Before we even start to read the image as a three-dimensional space, mise-en-scene offers many cues for guiding our attention and emphasizing elements in the frame.

Take something as simple as balancing the shot. Filmmakers often try to distribute various points of interest evenly around the frame. They assume that viewers will concentrate more on the upper half of the frame, probably because that's

"The audience is only going to look at the most overriding thing in the frame. You must take charge of and direct their attention. It's also the principle of magic: what is the single important thing? Make it easy for them to see it, and you're doing your job."

— David Mamet, director

4.113   *Mars Attacks!:* centering a single character . . .

4.114   . . . and balancing two.

where we tend to find characters' faces. Since the film frame is a horizontal rectangle, the director usually tries to balance the right and left halves. The extreme type of such balancing is bilateral symmetry. In the battle scene in *Life on a String,* Chen Kaige stages the action symmetrically (**4.112**).

More common than such near-perfect symmetry is a loose balancing of the shot's left and right regions. The simplest way to achieve compositional balance is to center the frame on the human body. Filmmakers often place a single figure at the center of the frame and minimize distracting elements at the sides, as in **4.113**. Many of our earlier illustrations display this flexible balance. Other shots may counterweight two or more elements, encouraging our eye to move back and forth, as in **4.114** and our *L'Avventura* dialogue (4.109, 4.110).

Balanced composition is the norm, but unbalanced shots can also create strong effects. In *Bicycle Thieves,* the composition emphasizes the father's new job by massing most of the figures on the right. They don't balance the son, but he seems even more vulnerable by being such an ineffective counterweight (**4.115**). A more drastic example occurs in Michelangelo Antonioni's *Il Grido* (**4.116**), where two strong elements, the hero and a tree trunk, are grouped on the right side of the shot. One could argue that the shot creates a powerful urge for the audience to see the woman's hidden face.

Sometimes the filmmaker will leave the shots a little unbalanced, in order to prime our expectation that something will change position in the frame. The cinema of the 1910s offers intriguing examples. Very often a doorway in the back of the set allowed the director to show that new characters were entering the scene, but

4.115 This composition from *Bicycle Thieves* emphasizes the father's new job by massing most of the figures on the right.

4.116 In *Il Grido,* instead of balancing the couple, the composition centers the man. If there were no tree in the frame, the shot would still be somewhat weighted to the right, but the unexpected vertical of the trunk makes that side even heavier.

4.117 From quite early in cinema history, filmmakers used unbalanced compositions to prepare the viewer for new narrative developments. In Yevgenii Bauer's *The Dying Swan* (1916), the young ballerina receives a tiara from an admirer.

4.118 She admires herself in a mirror, in a notably decentered framing.

4.119 As the ballerina lowers her arm, the door opens and her father appears.

4.120 Her father comes to the front area and balances the composition.

4.121 In V. I. Pudovkin's *Mother,* the spectator concentrates on the man's face rather than on the darkness surrounding it.

then figures closer to the camera had to be rearranged to permit a clear entrance. The result was a subtle unbalancing and rebalancing of the composition (**4.117–4.120**). In Chapter 6, we'll see how cutting can create a balance between two shots with relatively unbalanced compositions.

The filmmaker can guide our attention by use of another time-tested strategy, the principle of contrast. Our eyes are biased toward registering differences and changes. In most black-and-white films, light costumes or brightly lit faces stand out while darker areas tend to recede (**4.121**). If there are several light shapes in the frame, we'll tend to look from one to the other. But if the background is light, black elements will become prominent, as Sandro's hair does in our *L'Avventura* scene (4.109). The same principles work for color. A bright costume element shown against a more subdued setting is likely to draw the eye. Jiří Menzel exploits this principle in *Larks on a String* (**4.122**). Another pertinent principle is that when lightness values are equal, warm colors in the red-orange-yellow range tend to attract attention, while cool colors like purple and green are less prominent. In Yilmaz Güney's *Yol,* for example, the setting and the characters' outfits are already quite warm in hue, but the hot pink vest of the man in the central middle ground helps make him the primary object of attention (**4.123**).

Color contrasts don't have to be huge, because we're sensitive to small differences. What painters call a *limited palette* involves a few colors in the same range, as in our earlier example from Fellini's *Casanova* (4.39). Peter Greenaway's *The Draughtsman's Contract* employs a limited palette from the cooler end of the spectrum (**4.124**). An extreme case of the principle is sometimes called **monochromatic color design.** Here the filmmaker emphasizes a single color, varying it only in purity or lightness. We've already seen an example of monochromatic mise-en-scene in the white décor and costumes of *THX 1138* (4.40). In a monochromatic design, even the slightest fleck of a contrasting color will catch the viewer's attention. The color design of *Aliens* is dominated by metallic tones, so even a dingy yellow can mark the stiltlike loader as an important prop in the narrative (**4.125**).

Film has one resource that painting lacks. Our tendency to notice visual differences shifts into high gear when the image includes *movement.* In the *L'Avventura* scene, the turning of Claudia's head became a major event, but we are sensitive to far smaller motions in the frame. Normally, for instance we ignore the movement of scratches and dust on a film. But in David Rimmer's *Watching for the Queen,* in which the first image is an absolutely static photograph (**4.126**), the jumping bits of dust on the film draw our attention. In **4.127**, from Yasujiro Ozu's *Record of a Tenement Gentleman,* many items compete for our attention. But the moment that a scrap of

4.122 In *Larks on a String,* the junkyard setting provides earthy grays and blacks against which the characters' lighter clothes stand out sharply.

4.123 Warm colors guide the eye in *Yol.*

4.124   *The Draughtsman's Contract* uses a limited palette of green, black, and white.

4.125   *Aliens* uses warm colors like yellow sparingly.

newspaper flaps, it immediately attracts the eye because it is the only motion in the frame.

When several moving elements appear on the screen, as in a ballroom dance, we are likely to shift our attention among them, according to other cues or depending on our expectations about which one is most salient to the narrative action. In **4.128**, from John Ford's *Young Mr. Lincoln,* Lincoln is moving much less than the dancers we see in front of him. Yet he is framed centrally, as the major character, and the dancers pass rapidly through the frame. As a result, we are likely to concentrate on his gestures and facial expressions, however slight they might be compared to the energetic action in the foreground.

Scene Space   Looking at a film image as a two-dimensional picture helps us appreciate the artistry of filmmakers, but it requires some effort. We find it easier to immediately see the edges and masses on the screen as a three-dimensional space, like the one we live in. The elements of the image that create this impression are called *depth cues.*

Depth cues are what enabled us to understand the encounter of Sandro and Claudia as taking place in a realistic space, with layers and volume. We develop our understanding of depth cues from our experience of real locales and from our earlier experience with pictorial media. In cinema, depth cues are provided by lighting, setting, costumes, and staging—that is, by all the aspects of mise-en-scene.

Depth cues suggest that a space has both *volume* and several distinct *planes.* When we speak of an object as having volume, we mean that it is solid and occupies a three-dimensional area. A film suggests volume by shape, shading, and movement. In 4.104 and **4.129**, we do not think of the actors' faces as flat cutouts, like paper dolls. The shapes of those heads and shoulders suggest solid people. The

4.126   *Watching for the Queen* emphasizes scratches and dust.

4.127   A tiny movement in *Record of a Tenement Gentleman.*

4.128   Emphasizing a background figure in *Young Mr. Lincoln.*

4.129   Shading and shape suggest volume in Dreyer's *La Passion de Jeanne d'Arc.*

4.130   A flat composition in Norman McLaren's *Begone, Dull Care.*

attached shadows on the faces suggest the curves and recesses of the actors' features and give a modeling effect. We assume that if the actor in 4.104 turned her head, we would see a profile. Thus we use our knowledge of objects in the world to discern volume in filmic space.

An abstract film, because it can use shapes that are not everyday objects, can create compositions without a sense of volume. The shapes in **4.130** give us no depth cues for volume—they are unshaded, do not have a recognizable shape, and do not move in such a way as to reveal new views that suggest roundness.

Depth cues also pick out *planes* within the image. Planes are the layers of space occupied by persons or objects. Planes are described according to how close to or far away from the camera they are: foreground, middle ground, background.

Only a completely blank screen has a single plane. Whenever a shape—even an abstract one—appears, we will perceive it as being in front of a background. In 4.130, the four red S shapes are actually painted right on the frame surface, as is the lighter, textured area. Yet the textured area seems to lie behind the four shapes. The space here has only two planes, as in an abstract painting. This example, like our *L'Avventura* scene, suggests that one of the most basic depth cues is **overlap**. The curling S shapes have edges that overlap the background plane, block our vision of it, and thus seem to be closer to us. In 4.115, the people overlap the ladders, so we understand that they are closer to the camera than the ladders are, while in 4.116, the tree overlaps the figure of the woman.

Through overlap, a great many planes can be defined. In 4.56, from Jean-Luc Godard's *La Chinoise*, three distinct planes are displayed: the background of fashion cutouts, the woman's face that overlaps that background, and her hand, which overlaps her lower face. In the three-point lighting approach, edge-lighting accentuates the overlap of planes by emphasizing the contour of the object, thus sharply distinguishing it from the background. (See again 4.59, 4.64, and 4.66.)

Color differences also create overlapping planes. Because cool or pale colors tend to recede, filmmakers commonly use them for background planes such as setting. Similarly, because warm or saturated colors tend to come forward, such hues are often employed for costumes or other foreground elements, as in Sarah Maldoror's *Sambizanga* (**4.131**). (See also 4.29, 4.34, and 4.125.)

Animated films can achieve brighter and more saturated color than most live-action filming, so depth effects can be correspondingly more vivid. In Chuck Jones's *One Froggy Evening* (**4.132**), the luminous yellow of the umbrella and the

4.131   In *Sambizanga,* the heroine's dress has very warm and fairly saturated colors, making it stand out distinctly against the pale background.

4.132   Vivid colors emphasize the sense of extreme depth in *One Froggy Evening.*

frog's brilliant green skin make him stand out against the darker red of the curtain and the earth tones of the stage floor.

Because of the eye's sensitivity to differences, even quite muted color contrasts can suggest three-dimensional space. In *L'Argent* (4.21–4.23), Robert Bresson uses a limited, cool palette and relatively flat lighting. Yet the compositions pick out several planes by means of overlapping slightly different masses of black, tan, and light blue. Our shot from *Casanova* (4.39) articulates planes by means of slightly differing shades of red. In *The Draughtsman's Contract* (4.124), much of our sense of distant space is created by strong black verticals and by horizontal strips of various shades of green. Together these colors define distinct layers in this scene.

In cinema, *movement* is one of the most important depth cues, since it strongly suggests both planes and volumes (4.128). **Aerial perspective**, or the hazing of more distant planes, is yet another depth cue. Typically, our visual system assumes that sharper outlines, clearer textures, and purer colors belong to foreground elements. In landscape shots, the blurring and graying of distant planes can be caused by actual atmospheric haze, as in Güney's *The Wall* (**4.133**). Even when such haze is a minor factor, our vision typically assigns strong color contrasts to the foreground, as in the *Sambizanga* shot (4.131). In addition, very often lighting is manipulated in conjunction with lens focus to blur the background planes (**4.134**).

In **4.135**, the mise-en-scene provides several depth cues: overlap of edges, cast shadows, and **size diminution**. That is, figures and objects farther away from us are seen to get proportionally smaller; the smaller the figure appears, the farther away

4.133 Fog emphasizes the distance between the foreground and background trees in *The Wall*.

4.134 In Michael Curtiz's *The Charge of the Light Brigade*, aerial perspective is artificially created through diffused lighting of the background and a lack of clear focus beyond the foreground character.

4.135 Depth cues in Straub and Huillet's *The Chronicle of Anna Magdalena Bach*.

we believe it to be. This reinforces our sense of there being a deep space with considerable distances between the various planes.

The same illustration dramatically displays *linear perspective.* We will consider perspective relations in more detail in the next chapter, since they derive as much from properties of the camera lens as they do from mise-en-scene. For now, we can simply note that a strong impression of depth emerges when parallel lines converge at a distant vanishing point. *Off-center* linear perspective is illustrated in 4.135; note that the vanishing point is not the geometrical center. *Central* perspective is exemplified in 4.124 from *The Draughtsman's Contract.*

In many of the examples already given, you may have noticed that mise-en-scene serves not simply to direct our attention to foreground elements but rather to create a dynamic relation between foreground and background. In 4.56, for instance, Godard keeps our attention on the whole composition by using prominent backgrounds. Here the pictures behind the actress's head lead us to scan the various small shapes quickly.

The *La Chinoise* shot is a **shallow-space** composition. In such shots, the mise-en-scene suggests comparatively little depth, and the closest and most distant planes seem only slightly separated. The opposite tendency is **deep-space** composition, in which a significant distance seems to separate planes. Our earlier example from *The Chronicle of Anna Magdalena Bach* (4.135) exemplifies deep-space mise-en-scene. Often a director creates a deep-space composition by making the foreground plane quite large and the background plane quite distant (**4.136**).

Shallow and deep mise-en-scene are relative. Most compositions present a moderately deep space, falling between the extremes we have just considered. Sometimes a composition manipulates depth cues to make a space appear deeper or shallower than it really is—creating an optical illusion (**4.137**).

At this point, you might want to return to shots illustrated earlier in this chapter. You will notice that these images use depth cues of overlap, movement, cast shadows, aerial perspective, size diminution, and linear perspective to create distinctive foreground/background relations.

The fact that our vision is sensitive to differences allows filmmakers to guide our understanding of the mise-en-scene. All the cues to story space interact with one another, working to emphasize narrative elements, direct our attention, and set up dynamic relations among areas of screen space. We can see this interaction clearly in two shots from Carl Dreyer's *Day of Wrath.*

In the first shot, the heroine, Anne, is standing before a grillwork panel (**4.138**). She is not speaking, but since she is a major character in the film, the narrative already directs us to her. Setting, lighting, costume, and figure expression create

4.136   Several scenes of Wajda's *Ashes and Diamonds* create large foreground and distant background planes.

4.137   Leo Carax flattens space in *Boy Meets Girl* by making the actor in the foreground seem to blend into the advertisement on the wall behind.

pictorial cues that confirm our expectations. The setting yields a screen pattern of horizontal and vertical lines that intersect in the delicate curves of Anne's face and shoulders. The lighting yields a patch of brightness on the right half of the frame and a patch of darkness on the left, creating pictorial balance. Anne is the meeting point of these two areas. Her face becomes modeled by the relatively strong key lighting from the right, a little top lighting on her hair, and relatively little fill light. Coordinated with the lighting in creating the pattern of light and dark is Anne's costume—a black dress punctuated by white collar, and a black cap edged with white—that again emphasizes her face.

4.138 *Day of Wrath:* concentrating on a single figure.

The shot is comparatively shallow, displaying two major planes with little distance between them. The background sets off the more important element, Anne. The rigid geometrical grid in the rear makes Anne's slightly sad face the most expressive element in the frame, thus encouraging our eye to pause there. In addition, the composition divides the screen space horizontally, with the grid pattern running across the top half and the dark, severe vertical of Anne's dress dominating the lower half. As is common, the upper zone is the stronger because the character's head and shoulders occupy it. Anne's figure is positioned slightly off center, but with her face turned so as to compensate for the vacant area on the right. (Imagine how unbalanced the shot would look if she were turned to face us squarely and the same amount of space were left empty on the right.) Thus compositional balance reinforces the shot's emphasis on Anne's expression. In all, without using motion, Dreyer has channeled our attention by means of lines and shapes, lights and darks, and the foreground and background relations in the mise-en-scene.

In the second example, also from *Day of Wrath,* Dreyer coaxes our attention into a to-and-fro movement (**4.139**). Again, the plot guides us, since the characters and the cart are crucial narrative elements. Sound helps too, since Martin is at the moment explaining to Anne what the cart is used for. But mise-en-scene also plays a role. Size diminution and cast shadows establish basic foreground/background relations, with Anne and Martin on the front plane and the cart of wood in the background. The space is comparatively deep (though the foreground is not as exaggeratedly close as that in *Ashes and Diamonds,* 4.136). The prominence of the couple and the cart is reinforced by line, shape, and lighting contrasts. The figures are defined by hard edges and by dark costumes within the predominantly bright setting. Unlike most shots, this puts the human figures in the lower half of the frame, which gives that zone an unusual importance. The composition thus creates a vertical balance, counterweighting the cart with the couple. This encourages us to glance up and down between the two objects of our attention.

4.139 *Day of Wrath:* dividing attention between foreground and background figures.

Similar processes are at work in color films. In one shot of Yasujiro Ozu's *An Autumn Afternoon* (**4.140**), our attention is concentrated on the bride in the center foreground. Here many depth cues are at work. Overlap locates the two figures in two foreground planes, setting them against a series of more distant planes. Aerial perspective makes the tree foliage somewhat out of focus. Movement creates depth when the bride lowers her head. Perspective diminution makes the more distant objects smaller. The figure and the bright silver, red, and gold bridal costume stand out strikingly against the muted, cool colors of the background planes. Moreover, the colors bring back a red-and-silver motif that began in the very first shot of the film (**4.141**).

4.140 A simple shot from *An Autumn Afternoon* employs several depth cues.

In all these cases, compositional elements and depth cues have functioned to focus our attention on the narrative elements. But this need not always be the case. Bresson's *Lancelot du Lac* uses a limited palette of dark and metallic hues, and warmer colors tend to stand out (**4.142**). Such a distracting use of color becomes a stylistic motif in the film.

Time

Cinema is an art of time as well as space. So we shouldn't be surprised to find that many of our examples of two-dimensional composition and three-dimensional

4.141 The striped smokestacks establish a color motif for *An Autumn Afternoon.*

scenic space have unfolded over time. The director's control over mise-en-scene governs not only *what* we see but *when* we see it, and for how long. In our *L'Avventura* scene between Sandro and Claudia on the rooftop, the timing of the characters' movements—Sandro turning away just as Claudia turns toward us—contributes to the effect of a sudden, sharp revelation of her anxiety.

The director shapes the speed and direction of movement within the shot. Since our eyes are attuned to noticing changes, we can pick up the slightest cues. In **4.143**, from Chantal Akerman's *Jeanne Dielman, 23 quai du Commerce, 1080 Bruxelles,* the protagonist simply peels potatoes. This feminist film traces, in painstaking detail, the everyday routines of a Belgian housewife. The composition of this shot strongly centers Jeanne, and no competing movements distract us from her steady and efficient preparation of a meal. The same rhythm is carried throughout the film, so that when she does start to vary her habits, we are prepared to notice even the slight errors she makes under emotional pressure.

A far busier shot is **4.144**, from Busby Berkeley's *42nd Street*. This overhead view presents strongly opposed movements. The central and outer rings of dancers circle in one direction, while the second ring turns in a contrary direction. The dancers also swing strips of shiny cloth back and forth. The result is a partially abstract composition, but it's easy to grasp because the movement of the wheels within wheels has a geometrical clarity.

The dancers in *42nd Street* are synchronized to a considerable degree, but **4.145**, from Jacques Tati's *Play Time,* contains movements of differing speeds, with different visual accents. Moreover, they occur on different planes and follow

4.142   In *Lancelot du Lac,* a group of conversing knights is centered and balanced in the foreground planes, yet a pinkish-purple saddle blanket on a passing horse momentarily draws our eyes away from the action.

4.143   Slow, quiet movement in *Jeanne Dielman, 23 quai du Commerce, 1080 Bruxelles.*

4.144   Synchronized rhythm in *42nd Street.*

4.145   Competing rhythms of movement in a busy shot from *Play Time.*

contrasting trajectories. These diverse movements accord with Tati's tendency to cram his compositions with gags that compete for our attention.

As we have already seen, we scan any film frame for information. This scanning brings time sharply into play. Only a very short shot forces us to try to take in the image all at once. In most shots, we get an initial overall impression that creates formal expectations. These expectations are quickly modified as our eye roams around the frame.

As we'd expect, our scanning of the shot is strongly affected by the presence of movement. A static composition, such as our first shot from *Day of Wrath* (4.138), may keep pulling our attention back to a single element (here, Anne's face). In contrast, a composition emphasizing movement becomes more time-bound because our glance may be directed from place to place by various speeds, directions, and rhythms of movements. In the second image from *Day of Wrath* (4.139), Anne and Martin are turned from us (so that expression and gesture are minimized), and they are standing still. Thus the single movement in the frame—the cart—catches our attention. But when Martin speaks and turns, we look back at the couple, then back at the cart, and so on, in a shuttling, dynamic shift of attention.

Our time-bound process of scanning involves not only looking to and fro across the screen but also, in a sense, looking into its depths. A deep-space composition will often use background events to create expectations about what is about to happen in the foreground. "Composing in depth isn't simply a matter of pictorial richness," British director Alexander Mackendrick has remarked. "It has value in the narrative of the action, the pacing of the scene. Within the same frame, the director can organize the action so that preparation for what will happen next is seen in the background of what is happening now."

Our example from *The Dying Swan* (4.117-4.120) illustrates MacKendrick's point. The same principle is used in **4.146–4.148**, from *Three Kings*. Here the frame starts off unbalanced, and the fact that it includes a background doorway prepares us for the scene's dramatic development. In addition, any movement from

4.146   In this shot from *Three Kings,* Chief Elgin comes in to tell the partying GIs that their superior is coming. Normally, when a character is looking offscreen left, he or she is set a little off center toward the right. But Elgin is set to the left, leaving the tent flap behind him prominent. Without being aware of it, we expect some action to develop there.

4.147   Confirming Elgin's warning, the superior officer bursts into the background.

4.148   The officer comes forward, which is always a powerful way to command the viewer's attention. He moves aggressively into close-up, ramping up the conflict as he demands to know where the men got alcohol.

background to foreground is a strong attention-getter. At moments like these, the mise-en-scene is preparing us for what will happen, and by arousing our expectations, the style engages us with the unfolding action.

The *Dying Swan* and *Three Kings* examples also illustrate the power of *frontality.* In explaining one five-minute shot in his film *Adam's Rib,* George Cukor signaled this. He remarked how the defense attorney was positioned to focus our attention on her client, who's reciting the reasons she shot her husband (**4.149**). Katharine Hepburn "had her back to the camera almost the whole time, but that had a meaning: she indicated to the audience that they should look at Judy Holliday. We did that whole thing without a cut."

All other things being equal, the viewer expects that more story information will come from a character's face than from a character's back. The viewer's attention will thus usually pass over figures that are turned away and fasten on figures that are positioned frontally. A more distant view can exploit frontality, too. In Hou Hsiao-hsien's *City of Sadness,* depth staging centers the Japanese woman coming to visit the hospital, and a burst of bright fabric also draws attention to her (**4.150**). Just as important, the other characters are turned away from us. It's characteristic of Hou's style to employ long shots with small changes in figure movement. The subdued, delicate effect of his scenes depends on our seeing characters' faces in relation to others' bodies and the overall setting.

Frontality can change over time to guide our attention to various parts of the shot. We've already seen alternating frontality at work in our *L'Avventura* scene, when Sandro and Claudia turn to and away from us (4.109, 4.110). When actors are in dialogue, a director may allow frontality to highlight one moment of one actor's performance, then give another performer more prominence (**4.151, 4.152**). This device reminds us that mise-en-scene can borrow devices from theatrical staging.

4.149   In *Adam's Rib,* the wife who has shot her husband is given the greatest emphasis by three-point lighting, her animated gestures, and her frontal positioning. Interestingly, the exact center of the frame is occupied by a nurse in the background, but Cukor keeps her out of focus and unmoving so that she won't distract from Judy Holliday's performance.

4.150   Although she is farther from the camera, the woman visiting the hospital in *City of Sadness* draws our eye partly because she is the only one facing front.

4.151   In a conversation in *The Bad and the Beautiful,* our attention fastens on the studio executive on the right because the other two characters are turned away from us . . .

4.152   . . . but when the producer turns to the camera, his centered position and frontal posture emphasize him.

4.153   Mise-en-scene in the widescreen frame in *Rebel Without a Cause.*

4.154   Jim comes forward, drawing our attention and arousing expectations of a dramatic exchange.

4.155   Jim offers Plato his jacket, his action centered and his brightly lit white shirt making him the dominant player. Judy remains a secondary center of interest, segregated by the office window and highlighted by her bright red coat.

4.156   Judy turns abruptly, and her face's frontal position signals her interest in Jim.

A flash of frontality can be very powerful. In the opening scene of *Rebel Without a Cause,* three teenagers are being held at the police station (**4.153**). They don't know one another yet. When Jim sees that Plato is shivering, he drunkenly comes forward to offer Plato his sport coat (**4.154, 4.155**). Jim's frontality, forward movement, bright white shirt, and central placement emphasize his gesture. Just as Plato takes the coat, Judy turns and notices Jim for the first time (**4.156**). Like Claudia's sudden turn to the camera in our first example, this sudden revelation spikes our interest. It prepares us for the somewhat tense romance that will develop between them in later scenes. Overall, the scene's setting, lighting, costume, and staging cooperate to develop the drama.

The director can also achieve a strong effect by denying frontality, keeping us in suspense about what a character's face reveals. At a climactic moment in Kenji Mizoguchi's *Naniwa Elegy,* some of the cues for emphasis are reversed (**4.157, 4.158**). We get a long shot rather than a closer view, and the character is turned from us and moving away from the camera, through patches of darkness. Ayako is confessing to her suitor that she's been another man's mistress. Her withdrawal conveys a powerful sense of shame, and we, like her friend, have to judge her sincerity based on her posture and voice. In this and our other examples, several techniques of mise-en-scene dovetail from moment to moment in order to engage us more vividly with the action.

4.157   At the height of the drama in *Naniwa Elegy,* Kenji Mizoguchi has the heroine move away from us, into depth . .

4.158   . . . and as she passes through patches of distant darkness, our curiosity about her emotional state intensifies.

Narrative Functions of Mise-en-Scene in *Our Hospitality*

Our Hospitality, like most of Buster Keaton's films, exemplifies how mise-en-scene can economically advance the narrative and create a pattern of motifs. Since the film is a comedy, the mise-en-scene also creates gags. *Our Hospitality,* then, exemplifies what we will find in our study of every film technique: An individual element almost always has *several* functions, not just one.

Consider, for example, how the settings function within the plot of *Our Hospitality.* For one thing, they help divide the film into scenes and to contrast those scenes. The film begins with a prologue showing how the feud between the McKays and the Canfields results in the deaths of the young Canfield and the husband of the McKay family. We see the McKays living in a shack and are left in suspense about the fate of the baby, Willie. Willie's mother flees with her son from their southern home to the North (action narrated to us mainly by an intertitle).

The plot jumps ahead many years to begin the main action, with the grown-up Willie living in New York. There are a number of gags concerning early 19th-century life in the metropolis, contrasting sharply with the prologue scene. We are led to wonder how this locale will relate to the southern scenes, and soon Willie receives word that he has inherited his parents' home in the South. A series of amusing short scenes follows as he takes a primitive train back to his birthplace. During these scenes, Keaton uses real locales, but by laying out the railroad tracks in different ways, he exploits the landscapes for surprising and unusual comic effects we shall examine shortly.

The rest of the film deals with Willie's movements in and around the southern town. On the day of his arrival, he wanders around and gets into a number of comic situations. That night he stays in the Canfield house itself. Finally, an extended chase occurs the next day, moving through the countryside and back to the Canfield house for the settling of the feud. Thus the action depends heavily on shifts of setting that establish Willie's two journeys, as baby and as man, and later his wanderings to escape his enemies' pursuit. The narration is relatively unrestricted once Willie reaches the South, shifting between him and members of the Canfield family. We usually know more about where they are than Willie does, and the narrative generates suspense by showing them coming toward the places where Willie is hiding.

Specific settings fulfill distinct narrative functions. The McKay estate, which Willie envisions as a mansion, turns out to be a tumbledown shack. The McKay house is contrasted with the Canfield's palatial plantation home. In narrative terms, the Canfield home gains even more functional importance when the Canfield father forbids his sons to kill Willie on the premises: "Our code of honor forbids us to shoot him while he is a guest in our house." (Once Willie overhears this, he determines *never* to leave.) Ironically, the home of Willie's enemies becomes the only safe spot in town, and many scenes are organized around the Canfield brothers' attempts to lure Willie outside. At the end of the film, another setting takes on significance: the landscape of meadows, mountains, riverbanks, rapids, and waterfalls across which the Canfields pursue Willie. Finally, the feud ends back in the Canfield house itself, with Willie now welcomed as the daughter's husband. The pattern of development is clear: from the opening shootout at the McKay house that breaks up Willie's family to the final scene in the Canfield house with Willie becoming part of a new family. In such ways, every setting becomes highly motivated by the narrative's system of causes and effects, parallels and contrasts, and overall development.

The same narrative motivation marks the film's use of costume. Willie is characterized as a city boy through his dandified suit, whereas the southern gentility of the elder Canfield is represented through his white planter's suit. Props become important here: Willie's suitcase and umbrella succinctly summarize his role as visitor and wanderer, and the Canfields' ever-present pistols remind us of their goal of continuing the feud. Note also that a change of costume (Willie's disguising himself as a woman) enables him to escape from the Canfield household. At the end, the putting aside of the various guns by the characters signals the end of the feud.

Like setting, lighting in *Our Hospitality* has both general and specific functions. The film alternates scenes in darkness with scenes in daylight. The feuding in the prologue takes place at night; Willie's trip South and wanderings through the town occur in daylight; that night Willie comes to dinner at the Canfield's and stays as a guest; the next day, the Canfields pursue him; and the film ends that night with the marriage of Willie and the Canfield daughter. More specifically, the bulk of the film is evenly lit in the three-point method. Yet the somber action of the prologue takes place in hard sidelighting **(4.159, 4.160)**. Later, the murder scene is played out in flashes of light—lightning, gunfire—that fitfully punctuate the overall darkness. Because this sporadic lighting hides part of the action from us, it helps build suspense. The gunshots themselves are seen only as flashes in the darkness, and we must wait to learn the outcome—the deaths of both opponents—until the next flash of lightning.

Most economically of all, virtually every bit of the acting functions to support and advance the cause–effect chain of the narrative. The way Canfield sips and savors his julep establishes his southern ways; his southern hospitality in turn will not allow him to shoot a guest in his house. Similarly, Willie's every move expresses his diffidence or resourcefulness.

Even more concise is the way the film uses staging in depth to present two narrative events simultaneously. While the engineer drives the locomotive, the other cars pass him on a parallel track **(4.161)**. In other shots, Willie's awareness or ignorance of a situation is displayed through planes of depth **(4.162, 4.163)**. Thanks to such spatial arrangements, Keaton is able to pack together two story events, resulting in a tight narrative construction and in a relatively unrestricted narration. In 4.162, we know what Willie knows, and we expect that he will probably flee now that he understands the sons' plans. But in 4.163, we are aware, as Willie is not, that danger lurks around the corner; suspense results, as we wonder whether the Canfield boys' ambush will succeed.

4.159   In *Our Hospitality,* When the elder McKay flings off his hat to douse the lamp, the illumination changes from a soft blend of key, fill, and backlight . . .

4.160   . . . to a stark key light from the fireplace.

4.161   Within the same frame, we see both cause—the engineer's cheerful ignorance, made visible by frontality—and effect—the runaway cars.

4.162   The Canfield boys in the foreground make plans to shoot Willie, who overhears them in the background.

4.163   While Willie ambles along unsuspectingly in the background, one Canfield waits in the foreground to ambush him.

All of these devices for narrative economy considerably unify the film, but some other elements of mise-en-scene function as specific motifs. For one thing, there is the repeated squabble between the anonymous husband and wife. On his way to his estate, Willie passes a husband throttling his wife. Willie intervenes to protect her; the wife proceeds to thrash Willie for butting in. On Willie's way back, he passes the same couple, still fighting, but studiously avoids them. Nevertheless, the wife aims a kick at him as he passes. The mere repetition of the motif strengthens the film's narrative unity, but it functions thematically, too, as another joke on the contradictions surrounding the idea of hospitality.

Other motifs recur. Willie's first hat is too tall to wear in a jouncing railway coach. (When it gets crushed, he swaps it for the trademark flat Keaton hat.) Willie's second hat serves to distract the Canfields when Willie coaxes his dog to fetch it. There is also a pronounced water motif in the film. Water as rain conceals from us the murders in the prologue and later saves Willie from leaving the Canfield home after dinner ("It would be the death of anyone to go out on a night like this!"). Water as a river functions significantly in the final chase. And water as a waterfall appears soon after Willie's arrival in the South (4.164). This waterfall initially protects Willie by hiding him (4.165, 4.166) but later threatens both him and the Canfield daughters as they are nearly swept over it (4.172).

Two specific motifs of setting help unify the narrative. First there is the recurrence of an embroidered sampler hanging on the Canfield wall: "Love Thy Neighbor." It appears initially in the prologue of the film, when seeing it motivates Canfield's attempt to stop the feud. It then plays a significant role in linking the ending back to the beginning. The sampler reappears at the end when Canfield, enraged that Willie has married his daughter, glances at the wall, reads the inscription, and resolves to halt the years of feuding. His change in attitude is motivated by the earlier appearance of the motif.

The film also uses gun racks as a motif. In the prologue, each feuder goes to his mantelpiece to get his pistol. Later, when Willie arrives in town, the Canfields hurry to their gun rack and begin to load their pistols. Near the end of the film, when the Canfields return home after failing to find Willie, one of the sons notices that the gun rack is now empty. And, in the final shot, when the Canfields accept the marriage and lay down their arms, Willie produces from all over his person a staggering assortment of pistols taken as a precaution from the Canfields' own supply. Thus mise-en-scene motifs unify the film through their repetition, variation, and development.

Yet *Our Hospitality* is more than a film whose narrative system relates economically to patterns of mise-en-scene. It is a comedy, and one of the funniest. We should not be surprised to find, then, that Keaton uses mise-en-scene for gags. Indeed, so unified is the film that most of the elements that create narrative economy also function to yield comic effects.

The mise-en-scene bristles with many individually comic elements. Settings are exploited for amusement—the ramshackle McKay estate, the Broadway of 1830, the specially cut train tunnel that just fits the old-fashioned train and its smokestack (4.167). Costume gags also stand out. Willie's disguise as a woman is exposed by a gap in the rear of his skirt; later, Willie puts the same costume on a horse to distract the Canfields. Most strongly, comedy arises from the behavior of the figures. The railroad engineer's high kick unexpectedly swipes off his conductor's hat (4.168). The elder Canfield sharpens his carving knife with ferocious energy, just inches from Willie's head. When Willie lands at the bottom of the river, he stands there looking left and right, his hand shading his eyes, before he realizes where he is. Later, Willie scuds down the river, leaping out of the water like a fish and skidding across the rocks.

Perhaps the only aspect of mise-en-scene that competes with the comic brilliance of the figures' behavior is the film's use of deep space for gags. Many of the shots we have already examined function to create comedy as well: The engineer

4.164   After an explosion demolishes a dam, the water spills over a cliff and creates a waterfall.

4.165   The new waterfall begins to hide Willie as he sits fishing . . .

4.166   . . . and by the time the Canfields rush into the foreground, he is invisible.

stands firmly oblivious to the separation of train cars from the engine (see 4.161) just as Willie is unaware that the Canfield boy is lurking murderously in the foreground (4.163).

Even more striking, though, is the deep-space gag that follows the demolition of the dam. The Canfield boys have been searching the town for Willie. In the meantime, Willie sits on a ledge, fishing. As the water bursts from the dam and sweeps over the cliff, it completely engulfs Willie (4.165). At that very instant, the Canfield brothers step into the foreground from either side of the frame, still looking for their victim (4.166). The water's concealment of Willie reduces him to a neutral background for the movement of the Canfields. This sudden eruption of new action into the scene surprises us, rather than generating suspense, since we were not aware that the Canfield sons were so close by. Here surprise is crucial to the comedy.

However appealing the individual gags are, *Our Hospitality* patterns its comic aspects as strictly as it does its other motifs. The film's journey pattern often arranges a series of gags according to a formal principle of theme and variations. For instance, during the train trip South, a string of gags is based on the idea of people encountering the train. Several people turn out to watch it pass, a tramp rides the rods, and an old man chucks rocks at the engine. Another swift series of gags takes the train tracks themselves as its theme. The variations include a humped track, a donkey blocking the tracks, curled and rippled tracks, and finally no tracks at all.

But the most complex theme-and-variations series can be seen in the motif of "the fish on the line." Soon after Willie arrives in town, he is angling and hauls up a minuscule fish. Shortly afterward, a huge fish yanks him into the water **(4.169)**. Later in the film, through a series of mishaps, Willie becomes tied by a rope to one of the Canfield sons. Many gags arise from this umbilical-cord linkage, especially one that results in Canfield's being pulled into the water as Willie was earlier.

Perhaps the single funniest shot in the film occurs when Willie realizes that since the Canfield boy has fallen off the rocks **(4.170)**, so must he **(4.171)**. But even after Willie gets free of Canfield, the rope remains tied around his waist. So in the film's climax, Willie is dangling from a log over the waterfall **(4.172)**. Here again, one element fulfills multiple functions. The fish-on-the-line device advances the narrative, becomes a motif unifying the film, and takes its place in a pattern of parallel gags involving variations of Willie on the rope. In such ways, *Our Hospitality* becomes an outstanding example of the integration of cinematic mise-en-scene with narrative form.

4.167   The tunnel cut to fit the old-fashioned train.

4.168   As the engineer, Keaton's father, Joe, used his famous high-kick vaudeville stunt for this gag.

4.169   The motif begins as Willie is jerked into the water.

4.170   Tied to Willie, the Canfield boy falls off the cliff . . .

4.171   . . . and Willie braces himself to be pulled after.

4.172   Willie dangles like a fish on the end of a pole.

Summary

The viewer who wants to study mise-en-scene should look for it systematically. We should watch, first of all, for how setting, costume, lighting, and the behavior of the figures present themselves in a given film. As a start, we should try to trace only one sort of element—say, setting or lighting—through a scene.

We should also reflect on the patterning of mise-en-scene elements. How do they function? How do they constitute motifs that weave their ways through the entire film? In addition, we should notice how mise-en-scene is patterned in space and time to attract and guide our attention through the process of watching the film and to create suspense or surprise.

Finally, we should try to relate the system of mise-en-scene to the large-scale form of the film. Hard-and-fast prejudices about realism are of less value here than an openness to the great variety of mise-en-scene possibilities. Awareness of those possibilities will better help us to determine the functions of mise-en-scene.

Where to Go from Here

On the Origins of Mise-en-Scene

As a concept, mise-en-scene dates back to the 19th-century theater. For a historical introduction that is relevant to film, see Oscar G. Brockett and Robert R. Findlay, *Century of Innovation* (Englewood Cliffs, NJ: Prentice-Hall, 1973). The standard film works are Nicolas Vardac, *Stage to Screen* (Cambridge, MA: Harvard University Press, 1949), and Ben Brewster and Lea Jacobs, *Theatre to Cinema: Stage Pictorialism and the Early Feature Film* (Oxford: Oxford University Press, 1997).

On Realism in Mise-en-Scene

Many film theorists have seen film as a realistic medium par excellence. For such theorists as Siegfried Kracauer, André Bazin, and V. F. Perkins, cinema's power lies in its ability to present a recognizable reality. The realist theorist thus often values authenticity in costume and setting, naturalistic acting, and unstylized lighting. "The primary function of decor," writes V. F. Perkins, "is to provide a believable environment for the action" (*Film as Film* [Baltimore: Penguin, 1972], p. 94). André Bazin praises the Italian neorealist films of the 1940s for "faithfulness to everyday life in the scenario, truth to his part in an actor" (*What Is Cinema?* vol. 2 [Berkeley: University of California Press, 1970], p. 25).

Though mise-en-scene is always a product of selection and choice, the realist theorist may value the filmmaker who creates a mise-en-scene that *appears* to be reality. Kracauer suggests that even apparently unrealistic song-and-dance numbers in a musical can seem impromptu (*Theory of Film* [New York: Oxford University Press, 1965]), and Bazin considers a fantasy film such as *The Red Balloon* realistic because here "what is imaginary on the screen has the spatial density of something real" (*What Is Cinema?* vol. 1 [Berkeley: University of California Press, 1966], p. 48).

These theorists set the filmmaker the task of representing some historical, social, or aesthetic reality through the selection and arrangement of mise-en-scene. Though this book postpones the consideration of this problem—it lies more strictly in the domain of film theory—the realist controversy is worth your examination. Christopher Williams, in *Realism and the Cinema* (London: Routledge & Kegan Paul, 1980), reviews many issues in the area.

Computer Imaging and Mise-en-Scene

Digital, or *3D,* animation typically involves a few widely used programs, such as Maya for creating movement and Renderman for adding surface texture. Animators deal with specific needs of their projects by developing new software for such effects as fire, water, and moving foliage. The figures to be animated are created either by scanning every surface of a maquette (a detailed model, such as the dinosaur in 1.29) or by using motion capture ("mocap"), filming actors or animals in neutrally colored costumes covered with dots, which are the only things visible to the camera. The dots are connected by lines to create a "wire-frame" moving image, and the computer gradually adds more detailed layers to build a textured, three-dimensional, moving figure. Backgrounds can also be created digitally, using matte-painting programs. For figure animation, see *The Art of Maya: An Introduction to 3D Computer Graphics,* 3d ed. (Alias Systems, 2005), which includes a CD-ROM with introductory material.

For fiction feature films, 3D animation became viable with *digital compositing,* used for the T-1000 cyborg in *Terminator 2: Judgment Day.* Here a grid was painted on the actor's body, and the actor was filmed executing movements. As the film was scanned, the changing grid patterns were translated into a digital code similar to that used on compact discs. Then new actions could be created on the computer frame by frame. For a discussion, see Jody Duncan, "A Once and Future War," *Cinefex* 47 (August 1991): 4–59. Since *Terminator 2,* sophisticated software programs have enabled directors to create "actors" wholly from models that can be scanned into a computer and then animated. The most famous early example is the gallimimus herd in *Jurassic Park.* The phases of the imaging process for this film are explained in Jody Duncan, "The Beauty in the Beasts," *Cinefex* 55 (August 1993): 42–95. Both analog image synthesis and digital compositing were used in *The Matrix;* for background, see Kevin H. Martin, "Jacking into the Matrix," *Cinefex* 79 (October 1999): 66–89. The rendering of realistic human and humanlike characters depended on finding a way to create the elusively translucent quality of skin. Such figures as Jar Jar Binks in *Star Wars Episode 1: The Phantom Menace* and especially Gollum in *The Lord of the Rings* finally achieved this goal. See *Cinefex* 78 (July 1999), completely devoted to *The Phantom Menace;* Joe Fordham, "Middle-Earth Strikes Back," *Cinefex* 92 (January 2003): 70–142; and Joe Fordham, "Journey's End," *Cinefex* 96 (January 2004): 55–142.

The combination of live-action filming with computer animation has created a fresh range of cinematic effects. Méliès' urge to dazzle the audience with the magical powers of mise-en-scene continues to bear fruit.

Particular Aspects of Mise-en-Scene

On costume, see Elizabeth Lees, *Costume Design in the Movies* (London: BCW, 1976), and Edward Maeder, ed., *Hollywood and History: Costume Design in Film* (New York: Thames & Hudson, 1987). See also Vincent J.-R. Kehoe, *The Technique of the Professional Make-Up Artist* (Boston: Focal Press, 1995).

Léon Barsacq, with careful assistance by Elliott Stein, has produced the best history of setting to date, *Caligari's Cabinet and Other Grand Illusions: A History of Film Design* (New York: New American Library, 1976). Other major studies of decor in the cinema are Charles Affron and Mirella Jona Affron, *Sets in Motion: Art Direction and Film Narrative* (New Brunswick, NJ: Rutgers University Press, 1995); Dietrich Meumann, ed., *Film Architecture: Set Designs from "Metropolis" to "Blade Runner"* (Munich: Prestel, 1996); and C. S. Tashiro, *Pretty Pictures: Production Design and the History of Film* (Austin: University of Texas Press, 1998). For insightful interviews with set designers, see Vincent

LoBrutto, *By Design* (New York: Praeger, 1992), and Peter Ettedgui, *Production Design & Art Direction* (Woburn, MA: Focal Press, 1999). An excellent overview is offered by Vincent LoBrutto in *The Filmmaker's Guide to Production Design* (New York: Allworth, 2002). Pascal Pinteau's gorgeously illustrated *Special Effects: An Oral History* (New York: Abrams, 2003) covers not only models and digital effects but also make-up, setting, and even theme park rides.

A wide-ranging analysis of performance in film is Richard Dyer, *Stars* (London: British Film Institute, 1979). This book is complemented by Charles Affron, *Star Acting: Gish, Garbo, Davis* (New York: Dutton, 1977), and James Naremore, *Acting in the Cinema* (Berkeley: University of California Press, 1988). Useful practical guides are Patrick Tucker, *Secrets of Screen Acting* (New York: Routledge, 1994), and Tony Barr, *Acting for the Camera* (New York: Perennial, 1986). The ways in which a performance can be integrated with a film's overall form are considered in two other manuals, *The Film Director's Intuition: Script Analysis and Rehearsal Techniques,* by Judith Wilson (Studio City, CA: Michael Wiese, 2003), and Delia Salvi's *Friendly Enemies: Maximizing the Director–Actor Relationship* (New York: Billboard, 2003). Michael Caine's *Acting in Film: An Actor's Take on Movie Making* (New York: Applause Books) offers excellent and detailed discussion; see also the accompanying video, *Michael Caine on Acting in Film.*

Two fine surveys of lighting are Kris Malkiewicz, *Film Lighting: Talks with Hollywood's Cinematographers and Gaffers* (New York: Prentice-Hall, 1986); and Gerald Millerson, *Lighting for Television & Film,* 3d ed. (Boston: Focal Press, 1999). John Alton's *Painting with Light* (New York: Macmillan, 1949) and Gerald Millerson's *Technique of Lighting for Television and Motion Pictures* (New York: Hastings House, 1972) are useful older discussions, with emphasis on classical Hollywood practices. A useful reference book is Richard K. Ferncase's *Film and Video Lighting Terms and Concepts* (Newton, MA: Focal Press, 1995).

Depth

Art historians have long studied how a two-dimensional image can be made to suggest a deep space. A comprehensive introductory survey is William V. Dunning, *Changing Images of Pictorial Space: A History of Spatial Illusion in Painting* (Syracuse: Syracuse University Press, 1991). Dunning's history of Western painting emphasizes the manipulation of five techniques we have considered in this chapter: linear perspective, shading, the separation of planes, atmospheric perspective, and color perspective.

Though film directors have of course manipulated the image's depth and flatness since the beginning of cinema, critical understanding of these spatial qualities did not emerge until the 1940s. It was then that André Bazin called attention to the fact that certain directors staged their shots in unusually deep space. Bazin singled out F. W. Murnau (for *Nosferatu* and *Sunrise*), Orson Welles (for *Citizen Kane* and *The Magnificent Ambersons*), William Wyler (for *The Little Foxes* and *The Best Years of Our Lives*), and Jean Renoir (for practically all of his 1930s work). By offering us depth and flatness as analytical categories, Bazin increased our understanding of mise-en-scene. (See "The Evolution of the Language of Cinema," in *What Is Cinema?* vol. 1.) Interestingly, Sergei Eisenstein, who is often contrasted with Bazin, explicitly discussed principles of deep-space staging in the 1930s, as recorded by his faithful pupil, Vladimir Nizhny, in *Lessons with Eisenstein* (New York: Hill & Wang, 1962). Eisenstein asked his class to stage a murder scene in a single shot and without camera movement; the result was a startling use of extreme depth and dynamic movement toward the spectator. For a discussion, see David Bordwell, *The Cinema of Eisenstein* (Cambridge, MA: Harvard University Press, 1993), chaps. 4 and 6. For a general historical overview of depth in mise-en-scene, see David Bordwell's *On the History of Film Style* (Cambridge, MA: Harvard University Press, 1997), chap. 6.

Color Design

Two clear and readable discussions of color aesthetics in general are Luigina De Grandis, *Theory and Use of Color,* trans. John Gilbert (New York: Abrams, 1986), and Paul Zelanski and Mary Pat Fisher, *Colour for Designers and Artists* (London: Herbert Press, 1989).

For general discussion of the aesthetics of film color, see Raymond Durgnat, "Colours and Contrasts," *Films and Filming* 15, 2 (November 1968): 58–62; and William Johnson, "Coming to Terms with Color," *Film Quarterly* 20, 1 (Fall 1966): 2–22. The most detailed analysis of color organization in films is Scott Higgins, *Harnessing the Rainbow: Technicolor Design in the 1930s* (Austin: University of Texas Press, 2006).

Frame Composition and the Viewer's Eye

The film shot is like the painter's canvas: It must be filled up, and the spectator must be cued to notice certain things (and not to notice others). For this reason, composition in film owes much to principles developed in the graphic arts. A good basic study of composition is Donald L. Weismann, *The Visual Arts as Human Experience* (Englewood Cliffs, NJ: Prentice-Hall, 1974), which has many interesting things to say about depth as well. More elaborate discussions are to be found in Rudolf Arnheim, *Art and Visual Perception: A Psychology of the Creative Eye,* rev. ed. (Berkeley: University of California Press,

1974), and his *The Power of the Center: A Study of Composition in the Visual Arts,* 2d ed. (Berkeley: University of California Press, 1988).

André Bazin suggested that shots staged in depth and shot in deep focus give the viewer's eye greater freedom than do flatter, shallower shots: The viewer's eye can roam across the screen. (See Bazin, *Orson Welles* [New York: Harper & Row, 1978].) Noël Burch takes issue: "All the elements in any given film image are perceived as equal in importance" (Noël Burch, *Theory of Film Practice* [Princeton, NJ: Princeton University Press, 1981], p. 34). Psychological research on pictorial perception suggests, however, that viewers do indeed scan images according to specific cues. In cinema, static visual cues for "when to look where" are reinforced or undermined by movement of figures or of camera, by sound track and editing, and by the overall form of the film. The psychological research is outlined in Robert L. Solso, *Cognition and the Visual Arts* (Cambridge, MA: MIT Press, 1994), pp. 129–156. In *Figures Traced in Light: On Cinematic Staging* (Berkeley: University of California Press, 2005), David Bordwell studies how the filmmaker uses staging and frame composition to guide the viewer's scanning of the shot.

Websites

www.thescenographer.com/ Website for *The Scenographer* magazine, which deals with production design and costume design; has some online articles.

www.makeupmag.com/ Website for *Make-Up Artist Magazine,* professional journal for film and television workers; has some online articles.

www.16-9.dk/2003-06/side11_minnelli.htm/ In a well-illustrated article, "Medium Shot Gestures: Vincente Minnelli and *Some Came Running,*" Joe McElhaney provides a very good example of close analysis of long-take staging. The page is hosted by the Danish online magazine *16:9.*

Recommended DVD Supplements

DVDs often include galleries of designs for sets, costumes, and occasionally make-up. Documentaries on the subject include *Pulp Fiction*'s "Production Design Featurette." The unusually large, labyrinthine, enclosed spaceship interior in *Alien,* as well as the film's other sets, are discussed in the "Fear of the Unknown" and "The Darkest Reaches" segments. (The former also deals with costume design.) *Speed*'s "On Location" supplement deals with the 12 different buses that appeared at various stages of the film's action, as well as how the freeway locations were used.

Lighting is an area of mise-en-scene that receives relatively little coverage. An exception is "Painting with

Light," a documentary on cinematographer Jack Cardiff's work on the extraordinary color film *Black Narcissus*. A brief but informative look at lighting comes in the "Shooting on Location: Annie's Office" supplement for *Collateral*. In the "Here to Show Everybody the Light" section of the "Working like a Dog" supplement for *A Hard Day's Night*, director of photography Gilbert Taylor talks about how high-key lighting on the Beatles achieved the characteristic look of the images and about such challenges as rigging lighting equipment in a real train. *Toy Story*'s "Shaders and Lighting" section reveals how computer animation can simulate rim and key lighting.

Auditions are commonly included in DVD supplements, such as those for "The Making of *American Graffiti*" and especially *The Godfather*—where 72 minutes cover the casting, including many screen tests! Some discs go more deeply into aspects of acting. *Collateral*'s extras include a short segment, "Tom Cruise & Jamie Fox

Rehearse." "The Stunts," included with *Speed*, shows how the drivers' maneuvers with the vehicles involved in the accidents and near-misses were choreographed using models, as well as covering how decisions are made about whether to let stars do their own stunts. "Becoming an Oompa-Loompa" details the training Deep Roy underwent to play all the Oompa-Loompas in *Charlie and the Chocolate Factory*. A detailed exploration of the distinctive acting in the films of Robert Bresson is offered by Babette Mangolte's "The Models of *Pickpocket*," including lengthy interviews with the three main performers recalling the director's methods.

The *Dancer in the Dark* supplement "Choreography: Creating Vincent Paterson's Dance Sequences" takes an unusually close look at this particular type of staging. (This section can be best appreciated if you have watched the whole film or at least the musical numbers "Cvalda" [Track 9] and "I Have Seen It All" [Track 13].)

The Shot: Cinematography

I n controlling mise-en-scene the filmmaker stages an event to be filmed. But a comprehensive account of cinema as a medium cannot stop with simply what is put in front of the camera. The *shot* does not exist until patterns are inscribed on a strip of film. The filmmaker also controls the *cinematographic qualities* of the shot—not only *what* is filmed, but also *how* it is filmed. Cinematographic qualities involve three factors: (1) the photographic aspects of the shot, (2) the framing of the shot, and (3) the duration of the shot. This chapter surveys these three areas of artistic control.

The Photographic Image

Cinematography (literally, writing in movement) depends to a large extent on *photography* (writing in light). Sometimes the filmmaker eliminates the camera and simply works on the film itself; but even when drawing, painting, or scratching directly on film, punching holes in it, or growing mold on it, the filmmaker is creating patterns of light on celluloid. Most often, the filmmaker uses a camera to regulate how light from some object will be photochemically registered on the sensitized film. In any event, the filmmaker can select the range of tonalities, manipulate the speed of motion, and transform perspective.

The Range of Tonalities

An image may seem all grays or stark black and white. It may display a range of colors. Textures may stand out clearly or recede into a haze. The filmmaker may control all these visual qualities by manipulating the film stock, exposure, and developing procedures.

Types of **film stocks** are differentiated by the chemical qualities of the emulsion. The choice of film stock has many artistic implications. For one thing, the image will have more or less *contrast* depending partly on the stock used. Contrast refers to the degree of difference between the darkest and lightest areas of the frame. A high-contrast image displays bright white highlights, stark black areas, and a narrow range of grays in between. A low-contrast image possesses a wide range of grays, with no true white or black areas.

As we have already seen in Chapter 4, human vision is highly sensitive to differences in color, texture, shape, and other pictorial properties. Contrasts within the image enable filmmakers to guide the viewer's eye to important parts of the frame. Filmmakers control the degree of contrast in the image in various ways.

In general, a very fast film stock, one that is very sensitive to reflected light, will produce a contrasty look, while a slower, less light-sensitive one, will be low in contrast. The amount of light used on the set during shooting will also affect the image's degree of contrast. Moreover, the cinematographer may use particular developing procedures that increase or decrease contrast. For example, the strength and temperature of the chemicals and the length of time the film is left in the developing bath affect contrast. By manipulating the film stock, lighting factors, and developing procedures, filmmakers can achieve enormous variety in the look of the film image (**5.1–5.3**). Most black-and-white films employ a balance of grays, blacks, and whites.

Jean-Luc Godard's *Les Carabiniers* (**5.4**) offers a good example of what post-filming manipulations of film stock can accomplish. The shot's newsreel-like quality is heightened by both the film stock and lab work that increased contrast. "The positive prints," Godard has explained, "were simply made on a special Kodak high contrast stock. . . . Several shots, intrinsically too gray, were duped again sometimes two or three times, always to their highest contrast." The effect suggests old combat footage that has been recopied or shot under bad lighting conditions; the high-contrast look suited a film about the grubbiness of war.

> "Both [cinematographer] Floyd [Crosby] and I wanted [High Noon] to look like a documentary, or a newsreel from the period of the 1880s, if film had existed at that time—which, of course, it did not. I believe that we came close to our goal by using flat lighting, a grainy texture in the printing and an unfiltered white sky."
>
> — Fred Zinnemann, director

5.1　Most black-and-white films employ a balance of grays, blacks, and whites, as in this shot from *Casablanca.*

5.2　In *Breaking the Waves,* color manipulation created bleached-out images.

5.3　The dream sequence early in Ingmar Bergman's *Wild Strawberries* uses a combination of film stock, overexposure, and laboratory processing to create a bleached-out look.

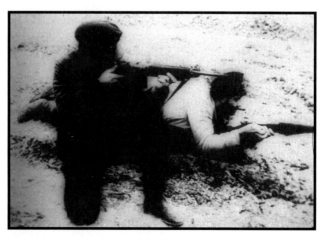

5.4　This shot from *Les Carabiniers* achieves a newsreel-like quality heightened by both the film stock and lab work that increased contrast.

5.5   The trolley scene in *Meet Me in St. Louis* shows off the vivid colors possible with the Technicolor process.

5.6   The use of blues in *Stalker* makes the action almost seem to be taking place underwater.

5.7   Lye manipulated Gasparcolor paper stock to create pure, saturated silhouettes that split and recombine in *Rainbow Dance*.

Different color film stocks yield varying color contrasts. Technicolor became famous for its sharply distinct, heavily saturated hues, as seen in such films as *Meet Me in St. Louis* (**5.5**). The richness of Technicolor was achieved by means of a specially designed camera and sophisticated printing process. To take another example, Soviet filmmakers used a domestically made stock that tends to lower contrast and give the image a murky greenish-blue cast. Andrei Tarkovsky exploited just these qualities in the monochromatic color design of his shadowy *Stalker* (**5.6**). Len Lye's abstract *Rainbow Dance* uses specific features of the English stock Gasparcolor (**5.7**).

The tonalities of color stock may also be altered by laboratory processes. The person assigned the role of *color timer* or *grader* has a wide choice about the color range of a print. A red patch in the image may be printed as crimson, pink, or almost any shade in between. Often the timer consults with the director to select a key tone that will serve as a reference point for color relations throughout the film. In addition, some prints can be made for purposes that require a different color balance. Today, most prints made for 35mm exhibition are printed somewhat dark, to create rich shadows and darker colors. But prints struck for transfer to video are made on special low-contrast stock in order to compensate for television's tendency to heighten contrast. The resulting image often has a lighter, brighter color range than seen in any theatrical print. Increasingly, cinematographers are using computer grading for selected shots or even an entire film. (See "A Closer Look," pp. 179–181.)

Certain procedures may also add color to footage originally shot in black and white. Before 1930, filmmakers often used tinting and toning. *Tinting* is accomplished by dipping the already developed film into a bath of dye. The dark areas remain black and gray, while the lighter areas pick up the color (**5.8**). *Toning* worked in an opposite fashion. The dye was added during the developing of the positive print. As a result, darker areas are colored, while the lighter portions of the frame remain white or only faintly colored (**5.9**).

Certain conventions grew up around tinting and toning. Night scenes, as in 5.9 (from *Cenere,* a 1916 Italian film) were often colored blue. Firelight was frequently colored red, while interiors were commonly amber. *The Wrath of the Gods* (1914) uses a pink tint to suggest the glow of an erupting volcano (5.8). Some later filmmakers revived these processes. Vera Chytilova employs a crimson toning in *Daisies* (**5.10**).

A rarer method of adding color is the difficult process of *hand coloring*. Here portions of black-and-white images are painted in colors, frame by frame. The ship's flag in Sergei Eisenstein's *Potemkin* was originally hand colored red against a blue sky. A modern use of hand coloring may be seen in Makavejev's *Innocence Unprotected* (**5.11**).

There are many other ways in which the filmmaker can manipulate the image's tonalities after filming. In *Reflections on Black,* Stan Brakhage scratched off the

5.8   Tinting creates a pinkish color across the entire frame in the 1914 film *The Wrath of the Gods.*

5.9   In *Cenere,* the deep blue of the dark areas and nearly white patches are characteristic of toning.

5.10   Toning in *Daisies.*

5.11   In *Innocence Unprotected,* stylized images are created by painting multiple colors within a shot.

emulsion in certain parts of the shot (**5.12**). Lars von Trier shot *Breaking the Waves* on 35mm film, then transferred the footage to video and used digital manipulation to drain out much of the color. He transferred the result back to film, resulting in desaturated images that tremble and shimmer (5.2).

The range of tonalities in the image is most crucially affected by the *exposure* of the image during filming. The filmmaker usually controls **exposure** by regulating how much light passes through the camera lens, though images shot with correct exposure can also be overexposed or underexposed in developing and printing. We commonly think that a photograph should be well exposed—neither underexposed (too dark, not enough light admitted through the lens) nor overexposed (too bright, too much light admitted through the lens). But even correct exposure usually offers some latitude for choice; it is not an absolute.

The filmmaker can manipulate exposure for specific effects. American *film noir* of the 1940s sometimes underexposed shadowy regions of the image in keeping with low-key lighting techniques. In *Vidas Secas,* Nelson Pereira dos Santos overexposed the windows of the prison cell to sharpen the contrast between the

5.12   By scratching the emulsion, Brakhage emphasizes the eye motif that runs through *Reflections on Black.*

prisoner's confinement and the world of freedom outside **(5.13)**. In the Moria sequence, *The Lord of the Rings: The Fellowship of the Ring* used overexposure in several shots. In **5.14**, the white glare was achieved by digital grading that simulated photographic overexposure.

Choices of exposure are particularly critical in working with color. For shots of *Kasba,* Kumar Shahani chose to emphasize tones within shaded areas, and so he exposed them and let sunlit areas bleach out somewhat **(5.15, 5.16)**.

Exposure can in turn be affected by **filters**—slices of glass or gelatin put in front of the lens of the camera or printer to reduce certain frequencies of light reaching the film. Filters thus alter the range of tonalities in quite radical ways. Before modern improvements in film stocks and lighting made it practical to shoot most outdoor night scenes at night, filmmakers routinely made such scenes by using blue filters in sunlight—a technique called *day for night* **(5.17)**. Hollywood cinematographers since the 1920s have sought to add glamour to close-ups, especially of women, by means of diffusion filters and silks. Filters applied during shooting or during printing can also alter the color image.

Digital cinematography doesn't employ film stock; the image is captured on an electrically charged sensor and recorded to tape or a hard drive. Still, the filmmakers must make choices about color, exposure, and tonal contrast that are comparable to those offered by film. All the other techniques we'll survey in this chapter have their equivalents in digital moviemaking.

Speed of Motion

A gymnast's performance seen in slow motion, ordinary action accelerated to comic speed, a tennis serve stopped in a freeze-frame—we are all familiar with the effects of the control of the speed of motion. Of course, the filmmaker who stages the event to be filmed can (within limits) dictate the pace of the action. But that pace can also be controlled by a photographic power unique to cinema: the control of the speed of movement seen on the screen.

The speed of the motion we see on the screen depends on the relation between the rate at which the film was shot and the rate of projection. Both **rates** are calculated in frames per second. The standard rate, established when synchronized-sound cinema came in at the end of the 1920s, was 24 frames per second. Today's 35mm cameras commonly offer the filmmaker a choice of anything between 8 and 64 frames per second (fps), with specialized cameras offering still wider range of choice.

5.13   Deliberate overexposure of windows in *Vidas Secas.*

5.14   In *The Fellowship of the Ring,* the overexposure of the wizard's staff makes the Fellowship a bright island threatened by countless orcs in the surrounding darkness.

5.15 In *Kasbah,* the vibrant hues of the store's wares stand out, while the countryside behind is overexposed . . .

5.16 . . . while at other moments underexposure for the shaded porches emphasizes the central outdoor area.

5.17 In *The Searchers,* this scene of the protagonists spying on an Indian camp from a bluff was shot in sunlight using day-for-night filters.

5.18 Cars become blurs of light when shot in fast motion for *Koyaanisqatsi.*

If the movement is to look accurate on the screen, the rate of shooting should correspond to the rate of projection. That's why silent films sometimes look jerky today: Films shot at anywhere from 16 to 20 frames per second are speeded up when shown at 24 frames per second. Projected at the correct speed, silent films can look as smooth as movies made today.

As the silent films indicate, if a film is exposed at fewer frames per second than the projection, the screen action will look speeded up. This is the *fast-motion* effect sometimes seen in comedies. But fast motion has long been used for other purposes. In F. W. Murnau's *Nosferatu,* the vampire's coach rushes skittishly across the landscape, suggesting his supernatural power. In Godfrey Reggio's *Koyaanisqatsi,* a delirious fast motion renders the hectic rhythms of urban life **(5.18)**. More recent films have used fast motion to grab our attention and accelerate the pace, whisking us through a setting to the heart of the action.

The more frames per second shot, the slower the screen action will appear. The resulting *slow-motion* effect is used notably in Dziga Vertov's *Man with a Movie Camera* to render sports events in detail, a function that continues to be important today. The technique can also be used for expressive purposes. In Rouben Mamoulian's *Love Me Tonight,* the members of a hunt decide to ride quietly home to avoid waking the sleeping deer; their ride is filmed in slow motion to create a comic depiction of noiseless movement. Today slow-motion footage often functions to suggest that the action takes place in a dream or fantasy, to express a lyrical quality, or to convey enormous power, as in a martial-arts film. Slow motion is also increasingly used for emphasis, becoming a way of dwelling on a moment of spectacle or high drama.

To enhance expressive effects, filmmakers can change the speed of motion in the course of a shot. Often the change of speed helps create special effects. In *Die Hard* a fireball bursts up an elevator shaft toward the camera. During the filming, the fire at the bottom of the shaft was filmed at 100 fps, slowing down its progress, and then shot at faster speeds as it erupted upward, giving the impression of an explosive acceleration. For *Bram Stoker's Dracula,* director Francis Ford Coppola wanted his vampire to glide toward his prey with supernatural suddenness. Cinematographer Michael Ballhaus used a computer program to control the shutter and the speed of filming, allowing smooth and instantaneous changes from 24 fps to 8 fps and back again.

Digital postproduction allows filmmakers to create the effect of variable shooting speeds through *ramping,* shifting speed of movement very smoothly and rapidly. In an early scene of Michael Mann's *The Insider,* researcher Jeffrey Wigand leaves the tobacco company that has just fired him. As he crosses the lobby toward a revolving door, his brisk walk suddenly slows to a dreamlike drifting. The point of this very noticeable stylistic choice becomes apparent only in the film's last shot. Lowell Bergman, the TV producer who has helped Wigand reveal that addictive substances are added to cigarettes, has been dismissed from CBS. He strides across the lobby, and as he passes through the revolving door, his movement glides into extreme slow motion. The repetition of the technique points out the parallels between two men who have lost their livelihoods as a result of telling the truth—two insiders who have become outsiders.

Extreme forms of fast and slow motion alter the speed of the depicted material even more radically. *Time-lapse* cinematography permits us to see the sun set in seconds or a flower sprout, bud, and bloom in a minute. For this, a very low shooting speed is required—perhaps one frame per minute, hour, or even day. For *high-speed* cinematography, which may seek to record a bullet shattering glass, the camera may expose hundreds, even thousands, of frames per second. Most cameras can be used for time-lapse shooting, but high-speed cinematography requires specially designed cameras.

After filming, the filmmaker can still control the speed of movement on the screen through various laboratory procedures. Until the early 1990s, the most common means used was the optical printer. This device rephotographs a film, copying all or part of each original frame onto another reel of film. The filmmaker can use the optical printer to skip frames (accelerating the action when projected), reprint a frame at desired intervals (slowing the action by *stretch printing*), stop the action (repeating a frame over and over, to freeze the projected image for seconds or minutes), or reverse the action. Some silent films are stretch-printed with every other frame repeated, so that they may run more smoothly at sound speed. We are familiar with freeze-framing, slow-motion, and reverse-motion printing effects from the *instant replays* of sports coverage and investigative documentaries. Many experimental films have made striking use of the optical printer's possibilities, such as Ken Jacobs's *Tom Tom the Piper's Son,* which explores the images of an early silent film by enlarging portions of its shots. The optical printer has largely been replaced by digital manipulations of the speed of movement.

Perspective

You are standing on railroad tracks, looking toward the horizon. The tracks not only recede but also seem to meet at the horizon. You glance at the trees and buildings along the tracks. They diminish by simple, systematic rule: the closer objects look larger, the farther objects look smaller—even if they are actually of uniform size. The optical system of your eye, registering light rays reflected from the scene, supplies a host of information about scale, depth, and spatial relations among parts of the scene. Such relations are called *perspective* relations.

5.19 In *Don't Look Now,* as the camera swivels to follow the walking character, the wide-angle lens makes a street lamp he passes appear to lean rightward . . .

5.20 . . . and then leftward.

The **lens** of a photographic camera does roughly what your eye does. It gathers light from the scene and transmits that light onto the flat surface of the film to form an image that represents size, depth, and other dimensions of the scene. One difference between the eye and the camera, though, is that photographic lenses may be changed, and each type of lens will render perspective in different ways. If two different lenses photograph the same scene, the perspective relations in the resulting images could be drastically different. A wide-angle lens could exaggerate the depth you see down the track or could make the foreground trees and buildings seem to bulge; a telephoto lens could drastically reduce the depth, making the trees seem very close together and nearly the same size.

The Lens: Focal Length   Control of perspective in the image is very important to the filmmaker. The chief variable in the process is the **focal length** of the lens. In technical terms, the focal length is the distance from the center of the lens to the point where light rays converge to a point of focus on the film. The focal length alters the perceived magnification, depth, and scale of things in the image. We usually distinguish three sorts of lenses on the basis of their effects on perspective:

1. *The short-focal-length* (**wide-angle**) *lens.*

In 35mm-gauge cinematography, a lens of less than 35mm in focal length is considered a wide-angle lens. Such lenses tend to distort straight lines lying near the edges of the frame, bulging them outward. Note the distortion in two frames from a shot in Nicholas Roeg's *Don't Look Now* (**5.19, 5.20**). When a wide-angle lens is used for a medium shot or close-up, the distortion of shape may become very evident (**5.21**).

The lens of short focal length has the property of exaggerating depth (**5.22**). Because distances between foreground and background seem greater, the wide-angle lens also makes figures moving to or from the camera seem to cover ground more rapidly.

2. *The middle-focal-length* (**normal**) *lens.*

A lens of medium focal length is 35 to 50mm. This normal lens seeks to avoid noticeable perspective distortion. With a normal lens, horizontal and vertical lines are rendered as straight and perpendicular. (Compare the bulging effect of the wide-angle lens.) Parallel lines should recede to distant vanishing points, as in our railroad tracks example. Foreground and background should seem neither stretched apart (as with the wide-angle lens) nor squashed together (as with the telephoto lens). A normal lens was used for **5.23**; contrast the sense of distance among the figures achieved in **5.22**.

3. *The long-focal-length* (**telephoto**) *lens.*

Whereas wide-angle lenses distort space laterally, longer lenses flatten the space along the camera axis. Cues for depth and volume are reduced. The planes seem squashed together, much as when you look through a telescope or binoculars. In **5.24**, from Chen Kaige's *Life on a String*, the long lens pushes the crowd members almost to the same plane. It also makes the rapids behind the men virtually a two-dimensional backdrop.

Today, the focal length of long lenses typically ranges from around 75 to 250mm or more. They are commonly used in the filming or televising of sports events, since they allow the cinematographer to magnify action at a distance. (For this reason, long lenses are also called telephoto lenses.) In a base-ball game there will invariably be shots taken from almost directly behind the umpire. You have probably noticed that such shots make catcher, batter, and pitcher look unnaturally close to one another. What a very long lens can do to space is dramatically illustrated throughout Godfrey Reggio's *Koyaanisqatsi* (**5.25**).

A long-focal-length lens also affects subject movement. Because it flattens depth, a figure moving toward the camera takes more time to cover what seems to

5.21   Wide-angle distortion in Mikhail Kalatozov's *The Cranes Are Flying.*

5.22   In this scene from *The Little Foxes,* the lens makes the characters seem farther from one another than we would expect in so relatively tight a grouping.

5.23   A shot made with a normal lens in *His Girl Friday.*

"I'm standing around waiting to see where the 50mm is going to be, or what size lens they're putting on, and in that unwritten book in my brain, I said, 'Don't ever let them shoot you full face, on a wide-angle lens, you'll end up looking like Dumbo.'"

— Tony Curtis, actor

"In New York, New York, *we shot only with a 32mm lens, the whole movie. We tried to equate the old style of framing, the old style meaning 1946–53."*

— Martin Scorsese, director

be a small distance. The *running-in-place* shots in *The Graduate* and other films of the 1960s and 1970s were produced by lenses of very long focal length. In *Tootsie,* the introduction of Michael Dorsey disguised as Dorothy Michaels occurs in a lengthy telephoto shot in order for us to recognize his altered appearance and to notice that none of the people around him finds "her" unusual (**5.26–5.28**).

Lens length can distinctly affect the spectator's experience. For example, expressive qualities can be suggested by lenses that distort objects or characters. We tend to see the man in **5.29** as looming, even aggressive. Moreover, choice of the lens can make a character or object blend into the setting (5.26) or stand out in sharp relief (5.29). Filmmakers may exploit the flattening effects of the long-focal-length lens to create solid masses of space (**5.30**), as in an abstract painting.

A director can use lens length to surprise us, as Kurosawa does in *Red Beard.* When the mad patient comes into the intern's room, a long-focal-length lens filming from behind him initially makes her seem to be quite close to him (**5.31**). But a cut to a more perpendicular angle shows that the patient and the intern are actually several feet apart and that he is not yet in danger (**5.32**).

There is one sort of lens that offers the director a chance to manipulate focal length and to transform perspective relations during a single shot. A **zoom lens** is optically designed to permit the continuous varying of focal length. Originally created for aerial and reconnaissance photography, zoom lenses gradually became a standard tool for newsreel filming. It was not, however, the general practice to zoom during shooting. The camera operator varied the focal length as desired and then started filming. In the late 1950s, however, the increased portability of cameras led to a trend toward zooming while filming.

"I tend to rely on only two kinds of lenses to compose my frames: very wide angle and extreme telephoto. I use the wide angle because when I want to see something, I want to see it completely, with the most detail possible. As for the telephoto, I use it for close-ups because I find it creates a real "encounter" with the actor. If you shoot someone's face with a 200-millimeter lens, the audience will feel like the actor is really standing in front of them. It gives presence to the shot. So I like extremes. Anything in between is of no interest to me."

— John Woo, director

Since then, the zoom has sometimes been used to substitute for moving the camera forward or backward. Although the zoom shot presents a mobile framing, the camera remains fixed. During a zoom, the camera remains stationary, and the lens simply increases or decreases its focal length. Onscreen, the zoom shot magnifies or demagnifies the objects filmed, excluding or including surrounding space, as in **5.33** and **5.34**, from Francis Ford Coppola's *The Conversation.* The zoom can produce interesting and peculiar transformations of scale and depth, as we shall see when we examine Michael Snow's *Wavelength.*

The impact that focal length can have on the image's perspective qualities is dramatically illustrated in Ernie Gehr's abstract experimental film *Serene Velocity.* The scene is an empty corridor. Gehr shot the film with a zoom lens, but he did not zoom while filming the shot. Instead, the zoom permitted him to change the lens's focal length between takes. As Gehr explains,

5.24   The long lens in Chen Kaige's *Life on a String.*

5.25   In *Koyaanisqatsi,* an airport is filmed from a great distance, and the long lens makes it appear that a plane is landing on a crowded highway.

5.26 In *Tootsie,* Dorothy becomes visible among the crowd at a considerable distance from the camera . . .

5.27 . . . and after taking 20 steps seems only slightly closer until . . .

5.28 . . . "she" finally grows somewhat larger, after a total of about 36 steps.

5.29 In Ilya Trauberg's *China Express,* a wide-angle lens creates foreground distortion.

5.30 In *Eternity and a Day,* a long lens makes the beach and sea appear as two vertical blocks.

5.31   In Kurosawa's *Red Beard,* the mad patient in the background seems threateningly to approach the intern . . .

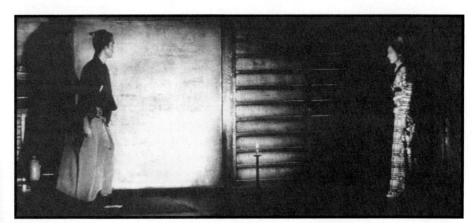

5.32   . . . until a cut reveals that she is across the room from him.

5.33   In the opening of *The Conversation,* a long, slow zoom-in arouses considerable uncertainty about its target . . .

5.34   . . . until it finally centers on a mime and our protagonist, surveillance technician Harry Caul.

[I] divided the mm range of the zoom lens in half and starting from the middle I recorded changes in mm positions. . . . The camera was not moved at all. The zoom lens was not moved during recording either. Each frame was recorded individually as a still. Four frames to each position. To give an example: I shot the first four frames at 50mm. The next four frames I shot at 55mm. And then, for a certain duration, approximately 60 feet, I went back and forth, four frames at 50mm, four frames at 55mm; four frames at 50mm, four frames at 55mm; etc. . . . for about 60 feet. Then I went to 45–60 [mm] and did the same for about 60 feet. Then to 40–65, and so on.

The resulting film presents an image whose perspective relations pulsate rhythmically—first with little difference in size and scale, but gradually with greater tension between a telephoto image and a wide-angle image (**5.35**). In a sense *Serene Velocity* takes as its subject the effect of focal length on perspective.

The Lens: Depth of Field and Focus   Focal length not only affects how shape and scale are magnified or distorted. It also affects the lens's **depth of field**—the range of distances before the lens within which objects can be photographed in sharp **focus**. A lens with a depth of field of 10 feet to infinity will render any object in that range clearly, but the sharpness of the image will decrease when the object moves closer to the lens (say, to 4 feet). All other things being equal, a short-focal-length (wide-angle) lens has a relatively greater depth of field than does a long-focal-length (telephoto) lens.

Depth of field should not be confused with the concept of deep space, discussed in Chapter 4. *Deep space* is a term for the way the filmmaker has staged the action on several different planes, *regardless of whether all of these planes are in focus.* In the case of *Our Hospitality,* those planes usually are in sharp focus, but in other films, not every plane of deep space is in focus. In this shot from *Simple Men* (**5.36**), we can see three planes of depth, but deep focus isn't used. The robber and the security guard she holds at pistol point in the middle ground are in focus. But the yellow railing forming a distinct foreground plane is out of focus. In the distant background, visible between the rails, stands the female robber's partner. He's out of focus, too. The example shows that deep space is a property of mise-en-scene, the techniques that affect what is placed in front of the camera. Depth of field depends on the camera itself, with the lens determining what layers of the mise-en-scene are in focus.

As the *Simple Men* example suggests, selective focus is often used to call attention to the main action and to deemphasize less significant parts of the surroundings. Often this involves centering the main character in the foreground and throwing the background out of focus (**5.37**). Deep space is a property of mise-en-scene, depending on how the image is composed. Depth of field is a property of the photographic lens, affecting what planes of the image are in focus.

If depth of field controls perspective relations by determining which planes will be in focus, what choices are open to the filmmaker? He or she may opt for what is usually called *selective focus*—choosing to focus on only one plane and letting the other planes blur. This is what director Hal Hurtley does in the *Simple Men* example. Selective focus typically draws the viewer's attention to the main character or object (**5.37**). The technique can be used for a more abstract compositional effect as well (**5.38**).

In Hollywood during the 1940s, partly due to the influence of *Citizen Kane,* filmmakers began using faster film, shorter-focal-length lenses, and more intense lighting to yield a greater depth of field. The contract-signing scene from *Citizen Kane* (**5.39**) offers a famous example. This practice came to be called **deep focus**.

Deep-focus cinematography became a major stylistic option in the 1940s and 1950s. A typical usage is illustrated in **5.40**. The technique was even imitated in animated cartoons (4.132, from Chuck Jones's *One Froggy Evening*). During the 1970s and 1980s, deep-focus cinematography was revived in Steven Spielberg's work, notably *Jaws* and *Close Encounters of the Third Kind,* and in the films of Brian De Palma (**5.41**). Today, extreme deep-focus effects can also be achieved digitally (**5.42**).

The filmmaker may also have the option of adjusting perspective while filming by **racking focus**, or *pulling focus.* A shot may begin with an object in the foreground sharply visible and the rear plane fuzzy, then rack focus so that the background elements come into crisp focus and the foreground becomes blurred. Alternatively, the focus can rack from background to foreground, as in **5.43** and **5.44**, from Bernardo Bertolucci's *Last Tango in Paris.*

Special Effects   The image's perspective relations may also be created by means of **special effects.** We have already seen (p. 117) that the filmmaker can create setting by use of models and computer-generated images. Alternatively,

5.35 In *Serene Velocity,* telephoto shots of a hallway are juxtaposed to wide-angle shots taken from the same spot.

"If I made big-budget films, I would do what the filmmakers of twenty years ago did: use 35, 40, and 50mm [lenses] with lots of light so I could have that depth of field, because it plays upon the effect of surprise. It can give you a whole series of little tricks, little hiding places, little hooks in the image where you can hang surprises, places where they can suddenly appear, just like that, within the frame itself. You can create the off-frame within the frame."

— Benoit Jacquot, director

5.36 In the first shot of *Simple Men,* the foreground railing and the man in the distance are out of focus, emphasizing the drama in focus in the middle ground.

5.37 Agnès Varda's *Vagabonde (Sans toi ni loi).*

5.38   Leos Carax's *Boy Meets Girl.*

5.39   In *Citizen Kane,* from one plane near the lens (Bernstein's head) through several planes in the middle ground to the wall far in the distance, everything is in sharp focus.

5.40   Anthony Mann's *The Tall Target.*

5.41   In *The Untouchables,* a conversation scene is played in the foreground while setting and distant figures are also kept in focus.

5.42   The small size of the chip in a digital video camera yields extreme depth of field. If this shot, from Agnès Varda's *The Gleaners and I,* had been made on film, either Varda's hand or the truck would have been far more out of focus.

separately photographed planes of action may be combined on the same strip of film to create the illusion that the two planes are adjacent. The simplest way to do this is through **superimposition**. Either by double exposure in the camera or in laboratory printing, one image is laid over another. Superimpositions have been used since the earliest years of the cinema. One common function is to render ghosts, which appear as translucent figures. Superimpositions also frequently provide a way of conveying dreams, visions, or memories. Typically, these mental images are shown against a close view of a face (**5.45**).

More complex techniques for combining strips of film to create a single shot are usually called **process**, or *composite,* **shots**. These techniques can be divided into *projection process work* and *matte process work.*

In projection process work, the filmmaker projects footage of a setting onto a screen, then films actors performing in front of the screen. Classical Hollywood filmmaking began this process in the late 1920s, as a way to avoid taking cast and crew on location. The Hollywood technique involved placing the actors against a translucent screen and projecting a film of the setting from behind the screen. The whole ensemble could then be filmed from the front (**5.46**).

Rear projection, as this system was known, seldom creates very convincing depth cues. Foreground and background tend to look starkly separate, partly because of the absence of cast shadows from foreground to background and partly because all background planes tend to seem equally diffuse (**5.47**).

5.43 In this shot from *Last Tango in Paris,* the woman, bench, and wall in the distance are in focus, while the man in the foreground is not . . .

5.44 . . . but after the camera racks focus, the man in the foreground becomes sharp and the background fuzzy.

5.45 In the opening of Quentin Tarantino's *Kill Bill, Vol. 1,* the Bride sees the first victim of her revenge, and her memory of a violent struggle is superimposed over a tight framing of her eyes.

5.46 *Boom Town.*

5.47 In Hitchcock's *Vertigo,* the seascape in the rear plane was shot separately and used as a back-projected setting for an embrace filmed under studio lighting.

Front projection, which came into use in the late 1960s, projects the setting onto a two-way mirror, angled to throw the image onto a high-reflectance screen. The camera photographs the actors against the screen by shooting through the mirror (**5.48**). The results of front projection can be clearly seen in the "Dawn of Man" sequence of *2001: A Space Odyssey,* the first film to use front projection extensively. (At one moment, a saber-toothed tiger's eyes glow, reflecting the projector's light.) Because of the sharp focus of the projected footage, front projection blends foreground and background planes fairly smoothly. The nonrealistic possibilities of front projection have been recently explored by Hans-Jürgen Syberberg. In his film of Wagner's opera *Parsifal* front projection conjures up colossal, phantasmagoric landscapes (**5.49**). Front and rear projection are rapidly being replaced by digital techniques. Here action is filmed in front of a large blue or green screen rather than a film image, with the background later added by digital manipulation.

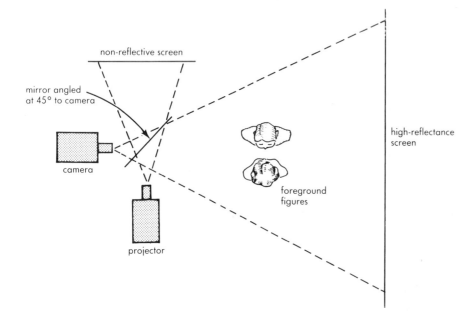

5.48   A front-projection system.

5.49   In Syberberg's film of Wagner's *Parsifal,* front projection conjures up colossal, phantasmagoric landscapes.

Composite filming can also be accomplished by **matte work**. A *matte* is a portion of the setting photographed on a strip of film, usually with a part of the frame empty. Through laboratory printing, the matte is joined with another strip of film containing the actors. One sort of matte involves a painting of the desired areas of setting, which is then filmed. The footage is combined with footage of action, segregated in the blank portions of the painted scenery. In this way, a matte can create an entire imaginary setting for the film. Stationary mattes of this sort have made glass shots virtually obsolete and were so widely used in commercial cinema that until the late 1990s the matte painter was a mainstay of production. In recent years, matte paintings have been made using computer programs, but they are used in the same way to create scenery (**5.50**).

With a matte painting, however, the actor cannot move into the painted portions of the frame without seeming to disappear. To solve this problem, the filmmaker can use a *traveling matte*. Here the actor is photographed against a blank, usually blue, background. In laboratory printing, the moving outline of the actor is cut out of footage of the desired background. After further lab work, the shot of the actor is jigsawed into the moving gap in the background footage. It is traveling mattes that present shots of Superman's flight or of spaceships hurtling through space (**5.51**). In 4.83, the robot is combined with live action in the background by means

5.50   In this shot from *The Fellowship of the Ring,* the distant part of the building, the cliffs, and the sky are all on a matte painting created by computer.

5.51   In *Star Wars: Episode IV—A New Hope,* the take-off of the *Millennium Falcon* was filmed as a model against a blue screen and matted into a shot of a building with imperial stormtroopers firing upward.

5.52   In *Who Framed Roger Rabbit?* a human director inhabits the same world as the cartoon characters starring in his film.

of a traveling matte. The animated figures in our shot from *Who Framed Roger Rabbit?* **(5.52)** were matted into live-action footage shot separately.

Before the perfecting of computer-generated imagery, traveling mattes were commonly used in all genres of mainstream cinema. Usually, they function to create a realistic-looking locale or situation. But they can also generate an abstract, deliberately unrealistic, image **(5.53)**.

For many films, different types of special effects will be combined. The above illustration from *The Fellowship of the Ring* (5.50) includes a partial full-size set with an actor at the left, a miniature set in the middle ground, a matte painting of the background elements, and computer-animated waterfalls and falling leaves. A single shot of a science fiction film might animate miniatures or models through stop action, convey their movements by a traveling matte, and add animated ray bursts in superimposition while a matte painting supplies a background. For the train crash in *The Fugitive,* front and rear projection were used simultaneously within certain shots.

You may have noticed that superimpositions, projection process work, and matte work all straddle two general bodies of film techniques. These special effects all require arrangement of the material before the camera, so to some extent they are aspects of mise-en-scene. But they also require control of photographic choices (such as refilming and making laboratory adjustments) and affect perspective

5.53   In *Rumble Fish,* a black-and-white film, Francis Ford Coppola uses traveling mattes to color the fish in an aquarium.

5.54   Computer-generated imagery created a gap in the freeway for the bus to leap in *Speed.*

5.55   The foreground plane of this shot from *The Chronicle of Anna Magdalena Bach* shows Bach, shot straight on, playing a harpsichord—yet the back-projected building behind him is shot from a low angle.

relations, so they involve cinematography as well. We have considered them here because, unlike effects employing models and miniatures, these effects are created through specifically photographic tricks. The general term for them, *optical effects,* stresses their photographic nature.

With the rise of computer-generated effects, the fusion of mise-en-scene and cinematography became even more seamless. Digital compositing allows the filmmaker to shoot some action with performers and then add backgrounds, shadows, or movement that would previously have required photographed mattes, multiple exposures, or optical printing. In *Speed,* the audience sees a city bus leap a broken freeway. The stunt was performed on a ramp designed for the jump, and the highway background was drawn digitally as a matte painting **(5.54)**. With the proliferation of specialized programs, computer-generated imagery (CGI) increasingly provides convincing effects that have all but replaced traditional optical printing. (See "A Closer Look.")

Like other film techniques, photographic manipulations of the shot are not ends in themselves. Rather, they function within the overall context of the film. Specific treatments of tonalities, speed of motion, or perspective should be judged less on criteria of realism than on criteria of function. For instance, most Hollywood filmmakers try to make their rear-projection shots unnoticeable. But in Jean-Marie Straub and Danièle Huillet's *The Chronicle of Anna Magdalena Bach,* the perspective relations are yanked out of kilter by an inconsistent rear projection **(5.55)**. Since the film's other shots have been filmed on location in correct perspective, this blatantly artificial rear projection calls our attention to the visual style of the entire film.

FROM MONSTERS TO THE MUNDANE:
Computer-Generated Imagery in *The Lord of the Rings*

The films adapted from J. R. R. Tolkien's trilogy *The Lord of the Rings (The Fellowship of the Ring, The Two Towers,* and *The Return of the King)* show how CGI can be used for impressive special effects: huge battle scenes, plausible monsters, and magical events. Less obviously, the films also indicate how, more and more, CGI shapes many aspects of production, from the spectacular to the mundane.

The director, Peter Jackson, started his career in horror and fantasy films in New Zealand, where he and his partners Jamie Selkirk and Richard Taylor formed a CGI firm, Weta Digital, in 1993. Most of the digital work for *Rings* was done at the Weta facility, although the film involved so much CGI that a few sequences were commissioned from other effects firms.

CGI was used at every stage of production. In preproduction, a sort of animated storyboard (a *previz,* for "previsualization") was made, consisting of *animatics,* or rough computer-generated versions of the scenes. Each of the three previzes was roughly as long as each finished film and helped to coordinate the work of the huge staff involved in both the digital and physical work of production.

During production of the three films, CGI helped create portions of the mise-en-scène. Many shots digitally stitched together disparate elements, blending full-size settings, miniature sets, and matte paintings (5.50). A total of 68 miniature sets were built, and computer manipulation was

required in each case to make them appear real or to allow camera movements through them. Computer paint programs could generate matte paintings (often based on location still photographs) for the sky, clouds, distant cliffs, and forests that appeared behind the miniatures.

Rings also drew on the rapidly developing capacity of CGI to create characters. The war scenes were staged with a small number of actual actors in costumes, while vast crowds of CGI soldiers appeared in motion alongside them. Like many companies working on digitally sophisticated films, the Weta team had to develop its own proprietary software programs. A crucial program was Massive (for "Multiple Agent Simulation System in Virtual Environment"). Using motion capture on a few *agents* (costumed actors), the team could build a number of different military maneuvers, assigning all of them to the thousands of crude, digitally generated figures. By giving each figure a rudimentary artificial intelligence—such as the ability to see an approaching soldier and identify it as friend or foe—Massive could generate a scene with figures moving in unpredictable patterns. (Many options were given to the digital soldiers, and the considerable variety resulted in more realistic crowds than had the earlier method of simply repeating the movements of a small number of agents.) Another new program, Grunt, rendered these figures into photorealistic soldiers, again by creating a variety of options as to weight, height,

5.56 Vast crowds of soldiers with individualized movements were generated by the Massive program for *The Two Towers*.

and so on and letting these combine randomly for each figure **(5.56)**.

The monsters encountered by the characters during their quest were more elaborately designed and executed than the troops. A detailed three-dimensional model of each creature was constructed and captured with a new scanning wand that could read into recesses and folds to create a complete image from all angles. Obtaining realistic movement from these figures demanded further computer manipulation, however. A new system, Character Mapper, captured motion from a human actor, then adjusted the mass and musculature to imaginary skeletons. This was used notably in the cave-troll sequence to give an impression of the large, squat creature swinging its limbs and flexing its muscles in a believable fashion.

Most of the speaking characters (with the important exception of the skeletal Gollum) were played by actors, but even here CGI was used. The main characters had digital look-alikes who served as stunt doubles, performing actions that were dangerous or impossible. In the cave-troll fight, the actors playing Legolas, Merry, and Pippin were all replaced by their digital doubles when they climbed or jumped on the troll's shoulders. A requirement specific to this story was the juxtaposition of full-size actors playing three-foot-tall hobbits with other characters considerably taller than themselves. The size difference was often created during filming by using small doubles or by placing the hobbits farther from the camera in false-perspective sets. Some scenes combining tall and short characters required camera movement, which, to avoid destroying the false perspective, was accomplished through *motion control*. Motion control uses a camera guided by computer calculations, and here it moved the foreground and background figures at different rates, proportionate to their size and distance from the lens.

In many cases, CGI created the kinds of special effects formerly generated on an optical printer. In *The Fellowship of the Ring,* such effects include Gandalf's fireworks, the flood at the Fords of Bruinen, the avalanche that hits the Fellowship on the mountain pass, and the flaming Eye of Sauron. The Elf Legolas's superhuman speed in archery was achieved by adding digital arrows to the actor's pantomime of firing.

Cinematography also depended on CGI. For the cave-troll scene, Jackson donned a virtual-reality helmet and planned camera positions by moving around a virtual set and facing a virtual troll. The camera positions were motion-captured and reproduced in the actual filming of the sequence—which has a rough, hand-held style quite different from the rest of the scenes.

CGI was required in postproduction as well. Filmmakers erased telephone poles in location shots and helicopter blades dipping into the aerial shots of the Fellowship's voyage across mountains. Specialized programs added details, such as the ripples caused by drops of dew falling into the water in the Mirror of Galadriel and the distant waterfalls seen behind Rivendell.

Perhaps most important, digital grading after filming manipulated 70 percent of the shots in *Fellowship* and 100 percent in *The Two Towers* and *The Return of the King*. Grading could alter the color of shots, giving each major location a distinctive look, such as the autumnal shades used for Rivendell. The faces of the characters were made to look pallid in the Mines of Moria, while the early scenes in the Shire were given a yellow glow that enhanced the sunshine and green fields. The grading also utilized a specially designed program, 5D Colossus, which allowed artists to adjust the color values of individual elements within a shot. Thus in the Lorien scene in which Galadriel shows Frodo her mirror, she glows bright white, contrasting with the deep blue tones of Frodo's figure and setting. This was achieved not only by aiming bright lights at her (which brightened nearby parts of the set as well), but also by digitally brightening only her figure in postproduction **(5.57)**. Thanks to digital grading, CGI techniques can go beyond the creation of imaginary creatures and large crowds to shape the visual style of an entire film.

Commenting on the special effects in the hobbit party scene in *Fellowship*, Visual Effects Supervisor Jim Rygiel and Weta Animation Design Supervisor Randall William Cook emphasize the range of uses for CGI. The party was shot on a set in a studio, but the treetops and sky were added by computer: "So we ended up replacing that whole sky and some of those trees and obviously adding the fireworks dragon and the smoke elements. So the showy stuff is obviously effects, but there's a lot of stuff that's hidden, like just the background behind Ian [Holm] and Elijah [Wood], which is every bit as much of a challenge."

Such ambitious applications of CGI required enormous technical facilities. At the end of *Fellowship*, Weta had 700 processors devoted solely to rendering images 24 hours a day. By the end of *Return*, there were 4200. The amount of digital information saved for the entire project was around 500 terabytes. As computer memory and speed continue to develop, the applications of CGI to many aspects of filmmaking—and not just on effects-heavy films like *The Lord of the Rings*—will expand as well.

5.57 In *The Fellowship of the Ring*, selective digital color grading makes one figure bright white while the rest of the scene has a uniform muted blue tone.

5.58   In *Daisies,* perspective cues create a comic optical illusion.

5.59   The Lumière camera provided flexibility in framing.

Similarly, **5.58** looks unrealistic unless we posit the man as being about two feet long. But director Vera Chytilova has used setting, character position, and deep focus to make a comic point about the two women's treatment of men. Such trick perspective was designed to be unnoticeable in *The Lord of the Rings,* where an adult actor playing a three-foot-tall hobbit might be placed considerably farther from the camera than an actor playing a taller character, yet the two appeared to be talking face to face. (See "A Closer Look," p. 179) The filmmaker chooses not only how to register light and movement photographically but also how those photographic qualities will function within the overall formal system of the film.

Framing

In any image, the frame is not simply a neutral border; it imposes a *certain vantage point* onto the material within the image. In cinema, the frame is important because it actively *defines* the image for us.

If we needed proof of the power of **framing**, we need only turn to the first major filmmaker in history, Louis Lumière. An inventor and businessman, Lumière and his brother Auguste devised one of the first practical cinema cameras (**5.59**). The Lumière camera, the most flexible of its day, also doubled as a projector. Whereas the bulky American camera invented by W.K.L. Dickson was about the size of an office desk (**5.60**), the Lumière camera weighed only 12 pounds and was small and portable. As a result of its lightness, the Lumière camera could be taken outside and could be set up quickly. Louis Lumière's earliest films presented simple events—workers leaving his father's factory, a game of cards, a family meal. But even at so early a stage of film history, Lumière was able to use framing to transform everyday reality into cinematic events.

Consider one of the most famous Lumière films, *The Arrival of a Train at La Ciotat* (1897). Had Lumière followed theatrical practice, he might have framed the shot by setting the camera perpendicular to the platform, letting the train enter the frame from the right side, broadside to the spectator. Instead, Lumière positioned the camera at an oblique angle. The result is a dynamic composition, with the train arriving from the distance on a diagonal (**5.61**). If the scene had been shot perpendicularly, we would have seen only a string of passengers' backs climbing aboard. Here, however, Lumière's oblique angle brings out many aspects of the passengers' bodies and several planes of action. We see some figures in the foreground, and some in the distance. Simple as it is, this single-shot film, less than a minute long, aptly illustrates how choosing a position for the camera makes a drastic difference in the framing of the image and how we perceive the filmed event.

Consider another Lumière short, *Baby's Meal* (1895). Lumière selected a camera position that would emphasize certain aspects of the event. A long shot would have situated the family in its garden, but Lumière framed the figures at a medium distance, which downplays the setting but emphasizes the family's gestures and facial expressions (**5.62**). The frame's control of the scale of the event has also controlled our understanding of the event itself.

5.60   The bulky camera of W.K.L. Dickson.

5.61   Louis Lumière's diagonal framing in *The Arrival of a Train at La Ciotat.*

5.62   *Baby's Meal.*

Framing can powerfully affect the image by means of (1) the size and shape of the frame; (2) the way the frame defines onscreen and offscreen space; (3) the way framing imposes the distance, angle, and height of a vantage point onto the image; and (4) the way framing can move in relation to the mise-en-scene.

Frame Dimensions and Shape

We are so accustomed to the frame as a rectangle that we should remember that it need not be one. In painting and photography, of course, images have frames of various sizes and shapes: narrow rectangles, ovals, vertical panels, even triangles and parallelograms. In cinema, the choice has been more limited. The primary choices involve the width of the rectangular image.

The ratio of frame width to frame height is called the **aspect ratio**. The rough dimensions of the ratio were set quite early in the history of cinema by Thomas Edison, Dickson, Lumière, and other inventors. The proportions of the rectangular frame were approximately four to three, yielding an aspect ratio of 1.33:1. Nonetheless, in the silent period, some filmmakers felt that this standard was too limiting. Abel Gance shot and projected sequences of *Napoleon* (1927) in a format he called *triptychs*. This was a wide-screen effect composed of three normal frames placed side by side. Gance used the effect sometimes to show a single huge expanse and sometimes to put three distinct images side by side (**5.63**). In contrast, the Soviet director Sergei Eisenstein argued for a square frame, which would make compositions along horizontal, vertical, and diagonal directions equally feasible.

The coming of sound in the late 1920s altered the frame somewhat. Adding the sound track to the filmstrip required adjusting either the shape or the size of the image. At first, some films were printed in an almost a square format, usually about 1.17:1 (**5.64**). But in the early 1930s, the Hollywood Academy of Motion Picture Arts and Sciences established the so-called **Academy ratio** of 1.33:1 (**5.65**). The Academy ratio was standardized throughout the world until the mid-1950s. For decades, standard television screens have also been in the 1.33:1 ratio, but wide-screen TVs are gradually gaining popularity.

Since the mid-1950s, a variety of *wide-screen* ratios has dominated 35mm filmmaking. The most common format in North America today is 1.85:1 (**5.66**). The 1.66:1 ratio (**5.67**) is more frequently used in Europe than in North America. A less common ratio, also widely used in European films, is 1.75:1 (**5.68**). A 2.35:1 ratio (**5.69**) was standardized by the CinemaScope anamorphic process during the 1950s. The 2.2:1 ratio was chiefly used for 70mm presentation (**5.70**), though as film stocks have improved, 70mm filming and projecting have largely disappeared.

The simplest way to create a wide-screen image is by **masking** it at some stage in production or exhibition (**5.71**). This masking is usually called a *hard matte*. Alternatively, many contemporary films are shot full-frame (that is, between 1.33:1 and 1.17:1) in the expectation that they will be masked when the film is shown.

5.63   A panoramic view from *Napoleon* joined images shot with three cameras.

COMMON ASPECT RATIOS OF 35MM FILM

1.17:1

5.64 *Public Enemy* shows the squarish aspect ratio of early sound films.

1.33 (1.37):1

5.65 *The Rules of the Game* was shot in Academy ratio.

1.85:1

5.66 *Me and You and Everyone We Know* uses a common North American ratio.

1.66:1

5.67 *Une chambre en ville.*

1.75:1

5.68 *Last Tango in Paris.*

2.35:1
(35mm anamorphic)

5.69 Anamorphic widescreen in *The Valiant Ones.*

2.2:1
(70mm)

5.70 *Ghostbusters.*

5.71   This frame from Agnès Varda's *Vagabond* was masked during filming or printing.

5.72   Martin Scorsese's *Raging Bull*. Note the microphone visible at the top edge.

5.73   A frame from Nicholas Ray's CinemaScope film *Bigger Than Life* squeezed . . .

5.74   . . . and as projected.

Sometimes this results in lights or sound equipment being visible in the full-frame image. In **5.72** you can clearly see the microphone bobbing down into the shot. This would not be seen in the theater, where the top and bottom of the frame would be masked by the aperture plate in the projector. The colored lines in our illustration show a projection framing at 1.85:1.

Another way to create a wide-screen image is by using an **anamorphic** process. Here a special lens squeezes the image horizontally, either during filming or in printing. A comparable lens is necessary to unsqueeze the image during projection. The image on the 35mm filmstrip is shown in **5.73**, while the image as projected on the screen is shown in **5.74**. The anamorphic aspect ratio, established by CinemaScope was 2.35:1, until the 1970s; for technical reasons, it was adjusted to 2.40:1. This is the aspect ratio of Panavision, today's most frequently used anamorphic system.

Wide-screen cinema, either masked or anamorphic, has significant visual effects. The screen becomes a band or strip, emphasizing horizontal compositions. The format was initially associated with genres of spectacle—Westerns, travelogues, musicals, historical epics—in which sweeping settings were important. But directors quickly learned that wide-screen has value for more intimate subjects, too.

The frame from Kurosawa's *Sanjuro* **(5.75)** shows how an anamorphic process (Tohoscope, the Japanese equivalent of CinemaScope) can be used to create significant foreground and background areas in a confined setting.

In some wide-screen compositions, the mise-en-scene draws the audience's attention to only one area of the image. A common solution is to put the important information slightly off center **(5.76)**, or even sharply off center **(5.77)**. Or the director may use the wide-screen format to multiply points of interest. Many scenes in Im Kwon-Taek's *Chunhyang* fill the frame with bustle and movement **(5.78)**.

5.75   Akira Kurosawa's *Sanjuro*.

5.76   Souleymare Cissé's *Yeelen*.

5.77   John McTiernan's *Die Hard*.

5.78 In this busy scene from *Chunhyang,* our eye shuttles around the widescreen frame according to who is speaking, who is facing us, and who responds to the speaker.

5.79 Gance's *La Roue.*

The rectangular frame, while by far the most common, has not prevented film-makers from experimenting with other image shapes within the rectangular frame. This has usually been done by attaching **masks** over either the camera's or the printer's lens to block the passage of light. Masks were quite common in the silent cinema. A moving circular mask that opens to reveal or closes to conceal a scene is called an **iris**. In *La Roue,* Gance employed a variety of circular and oval masks **(5.79)**. In **5.80**, a shot from Griffith's *Intolerance,* most of the frame is boldly blocked out to leave only a thin vertical slice, emphasizing the soldier's fall from the rampart. A number of directors in the sound cinema have revived the use of irises and masks. In *The Magnificent Ambersons* **(5.81)**, Orson Welles used an iris to close a scene; the old-fashioned device adds a nostalgic note to the sequence.

5.80 Griffith's *Intolerance.*

We also should mention experiments with *multiple-frame* imagery, often called *split-screen* imagery. In this process, two or more images, each with its own frame dimensions and shape, appear within the larger frame. From the early cinema on-ward, this device has been used to present scenes of telephone conversations **(5.82)**. Split-screen phone scenes were revived for phone conversations in *Bye Bye Birdie* **(5.83)** and other 1960s wide-screen comedies. Multiple-frame imagery is also use-ful for building suspense, as Brian De Palma has shown in such films as *Sisters.* We gain a godlike omniscience as we watch two or more actions at exactly the same moment. Peter Greenaway used split screen more experimentally in *Prospero's Books,* juxtaposing images suggested by Shakespeare's *The Tempest* **(5.84)**.

As usual, the filmmaker's choice of screen format can be an important factor in shaping the viewer's experience. Frame size and shape can guide the spectator's at-tention. It can be concentrated through compositional patterns or masking, or it can be dispersed by use of various points of interest or sound cues. The same possibil-ities exist with multiple-frame imagery, which must be carefully coordinated either to focus the viewer's notice or to send it ricocheting from one image to another.

5.81 Welles's *The Magnificent Ambersons.*

Onscreen and Offscreen Space

Whatever its shape, the frame makes the image finite. The film image is bounded, limited. From an implicitly continuous world, the frame selects a slice to show us, leaving the rest of the space *offscreen.* If the camera leaves an object or person and moves elsewhere, we assume that the object or person is still there, outside the frame. Even in an abstract film, we cannot resist the sense that the shapes and pat-terns that burst into the frame come from somewhere.

Film aesthetician Noël Burch has pointed out six zones of offscreen space: the space beyond each of the four edges of the frame, the space behind the set, and the space behind the camera. It is worth considering how many ways a filmmaker can imply the presence of things in these zones of offscreen space. A character can aim looks or gestures at something offscreen. As we'll see in Chapter 7, sound can of-fer potent clues about offscreen space. And, of course, something from offscreen can protrude partly into the frame. Virtually any film could be cited for examples

5.82 Philips Smalley's 1913 *Suspense* uses a three-way split screen.

5.83   Teenagers discuss the latest gossip in *Bye Bye Birdie*'s split-screen conversation.

5.84   The actor playing Ariel in *Prospero's Books* hovers over the scene in a separate space.

5.85   In *Jezebel*, the heroine, Julie, greets some friends in medium shot . . .

5.86   . . . when suddenly a huge fist holding a glass appears in the left foreground.

of all these possibilities, but attractive instances are offered by films that use off-screen space for surprise effects.

In a party scene in William Wyler's *Jezebel,* the heroine, Julie, is the main focus of attention until a man's hand comes abruptly into the frame **(5.85–5.88).** The intrusion of the hand abruptly signals us to the man's presence; Julie's glance, the camera movement, and the sound track confirm our new awareness of the total space. The director has used the selective powers of the frame to exclude something of great importance and then introduce it with startling effect.

More systematically, D. W. Griffith's *Musketeers of Pig Alley* makes use of sudden intrusions into the frame as a motif developing across the whole film. When a gangster is trying to slip a drug into the heroine's drink, we are not aware that the Snapper Kid has entered the room until a plume of his cigarette smoke wafts into the frame **(5.89).** At the film's end, when the Snapper Kid receives a payoff, a mysterious hand thrusts into the frame to offer him money **(5.90).** Griffith has exploited the surprise latent in our sudden awareness that figures are offscreen.

The use of the fifth zone of offscreen space, that behind the rear plane, is of course common; characters go out a door and are now concealed by a wall or a staircase. Somewhat rarer is the use of the sixth zone—offscreen space behind and near the camera. One lengthy example occurs in Abbas Kiarostami's *Under the Olive Trees.* The crew is shooting a film scene, and we watch through the lens of the camera. As the tensions between two young actors spoil take after take, the action is repeated many times **(5.91).** Eventually, shots begin to show the director and his crew behind the camera **(5.92).** After several repetitions, the director walks in from that offscreen space behind the camera and tries to resolve the problem **(5.93).** Because of our awareness of the space behind the camera, throughout the many

5.87   Julie looks off at its owner and comes forward . . .

5.88   . . . and the camera retreats slightly to frame her with the man who had toasted her.

5.89   *The Musketeers of Pig Alley.*

5.90   *The Musketeers of Pig Alley.*

5.91   The actors return to their positions for one of many retakes of a shot for the film-within-a-film in *Under the Olive Trees.*

5.92   Finally, a reverse shot reveals the crew behind the camera, trying to figure out what is causing the problem.

5.93   Eventually, the director walks into camera range and tries to talk the actors into playing their roles as he wants them to.

5.94 A straight-on angle in *The Chronicle of Anna Magdalena Bach.*

5.95 A high-angle framing from *Se7en.*

5.96 A low-angle framing from *Babe.*

retakes, we remain aware of the crew's growing frustration. In such ways, a film-maker can turn the necessary limitations of the frame edge to advantage.

Angle, Level, Height, and Distance of Framing

The frame implies not only space outside itself but also a position from which the material in the image is viewed. Most often, such a position is that of the camera filming the event. Even in an animated film, the shots may be framed as high or low angles, or long shots or close-ups, all of which simply result from the perspective of drawings selected to be photographed.

Angle   The frame positions us at some angle looking onto the shot's mise-en-scene. The number of such angles is infinite, since the camera might be placed anywhere. In practice, we typically distinguish three general categories: (1) the straight-on angle, (2) the high angle, and (3) the low angle. The straight-on angle is the most common **(5.94)**. The high-angle positions us looking down at the material within the frame **(5.95)**. The low-angle framing positions us as looking up at the framed materials **(5.96)**.

Level   The frame can be more or less level—that is, parallel to the horizon. If the framing is tipped to one side or the other, it's said to be **canted**. Canted framing is relatively rare, although a few films make heavy use of it, such as Orson Welles's *Mr. Arkadin,* Carol Reed's *The Third Man,* and Wong Kar-wai's *Fallen Angels* **(5.97)**. In Christopher Maclaine's *The End,* a canted framing makes a steep street in the foreground appear level and renders the houses in the background grotesquely out of kilter **(5.98)**.

Height   The framing usually gives us a sense of being stationed at a certain height in relation to the settings and figures. Camera angle is, of course, partly related to height: To frame from a high angle entails being at a vantage point higher than the material in the image.

But camera height is not simply a matter of camera angle. For instance, the Japanese filmmaker Yasujiro Ozu often positions his camera close to the ground to film characters or objects on the floor (4.140, 6.129, and 6.130). Note that this is not a matter of camera angle, for the angle is straight on; we still see the ground or floor. Filming from such a low height with a straight-on angle is an important quality of Ozu's distinctive visual style.

Distance   The framing of the image stations us not only at a certain angle and height and on a level plane or at a cant but also at a certain distance. Framing supplies a sense of being far away or close to the mise-en-scene of the shot. This aspect

5.97   A canted framing in *Fallen Angels.*

5.98   A startling canted framing in *The End.*

5.99   *The Third Man:* extreme long shot.

5.100   Long shot.

5.101   Medium long shot.

5.102   Medium shot.

5.103   Medium close-up.

5.104   Close-up.

of framing is usually called *camera distance*. In presenting the terms used for various distances, we'll use the standard measure: the human body. Our examples are all from *The Third Man*.

In the **extreme long shot**, the human figure is barely visible (**5.99**). This is the framing for landscapes, bird's-eye views of cities, and other vistas. In the **long shot**, figures are more prominent, but the background still dominates (**5.100**). Shots in which the human figure is framed from about the knees up are called **medium long shots (5.101)**. These are common, since they permit a nice balance of figure and surroundings.

The **medium shot** frames the human body from the waist up (**5.102**). Gesture and expression now become more visible. The **medium close-up** frames the body from the chest up (**5.103**). The **close-up** is traditionally the shot showing just the head, hands, feet, or a small object. It emphasizes facial expression, the details of a gesture, or a significant object (**5.104**). The **extreme close-up** singles out a portion of the face (often eyes or lips) or isolates and magnifies an object (**5.105**).

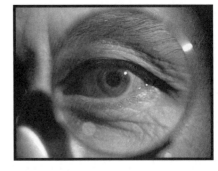

5.105   Extreme close-up.

Note that the size of the photographed material within the frame is as important as any real camera distance. From the same camera distance, you could film a long shot of a person or a close-up of King Kong's elbow. We would not call the shot in **5.106** (from *La Passion de Jeanne d'Arc*) a close-up just because only Jeanne's head appears in the frame; the framing is that of a long shot because in scale her head is relatively small. (If the framing were simply adjusted downward, her whole body would be visible.) In judging camera distance, the relative proportion of the material framed determines how we identify the shot.

Categories of framing are obviously matters of degree. There is no universal measure of camera angle or distance. No precise cut-off point distinguishes between a long shot and an extreme long shot, or a slightly low angle and a straight-on angle. Moreover, filmmakers are not bound by terminology. They don't worry if a shot does not fit into traditional categories. (Nevertheless abbreviations like MS for medium shot and CU for close-up are regularly used in screenplays, so

5.106   *La Passion de Jeanne d'Arc.*

5.107   In *Citizen Kane,* the low angle functions to isolate Kane and his friend against an empty background, his deserted campaign headquarters.

"I don't like close-ups unless you can get a kick out of them, unless you need them. If you can get away with attitudes and positions that show the feeling of the scene, I think you're better off using the close-up only for absolute punctuation—that's the reason you do it. And you save it— not like TV where they do everything in close-up."

— Howard Hawks, director, *His Girl Friday*

5.108   *North by Northwest.*

filmmakers do find these terms useful in their work.) In most cases, the concepts are clear enough for us to use them in talking about films.

Functions of Framing   Sometimes we're tempted to assign absolute meanings to angles, distances, and other qualities of framing. It is easy to claim that framing from a low angle automatically presents a character as powerful and that framing from a high angle presents him or her as dwarfed and defeated. Verbal analogies are especially seductive: A canted frame seems to mean that "the world is out of kilter."

The analysis of film as art would be a lot easier if technical qualities automatically possessed such hard-and-fast meanings, but individual films would thereby lose much of their uniqueness and richness. The fact is that framings have no absolute or general meanings. In *some* films, angles and distance carry such meanings as mentioned above, but in other films—probably most films—they do not. To rely on formulas is to forget that meaning and effect always stem from the film, from its operation as a system. The context of the film determines the function of the framings, just as it determines the function of mise-en-scène, photographic qualities, and other techniques. Consider three examples.

At many points in *Citizen Kane,* low-angle shots of Kane do convey his looming power, but the lowest angles occur at the point of Kane's most humiliating defeat—his miscarried gubernatorial campaign **(5.107)**. Note that angles of framing affect not only our view of the main figures but also the background against which those figures may appear.

If the cliché about high-angle framings were correct, **5.108**, a shot from *North by Northwest,* would express the powerlessness of Van Damm and Leonard. In fact, Van Damm has just decided to eliminate his mistress by pushing her out of a plane, and he says, "I think that this is a matter best disposed of from a great height." The angle and distance of Hitchcock's shot wittily prophesy how the murder is to be carried out.

Similarly, the world is hardly out of kilter in the shot from Eisenstein's *October* shown in **5.109**. The canted frame dynamizes the effort of pushing the cannon.

These three examples should demonstrate that we cannot reduce the richness of cinema to a few recipes. We must, as usual, look for the *functions* the technique performs in the particular *context* of the total film.

Camera distance, height, level, and angle often take on clear-cut narrative functions. Camera distance can establish or reestablish settings and character positions, as we shall see in the next chapter when we examine the editing of the first sequence of *The Maltese Falcon.* A framing can isolate a narratively important detail **(5.110, 5.111)**.

Framing also can cue us to take a shot as subjective. In Chapter 3, we saw that a film's narration may present story information with some degree of psychological depth (p. 90), and one option is a perceptual subjectivity that renders what a character sees or hears. When a shot's framing prompts us to take it as seen through a

5.109   A dramatic canted framing from *October.*

5.110   The tears of Henriette in *A Day in the Country* are visible in extreme close-up.

5.111   In *Day for Night,* a close framing emphasizes the precision with which the film director positions an actor's hands.

5.112 In *Fury,* the hero in his jail cell is seen through the bars from a slightly low angle . . .

5.113 . . . while the next shot, a high angle through the window toward the street outside, shows us what he sees, from his point of view.

5.114 In *The Maltese Falcon,* Kasper Gutman is frequently photographed from a low angle, emphasizing his obesity.

character's eyes, we call it an optically subjective shot, or a point-of-view (POV shot). Fritz Lang's *Fury* provides a clear example (**5.112, 5.113**).

Framings may serve the narrative in yet other ways. Across an entire film, the repetitions of certain framings may associate themselves with a character or situation. That is, framings may become motifs unifying the film (**5.114**). Throughout *La Passion de Jeanne d'Arc* Dreyer returns obsessively to extreme close-up shots of Jeanne (4.129).

Alternatively, certain framings in a film may stand out by virtue of their rarity. The ominously calm effect of the shot of the birds descending on Bodega Bay in Hitchcock's film *The Birds* arises from the abrupt shift from straight-on medium shots to an extreme long shot from very high above the town (6.34 and 6.35, p. 227). In a film composed primarily of long shots and medium shots, an extreme close-up will obviously have considerable force. Similarly, the early scenes of Ridley Scott's *Alien* present few shots depicting any character's point of view. But when Kane approaches the alien egg, we see close views of it as if through his eyes, and the creature leaps straight out at us. This not only provides a sudden shock; the abrupt switch to framings that restrict us to one character's range of knowledge emphasizes a major turning point in the plot.

Apart from their narrative significance, framings can add a visual interest of their own. Close-ups can bring out textures and details we might otherwise ignore. We can see the surreptitious gestures of a thief in the medium close-up from Robert Bresson's *Pickpocket* (**5.115**); a string of similar close shots makes up a dazzling, balletlike scene in this film. Long shots can permit us to explore vistas. Much of the visual delight of Westerns, of David Lynch's *The Straight Story,* or of Werner Herzog's documentary *Lessons of Darkness* (**5.116**) arises from long shots that make huge spaces manifest. By including a range of information, the long-shot framing encourages us to explore details or discover abstract patterns (**5.117**).

5.115 Bresson's *Pickpocket.*

5.116 In *Lessons of Darkness,* helicopter shots give the desolate burning oilfields of Kuwait after the 1991 Gulf War an eerie, horrifying grandeur.

5.118   René Clair in *Entr'acte* frames a ballerina from straight below, transforming the figure into an expanding and contracting flower.

5.117   In Hou Hsiao-hsien's *Summer at Grandpa's,* the boy from the city visits his disgraced uncle, and the neighborhood is presented as a welter of rooftops sheltering a spot of bright red.

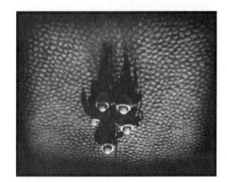

5.119   *La Passion de Jeanne d'Arc.*

Our eye also enjoys the formal play presented by unusual angles on familiar objects **(5.118)**. In *La Passion de Jeanne d'Arc,* the upside-down framings **(5.119)** are not motivated as a character's point of view; they exist as an exploration of framing in its own right. "By reproducing the object from an unusual and striking angle," writes Rudolf Arnheim, "the artist forces the spectator to take a keener interest, which goes beyond mere noticing or acceptance. The object thus photographed sometimes gains in reality, and the impression it makes is livelier and more arresting."

Framing may be used for comic effect, as Charlie Chaplin, Buster Keaton, and Jacques Tati have all shown. We have seen that in *Our Hospitality* Keaton stages many gags in depth. Now we can see that well-chosen camera angles and distances are also vital to the gags' success. For example, if the railroad scene shown in 4.161 were shot from the side and in extreme long shot, we would not see so clearly that the two parts of the train are on parallel tracks. Moreover, we could not see the engineer's unconcerned posture, which indicates his failure to realize what has happened. Similarly, the use of framing to create offscreen space is vital to the gag shown in 4.170 and 4.171. Here the gag is laid out in time rather than space. First Willie tugs on the rope; then an unseen effect of that tug becomes visible as the Canfield son hurtles past and disappears. Finally, Willie reacts and is himself dragged down into the abyss below the frameline. Try to imagine these moments and others in *Our Hospitality* framed in a different way, and you will see how our reaction to Keaton's humor depends on the careful combination of mise-en-scene and framing.

Similarly, in Tati's *Play Time,* mise-en-scene and camera position cooperate to create pictorial jokes **(5.120)**. The visual pun issues from the precisely chosen camera angle and distance, as well as from the mise-en-scene: the man's stooping posture as well as the door handles make him look like a goat. We cannot classify all the non-narrative functions of framing; we can only suggest that camera angle, level, height, and distance have the constant possibility of sharpening our awareness of purely visual qualities.

The Mobile Frame

All of the features of framing we have examined are present in paintings, photographs, comic strips, and other sorts of pictures. All images furnish instances of aspect ratios, in-frame and out-of-frame relations, angle, level, height, and distance of the frame's vantage point. But there is one resource of framing that is specific to

5.120   In *Play Time,* M. Hulot reacts with a start when he notices that a man locking a door seems suddenly to have sprouted horns (the door handles).

5.121   During a shot in Dreyer's *Ordet,* the camera pans right . . .

cinema (and video). In film, it is possible for the frame to *move* with respect to the framed material.

Mobile framing means that the framing of the object changes. The mobile frame changes the camera angle, level, height, or distance *during* the shot. Further, since the framing orients us to the material in the image, we often see ourselves as moving *along with* the frame. Through such framing, we may approach the object or retreat from it, circle it, or move past it.

Types of Mobile Framing   We usually refer to the ability of the frame to be mobile as *camera movement.* A mobile frame is usually achieved by moving the camera physically during production. There are several kinds of camera movement, each a specific effect onscreen.

The **pan** (short for *panorama*) movement rotates the camera on a vertical axis. The camera as a whole does not move to a new position. Onscreen, the pan gives the impression of a frame horizontally scanning space. It is as if the camera "turns its head" right or left **(5.121, 5.122)**.

The **tilt** movement rotates the camera on a horizontal axis. It is as if the camera's head were swiveling up or down. Again, the entire camera does not change position. Onscreen, the tilt movement yields the impression of unrolling a space from top to bottom or bottom to top **(5.123, 5.124)**.

In the **tracking** or **dolly shot**, the camera as a whole does change position, traveling in any direction along the ground—forward, backward, circularly, diagonally, or from side to side **(5.125, 5.126)**. Note how the figures remain in the same basic relationship to the frame as they stroll along a sidewalk, while the front of the house that they hope to buy remains visible behind them.

In the **crane shot**, the camera moves above ground level. Typically, it rises or descends, often thanks to a mechanical arm that lifts and lowers it. The mourning scene in *Ivan the Terrible* begins with a crane downward **(5.127, 5.128)**. A crane shot may move not only up and down, like an elevator, but forward and backward or from side to side **(5.129, 5.130)**. For *The Thin Red Line,* Terence Malick used a crane with a 72-foot arm to let the camera slither over tall grass during battle scenes. Variations of the crane shot are helicopter and airplane shots.

Pans, tilts, tracking shots, and crane shots are the most common framing movements, but virtually any kind of camera movement can be imagined (somersaulting, rolling, and so on). And as we shall see, types of camera movements can be combined.

Camera movements have held an appeal for filmmakers and audiences since the beginnings of cinema. Why? Visually, camera movements have several arresting effects. They often increase information about the space of the image. Objects become sharper and more vivid than in stationary framings. New objects or figures are usually revealed. Tracking shots and crane shots supply continually changing perspectives on passing objects as the frame constantly shifts its orientation.

5.122   . . . to keep the figures in frame as they cross a room.

"I realized that if I could just get to the really good scripts, I could approach it the way I approach literature—why the camera moves this way because of this motif—and then it became fascinating."

—Jodie Foster, director, *Little Man Tate*

"It's a compulsion of mine to move the camera, and I now know why. It enhances three-dimensionality. It puts you in the space, and if you move the camera the audience becomes aware of the space."

— George Miller, director, *The Road Warrior*

5.123   François Truffaut's *The Bride Wore Black* begins with a tilt down a church spire . . .

5.124   . . . to the church door.

5.125   During this lateral tracking shot in Erich von Stroheim's *Greed,* the camera moves rightward . . .

5.126   . . . along with the two characters.

5.127   In *Ivan the Terrible,* from a high-angle view of the bier, the camera cranes down . . .

5.128   . . . to end with a straight-on framing of Ivan seated at the bier's base.

Objects appear more solid and three-dimensional when the camera arcs (that is, tracks along a curved path) around them. Pan and tilt shots present space as continuous, both horizontally and vertically.

Moreover, it is difficult not to see camera movement as a substitute for *our* movement. The objects do not seem to swell or shrink. We seem to approach or retreat from them. We are not, of course, completely fooled. We never forget that we are watching a film in a theater. But camera movement provides several convincing cues for movement through space. Indeed, so powerful are these cues that filmmakers often make camera movements subjective—motivated narratively to represent the view through the eyes of a moving character. That is, camera movement can be a powerful cue that we are watching a point-of-view shot.

In commercial film production today, many camera movements are made with the camera on a dolly. Before the 1970s, it was standard practice to mount the dolly on rails for lengthy movements (hence the term *tracking*). In recent decades, however, a simple and popular means has been a gimbal-balanced camera mount patented as the Steadicam. This mount attaches the camera to the operator's body by means of a brace. The operator can walk with the camera, guiding the framing by minimal hand movements while viewing the image on a video monitor. Another operator adjusts focus by remote control.

The balancing mechanism allows the Steadicam to produce smooth mobile shots. It enables fluidity in tracking with actors climbing stairs, entering rooms, and riding bicycles or motorcycles (**5.131, 5.132**). Recently, directors have used a Steadicam on the set to supplement the principal camera by providing moving shots that can be cut into longer views. Some directors have taken advantage of the Steadicam to create elaborate moving shots lasting several minutes and traversing a series of spaces, as in the openings of Brian De Palma's *The Bonfire of the Vanities* and Paul Thomas Anderson's *Boogie Nights.* (For a Steadicam in use, see Fig. 5.206.)

Sometimes the filmmaker does not want smooth camera movements, preferring a bumpy, jiggling image. Commonly, this sort of image is achieved through use of the **hand-held** camera. That is, the operator does not anchor the machine on a tripod or dolly, but instead uses his or her body to act as the support without benefit of compensating equipment (**5.133**). This sort of camera movement became common in the late 1950s, with the growth of the *cinéma-vérité* documentary. One of the most famous early handheld traveling shots was in *Primary,* when a cameraman held the camera above his head and followed John F. Kennedy through a milling crowd (**5.134**).

Handheld shots have appeared in many fiction films as well. Because the technique originated in documentary filming, it can lend an air of authenticity to pseudo-documentaries like *The Blair Witch Project.* In other instances, the handheld camera movement functions to create subjective point of view (**5.135**). Sometimes the handheld shot intensifies a sense of abrupt movement, as if the action were glimpsed on the fly. For *julien donkey-boy,* Harmony Korine used lightweight, bouncy, mini-DV cameras to shoot Julian shuffling through his neighborhood (**5.136**).

5.129   At the end of Karel Reisz's *Morgan!* the camera moves diagonally up . . .

5.130   . . . and back to reveal that the hero's apparently innocuous flower garden proclaims his Communist sympathies.

5.131   In Martin Scorsese's *Raging Bull,* the Steadicam follows the protagonist out of his dressing room . . .

5.132   . . . and through a crowd up to the boxing ring.

5.133   Don Pennebaker hand-holds the camera while filming his *Keep on Rocking.*

5.134   John Kennedy greeting a Wisconsin crowd in *Primary.*

5.135   In Samuel Fuller's *The Naked Kiss,* a handheld subjective camera heightens the impact of a fight.

A static camera can simulate frame mobility. In animation, the actual camera stays in one position, but by filming individual cels frame by frame, the animator can create the effect of camera movement (**5.137–5.139**). Alternatively, a mobile frame effect can be achieved by photographing a still picture or a stopped frame of film and gradually enlarging or reducing any portion of that image, as is frequently done in optical printing or with CGI. Iris masking can open up to reveal a vista or close down to isolate a detail. The zoom lens can also be used to provide a mobile framing while the camera stays fixed.

How can we as viewers distinguish between a zoom and a tracking or craning movement? In general, animation, special effects, and the zoom lens reduce or blow up some portion of the image. Although the tracking shot and the crane shot do

5.136   As Julien walks, the handheld camera's jerky pace complements the explosions of color created by printing video up to 35mm.

5.137   A pan shot simulated by animation in *Peter Pan* begins with Peter and Captain Hook near a mast. Peter swings in to kick Hook . . .

5.138   . . . and the framing pans to follow as the two fly rightward . . .

5.139   . . . across the deck.

enlarge or reduce portions of the frame, this is not *all* that they do. In the genuine camera movement, static objects in different planes pass one another at different rates. We see different sides of objects, and backgrounds gain volume and depth.

In Alain Resnais's *La Guerre est finie,* a tracking shot (**5.140, 5.141**) gives the objects considerable volume. The wall has lost none of its bulk or solidity. Moreover, the street sign has not simply been enlarged. We also see it from a distinctly different angle.

In contrast, with a zoom enlargement, the mobile frame does not alter the aspects or positions of the objects filmed. In **5.142** and **5.143**, from Theo Angelopoulos's *Ulysses' Gaze,* a zoom enlarges our view of a large, broken statue of Lenin floating on a barge. Our vantage point on the statue is the same at the end of the shot as at the beginning: The top of the statue is still seen against the bottom of a row of small trees, and its feet are in exactly the same place in relation to the railing on the ship's prow. As the zoom occurs, the barge gradually looks closer to the line of trees than it had at the beginning. In sum, when the camera moves, we sense our own movement through the space. In a zoom, a bit of the space seems magnified or demagnified.

5.140   In *La Guerre est finie,* a street sign tilted slightly up on its right side . . .

5.141   . . . is tilted up distinctly at the left by the end of the track-in.

5.142   A distant view of a statue on a barge in *Ulysses' Gaze* . . .

5.143   . . . is enlarged by a zoom-in.

So far, we have isolated these different sorts of mobile framings in fairly pure states. But filmmakers frequently combine such framings within a single shot: The camera may track and pan at the same time or crane up while zooming. Still, every instance can be identified as a combination of the basic types.

Functions of Frame Mobility   Our catalogue of the types of mobile framings is of little use without a consideration of how such framing strategies function systematically within films. How does mobile framing relate to cinematic space and time? How do mobile framings create patterns of their own? In short, how does mobile framing interact with the form of the film?

1.   *The mobile frame and space*

The mobile frame affects onscreen and offscreen space considerably, as we've already seen in our earlier example from *Jezebel* (5.85–5.88). After the hand with the glass intrudes into close-up, the camera tracks back to frame the man standing in the foreground. The mobile frame also continually affects the angle, level, height, or distance of the framing. A crane up may change the angle from a low one to a high one; a track-in may change the distance from long shot to close-up.

We can, in general, ask several questions about how the mobile frame relates to space. Do the frame's movements depend on figure movement? For example, one of the commonest functions of camera movement is **reframing**. If a character moves in relation to another character, often the frame will slightly pan or tilt to adjust to the movement. In *His Girl Friday,* director Howard Hawks strives to balance his compositions through reframing (**5.144–5.146**). Since reframings are motivated by figure movement, they tend to be relatively unnoticeable. When you do start to notice them, you may be surprised at how frequently they appear. Almost any modern film is constantly reframing characters in conversation scenes.

Reframing is only one way that the mobile frame may depend on figure movement. The camera may also displace itself in order to follow figures or moving objects. A camera movement that is more than just a reframing and that follows a figure's movement is called—logically enough—a **following shot** (see 5.201–5.202, 5.208–5.209, and 5.213–5.222). A pan may keep a racing car centered, a tracking shot may follow a character from room to room, or a crane shot may pursue a rising balloon. In such cases frame mobility functions primarily to keep our attention fastened on the subject of the shot, and it subordinates itself to that subject's movement.

The mobile frame can move independently of the figures, too. Often, of course, the camera moves away from the characters to reveal something of significance to the narrative. A camera movement can point out an overlooked clue, a sign that comments on the action, an unnoticed shadow, or a clutching hand. The moving camera can establish a locale the characters will eventually enter. This is what

5.144   In *His Girl Friday,* when Hildy crosses from the left . . .

5.145   . . . to sit on a desk, the camera pans right to reframe her . . .

5.146   . . . and when Walter swivels his chair to face her, the camera reframes slightly leftward.

happens at the start of Otto Preminger's *Laura,* when the camera glides through Waldo Lydecker's sitting room, establishing him as a man of wealth and artistic tastes, before revealing the detective MacPherson. Similarly, at the beginning of *Back to the Future,* the camera prowls through Doc's empty house, hinting at his character and the narrative to come. In Jean Renoir's *Crime of M. Lange,* the moving camera characterizes Lange by leaving him and panning around to survey his room **(5.147–5.151)**. Lange is shown to be a fantasist, living in the world of Western lore he draws on for his cowboy stories.

Whether dependent on figure movement or independent of it, the mobile frame can profoundly affect how we perceive the space within the frame and offscreen. Different sorts of camera movements create different conceptions of space. In *Last Year at Marienbad,* Resnais often tracks into corridors and through doorways, turning a fashionable resort hotel into a maze. Alfred Hitchcock has produced some of the most famous single camera movements in film history. One track-and-crane shot moves from a high-angle long shot of a ballroom over the heads of the dancers to an extreme close-up of a drummer's blinking eyes (*Young and Innocent*). In *Vertigo,* an especially tricky combination track-*out* and zoom-*in* plastically distorts the shot's perspective and conveys the protagonist's dizziness. The device reappears in Spielberg's *Jaws,* when Sheriff Brody at the beach suddenly realizes that the shark has attacked a child. Simultaneously tracking and zooming in opposite directions has become common in modern Hollywood filmmaking (what director Sam Raimi calls the "warp-o cam"). In films such as *The Red and the White,* Miklós Jancsó specialized in lengthy camera movements that roam among groups of people moving across a plain. His shots use all of the resources of tracking, panning, craning, zooming, and racking focus to sculpt ever-changing spatial relations.

All of these examples illustrate various ways in which frame mobility affects our sense of space. Of any mobile framing, we can ask, How does it function to reveal or conceal offscreen space? Is the frame mobility dependent on figure

5.147   In *The Crime of M. Lange,* although the camera begins on Lange at work . . .

5.148   . . . it soon leaves him to show his cowboy pistols and hat . . .

5.149   . . . keeps going to show a map with Arizona outlined . . .

5.150   . . . pans past more guns . . .

5.151   . . . before returning to the excited author writing his Western tales

movement or independent of it? What particular trajectory does the camera pursue? Such questions will best be answered by considering how spatial effects of the camera movement function with respect to the film's overall form.

2.   *The mobile frame and time*

Frame mobility involves time as well as space, and filmmakers have realized that our sense of duration and rhythm is affected by the mobile frame. The importance of duration in camera movement, for example, can be sensed by comparing two Japanese directors, Yasujiro Ozu and Kenji Mizoguchi. Ozu prefers short camera movements in a single direction, as in *Early Summer* and *The Flavor of Green Tea over Rice.* Mizoguchi, alternatively, cultivates the leisurely, drawn-out tracking shot, often combining it with panning. That camera movements simply take less time in Ozu's films than in Mizoguchi's constitutes a major difference between the two directors' styles.

Since a camera movement consumes time on screen, it can create an arc of expectation and fulfillment. In the pan shot across M. Lange's study, Renoir makes us wonder why the camera strays from the main character, then answers the question by indicating Lange's fascination with the American West. Later in this chapter, we shall examine how our expectations are manipulated over time in the opening camera movements of Welles's *Touch of Evil.*

The velocity of frame mobility is important, too. A zoom or a camera movement may be relatively slow or fast. Richard Lester's *A Hard Day's Night* and *Help!* started a fad in the 1960s for very fast zoom-ins and -outs. In comparison, one of the most impressive early camera movements, D. W. Griffith's monumental crane shot in Belshazzar's feast in *Intolerance,* gains majesty and suspense through its inexorably slow descent toward the immense Babylonian set (4.12).

In general, a camera movement may create particular effects of its own. If the camera pans quickly from an event, we may be prompted to wonder what has happened. If the camera abruptly tracks back to show us something in the foreground that we had not expected, as in our earlier *Jezebel* example (5.85–5.88), we are taken by surprise. If the camera slowly moves in on a detail, gradually enlarging it but delaying the fulfillment of our expectations, the camera movement has contributed to suspense. In a narrative film, the velocity of mobile framing can be motivated by narrational needs. A quick track-in to a significant object can underline a key piece of story information.

Sometimes the speed of the mobile framing functions rhythmically. In Will Hindle's *Pastorale d'été* a gentle, bouncing beat is created by zooming in and slightly tilting up and down in time to Honegger's music. Often musical films make use of the speed of camera movement to underline qualities of a song or dance. During the "Broadway Rhythm" number in *Singin' in the Rain,* the camera cranes quickly back from Gene Kelly several times, and the speed of the movement is timed to accentuate the lyrics. Frame velocity can also create expressive qualities— a camera movement can be fluid, staccato, hesitant, and so forth. In short, the duration and speed of the mobile frame can significantly control our perception of the shot over time.

3.   *Patterns of mobile framing*

The mobile frame can create its own specific motifs within a film. For example, Hitchcock's *Psycho* begins and ends with a forward movement of the frame. In the film's first three shots, the camera pans right and then zooms in on a building in a cityscape (**5.152**). Two forward movements finally carry us under a window blind and into the darkness of a cheap hotel room (**5.153–5.155**). The camera's movement inward, the penetration of an interior, is repeated throughout the film, often motivated as a subjective point of view as when various characters move deeper and deeper into Norman Bates's mansion. The next-to-last shot of the film shows

"One thing I hate in films is when the camera starts circling characters. If three people are sitting at a table talking, you'll often see the camera circling them. I can't explain why, but I find it totally fake."

— Takeshi Kitano, director, *Sonatine*

5.152   The opening shot of *Psycho.*

5.153   The second shot concentrates on one building . . .

5.154   . . . as the camera moves lower and closer to a window . . .

5.155   . . . and reveals the heroine and her boyfriend in a lunchtime tryst.

5.156   *Psycho*'s next-to-last shot begins at a distance from Norman . . .

5.157   . . . and moves in so that we see his expression as we hear his thoughts.

5.158   A can used as a signal is initially seen sitting on a shelf . . .

5.159   . . . then is pulled over. It lands on a pillow and so makes no sound . . .

Norman sitting against a blank white wall, while we hear his interior monologue (**5.156**). The camera again moves forward into a close-up of his face (**5.157**). This shot is the climax of the forward movement initiated at the start of the film; the film has traced a movement into Norman's mind. Another film that relies heavily on a pattern of forward, penetrating movements is *Citizen Kane,* which depicts the same inexorable drive toward the revelation of a character's secret.

Other kinds of movements can repeat and develop across a film. Max Ophuls's *Lola Montès* uses both 360° tracking shots and constant upward and downward crane shots to contrast the circus arena with the world of Lola's past. In Michael Snow's ⟷ (usually called *Back and Forth*), the constant panning to and fro across a classroom, Ping-Pong fashion, determines the basic formal pattern of the film. It comes as a surprise when, near the very end, the movement suddenly becomes a repeated tilting up and down. In these and many other films, the mobile frame sets up marked repetitions and variations.

Functions of Mobile Framing: Grand Illusion and Wavelength   By way of summary, we can look at two contrasting films that illustrate possible relations of the mobile frame to narrative form. One uses the mobile frame in order to strengthen and support the narrative, whereas the other subordinates narrative form to an overall frame mobility.

Jean Renoir's *Grand Illusion* is a war film in which we almost never see the war. Heroic charges and doomed battalions, the staple of the genre, are absent. World War I remains obstinately offscreen. Instead, Renoir concentrates on life in a German POW camp to suggest how relations between nations and social classes are affected by war. The prisoners Maréchal and Boeldieu are both French; Rauffenstein is a German officer. Yet the aristocrat Boeldieu has more in common with Rauffenstein than with the mechanic Maréchal. The film's narrative form traces the death of the Boeldieu-Rauffenstein upper class and the precarious survival of Maréchal and his pal Rosenthal—their flight to Elsa's farm, their interlude of peace there, and their final escape back to France and presumably back to the war.

Within this framework, camera movement has several functions, all directly supportive of the narrative. First, and most typical, is its tendency to adhere to figure movement. When a character or vehicle moves, Renoir often pans or tracks to follow. The camera follows Maréchal and Rosenthal walking together after their escape; it tracks back when the prisoners are drawn to the window by the sound of marching Germans below. But it is the movements of the camera *independent* of figure movement that make the film more unusual.

When the camera moves on its own in *Grand Illusion,* we are conscious of it actively interpreting the action, creating suspense or giving us information that the characters do not have. For example, in one scene, a prisoner is digging in an escape tunnel and tugs a string signaling that he needs to be pulled out (**5.158**). Independent camera movement builds suspense by showing that the other characters have missed the signal and do not realize that he is suffocating (**5.159, 5.160**). Camera movement thus helps create a somewhat unrestricted narration.

Sometimes the camera is such an active agent that Renoir used repeated camera movements to create patterns of narrative significance. One such pattern is the movement to link characters with details of their environment. Often a sequence begins with a close-up of some detail, and the camera moves back to anchor this detail in its larger spatial and narrative context (**5.161, 5.162**).

More complicated is the scene of the Christmas celebration at Elsa's that begins with a close-up of the crèche and tracks back to show, in several stages, the interplay of reactions among the characters. Such camera movements are not simply decoration; beginning on a scenic detail before moving to the larger context makes narrative points economically, constantly emphasizing relationships among elements of Renoir's mise-en-scene. So does the rarer track-in to a detail at the *end*

5.160 . . . and the camera pans left to reveal that the characters have not noticed it.

5.161 Renoir begins the scene of Boeldieu and Maréchal discussing escape plans by framing a close-up of a caged squirrel . . .

5.162 . . . before tracking back to reveal the men beside the cage, thus creating a clear narrative parallel.

of a scene, as when after Boeldieu's death, Rauffenstein cuts the geranium, the one flower in the prison (**5.163, 5.164**).

Characters are tied to their environment by some even more ambitious moving-camera shots. These stress important narrative parallels. For example, tracking shots compare actions in two officers' bars—one French (**5.165–5.167**), one German (**5.168–5.170**). Through his camera movements, Renoir indicates a similarity between the two warring sides, blurring their national differences and stressing common desires. The camera movements, repeated in a systematic pattern, create the narrative parallel.

Or consider how two parallel tracking shots compare the war of the aristocrats and the war of the lower-class people. We are introduced to Rauffenstein's new position as commander of a POW camp through a lengthy tracking shot (**5.171–5.178**). During this movement, Renoir presents, wordlessly, the military mystique of grace on the battlefield that characterizes the aristocrat's war.

Late in the film, however, a parallel shot criticizes this one (**5.179–5.181**). That Elsa's war has none of Rauffenstein's glory is conveyed chiefly through a parallel created by the repeated camera movement. Moreover, these camera movements work together with mise-en-scene, as the narrative parallel is reinforced by the subtle use of objects as motifs—the crucifixes in 5.171 and 5.181, the photographs in 5.172 and 5.179, and the tables that end both shots. (Note the subtle use of the empty chairs upended on the table to reinforce the absence of Elsa's husband.)

Moving the camera independently of figure movement also links characters with one another. Again and again in the POW camp, the camera moves to join one man to his comrades, spatially indicating their shared condition. When the prisoners ransack the collection of women's clothes, one man decides to dress up

5.163 As Rauffenstein moves to the geranium in the window . . .

5.164 . . . Renoir tracks in to a close shot of the flower as he cuts it.

5.165 In the first scene, as Maréchal leaves the French officers' bar . . .

5.166 . . . Renoir pans and tracks left from the door to reveal pinups (just coming into the frame at the right) . . .

5.167 . . . and a poster.

5.168 One scene later, in the German officers' bar, a similar camera movement, this time toward the right, leaves the characters . . .

...two of Rhine wine, one of champagne and a half-bottle of Martell....

5.169 . . . and explores on its own . . .

5.170 . . . discovering some similar decorations.

5.171 Renoir begins on a crucifix and . . .

5.172 . . . tilts down to a military portrait on an altar, underlining the irony of a chapel commandeered as a bivouac.

5.173 The camera tracks past whips, spurs, and swords . . .

5.174 . . . to a servant preparing Rauffenstein's gloves.

5.175 He then walks away from the camera to close a window before returning . . .

5.176 . . . into the foreground as the camera pans left and tracks back to reveal . . .

5.177 . . . a breakfast table . . .

5.178 . . . at which Rauffenstein is revealed to be sitting.

5.179 This shot also begins on an object, a photograph of Elsa's dead husband . . .

5.180 . . . before tracking left past Elsa, who remarks, "Now the table is too large" . . .

5.181 . . . to reveal the kitchen table, where her daughter Lotte sits alone.

5.182 As the lead "female" singer whips off his wig and requests the "Marseillaise" from the musicians . . .

in them. When he appears, a stillness falls over the men. Renoir tracks silently over the prisoners' faces, each one registering a reticent longing.

A more elaborate linking movement occurs in the scene of the prison vaudeville show, when the men learn that the French have recaptured a city. Renoir presents the shot as a celebration of spatial unity, with the camera moving among the men as they begin defiantly to sing the "Marseillaise" (**5.182–5.188**). This complex camera movement circulates freely among the prisoners, suggesting their patriotic courage and unity in disobeying their captors.

In Elsa's cottage as well as in the prison, camera movement links characters. After feeding a cow, Maréchal enters the house, and a pan with him reveals Elsa scrubbing the floor. The culmination of the linking movement comes near the film's end, when Renoir pans from the Germans on one side of the border (**5.189**) to the distant French escapees on the other (**5.190, 5.191**). Even on this scale, Renoir's camera refuses to honor national divisions.

5.183 . . . the camera moves right as the singer turns toward the audience . . .

The French film critic André Bazin remarked: "Jean Renoir found a way to reveal the hidden meaning of people and things without destroying the unity that is natural to them." By placing emphasis and making comparisons, the mobile frame in *Grand Illusion* becomes as important as the mise-en-scene. The camera movements carve into space to create connections that enrich the film's narrative form.

In Michael Snow's experimental film *Wavelength,* the relation of narrative to the mobile frame is quite different. Instead of supporting narrative form, frame mobility dominates narrative, even deflecting our attention from narrative. The film begins with a long-shot framing of a loft apartment, facing one wall and window (**5.192**). In the course of the film, the camera zooms in abruptly a short distance and then holds that framing. It zooms in a bit more and then holds that (**5.193**). And so

5.184   . . . and farther right as others onstage sing along.

5.185   A tilt down shows two worried German guards . . .

5.186   . . . and a track back to the left reveals a row of French prisoners in the audience on their feet, singing.

5.187   The camera tracks forward past them to the musicians and singer again . . .

5.188   . . . then pans quickly left to face the entire audience.

5.189   As the Germans realize that Maréchal and Rosenthal have crossed over into Switzerland . . .

5.190   . . . Renoir pans to the right across the invisible border . . .

5.191   . . . to the two escapees, tiny dots in the huge landscape.

5.192   Early in *Wavelength,* much of the apartment is visible.

it goes throughout the film's 45-minute length. By the end, a photograph of ocean waves on the distant wall fills the frame in close-up.

Thus *Wavelength* is structured primarily around a single kind of frame mobility—the zoom-in. Its pattern of progression and development is not a narrative one, but one of exploration, through deliberately limited means, of how the zoom transforms the space of the loft. The sudden zooms create frequent abrupt shifts of perspective relations. In excluding parts of the room, the zoom-in also magnifies and flattens what we see; every change of focal length gives us a new set of spatial relations. The zoom places more and more space offscreen. The sound track, for the most part, reinforces the basic formal progression by emitting a single humming tone that rises consistently in pitch as the zoom magnifies the space more and more.

Within *Wavelength*'s basic pattern, though, there are two contrasting systems. The first is a series of filtered tints that plays across the image as abstract fields of color. These tints often work against the depth represented in the shot of the loft.

A second system evokes a sketchy narrative. At various intervals, characters enter the loft and carry on certain activities (talking, listening to the radio, making phone calls). There is even a mysterious death (a body lies on the floor in **5.194**). But these events remain unexplained in cause–effect terms and inconclusive as to closure (although at the film's end we do hear a sound that resembles a police siren). Furthermore, none of these actions swerves the mobile framing from its pre-determined course. The jerkily shifting and halting zoom continues, even when it excludes important narrative information. Thus *Wavelength* pulls in bits and pieces of narrative, but these fragments of action remain secondary, operating within the temporal progression of the zoom.

From the standpoint of the viewer's experience, *Wavelength*'s use of frame mobility arouses, delays, and gratifies unusual expectations. What plot there is briefly arouses curiosity (What are the people up to? What has led to the man's death, if he does die?) and surprise (the apparent murder). But in general, a story-centered suspense is replaced by a *stylistic* suspense: what will the zoom eventually frame? From this standpoint, the colored tints and even the plot work with the spasmodic qualities of the zoom to delay the forward progress of the framing. When the zoom finally reveals its target, our stylistic anticipations have come to fulfillment. The film's title stands revealed as a multiple pun, referring not only to the steadily rising pitch of the sound track but also to the distance that the zoom had to cross in order to reveal the photo—a "wave length."

Grand Illusion and *Wavelength* illustrate, in different ways, how frame mobility can guide and shape our perception of a film's space and time. Frame mobility may be motivated by larger formal purposes, as in Renoir's film, or it may itself become the principal formal concern, motivating other systems, as in Snow's film. What is important to realize is that by examining how filmmakers use the mobile frame within specific contexts, we can gain a fuller understanding of how our experience of a film is created.

Duration of the Image: The Long Take

In our consideration of the film image, we have emphasized spatial qualities—how photographic transformations can alter the properties of the image, how framing defines the image for our attention. But cinema is an art of time as well as space, and we have seen already how mise-en-scene and frame mobility operate in temporal as well as spatial dimensions. What we need to consider now is how the duration of the shot affects our understanding of it.

There is a tendency to consider the shot as recording real duration. Suppose a runner takes three seconds to clear a hurdle. If we film the runner, our projected film will also consume three seconds—or so the assumption goes. One film theorist, André Bazin, made it a major tenet of his aesthetic that cinema records real time. But the relation of shot duration to the time taken by the filmed event is not so simple.

First, obviously, the duration of the event on the screen may be manipulated during filming or post-production, as we discussed earlier in this chapter. Slow-motion or fast-motion techniques may present the runner's jump in 20 seconds or 2. Second, narrative films often permit no simple equivalence of real duration with screen duration, even within one shot. As Chapter 3 pointed out (pp. 80), story duration will usually differ considerably from plot duration and screen duration.

Consider a shot from Yasajiro Ozu's *The Only Son*. It is well past midnight, and we have just seen a family awake and talking; this shot shows a dim corner of the family's apartment, with none of the characters onscreen (**5.195**). But soon the light changes. The sun is rising. By the end of the shot, it is morning (**5.196**). This

5.193   Near the end, the sporadic zoom-ins have made details of the far wall visible.

5.194   The zoom-ins in *Wavelength* will soon eliminate the body on the floor from the frame.

5.195   A scene in *The Only Son* moves from night . . .

5.196   . . . to day in a single shot.

transitional shot consumes about a minute of screen time. It plainly does not record the duration of the story events; that duration would be at least five hours. To put it another way, by manipulating screen duration, the film's plot has condensed a story duration of several hours into a minute or so.

More recent films use tracking movements to compress longer passages of time in a continuous shot **(5.197, 5.198)**. The final shot of *Signs* moves away from an autumn view through a window (itself an echo of the opening shot's track-back from a window) and through a room, to reveal a winter landscape outside another window. Months of story time have passed during the tracking movement.

Functions of the Long Take

Every shot has some measurable screen duration, but in the history of cinema, directors have varied considerably in their choice of short or lengthy shots. In general, early cinema (1895–1905) tended to rely on shots of fairly long duration, since there was often only one shot in each film. With the emergence of continuity editing in the period 1905–1916, shots became shorter. In the late 1910s and early 1920s, an American film would have an average shot length of about 5 seconds. After the coming of sound, the average stretched to about 10 seconds.

Throughout the history of the cinema, some filmmakers have consistently preferred to use shots of greater duration than the average. In various countries in the mid-1930s, directors began to experiment with very lengthy shots. These filmmakers' usually lengthy shots—**long takes**, as they're called—represented a powerful creative resource.

5.197   In Roger Michell's *Notting Hill,* the protagonist's walk through the Portobello street market moves through autumn . . .

5.198   . . . winter, and spring.

Long take is not the same as *long shot,* which refers to the apparent distance between camera and object. As we saw in examining film production (p. 20), a *take* is one run of the camera that records a single shot. Calling a shot of notable length a long take rather than a long shot prevents ambiguity, since the latter term refers to a distanced framing, not to shot duration. In the films of Jean Renoir, Kenji Mizoguchi, Orson Welles, Carl Dreyer, Miklós Jancsó, Hou Hsiao-hsien, and Bèla Tarr, a shot may go on for several minutes, and it would be impossible to analyze these films without an awareness of how the long take can contribute to form and style. One long take in Andy Warhol's *My Hustler* follows the seductive exchange of two gay men as they groom themselves in a bathroom (**5.199**). The shot, which runs for about 30 minutes, constitutes much of the film's second half.

5.199　A long take in *My Hustler.*

Usually, we can regard the long take as an alternative to a series of shots. The director may choose to present a scene in one or a few long takes or to present the scene through several shorter shots. When an entire scene is rendered in only one shot, the long take is known by the French term *plan-séquence,* or *sequence shot.*

Most commonly, filmmakers use the long take selectively. One scene may rely heavily on editing, while another is presented in a long take. This permits the director to associate certain aspects of narrative or non-narrative form with the different stylistic options. A vivid instance occurs in the first part of Fernando Solanas and Octavio Getino's *Hour of the Furnaces.* Most of the film relies on editing of newsreel and staged shots to describe how European and North American ideologies penetrate developing nations. But the last shot of the film is a slow zoom-in to a photograph of the corpse of Che Guevera, symbol of guerrilla resistance to imperialism. Solanas made the shot a long take, holding it for three minutes to force the viewer to dwell on the cost of resistance (**5.200**).

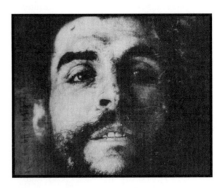

5.200　The final three-minute shot of *Hour of the Furnaces.*

Mixing long takes and shorter shots also creates parallels and contrasts among scenes. Bazin pointed out that *Citizen Kane* oscillates between long takes in the dialogue scenes and rapid editing in the "News on the March" newsreel and other sequences. Hitchcock, Mizoguchi, Renoir, and Dreyer often vary shot duration, depending on the scene's function in the entire film.

Alternatively, the filmmaker may decide to build the entire film out of long takes. Hitchcock's *Rope* is famous for containing only eleven shots, most running between four and ten minutes. Similarly, each scene in *Winterwind, Agnus Dei, Red Psalm,* and other films by Miklós Jancsó is a single shot. In such cases, the long take becomes a large-scale part of a film. And in such a context, editing can have great force. After a seven- or eight-minute shot, an elliptical cut can prove quite disorienting. Gus van Sant's *Elephant* traces events around a high-school shooting rampage, and it presents most scenes in very long takes following students through the hallways. Moreover, *Elephant*'s plot doesn't present the events in chronological order. The narration flashes back to show other school days, the boys' lives at home, and their preparations for the killings. So when a cut interrupts a long take, the audience must reflect for a moment to determine how the new shot's action fits into the plot. The effect of the editing is unusually harsh, because the cuts tend to break the smooth rhythm of the sustained traveling shots (**5.201–5.203**).

Could a feature-length movie consist of one long take? Many directors have dreamed of this possibility, but the lengths of film reels have prevented it. A 35mm camera reel typically runs for only 11 minutes, so Hitchcock tried to hide some of *Rope*'s obligatory cuts. Extended 16mm reels of the type Warhol used in *My Hustler* (5.199) can run up to 30 minutes. With digital video, however, it is possible to shoot for over two hours on a single tape, and the Russian director Aleksander Sokurov seized this opportunity in his *Russian Ark.* The film consists of a single shot nearly 90 minutes long, as a Steadicam follows over 2000 actors in period costume through St. Petersburg's immense Winter Palace. *Russian Ark* takes us through several eras of Russian history, culminating in a stupendous ballroom dance and a

5.201   In a shot lasting two minutes, the camera follows Michelle into the library, where she starts reshelving books. Many of the long takes in *Elephant* frame the walking characters from behind. This conceals their facial expressions from us and emphasizes the school environment they move through.

5.202   Michelle turns as we hear a rifle being cocked.

5.203   We expect a reverse shot to reveal what she sees. Instead, we get a flashback to earlier that day when the two boys showered together before going to school on their deadly mission.

crowd drifting off into a wintry night (**5.204–5.206**). Sokurov rehearsed *Russian Ark* for several months and completed the take used in the film on the fourth try.

The Long Take and the Mobile Frame

The *Elephant* example suggests that a long take is likely to rely on camera movement. Panning, tracking, craning, or zooming to present continually changing vantage points that are comparable in some ways to the shifts of view supplied by editing.

Very often, frame mobility breaks the long-take shot into significant smaller units. In Mizoguchi's *Sisters of Gion,* one long take shows a young woman, Omocha, luring a businessman into becoming her patron (**5.207–5.212**). Though there is no cutting, the camera and figure movements demarcate important stages of the scene's action.

As in this example, long takes tend to be framed in medium or long shots. The camera lingers on a fairly dense visual field, and the spectator has more opportunity to scan the shot for particular points of interest. This is recognized by Steven Spielberg, a director who has occasionally exploited lengthy takes:

> I'd love to see directors start trusting the audience to be the film editor with their eyes, the way you are sometimes with a stage play, where the audience selects who they would choose to look at while a scene is being played. . . . There's so much cutting and so many close-ups being shot today I think directly as an influence from television.

5.204   In *Russian Ark,* one episode takes place in the palace theater, with Catherine the Great pronouncing the rehearsal satisfactory.

5.205   An hour or so later, still within the same shot, hundreds of aristocrats and officers descend a staircase toward the impending devastation of the Russian Revolution.

5.206   Crew members moving through the Hermitage Museum, filming *Russian Ark* with a digital camera mounted on a Steadicam (photography by Alexander Belenkiy).

As we have seen in the previous chapter, however, the director can guide the audience's scanning of the frame through all of the technical resources of mise-en-scene. This is another way of saying that using the long take often puts more emphasis on performance, setting, lighting, and other mise-en-scene factors.

The example from *Sisters of Gion* illustrates another important feature of the long take. Mizoguchi's shot reveals a complete internal logic—a beginning, middle, and end. As a part of a film, the long take can have its own formal pattern, its own development, its own trajectory and shape. Suspense develops; we start to ask how the shot will continue and when it will end.

The classic example of how the long take can constitute a formal pattern in its own right is the opening sequence of Welles's *Touch of Evil* (**5.213–5.224**). This opening shot makes plain most of the features of the long take. It offers an alternative to building the sequence out of many shots, and it stresses the cut that finally comes (occurring at the sound of the explosion of the car).

Most important, the shot has its own internal pattern of development. We expect that the bomb shown at the beginning will explode at some point, and we wait for that explosion through the duration of the long take. The shot establishes the geography of the scene (the border between Mexico and the United States). The camera movement, alternately picking up the car and the walking couple, weaves together two separate lines of narrative cause and effect that intersect at the border station. Vargas and Susan are thus drawn into the action involving the bombing. Our expectation is fulfilled when the end of the shot coincides with the explosion (offscreen) of the bomb. The shot has guided our response by taking us through a suspenseful development. The long take can present, in a single chunk of time, a complex pattern of events moving toward a goal, and this ability shows that shot duration can be as important to the image as photographic qualities and framing are.

5.207   In *Sisters of Gion*, the long take begins with Omocha and the businessman seated. The camera follows as . . .

5.208   . . . she moves to the opposite end of the room . . .

5.209   . . . and sits at a small table facing him.

5.210   A second phase of the shot begins as she begins to appeal to his sympathy and he moves to the table . . .

5.211   . . . and sits down to console her.

5.212   Finally, the camera moves into a tighter shot as she sits beside him and he succumbs to her advances.

5.213   The opening shot of *Touch of Evil* begins with a close-up of a hand setting the timer of a bomb.

5.214   The camera tracks immediately right to follow first the shadow . . .

5.215   . . . and then the figure of an unknown assassin planting the bomb in a car.

5.216   The camera then cranes up to a high angle as the assassin flees and the victims arrive and set out in the car.

5.217   As the camera rounds the corner, it plans to rejoin the car, and tracks back to follow it.

5.218   The car passes Vargas and his wife, Susan, and the camera starts to follow them, losing the car and tracking diagonally backward with the couple through the crowd.

5.219   The camera tracks backward until both the occupants of the car and Susan and Vargas meet again . . .

5.220   . . . and a brief scene with the border guard ensues.

5.221   After tracking left with the car, the camera again encounters Susan and Vargas and tracks forward toward them . . .

5.222   . . . bringing them into medium shot as they begin to kiss.

5.223   Their embrace is interrupted by the offscreen sound of an explosion, and they turn to look leftward.

5.224   The next shot zooms in to show the car in flames.

Summary

The film shot, then, is a very complex unit. Mise-en-scene fills the image with material, arranging setting, lighting, costume, and staging within the formal context of the total film. Within that formal context, the filmmaker also controls the cinematographic qualities of the shot—how the image is photographed and framed, how long the image lasts on the screen.

You can sensitize yourself to these cinematographic qualities in much the same way that you worked on mise-en-scene. Trace the progress of a single technique—say, camera distance—through an entire scene. Notice when a shot begins and ends, observing how the long take may function to shape the film's form. Watch for camera movements, especially those that follow the action (since those are usually the hardest to notice). Once you are aware of cinematographic qualities, you can move to an understanding of their various possible functions within the total film.

Film art offers still other possibilities for choice and control. Chapters 4 and 5 focused on the shot. The filmmaker may also juxtapose one shot with another through editing, and that's the subject of Chapter 6.

Where to Go from Here

General Works

The standard contemporary references on cinematography are Rob Hummel, ed., *The American Cinematographer Manual,* 8th ed. (Hollywood: American Society of Cinematographers, 2001), and Kris Malkiewicz, *Cinematography: A Guide for Film Makers and Film Teachers,* 3d ed. (New York: Fireside, 2000). Cinematographers can be articulate about their craft, and we can learn a lot from their interviews. See Vincent LoBrutto, *Principal Photography: Interviews with Feature Film Cinematographers* (Westport, CT: Praeger, 1999); Pauline Rogers, *Contemporary Cinematographers on Their Art* (Boston: Focal Press, 1999); Benjamin Bergery, *Reflections: Twenty-One Cinematographers at Work* (Hollywood: ASC Press, 2002); and Peter Ettedgui, *Cinematography: Screencraft* (Hove, England: RotoVision, 1998). In the Rogers collection, Dean Cundey recalls that the camera movements in *Who Framed Roger Rabbit?* posed problems for adding animation. "If Roger was to go from one part of the room to another, hopping onto a chair, we had to find a way for the camera operator to track that movement. We developed full-size rubber characters to stage the action. The operator could then see movement in real time. He would associate movement with dialogue." A monthly magazine, *American Cinematographer,* contains detailed articles on current cinematography around the world.

Alternative points of view on cinematography may be found in Stan Brakhage, "A Moving Picture Giving and Taking Book," in *Brakhage Scrapbook: Collected Writings 1964–1980,* ed. Robert A. Haller (New Paltz,

NY: Documentext, 1982), pp. 53–77; Dziga Vertov, *Kino-Eye: The Writings of Dziga Vertov,* ed. Annette Michelson (Berkeley: University of California Press, 1984); and Maya Deren, "An Anagram of Ideas on Art, Form, and Film" and "Cinematography," in George Amberg, ed., *The Art of Cinema* (New York: Arno, 1972).

Color Versus Black and White

Today most films are shot on color stock and most viewers have come to expect that movies will be in color. At many points in film history, however, color and black-and-white film have been used to carry different meanings. In 1930s and 1940s American cinema, color tended to be reserved for fantasies (for example, *The Wizard of Oz*), historical films or films set in exotic locales (*Becky Sharp, Blood and Sand*), or very lavish musicals (*Meet Me in St. Louis*). Black and white was then considered more realistic. But now that most films are in color, filmmakers can call on black and white to suggest a historical period (as witnessed by two such different films as Straub and Huillet's *Chronicle of Anna Magdalena Bach* and Tim Burton's *Ed Wood*). Such rules of thumb as "color for realism" have no universal validity; as always, it is a matter of context, the function of color or black-and-white tonalities within a specific film.

A basic history is R. T. Ryan, *A History of Motion Picture Color Technology* (New York: Focal Press, 1977). The most influential early process is considered in Fred E. Basten's *Glorious Technicolor: The Movies' Magic Rainbow* (Camarillo, CA: Technicolor, 2005). Len Lye explains the elaborate process behind the color design of

Rainbow Dance in Wystan Curnow and Roger Horrocks, eds., *Figures of Motion: Len Lye/Selected Writings* (Auckland: Auckland University Press, 1984), pp. 47–49.

Film theorists have debated whether color film is artistically less pure than black and white. One argument against color may be found in Rudolf Arnheim, *Film as Art* (Berkeley: University of California Press, 1957). Arnheim's argument is disputed by V. F. Perkins in *Film as Film* (Baltimore: Penguin, 1972).

Special-Effects Cinematography

Part of the reason that major film studios tout themselves as the "magic factories" is that special-effects cinematography demands the complexity and expense that only a big firm can support. Special effects require the time, patience, and rehearsal afforded by control over mise-en-scène. It is, then, no surprise that Méliès, the first person to exploit fully the possibilities of studio filmmaking, excelled at special-effects cinematography. Nor is it surprising that when UFA, the gigantic German firm of the 1920s, became the best-equipped film studio in Europe, it invested heavily in new special-effects processes. Similarly, as Hollywood studios grew from the mid-1910s on, so did their special-effects departments. Engineers, painters, photographers, and set designers collaborated to contrive fantastic visual novelties. In these magic factories, most of the history of special effects has been made.

But such firms were not motivated by sheer curiosity. The costs of elaborate back projection and matte work were usually investments. First, expensive as they were, such tricks often saved money in the long run. Instead of building a huge set, one could photograph the actors through a glass with the setting painted on it. Instead of taking players to the desert, one could film them against a back projection of the pyramids. Second, special effects made certain film genres possible. The historical epic—whether set in Rome, Babylon, or Jerusalem—was unthinkable unless special effects were devised to create huge vistas and crowds. The fantasy film, with its panoply of ghosts, flying horses, and invisible or incredibly shrinking people, demanded that superimposition and matte processes be improved. The science fiction film genre could scarcely exist without a barrage of special effects. For the major studios, the "factory" principle was responsible for the "magic."

The best survey of the subject is Richard Rickitt's sumptuously illustrated *Special Effects: The History and the Technique* (New York: Billboard, 2000). Illuminating case studies can be found in Linwood G. Dunn and George E. Turner, eds., *The ASC Treasury of Visual Effects* (Hollywood: American Society of Cinematographers, 1983). See also Mark Cotta Vaz and Patricia Rose Duignan, *Industrial Light & Magic: Into the Digital Realm* (New York: Ballantine Books, 1996). An extensive and well-illustrated history of matte paintings, including the move to the digital creation of environments, is Mark Cotta Vaz and Craig Barron's *The Invisible Art: The Legends of Movie Matte Painting* (San Francisco: Chronicle Books, 2002); this book includes a CD-ROM with examples of matte paintings. Articles on particular films' use of special effects appear regularly in *American Cinematographer* and *Cinefex.*

Aspect Ratio

The aspect ratio of the film image has been debated since the inception of cinema. The Edison-Lumière ratio (1.33:1) was not generally standardized until 1911, and even after that other ratios were explored. Many cinematographers believed that 1.33:1 was the perfect ratio (perhaps not aware that it harks back to the "golden section" of academic painting). With the large-scale innovation of widescreen cinema in the early 1950s, cries of distress were heard. Most camera operators hated it. Lenses often were not sharp, lighting became more complicated, and as Lee Garmes put it, "We'd look through the camera and be startled at what it was taking in." Yet some directors—Nicholas Ray, Akira Kurosawa, Samuel Fuller, François Truffaut, Jean-Luc Godard—created fascinating compositions in the wide-screen ratio. The systems are exhaustively surveyed in Robert E. Carr and R. M. Hayes's *Wide Screen Movies: A History and Filmography of Wide Gauge Filmmaking* (Jefferson, NC: McFarland, 1988).

The most detailed defense of the aesthetic virtues of the widescreen image remains Charles Barr's "CinemaScope: Before and After," *Film Quarterly* 16, 4 (Summer 1963): 4–24. *The Velvet Light Trap* 21 (1985) contains several articles on the history and aesthetics of widescreen cinema, including an article on Barr's essay and second thoughts by Barr.

During the 1980s, two variants on traditional film gauges were designed in response to widescreen demands. One innovation is Super 35mm, which expands the image area within the traditional 35mm format. It allows filmmakers to make a release print at either 2.40:1 (anamorphic) ratio or 1.85:1 matted. For small-budget projects, there is Super 16mm, which can be blown up to make 35mm release prints more easily than from normal 16mm. Super 16mm provides 40 percent more image area and creates a wider frame that can be matted to the 1.85:1 aspect ratio favored in 35mm exhibition.

The Subjective Shot

Sometimes the camera, through its positioning and movements, invites us to see events through the eyes of a character. Some directors (Howard Hawks, John Ford, Kenji Mizoguchi, Jacques Tati) seldom use the subjective shot, but others use it constantly. Hitchcock relies on it often, as we indicated when we examined the dinner table scene in *Shadow of a Doubt* back in Chapter 1 (pp. 3–7). As 5.135 indicated, Samuel Fuller's *Naked Kiss* starts with shocking subjective shots:

> We open with a direct cut. In that scene, the actors utilized the camera. They held the camera; it was strapped on them. For the first shot, the pimp has the camera strapped on his chest. I say to [Constance] Towers, "Hit the camera!" She hits the camera, the lens. Then I reverse it. I put the camera on her, and she whacks the hell out of him. I thought it was effective. (Quoted in Eric Sherman and Martin Rubin, *The Director's Event* [New York: Signet, 1969], p. 189)

Filmmakers began experimenting with the "first-person camera" or the "camera as character" quite early. *Grandma's Reading Glass* (1901) features subjective point-of-view shots. Keyholes, binoculars, and other apertures were often used to motivate optical point of view. In 1919, Abel Gance used many subjective shots in *J'accuse*. The 1920s saw many filmmakers taking an interest in subjectivity, seen in such films as E. A. Dupont's *Variety* (1925), F. W. Murnau's *The Last Laugh* (1924) with its famous drunken scene, and Abel Gance's *Napoleon* (1927). Some believe that in the 1940s, the subjective shot—especially subjective camera movement—got completely out of hand in Robert Montgomery's *Lady in the Lake* (1946). For almost the entire film, the camera represents the vision of the protagonist, Philip Marlowe; we see him only when he glances in mirrors. "Suspenseful! Unusual!" proclaimed the advertising. "YOU accept an invitation to a blonde's apartment! YOU get socked in the jaw by a murder suspect!"

The history of the technique has teased film theorists into speculating about whether the subjective shot evokes identification from the audience. Do we think we *are* Philip Marlowe? The problem of audience identification with a point-of-view shot remains a difficult one in film theory. A useful discussion is Edward Branigan's *Point of View in the Cinema: A Theory of Narration and Subjectivity in Classical Film* (New York: Mouton, 1984).

Real Time and the Long Take

When the camera is running, does it record real time? If so, what artistic implications follow from that?

André Bazin argued that cinema is an art that depends on actual duration. Like photography, Bazin claimed, cinema is a *recording process*. The camera registers, photochemically, the light reflected from the object. Like the still camera, the movie camera records space. But unlike the still camera, the movie camera can also record *time*. "The cinema is objectivity in time. . . . Now, for the first time, the image of things is likewise the image of their duration, change mummified as it were" (*What Is Cinema?* vol. 1 [Berkeley: University of California Press, 1966], pp. 14–15). On this basis, Bazin saw editing as an intrusive interruption of the natural continuity of duration. He thus praised long-take directors such as Jean Renoir, Orson Welles, William Wyler, and Roberto Rossellini as artists whose styles respected concrete moment-to-moment life.

Bazin should be credited with calling our attention to the possibilities latent in the long take at a time when other film theorists considered it theatrical and uncinematic. Yet the problem of real time in film seems more complicated than Bazin thought. For example, a five-minute long take may not present five minutes in the story. The shot that tracks the protagonist of *Notting Hill* through changing seasons lasts about 100 seconds on the screen, but it covers about a year of story time. The 91-minute shot that constitutes *Russian Ark* shifts the viewer backward and forward through Russian history. Mise-en-scene cues can override the camera's recording of real duration, giving the film a flexible time frame. As usual, a film's overall formal context assigns concrete functions to particular stylistic elements.

Websites

www.theasc.com/ The official site of the American Society of Cinematographers, tied to this association's activities and its journal, *American Cinematographer.* Includes some online articles.

www.soc.org/magazine.html/ The official site of the Society of Operating Cameramen, with an archive of many articles. Especially good are Rick Meyer's essays on the history of wide-screen processes.

www.cinematography.net/ An extensive discussion site about professional cinematography.

www.widescreenmuseum.com/ A vast site (950 pages, 3000 images) devoted to wide-screen processes, past and present, as well as color and sound technology.

Recommended DVD Supplements

The 1993 documentary *Visions of Light: The Art of Cinematography,* which includes numerous interviews with cinematographers and brief clips from a wide variety of films, is available on DVD (Image Entertainment). In "Painting with Light," cinematographer Jack Cardiff talks about his use of Technicolor in *Black Narcissus*. Raoul Coutard discusses anamorphic wide-screen and color processes in an interview on the *Contempt* DVD (which also includes a "Widescreen vs. Full-Frame Demonstration"). *Oklahoma!*'s disc contains a very good comparison featurette, "CinemaScope vs. Todd-AO," as well as a short originally shown in theaters before *Oklahoma!* to introduce the new wide-screen process, "The Miracle of Todd-AO."

A rare demonstration of laboratory work comes in "Day 66: Journey of a Roll of Film," in *King Kong: Peter Jackson's Production Diaries,* which includes the use of a Telecine machine to make a digital intermediate. The process of selective digital grading, which we discuss on page 181, is explained in "Digital Grading," on the *Lord of the Rings: The Fellowship of the Ring* supplements.

The "Outward Bound" chapter on the *Alien* disc provides a clear demonstration of how models were shot to look realistic in the pre-CGI, pre-green-screen era. *Speed*'s "Visual Effects" track covers motion control, the digital matte work and other tricks showing the bus jumping the freeway gap, and a huge miniature used for the final train crash. The "Special Effects Vignettes" for *Cast Away* do a particularly good job of tracing through the various layers that build up as CGI shots are created. "Visual FX: MTA Train" gives a brief but informative look at green-screen work in *Collateral*'s train scene; it shows how effects can be used not only for flashy action but also for such subtle purposes as varying the colors and lights seen through the windows as the mood of the scene shifts. "Designing the Enemy: Tripods and Aliens" (*War of the Worlds*) reveals how computers can be used to design digital figures. Each of the *Lord of the Rings* DVD sets contains extensive special-effects descriptions, and *The Return of the King* supplements include a segment on one of the most complex CGI scenes ever created: "Visual Effects Demonstration: 'The Mûmakil Battle.'"

"No Feat But What We Make," a *Terminator 2: Judgment Day* supplement, offers an excellent history of the early development of digital special effects in *The Abyss* and *Terminator 2,* and includes director James Cameron discussing perspective. "The Making of *Jurassic Park*" covers some of the same material and moves forward to the transitions from animation of shiny surfaces to the creation of realistic dinosaurs.

With the recent increase in multiple-camera shooting in epic films, DVD supplements sometimes include sequences juxtaposing the views from those cameras shown in split-screen. These tend not to provide much information about the process, but the "Interactive Multi-Angle Battle Scene Studies" for *Master and Commander* helpfully give readouts of lens length and shooting speed (revealing how common it has become for shots of violent action to be done with varying degrees of slow motion). Similarly, *Speed*'s "Action Sequences: Multi-angle Stunts," provides a frames-per-second readout in its demonstration. *Dancer in the Dark*'s extreme use of multiple-camera shooting for the music numbers is explained in "100 Cameras: Capturing Lars von Trier's Vision."

The ultimate supplement dealing with long takes is "In One Breath," which documents the filming of the single elaborate shot that makes up *Russian Ark.*

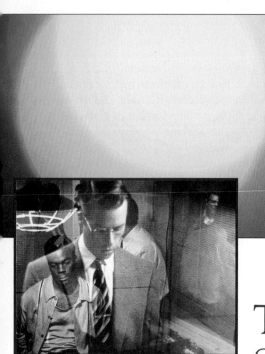

The Relation of Shot to Shot: Editing

S ince the 1920s, when film theorists began to realize what **editing** can achieve, it has been the most widely discussed film technique. This hasn't been all to the good, for some writers have mistakenly found in editing the key to good cinema (or even *all* cinema). Yet many films, particularly in the period before 1904, consist of only one shot and hence do not depend on editing at all. Experimental films sometimes deemphasize editing by making each shot as long as the amount of film a camera will hold, as with Michael Snow's *La Région centrale* and Andy Warhol's *Eat, Sleep,* and *Empire.* Such films are not necessarily less "cinematic" than others that rely heavily on editing.

Still, we can see why editing has exercised such an enormous fascination for film aestheticians, for as a technique it's very powerful. The ride of the Klan in *The Birth of a Nation,* the Odessa Steps sequence in *Potemkin,* the hunt sequence in *The Rules of the Game,* the shower murder in *Psycho,* the diving sequence in *Olympia,* Clarice Starling's discovery of the killer's lair in *The Silence of the Lambs,* the tournament sequence in *Lancelot du Lac,* the reconstruction of the Dallas assassination in *JFK*—all of these celebrated moments derive much of their effect from editing.

Perhaps even more important, however, is the role of editing within an entire film's stylistic system. An ordinary Hollywood film typically contains between 1000 and 2000 shots; an action-based movie can have 3000 or more. This fact alone suggests that editing strongly shapes viewers' experiences, even if they aren't aware of it. Editing contributes a great deal to a film's organization and its effects on spectators.

What Is Editing?

Editing may be thought of as the coordination of one shot with the next. As we have seen, in film production, a shot is one or more exposed frames in a series on a continuous length of film stock. The film editor eliminates unwanted footage, usually by discarding all but the best take. The editor also cuts superfluous frames, such as those showing the clapboard (p. 20), from the beginnings and endings of shots. She or he then joins the desired shots, the end of one to the beginning of another.

These joins can be of different sorts. A **fade-out** gradually darkens the end of a shot to black, and a **fade-in** accordingly lightens a shot from black. A **dissolve** briefly superimposes the end of shot A and the beginning of shot B (**6.1–6.3**). In a **wipe**, shot B replaces shot A by means of a boundary line moving across the screen (**6.4**). Here both images are briefly on the screen at the same time, but they do not blend, as in a dissolve. In the production process, fades, dissolves, and wipes are optical effects and are marked as such by the editor. They are typically executed in the laboratory or, more recently, through digital manipulation.

The most common means of joining two shots is the **cut**. Until the rise of digital editing in the 1990s, a cut was made by splicing two shots together by means of cement or tape. Some filmmakers "cut" during filming by planning for the film to emerge from the camera ready for final showing. Here the physical junction from shot to shot is created in the act of shooting. Such editing in the camera, however, is rare and is mainly confined to experimental and amateur filmmaking. Editing after shooting is the norm. Today most editing is done on computer, using footage stored on discs or a hard drive, so that the cuts (or *edits,* in video terminology) can be made without touching film. The final version of the film is prepared for printing by cutting and splicing the negative footage.

As viewers, we perceive a shot as an uninterrupted segment of screen time, space, or graphic configurations. Fades, dissolves, and wipes are perceived as gradually one shot and replacing it with another. Cuts are perceived as instantaneous changes from one shot to another.

Consider an example of cutting—four shots from the first attack on Bodega Bay in Alfred Hitchcock's *The Birds* (**6.5–6.8**):

1. *Medium shot, straight-on angle.* Melanie, Mitch, and the Captain standing by the restaurant window talking. Melanie on extreme right, bartender in background (6.5).

2. *Medium close-up.* Melanie by the Captain's shoulder. She looks to right (out offscreen window) and up, as if following with her eyes. Pan right with her as she turns to window and looks out (6.6).

3. *Extreme long shot.* Melanie's point of view. Gas station across street, phone booth in left foreground. Birds dive-bomb attendant, right to left (6.7).

4. *Medium close-up.* Melanie, profile. The Captain moves right into shot, blocking out bartender; Mitch moves right into extreme foreground. All in profile look out window (6.8).

Each of these four shots presents a different segment of time, space, and pictorial information. The first shot shows three people talking. An instantaneous change—a cut—shifts us to a medium close-up shot of Melanie. Here space has changed (Melanie is isolated and larger in the frame), time is continuous, and the graphic configurations have changed (the arrangements of the shapes and colors vary). Another cut takes us instantly to what she sees. The gas station shot (6.7) presents a very different space, a successive bit of time, and a different graphic configuration.

> "Editing is the basic creative force, by power of which the soulless photographs (the separate shots) are engineered into living, cinematographic form."
>
> — V. I. Pudovkin, director

> "You can definitely help performances in the cutting room, by intercutting reaction, maybe re-recording lines, adding lines over reaction shots. And you can help a film's structure by moving sequences about and dropping scenes that hold up pacing. And sometimes you can use bits and pieces from different takes, which also helps a lot. What you can do in the editing room to help a film is amazing."
>
> — Jodie Foster, actor and director

6.1   The first shot of *The Maltese Falcon* leads to . . .

6.2   . . . a dissolve to . . .

6.3   . . . the second shot.

6.4   A wipe joins the last shot of one scene with the first of the next in *Seven Samurai.*

6.5   *The Birds:* shot 1.

6.6   *The Birds:* shot 2.

6.7   *The Birds:* shot 3.

6.8   *The Birds:* shot 4.

Another cut returns us to Melanie (6.8), and again we are shifted instantly to another space, the next slice of time, and a different graphic configuration. Thus the four shots are joined by three cuts.

Hitchcock could have presented the *Birds* scene without editing—as Jean Renoir might in a similar situation (5.168–5.170). Imagine a camera movement that frames the four people talking, tracks in and rightward to Melanie as she turns, pans rightward to the window to show the dive-bombing gull, and pans leftward back to catch the group's expressions. This would constitute one shot. The camera movements, no matter how fast, would not present the marked and abrupt shifts that cuts produce. Now imagine a deep-space composition of the sort that Orson Welles might use (5.39), presenting Mitch in the foreground, Melanie and the window in the middle ground, and the gull attack in the distance. Again, the scene could now be played in one shot, for we would have no abrupt change of time or space or graphics. And the movements of the figures would not yield the jumps in time, space, and composition provided by editing.

Although many films today are shot with several cameras running simultaneously, throughout film history most sequences have been shot with only one camera. In the *Birds* scene, for example, the shots were taken at different times and places— one (shot 3) outdoors, the others in a sound stage (and these perhaps on different days). A film editor thus must assemble a large and varied batch of footage. To ease this task, most filmmakers plan for the editing phase during the preparation and shooting phases. Shots are taken with an idea of how they will eventually fit together. In fictional filming, scripts and storyboards help plan editing, while documentary filmmakers often shoot with an eye to how the footage will be cut.

Dimensions of Film Editing

Editing offers the filmmaker four basic areas of choice and control:

1. Graphic relations between shot A and shot B
2. Rhythmic relations between shot A and shot B
3. Spatial relations between shot A and shot B
4. Temporal relations between shot A and shot B

Graphic and rhythmic relationships are present in the editing of any film. Spatial and temporal relationships may be irrelevant to the editing of films using abstract form, but they are present in the editing of films built out of nonabstract images (that is, the great majority of motion pictures). Let's trace the range of choice and control in each area.

Graphic Relations Between Shot A and Shot B

The four shots from *The Birds* may be considered purely as graphic configurations, as patterns of light and dark, line and shape, volumes and depths, movement and stasis—*independent of* the shots' relation to the time and space of the story. For instance, Hitchcock did not drastically alter the overall brightness from shot to shot, because the scene takes place during the day. But if the scene had been set at night, he could have cut from the uniformly lit second shot in the bar (6.6, Melanie turning to the window) to a shot of the gas station swathed in darkness. Moreover, Hitchcock usually keeps the most important part of the composition roughly in the center of the frame. (Compare Melanie's position in the frame with that of the gas station in 6.7.) He could, however, have cut from a shot in which Melanie was in, say, upper frame left to a shot locating the gas station in the lower right of the frame.

Hitchcock also plays off certain color differences. Melanie's hair and outfit make her a predominantly yellow and green figure, whereas the shot of the gas station is dominated by drab bluish grays set off by touches of red in the gas pumps. Alternatively, Hitchcock could have cut from Melanie to another figure composed of similar colors. Furthermore, the movement in Melanie's shot—her turning to the window—does not blend into the movements of either the attendant or the gull in the next shot, but Hitchcock could have echoed Melanie's movement in speed, direction, or frame placement by movement in the next shot.

In short, editing together any two shots permits the interaction, through similarity and difference, of the *purely pictorial* qualities of those two shots. The four aspects of mise-en-scene (lighting, setting, costume, and the behavior of the figures in space and time) and most cinematographic qualities (photography, framing, and camera mobility) all furnish potential graphic elements. Thus every shot provides possibilities for purely graphic editing, and every cut creates some sort of graphic relationship between two shots.

Graphics may be edited to achieve smooth continuity or abrupt contrast. The filmmaker may link shots by graphic similarities, thus making what we can call a **graphic match**. Shapes, colors, overall composition, or movement in shot A may be picked up in the composition of shot B. A minimal instance is the cut that joins the first two shots of David Byrne's *True Stories* (**6.9, 6.10**). More dynamic graphic matches appear in Akira Kurosawa's *Seven Samurai*. After the samurai have first arrived at the village, an alarm sounds and they race to discover its source. Kurosawa cuts together six shots of different running samurai, which he dynamically matches by means of composition, lighting, setting, figure movement, and panning camera movement. (We show the first three in **6.11–6.13**.)

Filmmakers often call attention to graphic matches at transitional moments (**6.14–6.16**). Such precise graphic matching is relatively rare. Still, an approximate graphic continuity from shot A to shot B is typical of most narrative cinema. The director will usually strive to keep the center of interest roughly constant across the cut, to maintain the overall lighting level, and to avoid strong color clashes from shot to shot. In Juzo Itami's *Tampopo,* an aspiring cook is trying to learn the secret of good noodles, and she questions a successful cook. Their confrontation is presented through head-on framings. Alternating shots keep each main character's face in the right center of each frame (**6.17, 6.18**).

Editing need not be graphically continuous. Mildly discontinuous editing may appear in wide-screen compositions organized around characters facing one another. A scene from Quentin Tarantino's *Pulp Fiction* places the two hitmen opposite each other in a restaurant booth, each framed distinctly off-center (**6.19, 6.20**). Compared to the *Tampopo* example, the cut here creates greater graphic discontinuity. Note, however, that the cut does balance the frame area from shot to shot: each man fills the space left empty in the previous shot. In addition, each man's face is just above the horizontal center of each frame, so that the spectator's eye can easily

6.9 A shot from *True Stories* with the Texas horizon midway up the frame is graphically matched . . .

6.10 . . . with a shot where the waterline of ancient seas is in the same position.

6.11   *Seven Samurai.*

6.12   *Seven Samurai.*

6.13   *Seven Samurai.*

6.14   In *Aliens,* the curved outline of Ripley's sleeping face . . .

6.15   . . . is graphically matched by means of a dissolve . . .

6.16   . . . to the outline of the earth.

6.17   The woman and her friend, the cowboy truck driver . . .

6.18   . . . confront the enraged cook and his assistants. The key characters are made prominent by being placed in the same area of each shot.

adjust to the changing composition. If asked afterward, many viewers would probably not recall that these compositions were unbalanced.

Graphically discontinuous editing can be more noticeable. Orson Welles frequently sought a clash from shot to shot, as in *Citizen Kane* when the dark long shot of Kane's bedroom is followed by the bright opening title of the "News on the March" reel. Similarly, in *Touch of Evil,* Welles dissolves from a shot of Menzies looking out a window on frame right **(6.21)** to a shot of Susan Vargas looking out a different window on frame left **(6.22)**. The clash is further accentuated by the contrasting screen positions of the window reflections. Alain Resnais's *Night and Fog* began something of a fad by utilizing an extreme but apt graphic conflict: color footage of an abandoned concentration camp today is cut together with black-and-white newsreel shots of the camps in the period 1942–1945. Resnais balanced such

6.19 As Tarantino cuts between Vincent and . . .

6.20 . . . Jules, our eye must move back and forth across the screen.

6.21 *Touch of Evil:* graphic discontinuity.

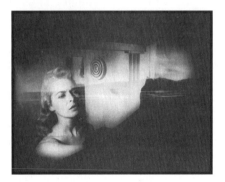

6.22 *Touch of Evil.*

contrasts by finding striking similarities in shape, as when a tracking shot of fence posts graphically matches a low-angle shot of marching Nazi legs.

A director may call on editing to create a graphic conflict between color qualities. In *Paris, Texas,* the protagonist discovers his wife working in an erotic peepshow. Wim Wenders follows the couple's conversation by cutting from the customer's side of the glass to the performer's **(6.23, 6.24)**. Although both people are visible in each shot, the cutting stresses their separation by harsh color contrasts.

Later in the *Birds* sequence discussed above, Hitchcock puts graphic conflict to good use. Gasoline spurting from the pump has flowed across the street to a parking lot, and Melanie, along with several other people at the restaurant window, has seen a man accidentally set the gasoline alight. His car ignites, and an explosion of flame engulfs him. What we see next is Melanie watching helplessly as the flame

6.23   In *Paris, Texas,* the wife's light-blue, almost washed-out, stage setting, as seen from the husband's side of the glass, clashes . . .

6.24   . . . with the blackness and the aluminum-foil reflections in the next shot.

races along the trail of gas toward the station. Hitchcock cuts the shots as shown in **6.25–6.35**:

Shot 30	(Long shot)	High angle. Melanie's POV. Flaming car, spreading flames (6.25).	73 frames
Shot 31	(Medium close-up)	Straight-on angle. Melanie, immobile, looking off left, mouth open (6.26).	20 frames
Shot 32	(Medium shot)	High angle. Melanie's POV. Pan with flames moving from lower right to upper left of trail of gasoline (6.27).	18 frames
Shot 33	(Medium close-up)	as 31. Melanie, immobile, staring down center (6.28).	16 frames
Shot 34	(Medium shot)	High angle. Melanie's POV. Pan with flames moving from lower right to upper left (6.29).	14 frames
Shot 35	(Medium close-up)	as 31. Melanie, immobile, looking off right, staring aghast (6.30).	12 frames
Shot 36	(Long shot)	Melanie's POV. Gas station. Flames rush in from right. Mitch, sheriff, and attendant run out left (6.31).	10 frames
Shot 37	(Medium close-up)	as 31. Melanie, immobile, stares off extreme right (6.32).	8 frames
Shot 38	(Long shot)	as 36. Melanie's POV. Cars at station explode (6.33).	34 frames
Shot 39	(Medium close-up)	as 31. Melanie covers face with hands (6.34).	33 frames
Shot 40	(Extreme long shot)	Extreme high angle on city, flaming trail in center. Gulls fly into shot (6.35).	

In graphic terms, Hitchcock has exploited two possibilities of contrast. First, although each shot's composition centers the action (Melanie's head, the flaming trail), the movements thrust in different directions. In shot 31, Melanie looks to the lower left, whereas in shot 32, the fire moves to the upper left. In shot 33, Melanie is looking down center, whereas in the next shot, the flames still move to the upper left, and so on.

More important—and what makes the sequence impossible to recapture on the printed page—is a crucial contrast of mobility and stasis. The shots of the flames

6.25   *The Birds:* shot 30.

6.26   *The Birds:* shot 31.

6.27   *The Birds:* shot 32.

6.28   *The Birds:* shot 33.

6.29   *The Birds:* shot 34.

6.30   *The Birds:* shot 35.

6.31   *The Birds:* shot 36.

6.32   *The Birds:* shot 37.

6.33   *The Birds:* shot 38.

6.34   *The Birds:* shot 39.

6.35   *The Birds:* shot 40.

present movement of both the subject (the flames rushing along the gas) and the camera (which pans to follow). But the shots of Melanie could almost be still photographs, since they are absolutely static. She does not turn her head in any shot, and the camera does not track in or away from her. We must infer the progress of her attention. By making movement conflict with countermovement and with stillness, Hitchcock has powerfully exploited the graphic possibilities of editing.

Rhythmic Relations Between Shot A and Shot B

Each shot, being a strip of film, is of a certain length, measured in frames, feet, or meters. And the shot's physical length corresponds to a measurable duration onscreen. As we know, at sound speed, 24 frames last one second in projection. A shot can be as short as a single frame, or it may be thousands of frames long, running for many minutes when projected. Editing thus allows the filmmaker to determine the duration of each shot. When the filmmaker adjusts the length of shots in relation to one another, she or he is controlling the *rhythmic* potential of editing.

Cinematic rhythm as a whole derives not only from editing but from other film techniques as well. The filmmaker relies on movement in the mise-en-scene, camera position and movement, the rhythm of sound, and the overall context to determine the editing rhythm. Nevertheless, the patterning of shot lengths contributes considerably to what we intuitively recognize as a film's rhythm.

Sometimes the filmmaker will use shot duration to create a stressed, accented, moment. In one sequence of *The Road Warrior,* a ferocious gang member butts his head against that of a victim. At the moment of contact, director George Miller cuts in a few frames of pure white. The result is a sudden flash that suggests violent impact. Alternatively, a shot's duration can be used to deaccentuate an action. During test screenings of *Raiders of the Lost Ark,* Steven Spielberg discovered that after Indiana Jones shoots the gigantic swordsman, several seconds had to be added to allow the audience's reaction to die down before the action could resume.

More commonly, the rhythmic possibilities of editing emerge when several shot lengths form a discernible pattern. A steady beat can be established by making all of the shots approximately the same length. The filmmaker can also create a dynamic pace. Lengthening shots can gradually slow the tempo, while successively shorter shots can accelerate it.

Consider how Hitchcock handles the tempo of the first gull attack in *The Birds.* Shot 1, the medium shot of the group talking (6.5), consumes almost a thousand frames, or about 41 seconds. But shot 2 (6.6), which shows Melanie looking out the window, is much shorter—309 frames (about 13 seconds). Even shorter is shot 3 (6.7), which lasts only 55 frames (about $2\frac{1}{3}$ seconds). The fourth shot (6.8), showing Melanie joined by Mitch and the Captain, lasts only 35 frames (about $1\frac{1}{2}$ seconds). Clearly, Hitchcock is accelerating the pace at the beginning of what will be a tense sequence.

In what follows, Hitchcock makes the shots fairly short, but subordinates the length of the shot to the rhythm of the dialogue and the movement in the images. As a result, shots 5–29 (not shown here) have no fixed pattern of lengths. But once the essential components of the scene have been established, Hitchcock returns to strongly accelerating cutting.

In presenting Melanie's horrified realization of the flames racing from the parking lot to the gas station, shots 30–40 (6.25–6.35) climax the rhythmic intensification of the sequence. As the description on page 225 shows, after the shot of the spreading flames (shot 30, 6.25), each shot decreases in length by 2 frames, from 20 frames ($\frac{4}{5}$ of a second) to 8 frames ($\frac{1}{3}$ of a second). Two shots, 38 and 39, then punctuate the sequence with almost identical durations (a little less than $1\frac{1}{2}$ seconds apiece). Shot 40 (6.35), a long shot that lasts over 600 frames, functions as both a pause and a suspenseful preparation for the new attack. The scene's variations in rhythm alternate between rendering the savagery of the attack and generating suspense as we await the next onslaught.

"I noticed a softening in American cinema over the last twenty years, and I think it's a direct influence of TV. I would even say that if you want to make movies today, you'd be better off studying television than film because that's the market. Television has diminished the audience's attention span. It's hard to make a slow, quiet film today. Not that I would want to make a slow, quiet film anyway!"

— Oliver Stone, director

We have had the luxury of counting frames on the actual strip of film. The theater viewer cannot do this, but she or he does feel the shifting tempo in this sequence because of the changing shot durations. In general, by controlling editing rhythm, the filmmaker controls the amount of time we have to grasp and reflect on what we see. A series of rapid shots, for example, leaves us little time to think about what we're watching. In the *Birds* sequence, Hitchcock's editing impels the viewer's perception to move at a faster and faster pace. Quickly grasping the progress of the fire and understanding Melanie's changes in position become essential factors in the rising excitement of the scene.

Hitchcock is not, of course, the only director to use rhythmic editing. Its possibilities were initially explored by such directors as D. W. Griffith (especially in *Intolerance*) and Abel Gance. In the 1920s, the French Impressionist filmmakers and the Soviet Montage school explored the rhythmic possibilities of strings of short shots (pp. 450–452, 453–456). When sound films became the norm, pronounced rhythmic editing survived in dramas such as Lewis Milestone's *All Quiet on the Western Front* and in musical comedies and fantasies such as René Clair's *À Nous la liberté* and *Le Million,* Rouben Mamoulian's *Love Me Tonight,* and Busby Berkeley's dance sequences in *42nd Street* and *Footlight Parade.* Rhythm remains a fundamental resource of the editor, most notably in the use of fast cutting to build up excitement during an action sequence, a television advertisement, or a music video.

Spatial Relations Between Shot A and Shot B

Editing usually serves not only to control graphics and rhythm but also to construct film space. Exhilaration in this newly discovered power can be sensed in the writings of such filmmakers as the Soviet director Dziga Vertov: "I am Kino-eye. I am builder. I have placed you . . . in an extraordinary room which did not exist until just now when I also created it. In this room there are twelve walls, shot by me in various parts of the world. In bringing together shots of walls and details, I've managed to arrange them in an order that is pleasing."

Such elation is understandable. Editing permits the filmmaker to juxtapose *any* two points in space and thus imply some kind of relationship between them.

The director might, for instance, start with a shot that establishes a spatial whole and follow this with a shot of a part of this space. This is what Hitchcock does in shot 1 and shot 2 of the *Birds* sequence (6.5, 6.6): a medium long shot of the group of people followed by a medium shot of only one, Melanie. Such analytical breakdown is a very common editing pattern.

Alternatively, the filmmaker could construct a whole space out of component parts. Hitchcock does this later in the *Birds* sequence. Note that in 6.5–6.8 and in shots 30–39 (6.25–6.34), we do not see an establishing shot including Melanie *and* the gas station. In production, the restaurant window need not have been across from the station at all; they could have been filmed in different towns or even countries. Yet we are compelled to believe that Melanie is across the street from the gas station. The bird cry offscreen and the mise-en-scene (the window and Melanie's sideways glance) contribute considerably as well. It is, however, primarily the editing that creates the spatial whole of restaurant-and-gas-station.

Such spatial manipulation through cutting is fairly common. In documentaries compiled from newsreel footage, for example, one shot might show a cannon firing, and another shot might show a shell hitting its target; we infer that the cannon fired the shell, though the shots may show entirely different battles. Again, if a shot of a speaker is followed by a shot of a cheering crowd, we assume a spatial coexistence.

The possibility of such spatial manipulation was examined by the Soviet filmmaker Lev Kuleshov. During the 1920s, Kuleshov conducted informal experiments by assembling shots of separate dramatic elements. The most famous of these experiments involved cutting neutral shots of an actor's face with other shots (variously reported as shots of soup, nature scenes, a dead woman, and a baby). The reported result was that the audience immediately assumed that the actor's expression changed and that the actor was reacting to things present in the same space as himself. Similarly, Kuleshov cut together shots of actors "looking at each other" but on Moscow streets miles apart, then meeting and strolling together—and looking at the White House in Washington. Although filmmakers had used such cutting before Kuleshov's work, film scholars call the *Kuleshov effect* any series of shots that *in the absence of an establishing shot* prompts the spectator to infer a spatial whole on the basis of seeing only portions of the space.

The Kuleshov effect can conjure up robust cinematic illusions. In Corey Yuen's *Legend of Fong Sai-Yuk,* a martial-arts bout between the hero and an adept woman begins on a platform but then moves into the audience—or rather, onto the audience. The two fight while balancing on the heads and shoulders of the crowd. Yuen's rapid editing conveys the scene's point by means of the Kuleshov effect **(6.36, 6.37)**. (In production, this meant that the combatants could be hung on wires or bars suspended outside the frame, as in 6.37.) Across many shots, Yuen provides only a few brief full-figure framings showing Fong Sai-Yuk and the woman.

While the viewer doesn't normally notice the Kuleshov effect, a few films call attention to it. Carl Reiner's *Dead Men Don't Wear Plaid* mixes footage filmed in the present with footage from Hollywood movies of the 1940s. Thanks to the Kuleshov effect, *Dead Men* creates unified scenes in which Steve Martin converses with characters who were originally featured in other films. In *A Movie,* Bruce Conner makes a joke of the Kuleshov effect by cutting from a submarine captain peering through a periscope to a woman gazing at the camera, as if they could see each other **(6.38, 6.39)**.

In the Kuleshov effect, editing cues the spectator to infer a single locale. Editing can also emphasize action taking place in separate places. In *Intolerance,* D. W. Griffith cuts from ancient Babylon to Gethsemane and from France in 1572 to

"Editing is very interesting and absorbing work because of the illusions you can create. You can span thirty years within an hour and a half. You can stretch a moment in slow motion. You can play with time in extraordinary ways."

— Paul Hirsch, editor

6.36   In *The Legend of Fong Sai-Yuk,* a shot of the woman's upper body is followed by . . .

6.37   . . . a shot of her legs and feet, supported by unwilling bystanders.

6.38   In *A Movie,* a shot from one film leads to . . .

6.39   . . . a shot from another, creating a visual joke.

America in 1916. Such parallel editing, or **crosscutting**, is a common way films construct a variety of spaces.

More radically, the editing can present spatial relations as being ambiguous and uncertain. In Carl Dreyer's *La Passion de Jeanne d'Arc,* for instance, we know only that Jeanne and the priests are in the same room. Because the neutral white backgrounds and the numerous close-ups provide no orientation to the entire space, we can seldom tell how far apart the characters are or precisely who is beside whom. We'll see later how films can create even more extreme spatial discontinuities.

Temporal Relations Between Shot A and Shot B

Like other film techniques, editing can control the time of the action denoted in the film. In a narrative film especially, editing usually contributes to the plot's manipulation of story time. You will recall that Chapter 3 pointed out three areas in which plot time can cue the spectator to construct the story time: order, duration, and frequency. Our *Birds* example (6.5–6.8) shows how editing reinforces all three areas of control.

First, there is the *order* of presentation of events. The men talk, then Melanie turns away, then she sees the gull swoop, then she responds. Hitchcock's editing presents these story events in the 1-2-3-4 order of his shots. But he could have shuffled the shots into any order at all, even reverse (4-3-2-1). This is to say that the filmmaker may control temporal succession through the editing.

Such manipulation of events leads to changes in story–plot relations. We are most familiar with such manipulations in **flashbacks**, which present one or more shots out of their presumed story order. In *Hiroshima mon amour,* Resnais uses the protagonist's memory to motivate a violation of temporal order. Three shots (**6.40–6.42**) suggest visually that the position of her current lover's hand triggers a recollection of another lover's death years before. In contemporary cinema, brief flashbacks to key events may brutally interrupt present-time action. *The Fugitive* uses this technique to return obsessively to the murder of Dr. Kimball's wife, the event that initiated the story's action.

A much rarer option for reordering story events is the **flash-forward**. Here the editing moves from the present to a future event and then returns to the present. A small-scale instance occurs in *The Godfather.* Don Vito Corleone talks with his sons Tom and Sonny about their upcoming meeting with Sollozzo, the gangster who is asking them to finance his narcotics traffic. As the Corleones talk in the present, shots of them are interspersed with shots of Sollozzo going to the meeting in the future (**6.43–6.45**). The editing is used to provide exposition about Sollozzo while also moving quickly to the Don's announcement, at the gangsters' meeting, that he will not involve the family in the drug trade.

Filmmakers may use flash-forwards to tease the viewer with glimpses of the eventual outcome of the story action. The end of *They Shoot Horses, Don't They?* is hinted at in brief shots that periodically interrupt scenes in the present. Such flashforwards create a sense of a narration with a powerful range of story knowledge.

We may assume, then, that if a series of shots traces a 1-2-3 order in the presentation of story events, it is because the filmmaker has chosen to do that, not because of any necessity of following this order.

Editing also offers ways for the filmmaker to alter the *duration* of story events as presented in the film's plot. **Elliptical editing** presents an action in such a way that it consumes less time on the screen than it does in the story. The filmmaker can create an *ellipsis* in three principal ways.

Suppose a director wants to show a man climbing a flight of stairs, but doesn't want to show the entire duration of his climb. The director could use a conventional *punctuation* shot change, such as a dissolve or a wipe or a fade. In the classical filmmaking tradition, such a device signals that some time has been omitted. Our director could simply dissolve from a shot of the man starting at the bottom of the stairs to a shot of him reaching the top.

6.40   In *Hiroshima mon amour,* a view of the protagonist's Japanese lover asleep is followed by . . .

6.41   . . . a shot of her looking at him, leading to . . .

6.42   . . . a flashback of her dead German lover's hand.

"I saw Toto the Hero, the first film of the Belgian ex-circus clown Jaco van Dormael. What a brilliant debut. He tells the story with the camera. His compression and ellipses and clever visual transitions make it one of the most cinematic movies in a long time. The story spans a lifetime and kaleidoscopic events with such a lightness and grace that you want to get up and cheer."
— John Boorman, director

6.43   In *The Godfather,* the Corleones discuss their upcoming meeting with Sollozzo.

6.44   Flash-forward: Sollozzo arrives at the meeting, greeted by Sonny.

6.45   The next shot returns us to the family conversation, where Don Vito ponders what he will tell Sollozzo.

Alternatively, the filmmaker could show the man at the bottom of the staircase and let him walk up out of the frame, hold briefly on the empty frame, then cut to an empty frame of the top of the stairs and let the man enter the frame. The *empty frames* on either side of the cut cover the elided time.

Also, the filmmaker can create an ellipsis by means of a *cutaway:* a shot of another event elsewhere that will not last as long as the elided action. In our example, the director might start with the man climbing but then cut away to a woman in her apartment. We could then cut back to the man much farther along in his ascent.

It's also possible to expand story time. If the action from the end of one shot is partly repeated at the beginning of the next, we have **overlapping editing**. This prolongs the action, stretching it out past its story duration. The Russian filmmakers of the 1920s made frequent use of temporal expansion through such overlapping editing, and no one mastered it more thoroughly than Sergei Eisenstein. In *Strike,* when factory workers bowl over a foreman with a large wheel hanging from a crane, two shots expand the action (**6.46–6.48**). In *October,* Eisenstein overlaps several shots of rising bridges in order to stress the significance of the moment.

We're accustomed to seeing a scene present action only once. Occasionally, however, a filmmaker may go beyond expanding an action to repeat it in its entirety. The very rarity of this technique may make it a powerful editing resource. In Bruce Conner's *Report,* there is a newsreel shot of John and Jacqueline Kennedy riding a limousine down a Dallas street. The shot is systematically repeated, in part or in whole, over and over, building up tension in our expectations as the shot seems to move by tiny increments closer to the moment of the inevitable assassination. Occasionally in *Do The Right Thing,* Spike Lee cuts together two takes of the same action, as when we twice see a garbage can fly through the air and break the pizzeria window at the start of the riot. Jackie Chan often shows his most virtuosic stunts three or four times in a row from different angles to allow the audience to marvel at his daring (**6.49–6.51**).

Graphics, rhythm, space, and time, then, are at the service of the filmmaker through the technique of editing. They offer potentially unlimited creative possibilities. Yet most films we see make use of a very narrow set of editing possibilities—so narrow, indeed, that we can speak of a dominant editing style throughout film history. This is what is usually called **continuity editing**. Still, the most familiar way to edit a film isn't the only way to edit a film, and so we'll also consider some alternatives to continuity editing.

Continuity Editing

Around 1900–1910, as filmmakers started to use editing, they sought to arrange their shots so as to tell a story coherently and clearly. Thus editing, supported by specific strategies of cinematography and mise-en-scene, was used to ensure *narrative continuity.* So powerful is this style that, even today, anyone working in narrative filmmaking around the world is expected to be thoroughly familiar with it.

As its name implies, the basic purpose of the continuity system is to allow space, time, and action to continue in a smooth flow over a series of shots. All of the possibilities of editing we have already examined are turned to this end. First, graphic qualities are usually kept roughly continuous from shot to shot. The figures are balanced and symmetrically deployed in the frame; the overall lighting tonality remains constant; the action occupies the central zone of the screen.

Second, the rhythm of the cutting is usually made dependent on the camera distance of the shot. Long shots are left on the screen longer than medium shots, and medium shots are left on longer than close-ups. The assumption is that the spectator needs more time to take in the shots containing more details. In scenes of physical action like the fire in *The Birds,* accelerated editing rhythms may be present, but in general, shorter shots will tend to be closer views.

Since the continuity style seeks to present a story, it's chiefly through the handling of space and time that editing furthers narrative continuity.

Spatial Continuity: The 180° System

In the continuity style the space of a scene is constructed along what is called variously the **axis of action**, the *center line,* or the *180° line.* The scene's action—a person walking, two people conversing, a car racing along a road—is assumed to take place along a clear-cut vector. This axis of action determines a half-circle, or 180° area, where the camera can be placed to present the action. Consequently, the filmmaker will plan, film, and edit the shots so as to respect this center line. The camera work and mise-en-scene in each shot will be manipulated to establish and reiterate the 180° space.

6.46   In *Strike,* a wheel swings toward the foreman . . .

6.47   . . . then swings toward him again . . .

6.48   . . . and then again before striking him.

6.49   In *Police Story,* chasing the gangsters through a shopping mall, Jackie Chan leaps onto a pole several stories above them . . .

6.50   . . . and slides down in a shower of exploding lights.

6.51   Cut to a new angle: Jackie leaps again, leading to an instant replay of the risky stunt.

"The way [Howard] Hawks constructs a continuity of space is remarkable, and generally holds you 'inside' it. There is no possible way of escape, unless the film decides to provide you with one. My theory is that his films are captivating because they build a sense of continuity which is so strong that it allows the complete participation of the audience."

— Slobodan Sijan, director

Consider the bird's-eye view in **6.52.** We have a girl and a boy conversing. The axis of action is the imaginary line connecting the two people. Under the continuity system, the director would arrange the mise-en-scene and camera placement so as to establish and sustain this line. The camera can be put at any point as long as it stays on the same *side* of the line (hence the 180° term). A typical series of shots for coverage of the scene would be these: (1) a medium shot of the girl and boy, (2) a shot over the girl's shoulder, favoring the boy, and (3) a shot over the boy's shoulder, favoring the girl. But to cut to a shot from camera position X, or from any position within the tinted area, would be considered a

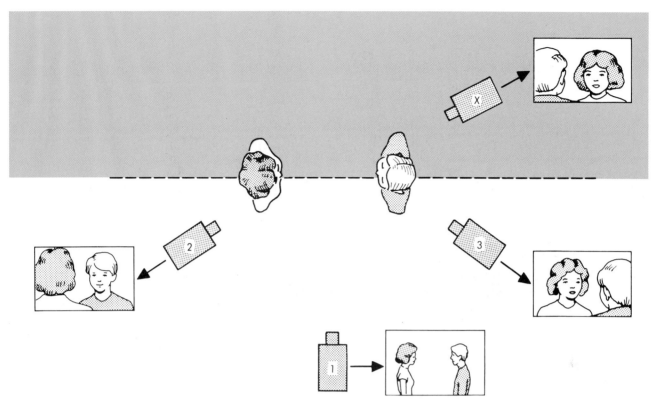

6.52 A conversation scene and the axis of action.

violation of the system because it *crosses* the axis of action. Indeed, some handbooks of film directing call shot X flatly wrong. To see why, we need to examine what happens if a filmmaker follows the **180° system**.

The 180° system ensures that relative positions in the frame remain consistent. In the shots taken from camera positions 1, 2, and 3, the characters remain in the same positions in the frame relative to each other. Even though we see them from different angles, the girl is always on the left and the boy is always on the right. But if we cut to shot X, the characters will switch positions in the frame. An advocate of traditional continuity would claim that shot X confuses us: have the two characters somehow swiveled around each other?

The 180° system ensures consistent eyelines. In shots 1, 2, and 3, the girl is looking right and the boy is looking left. Shot X violates this pattern by making the girl look to the left.

The 180° system ensures consistent screen direction. Imagine now that the girl is walking left to right; her path constitutes the axis of action. As long as our shots do not cross this axis, cutting them together will keep the **screen direction** of the girl's movement constant, from left to right. But if we *cross* the axis and film a shot from the other side, the girl will now appear on the screen as moving from *right to left.* Such a cut could be disorienting.

Consider a similar situation to that in 6.52, a standard scene of two cowboys meeting for a shootout on a town street (**6.53**). Cowboy A and cowboy B form the 180° line, but here A is walking from left to right and B is approaching from right to left, both seen in the shot taken from camera position 1. A closer view, from camera position 2, shows B still moving from right to left. A third shot, from camera position 3, shows A walking, as he had been in the first shot, from left to right.

But imagine that this third shot was instead taken from position X, on the opposite side of the line. A is now seen as moving from right to left. Has he taken fright and turned around while the second shot, of B, was on the screen? The filmmakers may want us to think that he is still walking toward his adversary, but

"*. . . what I call 'new brutalism' in cinema . . . is a form of naïveté, because it's made by people who I think don't really have a grasp of cinema's history. It's the MTV kind of editing, where the main idea is that the more disorienting it is, the more exciting. And you see it creeping into mainstream cinema more and more. You look at something like* Armageddon *and you see all the things that would have been forbidden in classical cinema, like crossing the line, camera jumping from side to side. It is a way to artificially generate excitement, but it doesn't really have any basis to it. And I find it kind of sad, because it's like an old man trying to dress like a teenager.*"

— John Boorman, director

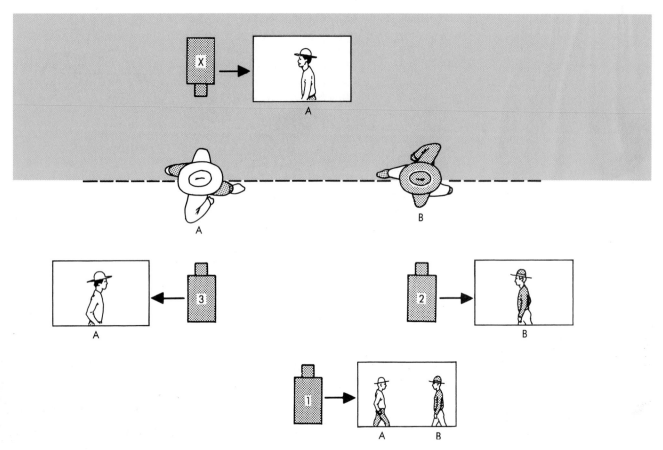

6.53   A Western shootout and the axis of action.

the change in screen directions could make us think just the opposite. A cut to a shot taken from any point in the colored area would create this change in direction. Such breaks in continuity can be confusing.

Even more disorienting would be crossing the line while establishing the scene's action. In our shootout, if the first shot shows A walking from left to right and the second shot shows B (from the other side of the line) also walking left to right, we would probably not be sure that they were walking toward each other. The two cowboys would seem to be walking in the same direction at different points on the street, as if one were following the other. We would very likely be startled if they suddenly came face to face within the same shot.

The 180° system prides itself on delineating space clearly. The viewer should always know *where the characters are* in relation to one another and to the setting. More important, the viewer always knows *where he or she is* with respect to the story action. The space of the scene, clearly and unambiguously unfolded, does not jar or disorient, because such disorientation, it is felt, will distract the viewer from the center of attention: the narrative chain of causes and effects.

Continuity Editing in *The Maltese Falcon*

We saw in Chapter 3 that the classical Hollywood mode of narrative subordinates time, motivation, and other factors to the cause–effect sequence. We also saw how mise-en-scene and camera work may present narrative material. Now we can note how, on the basis of the 180° principle, filmmakers have developed the continuity system as a way to build up a smoothly flowing space that remains subordinate to narrative action. Let's consider a concrete example: the opening of John Huston's film *The Maltese Falcon*.

The scene begins in the office of detective Sam Spade. In the first two shots, this space is established in several ways. First, there is the office window (shot 1a, **6.54**), from which the camera tilts down to reveal Spade (shot 1b, **6.55**) rolling a cigarette. As Spade says, "Yes, sweetheart?" shot 2 **(6.56)** appears. This is important in several respects. It is an **establishing shot**, delineating the overall space of the office: the door, the intervening area, the desk, and Spade's position. Note also that shot 2 establishes a 180° line between Spade and his secretary, Effie; Effie could be the girl in 6.52, and Spade could be the boy. The first phase of this scene will be built around staying on the same side of this 180° line.

Once laid out for us in the first two shots, the space is analyzed into its components. Shots 3 **(6.57)** and 4 **(6.58)** show Effie and Spade talking. Because the 180° line established at the outset is adhered to (each shot presents the two from the same side), we know their location and spatial relationships. In cutting together medium shots of the two, however, Huston relies on two other common tactics within the 180° system.

The first is the **shot/reverse-shot** pattern. Once the 180° line has been established, we can show first one end point of the line, then the other. Here we cut back and forth from Effie to Spade. A reverse shot is not literally the reverse of the first framing. It's simply a shot of the opposite end of the axis of action, usually showing a three-quarters view of the subject. In our bird's-eye view diagram (6.52), shots 2 and 3 form a shot/reverse-shot pattern, as 6.57 and 6.58 do here. Earlier examples in this chapter of shot/reverse-shot cutting are 6.17, 6.18 and 6.19, 6.20.

The second tactic Huston uses here is the **eyeline match**. That is, shot A presents someone looking at something offscreen; shot B shows us what is being looked at. In neither shot are *both* looker and object present. In the *Maltese Falcon* opening, the cut from the shot of Effie (shot 3, 6.57) to the shot of Spade at his desk (shot 4, 6.58) is an eyeline match. The shots from *The Birds* of Melanie watching the bird attack and fire also create eyeline matches, as do the examples of editing balancing frame compositions (6.17, 6.18 and 6.19, 6.20).

Note that shot/reverse-shot editing need not employ eyeline matches. You could film both ends of the axis in a shot/reverse-shot pattern without showing the characters looking at each other. (In 6.58, Spade is not looking at Effie.) On the whole, however, most shot/reverse-shot cuts also utilize the eyeline match.

The eyeline match is a simple idea but a powerful one, since the *directional* quality of the eyeline creates a strong spatial continuity. To be looked at, an object must be near the looker. The eyeline match presumably created the effects Kuleshov identified in his construction of false spaces through editing. That is, the expressionless actor seems to be looking at whatever we see in the next shot, and the audience assumes that the actor is reacting accordingly.

Within the 180° system, the eyeline match, like constant screen direction, can stabilize space. Note how in shot 3, Effie's glance off right reiterates Spade's

6.54 *The Maltese Falcon:* shot 1a.

6.55 *The Maltese Falcon:* shot 1b.

6.56 *The Maltese Falcon:* shot 2.

6.57 *The Maltese Falcon:* shot 3.

6.58 *The Maltese Falcon:* shot 4.

6.59   *The Maltese Falcon:* shot 5a.

6.60   *The Maltese Falcon:* shot 5b.

6.61   *The Maltese Falcon:* shot 6a.

6.62   *The Maltese Falcon:* shot 6b.

position even though he is not onscreen. And though Spade does not look up after the cut to shot 4, the camera position remains adamantly on the same side of the axis of action (indeed, the position is virtually identical to that in shot 1b). We know that Effie is offscreen left. Thus the breakdown of the scene's space is completely consistent, this consistency ensured by adherence to the 180° system. Thanks to the shot/reverse-shot pattern and the eyeline match, we understand the characters' locations even when they aren't in the same frame.

The spatial consistency is reaffirmed in shot 5, which presents the same framing as did shot 2. The office is shown again (shot 5a, **6.59**), when the new character, Brigid O'Shaughnessy, enters. Spade stands to greet her, and the camera reframes his movement by a slight tilt upward (shot 5b, **6.60**). Shot 5 is a **reestablishing shot**, since it reestablishes the overall space that was analyzed into shots 3 and 4. The pattern, then, has been *establishment/breakdown/reestablishment*—one of the most common patterns of spatial editing in the classical continuity style.

Let's pause to examine how this pattern has functioned to advance the narrative. Shot 1 has suggested the locale and, more important, has emphasized the protagonist by linking him to the sign on the window. Offscreen sound and Spade's "Yes, sweetheart?" motivate the cut to shot 2. This establishing shot firmly anchors shot 1 spatially. It also introduces the source of the offscreen sound—the new character, Effie. The shot changes at precisely the moment when Effie enters. We are thus unlikely to notice the cut, because our expectations lead us to want to see what happens next. The area near the door has been shown when the cause–effect chain makes it important, not before.

Shots 3 and 4 present the conversation between Spade and Effie, and the shot/reverse shot and the eyeline match reassure us as to the characters' locations. We may not even notice the cutting, since the style works to emphasize the dramatic flow of the scene—what Effie says and how Spade reacts. In shot 5, the overall view of the office is presented again, precisely at the moment when a new character enters the scene, and this in turn situates her firmly in the space. Thus narrative elements—the dialogue, the entrance of new characters—are emphasized by adhering to the 180° system. The editing subordinates space to action.

We can trace the same procedures, with one additional variation, in the shots that follow. In shot 5, Brigid O'Shaughnessy enters Spade's office. Shot 6 presents a reverse angle on the two of them as she comes toward him (shot 6a, **6.61**). She sits down alongside his desk (shot 6b, **6.62**). Up to this point, the 180° line ran between Spade and the doorway. Now the axis of action runs from Spade to the client's chair by his desk. Once established, this new line will not be violated.

The extra factor here is a third tactic for ensuring spatial continuity—the **match on action**, a very powerful device. Assume that a person starts to stand up in shot 1. We can wait until the character is standing up and has stopped moving before cutting to shot 2. But we can instead show the person's movement *beginning* in shot 1, and then we can cut to shot 2, which shows the continuation of the movement. We would then have a match on action, the editing device that carries a movement across the break between two shots.

To appreciate the skill involved in making a match on action, recall that most films are shot with a single camera. In filming shots whose action will be matched at the editing stage, it is possible that the first shot, in which the movement starts, will be filmed hours or days apart from the second, in which the movement is continued. Thus matching action is not simply a matter of cutting together two complete versions of the same scene from different vantage points. The director and the crew must keep notes about matters of camera work, mise-en-scene, and editing so that all the details can be fitted together in the assembly phase of production.

In the *Maltese Falcon* scene, the cut from the end of shot 5 (6.60) to the beginning of shot 6 (6.61) uses a match on action, the action being Brigid's walk toward Spade's desk. Again, the 180° system aids in concealing the match, since it keeps screen direction constant: Brigid moves from left to right in both shots. As

6.63   *The Maltese Falcon:* shot 7.

6.64   *The Maltese Falcon:* shot 8.

6.65   *The Maltese Falcon:* shot 9.

6.66   *The Maltese Falcon:* shot 10.

6.67   *The Maltese Falcon:* shot 11.

6.68   *The Maltese Falcon:* shot 12.

6.69   *The Maltese Falcon:* shot 13.

6.70   *The Maltese Falcon:* shot 14.

6.71   *The Maltese Falcon:* shot 15.

you'd expect, the match on action is a tool of narrative continuity. It takes a practiced eye to spot a smooth match on action; so powerful is our desire to follow the action flowing across the cut that we ignore the cut itself.

Except for the match on action, the editing in the rest of the scene uses the same tactics we have already seen. When Brigid sits down, a new axis of action has been established (shot 6b, 6.62). This enables Huston to break down the space into closer shots (shots 7–13, **6.63–6.69**). All of these shots use the shot/reverse-shot tactic: The camera frames, at an oblique angle, one end point of the 180° line, then frames the other. (Note the shoulders in the foreground of shots 7, 8, and 10—6.63, 6.64, and 6.66.) Here again, the editing of space presents the dialogue action simply and unambiguously.

Beginning with shot 12, Huston's cuts also create eyeline matches. Spade looks off left at Brigid (shot 12, 6.68). She looks off left as the door is heard opening (shot 13, 6.69). Archer, just coming in, looks off right at them (shot 14, **6.70**), and they both look off at him (shot 15, **6.71**). The 180° rule permits us always to know who is looking at whom.

Huston could have played the entire conversation in one long take, remaining with shot 6b (6.62). Why has he broken the conversation into seven shots? Most

6.72   *The Maltese Falcon:* shot 16a.

6.73   *The Maltese Falcon:* shot 16b.

6.74   *The Maltese Falcon:* shot 17.

6.75   In Ron Howard's *Parenthood,* eyeline-matched shot/reverse shots present a conversation . . .

6.76   . . . with the women in the foreground establishing the axis of action.

evidently, the analytical cutting controls our attention. We'll look at Brigid or Spade at exactly the moment Huston wants us to. In the long take and the more distant framing, Huston would have to channel our attention in other ways, perhaps through staging or sound.

Furthermore, the shot/reverse-shot pattern emphasizes the development of Brigid's story and Spade's reaction to it. As she gets into details, the cutting moves from over-the-shoulder shots (6.63, 6.64) to framings that isolate Brigid (6.65 and 6.67) and eventually one that isolates Spade (6.68). These shots come at the point when Brigid, in an artificially shy manner, tells her story, and the medium close-ups arouse our curiosity about whether she's telling the truth. The shot of Spade's re-action (6.68) suggests that he's skeptical. In short, the analytical editing cooperates with framing and figure behavior to focus our attention on Brigid's tale, to let us study her demeanor, and to get a hint as to Spade's response.

When Archer enters, the breakdown of the space stops for a moment, and Huston reestablishes the locale. Archer is integrated into the action by means of a right-ward pan shot (shots 16a and 16b, **6.72** and **6.73**). His path is consistent with the scene's first axis of action, that running between Spade and the doorway. Moreover, the framing on him is similar to that used for Brigid's entrance earlier. (Compare shot 16b with 6a [6.73 and 6.61].) Such repetitions allow the viewer to concentrate on the new information, not the manner in which it is presented.

Now firmly established as part of the scene, Archer hitches himself up onto Spade's desk. His position puts him at Spade's end of the axis of action (shot 17, **6.74**). The rest of the scene's editing analyzes this new set of relationships without ever crossing the 180° line.

The viewer is not supposed to notice all this. Throughout, the shots present space to emphasize the cause–effect flow—the characters' actions, entrances, dialogue, reactions. The editing has economically organized space to convey narrative continuity.

The continuity system, in exactly these terms, remains in force today. Most narrative films still draw on 180° principles (**6.75, 6.76**).

Continuity Editing: Some Fine Points

The continuity system can be refined in various ways. If a director arranges several characters in a circular pattern—say, sitting around a dinner table—then the axis of action will probably run between the characters of greatest importance at the moment. In **6.77** and **6.78**, from Howard Hawks's *Bringing Up Baby,* the important interaction is occurring between the two men, so we can cut from one side of the woman in the fore-ground to the other side in order to get consistent shot/reverse shots. When one man leaves the table, however, a semicircular arrangement of figures in space is created, so that a new axis of action can be established between the two women. Now we can get shot/reverse-shot exchanges running down the length of the table (**6.79, 6.80**).

6.77 In *Bringing Up Baby,* the shot/reverse shot between the man on the right . . .

6.78 . . . and the one on the left gives way to . . .

6.79 . . . a shot/reverse shot between the woman on the left . . .

6.80 . . . and the one on the right.

Both the *Maltese Falcon* and the *Bringing Up Baby* examples show that in the course of a scene the 180° line may shift as the characters move around the setting. In some cases, the filmmaker may create a new axis of action that allows the camera to take up a position that would have been across the line in an earlier phase of the scene.

The power of the axis of action and the eyelines it can create is so great that the filmmaker may be able to eliminate an establishing shot, thus relying on the Kuleshov effect. In Spike Lee's *She's Gotta Have It,* Nola Darling holds a Thanksgiving dinner for her three male friends. Lee never presents a shot showing all four in the same frame. Instead, he uses medium long shots including all the men (for example, **6.81**), over-the-shoulder shot/reverse shots among them (for example, **6.82**), and eyeline-matched medium close-ups of them. Nola is given her own medium close-ups (**6.83**).

Through eyelines and body orientations, Lee's editing keeps the spatial relations completely consistent. For example, each man looks in a different direction when addressing Nola (**6.84, 6.85**). This cutting pattern enhances the dramatic action by making all the men equal competitors for her. They are clustered at one end of the table, and none is shown in the same frame with her. In addition, by organizing the angles around her overall orientation to the action (as in **6.86**, an optical point-of-view shot), Lee keeps Nola the pivotal character. Further, the longer shot and her separate medium close-ups intensify the progression of the scene: The men are on display, and Nola is coolly judging each one's behavior.

Another felicity in the 180° system is the **cheat cut**. Sometimes a director may not have perfect continuity from shot to shot because he or she has composed each shot for specific reasons. Must the two shots match perfectly? Again, narrative motivation decides the matter. Given that the 180° system emphasizes story action, the director has some freedom to "cheat" mise-en-scene from shot to shot—that is, to mismatch slightly the positions of characters or objects.

6.81   *She's Gotta Have It.*

6.82   *She's Gotta Have It.*

6.83   *She's Gotta Have It.*

6.84   *She's Gotta Have It.*

6.85   *She's Gotta Have It.*

6.86   *She's Gotta Have It.*

6.87   In this shot from *Jezebel,* the top of Julie's head is even with the man's chin . . .

6.88   . . . but in the second shot she seems to have grown several inches.

Consider two shots from William Wyler's *Jezebel.* Neither character moves during either shot, but Wyler has blatantly cheated the position of Julie (**6.87, 6.88**). Yet most viewers would not notice the discrepancy since it's the dialogue that is of paramount importance in the scene; here again, the similarities between shots outweigh the differences of position. Moreover, a change from a straight-on angle to a slightly high angle helps hide the cheat. There is, in fact, a cheat in the *Maltese Falcon* scene, too, between shots 6b and 7. In 6b (6.62), as Spade leans forward, the back of his chair is not near him. Yet in shot 7 (6.63), it has been cheated to be just behind his left arm. Here again, the primacy of the narrative flow overrides such a cheat cut.

One more fine point in spatial continuity is particularly relevant to a film's narration. We have already seen that a camera framing can strongly suggest a character's optical point of view, as in our earlier example from *Fury* (5.112, 5.113). That example depends on a cut from the person looking (5.112) to what he sees (5.113). We have also seen an instance of POV cutting in the *Birds* sequence discussed on pp. 225–228. Now we are in a position to see how optical POV is consistent with continuity editing, creating a variety of eyeline-match editing known as *point-of-view cutting.*

Consider Alfred Hitchcock's *Rear Window,* which is built around the situation of the solitary photographer Jeff watching events taking place in an apartment across the courtyard. Hitchcock uses a standard eyeline-match pattern, cutting from a shot of Jeff looking (**6.89**) to a shot of what he sees (**6.90**). Since there is no establishing shot that shows both Jeff and the opposite apartment, the Kuleshov effect operates here: our mind connects the two images. More specifically, the second shot represents Jeff's optical viewpoint, and this is filmed from a position on his end of the axis of action (**6.91**). We are strongly restricted to what Jeff sees and what (he thinks) he knows.

As *Rear Window* goes on, the subjectivity of the POV shots intensifies. Becoming more eager to examine the details of his neighbor's life, Jeff begins to use binoculars and a photographic telephoto lens to magnify his view. By using shots taken with lenses of different focal lengths, Hitchcock shows how each new tool enlarges what Jeff can see (**6.92–6.95**). Hitchcock's cutting adheres to spatial continuity rules and exploits their POV possibilities in order to arouse curiosity and suspense.

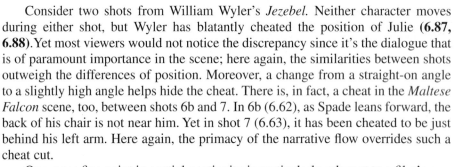

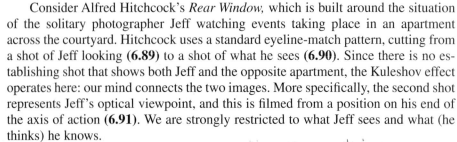

6.89   In *Rear Window,* Jeff looks out his window and . . .

6.90   . . . the next shot shows what he sees from his optical POV.

6.92   When Jeff looks through his binoculars . . .

6.93   . . . we see a telephoto POV shot of his neighbor.

6.94   When he employs a powerful photographic lens . . .

6.95   . . . the resulting POV shot enlarges his neighbor's activities even more.

6.91   An overhead diagram of the *Rear Window* POV shot.

More Refinements: Crossing the Axis of Action

Most continuity-based filmmakers prefer not to cut across the axis of action. They would rather move the actors around the setting and create a new axis. Still, can you ever legitimately cut across an established axis of action? Yes, sometimes. A scene occurring in a doorway, on a staircase, or in other symmetrical settings may occasionally break the line. Sometimes, too, the filmmakers can get across the axis by taking one shot *on the line itself* and using it as a transition. This strategy is rare in dialogue sequences, but it can be seen in chases and outdoor action. By filming on the axis, the filmmaker presents the action as moving directly toward the camera (a *head-on* shot) or away from it (a *tail-on* shot). The climactic chase of *The Road Warrior* offers several examples. As marauding road gangs try to board a fleeing gasoline truck, George Miller uses many head-on and tail-on shots of the vehicles (**6.96–6.100**).

Also, we should note that continuity-based films occasionally violate screen direction without confusing the viewer. This usually occurs when the scene's action is very well defined. For example, during a chase in John Ford's *Stagecoach*, there is no ambiguity about the Ringo Kid's leaping from the coach to the horses (**6.101, 6.102**). We wouldn't be likely to assume that the coach had turned around suddenly, as in the possible misinterpretation of the shootout scene with the two cowboys (6.53).

6.96   Near the climax of the chase in *The Road Warrior,* Max is driving left to right along the road . . .

6.97   . . . and in later shots he is still driving toward the right. An attacking thug perched on the front of the truck turns and looks off right in horror . . .

6.98   . . . realizing that another vehicle, moving right to left, is coming toward them on a collision course.

6.99   Several quick shots facing head-on to the vehicles show the crash . . .

6.100   . . . and a long shot shows the truck again, now moving right to left.

6.101   In *Stagecoach*, in a long shot where all movement is toward the right, the hero begins leaping from the driver's seat down onto the horse team . . .

6.102   . . . and in the next shot both he and the coach are moving leftward.

6.103   In *The Battle of Elderbush Gulch,* Griffith cuts from a shot of the cavalry . . .

6.104   . . . to a view inside the besieged cabin . . .

6.105   . . . back to the cavalry . . .

6.106   . . . and then back to the cabin.

Crosscutting

The continuity system shows that editing can endow the film's narration with a great range of knowledge. A cut can take us to any point on the correct side of the axis of action. Editing can even create omniscience, that godlike knowledge that some films seek to present. The outstanding technical device here is *crosscutting,* first extensively explored by D. W. Griffith in his last-minute rescue scenes. In *The Battle at Elderbush Gulch,* a cavalry troop is riding to rescue some settlers trapped in a cabin and battling the Indians outside (**6.103–6.106**). After 11 additional shots of the cavalry, various parts of the cabin interior, and the Indians outdoors, a 12th shot shows the cavalry riding in from the distance behind the cabin.

Crosscutting gives us an unrestricted knowledge of causal, temporal, or spatial information by alternating shots from one line of action in one place with shots of other events in other places. Crosscutting thus creates some spatial discontinuity, but it binds the action together by creating a sense of cause and effect and temporal simultaneity. In *Jerry Maguire,* for example, crosscutting interweaves the action of sports agent Jerry and his rival racing to sign up the same clients (**6.107–6.110**).

Fritz Lang's *M* goes further, intercutting three lines of action. While the police seek the child murderer, gangsters prowl the streets looking for him as well, and we also occasionally see the murderer himself. Crosscutting ties together the different lines of action, bringing out a temporal simultaneity and the causal process of the pursuit. The crosscutting also gives us a range of knowledge greater than that of any one character. We know that the gangsters are after the murderer, but the police and the murderer do not. Crosscutting also builds up suspense, as we form expectations that are only gradually clarified and fulfilled. It may create parallels as well, and

6.107 In *Jerry Maguire,* from a shot of Jerry seething with tension . . .

6.108 . . . there is a cut to his confident rival and his assistant . . .

6.109 . . . we then cut back to Jerry placing a phone call . . .

6.110 . . . and his rival doing the same.

Lang exploits this possibility by suggesting analogies between the police and the crooks. Whatever other functions it may have, though, crosscutting remains primarily a means of presenting narrative actions that are occurring in several locales at roughly the same time.

All the devices of spatial continuity show how film technique draws the spectator into an active process. We assume that setting, character movement, and character position will be consistent and coherent. Our prior knowledge of filmic conventions lets us form strong expectations about what shot will follow the one we are seeing. We also make inferences on the basis of cues, so that when Brigid and Spade look off left, we infer that someone is entering the room, and we expect to see a shot of that person.

What makes the continuity system invisible is its ability to draw on a range of skills that we have learned so well that they seem automatic. This makes spatial continuity editing a powerful tool for the filmmaker who wishes to reinforce habitual expectations. In recent decades, Hollywood filmmakers have developed ways to make traditional continuity techniques more forceful. (See "A Closer Look.") Because continuity editing has been so widely used for so long, it also becomes a central target for the filmmaker who wants to use film style to challenge or change our normal viewing activities.

Temporal Continuity: Order, Frequency, and Duration

In the classical continuity system, time, like space, is organized according to the development of the narrative. We know that the plot's presentation of the story typically involves manipulation of time. Continuity editing seeks to support and sustain this temporal manipulation.

INTENSIFIED CONTINUITY: *L.A. Confidential* and Contemporary Editing

By the 1930s, the continuity system was the standard approach to editing in most of the world's commercial film-making. But it underwent changes over the years. Today's editing practices abide by the principles of continuity but amplify them in certain ways.

Most obviously, mainstream films are now cut much faster than in the period between 1930 and 1960. Then, a film typically consisted of 300–500 shots, but in the years after 1960, the cutting pace picked up. Today a two-hour film might have over 2000 shots, and action films routinely contain 3000 or more. The average shot in *The Bourne Supremacy* lasts less than two seconds. Partly because of the faster editing, scenes are built out of relatively close views of individual characters, rather than long-shot framings. Establishing shots tend to be less common, sometimes appearing only at the end of a scene. Telephoto lenses, which enlarge faces, help achieve tight framings, and modern widescreen formats allow two or more facial close-ups to occupy the screen. Also, the camera tends to move very frequently, picking out one detail after another.

The accompanying shots from *L.A. Confidential* show several of these tendencies at work. After arresting three black suspects, Lieutenant Ed Exley prepares to wring a confession from them.

The scene takes less than a minute but employs nine shots, two with significant camera movement. (The film contains nearly 2000 shots, an average of four seconds apiece.) Director Curtis Hanson shifts the emphasis among several key characters by coordinating his editing with anamorphic widescreen, staging in depth, close-ups and medium-close-ups, rack-focus, and mobile framing **(6.111–6.122)**. Interestingly, the actors make no expressive use of their hands or bodies; the performances are almost completely facial.

Why did this intensified form of continuity become so common? Some historians trace it to the influence of television. Movies were broadcast by TV networks in the 1960s, transmitted by cable and satellite in the 1970s, and available on home video in the 1980s and 1990s. As people saw movies on home screens rather than in theaters, filmmakers reshaped their techniques. Constantly changing the image by cutting and camera movement could keep the viewer from switching channels or picking up a magazine. On smaller screens, faster cutting is easier to follow, and closer views look better than long shots, which tend to lose detail. Intensified continuity was shaped by many factors, such as the arrival of computer-based editing, but television was a major influence.

6.111 Shot 1: The scene begins by presenting only a portion of the space. A reflection shows Exley waiting and his colleagues milling about outside the interrogation room. This image singles out the core dramatic action to come—Exley's brutal confrontation with the suspects.

6.112 Shot 2: A match on Exley's action of turning gives us a fuller view of the policemen and establishes two other main characters: Jack Vincennes on the left and Bud White in the background, watching. This is only a partial establishing shot; a later camera movement will acquaint us with the layout of the interrogation rooms.

6.113 Shot 3: Hanson underscores White's presence by cutting to a telephoto shot of him saying that the suspects killed his partner.

6.114 Shot 4: In an echo of the opening framing, Exley now stands at the second interrogation room, seen in another reflection. The shot also reiterates Vincennes's presence, which will provide an important reaction later.

6.115 The camera tracks with Exley moving right to study the suspect in the third room. White's reflection can be seen in frame center. The camera movement has linked the three main detectives on the case while also establishing the three rooms as being side by side. At the end of the camera movement, Exley turns, and . . .

6.116 Shot 5: . . . a two-shot establishes his superior, Smith, on the scene. As Smith explains that the suspects' shotguns put them at the murder scene, the camera racks focus to him, putting Exley out of focus.

6.117 Shot 6: A cutaway to White listening—again, a tight facial shot taken with a telephoto lens—reminds us of his presence. He is only an observer in this phase of the scene, but as the questioning heats up, he will burst in to attack a suspect.

6.118 Shot 7: Returning to the two-shot shows Smith demanding that Exley make the men confess.

6.119 Shot 8: A reverse-angle on Exley, the first shot in the scene devoted to his face alone, underscores his determination: "Oh, I'll break them, sir."

6.120 Shot 9: A cut back to the two-shot supplies Smith's satisfied reaction.

6.121 Exley turns away. The lens shifts focus to catch his grim face in the foreground, preparing us for the brutality he will display.

6.122 Exley walks out of the shot. The camera tilts down slightly and racks focus to display Vincennes's skeptical expression. The telephoto lens, accentuated by the rack-focus, has supplied close views of Smith, then Exley, and then Vincennes in a single shot.

To get specific, recall our distinction among temporal order, frequency, and duration. Continuity editing typically presents the story events in a 1-2-3 order. Spade rolls a cigarette, then Effie comes in, then he answers her, and so on. The most common violation of 1-2-3 order is a flashback, signaled by a cut or dissolve. Furthermore, classical editing also often presents only *once* what happens *once* in the story; in continuity style, it would be a gross mistake for Huston to repeat the shot of, say, Brigid sitting down (6.62). Again, though, flashbacks are the most common way of motivating the repetition of a scene already witnessed. So chronological sequence and one-for-one frequency are the standard methods of handling order and frequency within the continuity style of editing. There are occasional exceptions, as we saw in our examples from *The Godfather, Do The Right Thing* and *Police Story* (pp. 231, 232).

What of duration? In the classical continuity system, story duration is seldom expanded; that is, screen time is seldom made greater than story time. Usually, duration is in complete continuity (plot time equaling story time) or is elided (story time being greater than plot time). Let's first consider complete continuity, the most common possibility. Here a scene occupying five minutes in the story also occupies five minutes when projected on the screen.

The first scene of *The Maltese Falcon* displays three cues for *temporal continuity*. First, the narrative progression of the scene has no gaps. Every movement by the characters and every line of dialogue is presented. Second, there is the sound track. Sound issuing from the story space (what we call *diegetic* sound) is a standard indicator of temporal continuity, especially when, as in this scene, the sound bleeds over each cut. Third, there is the match on action between shots 5 and 6. So powerful is the match on action that it creates both spatial *and* temporal continuity. The reason is obvious: If an action carries across the cut, the space and time are assumed to be continuous from shot to shot. In all, an absence of ellipses in the story action, diegetic sound overlapping the cuts, and matching on action are three primary indicators that the duration of the scene is continuous.

Sometimes, however, a second possibility will be explored: *temporal ellipsis*. The ellipsis may omit seconds, minutes, hours, days, years, or centuries. Some ellipses are of no importance to the narrative development and so are concealed. A classical narrative film doesn't show the entire time it takes a character to dress, wash, and breakfast in the morning. Shots of the character going into the shower, putting on shoes, or frying an egg might be combined so as to eliminate the unwanted bits of story time. As we saw on pp. 229–231, optical punctuations, empty frames, and cutaways are frequently used to cover short temporal ellipses.

But other ellipses are important to the narrative. The viewer must recognize that time has passed. For this task, the continuity style has built up a varied repertoire of devices. Often, dissolves, fades, or wipes are used to indicate an ellipsis between shots, usually the end of one scene and the beginning of the next. The Hollywood rule is that a dissolve indicates a brief time lapse and a fade indicates a much longer one. Contemporary filmmakers usually employ a cut for such transitions. For example, in *2001,* Stanley Kubrick cuts directly from a bone spinning in the air to a space station orbiting the earth, one of the boldest graphic matches in narrative cinema. The cut eliminates millions of years of story time.

In other cases, it's necessary to show a large-scale process or a lengthy period—a city waking up in the morning, a war, a child growing up, the rise of a singing star. Here classical continuity uses another device for temporal ellipsis: the **montage sequence**. (This should not be confused with the concept of *montage* in Sergei Eisenstein's film theory.) Brief portions of a process, informative titles (for example, "1865" or "San Francisco"), stereotyped images (such as the Eiffel Tower), newsreel footage, newspaper headlines, and the like can be joined by dissolves and music to create a quick, regular rhythm and to compress a lengthy series of actions into a few moments.

American studio films of the 1930s established some montage clichés—calendar pages fluttering away, newspaper presses pounding out an Extra—but in the

"Now nobody trusts the actor's performance. If an actor has a scene where they are sitting in the distance, everybody says, 'What are you shooting? It has to be close-up!' This is ridiculous. You have the position of the hand, the whole body—this is the feeling of a movie. I hate movies where everybody has big close-ups all the time. . . . This is television. I have talking heads on my television set in my home all the time."

— Miroslav Ondříček, editor

6.123   In *May Time*, Slavko Vorkapich uses superimpositions (here, the singer, sheet music, and a curtain rising) and rapid editing to summarize an opera singer's triumphs. *Citizen Kane* ironically refers to this passage in the montage sequences showing Susan Alexander's failures.

hands of deft editors, such sequences became small virtuoso pieces. The driving pace of gangster films like *Scarface* and *The Roaring Twenties* owes a lot to dynamic montage sequences. Slavko Vorkapich, an experimental filmmaker, created somewhat abstract, almost delirious summaries of wide-ranging actions such as stock market crashes, political campaigns, and an opera singer's career **(6.123)**. Montage sequences have been a mainstay of narrative filmmaking ever since. *Jaws* employs montage to summarize the start of tourist season through brief shots of vacationers arriving at the beach. A montage sequence in *Spider-Man* shows Peter Parker sketching his superhero costume, inspired by visions of the girl he loves. All these instances also remind us that because montage sequences usually lack dialogue, they tend to come wrapped in music. In *Tootsie,* a song accompanies a series of magazine covers showing the hero's rise to success as a soap opera star.

In sum, the continuity style uses the temporal dimension of editing primarily for narrative purposes. Through prior knowledge, the spectator expects the editing to present story events in chronological order, with only occasional rearrangement through flashbacks. The viewer expects that editing will respect the frequency of story events. And the viewer assumes that actions irrelevant to story causality will be omitted or at least abridged by judicious ellipses. All these expectations allow the viewer to follow the story with minimal effort.

At least, this is how the classical Hollywood continuity system has treated storytelling. Like graphics, rhythm, and space, time is organized to permit the unfolding of cause and effect, and the arousal of curiosity, suspense, and surprise. But there are many alternatives to the continuity style of editing, and these are worth a look.

Alternatives to Continuity Editing

Graphic and Rhythmic Possibilities

Powerful and pervasive as it is, the continuity style remains only *one* style, and many filmmakers have explored other editing possibilities.

Films using abstract or associational form have frequently granted the graphic and rhythmic dimensions of editing great weight. Instead of joining shot 1 to shot 2 primarily on the basis of the spatial and temporal functions that the shot fulfills in presenting a story, you could join them on the basis of purely graphic or rhythmic qualities—independent of the time and space they represent. In films such as *Anticipation of the Night, Scenes from Under Childhood,* and *Western History,* experimentalist Stan Brakhage uses purely graphic means of joining shot to shot: Continuities and discontinuities of light, texture, and shape motivate the editing.

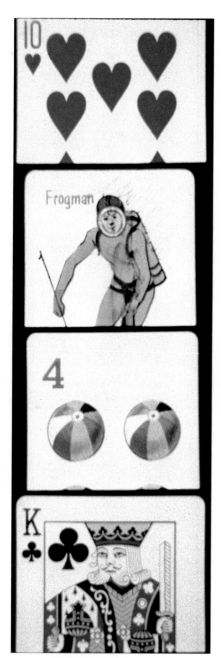

6.124 The stretches of single-frame shots in *Fist Fight* create a flickering effect on the screen.

Similarly, parts of Bruce Conner's *Cosmic Ray, A Movie,* and *Report* cut together newsreel footage, old film clips, film leader, and black frames on the basis of graphic patterns of movement, direction, and speed.

Many non-narrative films have completely subordinated the space and time presented in each shot to the rhythmic relations among shots. *Single-frame films* (in which each shot is only one frame long) are the most extreme examples of this overriding rhythmic concern. Two famous examples are Robert Breer's *Fist Fight* (**6.124**) and Peter Kubelka's *Schwechater.*

As early as 1913, some painters were contemplating the pure-design possibilities offered by film, and many works of the European avant-grade movements of the 1920s combined an interest in abstract graphics with a desire to explore rhythmic editing. Perhaps the most famous of these is the Fernand Léger–Dudley Murphy film *Ballet mécanique.* In Chapter 10, we'll see how *Ballet mécanique* juxtaposes its shots on the basis of graphic and rhythmic qualities.

The graphic and rhythmic possibilities of editing haven't been neglected in the story film, either. Some narrative filmmakers occasionally subordinate narrative concerns to graphic pattern. The most famous examples are probably the films for which Busby Berkeley choreographed elaborate dance numbers. In *42nd Street, Gold Diggers of 1933, Footlight Parade, Gold Diggers of 1935,* and *Dames,* the narrative periodically grinds to a halt and the film presents intricate dances that are arranged, shot, and edited with a concern for the pure configuration of dancers and background (4.144, from *42nd Street*).

More complexly related to the narrative is the graphic editing of Yasujiro Ozu. Ozu's cutting is often dictated by a much more precise graphic continuity than we find in the classical continuity style. In two scenes from *An Autumn Afternoon,* Ozu creates graphic matches on men sitting opposite each other in restaurants (**6.125–6.128**). In *Ohayu,* Ozu uses color for the same purpose, cutting from laundry on a line to a domestic interior and matching on a red shape in the upper left of each shot (a shirt, a lamp; **6.129, 6.130**).

Some narrative films have momentarily subordinated spatial and temporal editing to rhythmic cutting. In the 1920s, both the French Impressionist school and the Soviet avant-garde frequently made story progression secondary to purely rhythmic editing. In such films as Abel Gance's *La Roue,* Jean Epstein's *Coeur fidèle* and *La Glace à trois faces,* and Alexandre Volkoff's *Kean,* accelerated editing renders the tempo of an onrushing train, a whirling carousel, a racing automobile, and a drunken dance. Kuleshov's *The Death Ray* and, as we shall see, Eisenstein's *October* occasionally make rhythm dominate narrative space and time. We can find strong passages of rhythmic editing in Rouben Mamoulian's *Love Me Tonight,* René Clair's *Le Million,* and several films of Ozu and Hitchcock, as well as in *Assault on Precinct 13* and *The Terminator.* Pulsating rhythmic editing is prominent in films influenced by music videos, such as *The Crow* and *Romeo + Juliet.* As we saw with graphics, rhythmic editing may override the spatial and temporal dimensions; when this happens, narrative becomes less important.

Spatial and Temporal Discontinuity

How can you tell a story without adhering to the continuity rules? Let's sample some ways filmmakers have created distinct editing styles by use of what might be considered spatial and temporal discontinuities.

One option is to use spatial continuity in ambiguous ways. In *Mon Oncle d'Amérique,* Resnais intercuts the stories of his three main characters with shots of each character's favorite star, taken from French films of the 1940s. At one point, as René's pesky office mate calls to him, we get the coworker in one shot (**6.131**). But Resnais cuts to a shot of Jean Gabin in an older film, turning in reverse shot (**6.132**). Only then does Resnais supply a shot of René turning to meet his questioner (**6.133**). The film does not definitely present the Gabin shot as a fantasy image; we can't tell

6.125   In *An Autumn Afternoon,* Ozu cuts from one man drinking sake directly . . .

6.126   . . . to another caught in almost exactly the same position, costume, and gesture.

6.127   Later he cuts from one man to another, maintaining very similar compositions. Even their beer bottles . . .

6.128   . . . sit in nearly the same position on frame left, their labels graphically matched as well.

6.129   In *Ohayu,* Ozu creates a playful graphic match by cutting from an outdoor scene with a bright red sweater in the upper left . . .

6.130   . . . to an interior with a vivid red lampshade in the same position.

whether René imagines himself as his favorite star confronting his coworker, or whether the film's narration draws the comparison independent of René's state of mind. The cut relies on the cues of shot/reverse shot but uses them to create a momentarily jarring discontinuity that triggers ambiguity.

More drastically, a filmmaker could violate or ignore the 180° system. The editing choices of filmmakers Jacques Tati and Yasujiro Ozu are based on what we might call 360° space. Instead of an axis of action that dictates that the camera be placed within an imaginary semicircle, these filmmakers work as if the action were not a line but a point at the center of a circle and as if the camera could be placed at any point on the circumference. In *Mr. Hulot's Holiday, Play Time,* and *Traffic,* Tati systematically films from almost every side; edited together, the shots present multiple spatial perspectives on a single event. Similarly, Ozu's scenes construct a 360° space that produces what the continuity style would consider grave editing errors. Ozu's films often do not yield consistent relative positions and screen directions; the eyeline matches are out of joint, and the only consistency is the *violation* of the 180° line. One of the gravest sins in the classical continuity style is to match on action while breaking the line, yet Ozu does this comfortably in *Early Summer* (**6.134, 6.135**).

Such spatially discontinuous cutting affects the spectator's experience as well. The defender of classical editing would claim that spatial continuity rules are necessary for the clear presentation of a narrative. But anyone who has seen a film by Ozu or Tati can testify that no narrative confusion arises from their continuity violations. Though the spaces do not flow as smoothly as in the Hollywood style (this is indeed part of the films' fascination), the causal developments remain intelligible. The inescapable conclusion is that the continuity system is only *one* way to tell

6.131   *Mon Oncle d'Amérique.*

6.132   *Mon Oncle d'Amérique.*

6.133   *Mon Oncle d'Amérique.*

6.134   In *Early Summer,* Ozu cuts on the grandfather's gesture of drinking . . .

6.135   . . . directly to the opposite side of the characters.

a story. Historically, this system has been the dominant one, but artistically, it has no priority over other styles.

There are two other notable devices of discontinuity. In *Breathless,* Jean-Luc Godard violates conventions of spatial, temporal, and graphic continuity by his systematic use of the **jump cut**. Though this term is often loosely used, its primary meaning is this: when two shots of the same subject are cut together but are not sufficiently different in camera distance and angle, there will be a noticeable jump on the screen. Classical continuity avoids such jumps by generous use of shot/reverse shots and by the *30° rule* (advising that every camera position be varied by at least 30° from the previous one). But an examination of shots from *Breathless* suggests the consequences of Godard's jump cuts (**6.136, 6.137**). Far from flowing unnoticeably, such cuts are very visible, and they disorient the spectator.

A second violation of continuity is created by the **nondiegetic insert**. Here the filmmaker cuts from the scene to a metaphorical or symbolic shot that is not part of the space and time of the narrative. Clichés abound here (**6.138, 6.139**). More complex examples occur in the films of Eisenstein and Godard. In Eisenstein's *Strike,* the massacre of workers is intercut with the slaughter of a bull. In Godard's *La Chinoise,* Henri tells an anecdote about the ancient Egyptians, who, he claims, thought that "their language was the language of the gods." As he says this (**6.140**), Godard cuts in two close-ups of relics from the tomb of King Tutankhamen (**6.141, 6.142**). As nondiegetic inserts, coming from outside the story world, these shots construct a running, often ironic, commentary on the action, and they prompt the spectator to search for implicit meanings. Do the relics corroborate or challenge what Henri says?

Though both the jump cut and the nondiegetic insert can be used in a narrative context (as in the *Fury* example), they tend to weaken narrative continuity. The jump cut interrupts the story with abrupt gaps, while the nondiegetic insert suspends story action altogether. It is no accident that both devices have been

6.136 In *Breathless,* in the jump cut from this shot of Patricia . . .

6.137 . . . to this one, the background has changed and some story time has gone by.

6.138 In *Fury,* Lang cuts from housewives gossiping . . .

prominently used by the contemporary filmmaker most associated with the challenge to classical narrative, Jean-Luc Godard. In Chapter 11, we'll examine the nature of this challenge by analyzing *Breathless.*

There are still other alternatives to classical continuity, especially in the temporal dimension. Although the classical approach to order and frequency of story events may seem the best option, it is only the most familiar. Story events do not have to be edited in 1-2-3 order. In Resnais's *La Guerre est finie,* scenes cut in conventional continuity are interrupted by images that may represent flashbacks, or fantasy episodes, or even future events. Editing can also play with variable frequency for narrative purposes; the same event can be shown repeatedly. In *La Guerre est finie,* the same funeral is depicted in different hypothetical ways, with the protagonist either present or absent.

6.139 . . . to shots of clucking hens.

Again, Godard offers a striking example of how editing can manipulate both order and frequency. In *Pierrot le fou,* as Marianne and Ferdinand flee her apartment Godard scrambles the order of the shots (**6.143–6.146**). Godard also plays with frequency by repeating one gesture—Ferdinand jumping into the car—but showing it *differently* each time. Such manipulation of editing blocks our normal expectations about story action and forces us to concentrate on the very process of piecing together the film's narrative.

The editing may also take liberties with story duration. Although complete continuity and ellipsis are the most common ways of rendering duration, expansion—stretching a moment out, making screen time greater than story time—remains a distinct possibility. François Truffaut uses such expansions in *Jules and Jim* to underscore narrative turning points, as when the heroine Catherine lifts her veil or jumps off a bridge.

Filmmakers have found creative ways to rework the most basic tenets of the continuity system. We've indicated, for example, that a match on action strongly

6.140 A diegetic shot in *La Chinoise* is followed by . . .

6.141 . . . nondiegetic shots of the lion bed of King Tutankhamen . . .

6.142 . . . and his golden mask.

6.143   In *Pierrot le fou,* initially, Ferdinand jumps into the car as Marianne pulls away . . .

6.144   . . . but then the couple are seen back in their apartment.

6.145   Next the car races down a street . . .

6.146   . . . and then Marianne and Ferdinand climb onto a rooftop, an event that occurred before they drove off.

suggests that time continues across the cut. Yet Alain Resnais creates an impossible continuous action in *Last Year at Marienbad.* Small groups of guests are standing around the hotel lobby; one medium shot frames a blonde woman beginning to turn away from the camera (**6.147**). In the middle of her turn, there is a cut to her, still turning but in a different setting (**6.148**). The smooth match on action, along with the woman's graphically matched position in the frame, imply that she is moving continuously, yet the change of setting contradicts this impression. As we'll see in Chapter 10, experimental films push ambiguous or contradictory editing even further.

Our examples indicate that some discontinuities of temporal order, duration, and frequency can become perfectly intelligible in a narrative context. On the other hand, with the jump cut, the nondiegetic insert, and the inconsistent match on action, temporal dislocations can also push away from traditional notions of story altogether and create ambiguous relations among shots.

As an example of the power of spatial and temporal discontinuities in editing, let's look at a famous example: Sergei Eisenstein's *October.*

Functions of Discontinuity Editing: *October*

For many Soviet filmmakers of the 1920s, editing was a major means of organizing the entire form of the film; it did not simply serve the narrative progression, as in the continuity system. Eisenstein's *Strike, Potemkin, October,* and *Old and New* tried to build a film on the basis of certain editing devices. Rather than subordinate his editing patterns to the mapping out of a story, Eisenstein conceived of these films as editing constructions.

Eisenstein deliberately opposed himself to continuity editing, seeking out and exploiting what Hollywood would consider discontinuities. He often staged, shot, and cut his sequences for the maximum *collision* from shot to shot, and sequence to sequence, since he believed that only through being forced to synthesize such conflicts could the viewer participate in actively understanding the film.

No longer bound by conventional dramaturgy, Eisenstein's films roam freely through time and space to construct an intricate pattern of images calculated to stimulate the viewer's senses, emotions, and thinking. A short passage from *October* can illustrate how he uses editing discontinuities.

The sequence is the third one in the film (and comprises no fewer than 125 shots). The story action is simple. The bourgeois Provisional Government has taken power in Russia after the February Revolution, but instead of withdrawing from World War I, the government has continued to support the Allies. This maneuver has left the Russian people no better off than under the czar. In classical Hollywood cinema, this story might have been shown through a montage sequence of newspaper headlines smoothly linked to a scene wherein a protagonist complains that the Provisional Government has not changed a thing. *October*'s protagonist, though, is not one person but the entire Russian people, and the film does not usually use dialogue scenes to present its story points. Rather, *October* seeks to go beyond a simple presentation of story events by making the audience actively

6.147   In *Last Year at Marienbad,* a match on action . . .

6.148   . . . across two settings.

assemble those events. So the film confronts us with a disorienting and disjunctive set of images.

The sequence begins with shots showing the Russian soldiers on the front casting down their rifles and fraternizing freely with German soldiers (**6.149**). Eisenstein then cuts back to the Provisional Government, where a flunky extends a document to an unseen ruler (**6.150**); this document pledges the government to aid the Allies. The soldiers' fraternization is suddenly disrupted by a bombardment (**6.151**). The soldiers run back to the trenches and huddle as dirt and bomb fragments rain down on them. Eisenstein then cuts to a series of shots of a cannon being lowered off a factory assembly line. For a time, the narration crosscuts these images with the soldiers on the battlefield (**6.152, 6.153**). In the last section of the sequence, the shots of the cannon are crosscut with hungry women and children standing in breadlines in the snow (**6.154**). The sequence ends with two intertitles: "All as before . . ."/ "Hunger and war."

Graphically, there are some continuities. When the soldiers fraternize, many shots closely resemble one another graphically, and one shot of a bursting bomb is graphically matched in its movement with men bustling into a trench. But the *dis*continuities are more noteworthy. Eisenstein cuts from a laughing German soldier facing right to a menacing eagle statue, facing left, at the government headquarters (**6.155, 6.156**). There is a bold jump cut: The flunky is bowing; then suddenly he is standing up (**6.157, 6.158**). A static shot of rifles thrust into the snow cuts to a long shot of a bursting shell (**6.159, 6.160**). When the soldiers race back to the trenches, Eisenstein often opposes their direction of movement from shot to shot. Moreover, the cutting contrasts shots of the cannon slowly *descending* with shots of the men crouching in the trenches looking *upward* (6.152, 6.153). In the last phase of the sequence, Eisenstein juxtaposes the misty, almost completely static shots of the women and children with the sharply defined, dynamically moving

6.149   In *October*, Russian and German soldiers talk, drink, and laugh together on the battlefield.

6.150   *October:* at the Provisional Government's headquarters.

6.151   *October:* a bombardment at the front.

6.152   In *October*, a cannon in a factory intercut . . .

6.153   . . . with soldiers at the front.

6.154   In *October*, a breadline intercut with the war scenes.

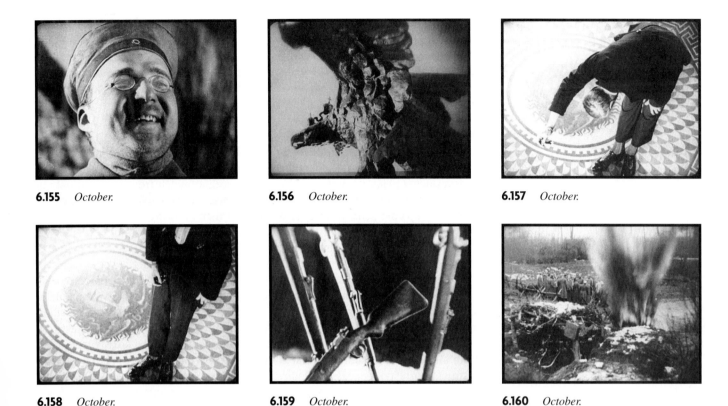

6.155   *October.*

6.156   *October.*

6.157   *October.*

6.158   *October.*

6.159   *October.*

6.160   *October.*

shots of factory workers lowering the cannon (**6.161**). Such graphic discontinuities recur throughout the film, especially in scenes of dynamic action, and stimulate perceptual conflict in the audience. To watch an Eisenstein film is to submit oneself to such percussive, pulsating graphic editing.

Eisenstein also makes vigorous use of temporal discontinuities. The sequence as a whole is opposed to Hollywood rules in its refusal to present the order of events unambiguously. Does the crosscutting of battlefield and government, and factory and street indicate simultaneous action? (Consider, for example, that the women and children are seen at night, whereas the factory appears to be operating in the daytime.) It is impossible to say if the battlefield events take place before or after or during the women's vigil. Eisenstein has sacrificed the delineation of 1-2-3 order so that he can present the shots as emotional and conceptual units.

Duration is likewise variable. The soldiers fraternize in fairly continuous time, but the Provisional Government's behavior presents drastic ellipses; this permits Eisenstein to identify the government as the unseen cause of the bombardment that ruptures the peace. At one point, Eisenstein uses one of his favorite devices, a temporal expansion: there is an overlapping cut as a soldier drinks from a bottle. The cut recalls the expanded sequence of the wheel knocking over the foreman in *Strike* (6.46–6.48). At another point, the gradual collapse of the women and children waiting in line is elided. We see them standing, then later lying on the ground. Even frequency is made discontinuous: It is difficult to say whether we are seeing several cannons lowered off the assembly line or only one descending cannon shown several times. Again, Eisenstein seeks a specific *juxtaposition* of elements, not obedience to a time line. Editing's manipulation of order, duration, and frequency subordinates straightforward story time to specific conceptual relationships. Eisenstein creates these relations by juxtaposing disparate lines of action through editing.

Spatially, the *October* sequence runs from rough continuity to extreme discontinuity. Although at times the 180° rule is respected (especially in the shots of women and children), never does Eisenstein begin a section with an establishing

6.161   *October.*

shot. Reestablishing shots are rare, and seldom are the major components of the locales shown together in one shot.

Throughout, the classical continuity of space is broken by the intercutting of the different locales. To what end? By violating space in this manner, the film invites us to make emotional and conceptual connections. For example, crosscutting to the Provisional Government makes it the source of bombardment, a meaning reinforced by the way the first explosions are followed by the jump cut of the government flunky.

More daringly, by cutting from the crouching soldiers to a descending cannon, Eisenstein powerfully depicts the men being crushed by the warmaking apparatus of the government. This is reinforced by a false eyeline match from soldiers looking upward, *as if* at the lowering cannon—false because, of course, the two elements are in entirely separate settings (6.152, 6.153). By then showing the factory workers lowering the cannon (6.161), the cutting links the oppressed soldiers to the oppressed proletariat. Finally, as the cannon hits the ground, Eisenstein crosscuts images of it with the shots of the starving families of the soldiers and the workers. They, too, are shown as crushed by the government machine. As the cannon wheels come ponderously to the floor, Einstein cuts to the women's feet in the snow, and the machine's heaviness is linked by titles ("one pound," "half a pound") to the steady starvation of the women and children. Although all of the spaces are in the story, such discontinuities create a running political commentary on the story events.

In all, then, Eisenstein's spatial editing, like his temporal and graphic editing, constructs correspondences, analogies, and contrasts that ask us to *interpret* the story events. The interpretation is not simply handed to the viewer; rather, the editing discontinuities push the viewer to work out implicit meanings. This sequence, like others in *October,* demonstrates that there are powerful alternatives to the principles of classical continuity.

Summary

When any two shots are joined, we can ask several questions:

1. How are the shots graphically continuous or discontinuous?

2. What rhythmic relations are created?

3. Are the shots spatially continuous? If not, what creates the discontinuity? (Crosscutting? Ambiguous cues?) If the shots are spatially continuous, how does the 180° system create the continuity?

4. Are the shots temporally continuous? If so, what creates the continuity? (For example, matches on action?) If not, what creates the discontinuity? (Ellipsis? Overlapping cuts?)

More generally, we can ask the question we ask of every film technique: How does this technique *function* with respect to the film's narrative form? Does the film use editing to lay out the narrative space, time, and cause–effect chain in the manner of classical continuity? How do editing patterns emphasize facial expressions, dialogue, or setting? Do editing patterns withhold narrative information? In general, how does editing contribute to the viewer's experience of the film?

Some practical hints: You can learn to notice editing in several ways. If you are having trouble noticing cuts, try watching a film or TV show and tapping with a pencil each time a shot changes. Once you recognize editing easily, watch any film with the sole purpose of observing one editing aspect—say, the way space is presented or the control of graphics or time. Sensitize yourself to rhythmic editing by noting cutting rates; tapping out the tempo of the cuts can help.

Watching 1930s and 1940s American films can introduce you to classical continuity style; try to predict what shot will come next in a sequence. (You'll be surprised at how often you're right.) When you watch a film on video, try turning off the sound; editing patterns become more apparent this way. When there is a violation of continuity, ask yourself whether it is accidental or serves a purpose. When you see a film that does not obey classical continuity principles, search for its unique editing patterns. Use the slow-motion, freeze, and reverse controls on a videocassette machine or DVD player to analyze a film sequence as this chapter has done. (Almost any film will do.) In such ways as these, you can considerably increase your awareness and understanding of the power of editing.

Where to Go from Here

What Editing Is

Professional reflections on the work of the film editor include Ralph Rosenblum, *When the Shooting Stops . . . The Cutting Begins: A Film Editor's Story* (New York: Penguin, 1980); Edward Dmytryk, *On Film Editing* (Boston: Focal Press, 1984); Vincent Lo Brutto, *Selected Takes: Film Editors on Film Editing* (New York: Praeger, 1991); Gabriella Oldham, *First Cut: Conversations with Film Editors* (Berkeley: University of California Press, 1992); and Declan McGrath, *Editing and Post-Production* (Hove, England: RotoVision, 2001). See also Ken Dancyger, *The Technique of Film and Video Editing* (Boston: Focal Press, 1993).

Walter Murch, one of the most thoughtful and creative editors in history, provides a rich array of ideas in *In the Blink of an Eye: A Perspective on Film Editing,* 2d ed. (Los Angeles: Silman-James, 2001). Murch, who worked on *American Graffiti, The Godfather, Apocalypse Now,* and *The English Patient,* has always conceived image and sound editing as part of the same process. He shares his thoughts in an extended dialogue with prominent novelist Michael Ondaatje in *The Conversations: Walter Murch and the Art of Editing Film* (New York: Knopf, 2002). Ever the experimenter, Murch tried using an inexpensive digital program to edit a theatrical feature. The result is traced in detail in Charles Koppelman, *Behind the Seen: How Walter Murch Edited* Cold Mountain *Using Apple's Final Cut Pro and What This Means for Cinema* (Berkeley, CA: New Riders, 2005). You can listen to Murch discussing his work on the National Public Radio program *Fresh Air,* available at www.npr.org.

We await a large-scale history of editing, but André Bazin sketches a very influential account in "The Evolution of Film Language," in *What Is Cinema?* vol. 1 (Berkeley: University of California Press, 1967), pp. 23–40. Editing in early U.S. cinema is carefully analyzed by Charlie Keil in *Early American Cinema in Transition: Story, Style, and Filmmaking, 1907–1913* (Madison: University of Wisconsin Press, 2001). Profes-

sional editor Don Fairservice offers a thoughtful account of editing in the silent and early sound eras in *Film Editing: History, Theory and Practice* (Manchester: Manchester University Press, 2001). Several sections of Barry Salt's *Film Style and Technology: History and Analysis* (London: Starword, 1992) are devoted to changes in editing practices.

Documentary films characteristically rely on editing, perhaps more than fictional films do. A set of cutting conventions has developed. For example, it is common to intercut talking-head shots of conflicting experts as a way of representing opposing points of view. Interestingly, in making *The Thin Blue Line,* Errol Morris instructed his editor Paul Barnes, to avoid cutting between the two main suspects. "He didn't want the standard documentary good guy/bad guy juxtaposition. . . . He hated when I intercut people telling the same story, or people contradicting or responding to what someone has just said" (Oldham, *First Cut,* p. 144). Morris apparently wanted to give each speaker's version a certain integrity, letting each stand as an alternative account of events.

Dimensions of Film Editing

Very little has been written on graphic aspects of editing. See Vladimir Nilsen, *The Cinema as a Graphic Art* (New York: Hill & Wang, 1959), and Jonas Mekas, "An Interview with Peter Kubelka," *Film Culture* 44 (Spring 1967): 42–47.

What we are calling rhythmic editing incorporates the categories of metric and rhythmic montage discussed by Sergei Eisenstein in "The Fourth Dimension in Cinema," in *Selected Works,* vol. I, pp. 181–94. For a sample analysis of a film's rhythm, see Lewis Jacobs, "D. W. Griffith," in *The Rise of the American Film* (New York: Teachers College Press, 1968), chap. 11, pp. 171–201. Television commercials are useful to study for rhythmic editing, for their highly stereotyped imagery permits the editor to cut the shots to match the beat of the jingle on the sound track.

The Kuleshov experiments have been variously described. The two most authoritative accounts are in V. I. Pudovkin, *Film Technique* (New York: Grove Press, 1960), and Ronald Levaco, trans. and ed., *Kuleshov on Film: Writings of Lev Kuleshov* (Berkeley: University of California Press, 1974), pp. 51–55. For a summary of Kuleshov's work, see Vance Kepley, Jr., "The Kuleshov Workshop," *Iris* 4, 1 (1986): 5–23. Can the effect actually suggest an expressionless character's emotional reaction? Two film researchers tried to test it, and their skeptical conclusions are set forth in Stephen Prince and Wayne E. Hensley, "The Kuleshov Effect: Recreating the Classic Experiment," *Cinema Journal* 31, 2 (Winter 1992): 59–75. During the 1990s, two Kuleshov experiments, one complete and one fragmentary, were discovered. For a description and historical background on one of them, see Yuri Tsivian, Ekaterina Khokhlova, and Kristin Thompson, "The Rediscovery of a Kuleshov Experiment: A Dossier," *Film History* 8, 3 (1996): 357–67.

Continuity Editing

For a historical discussion of continuity editing, see Chapter 12 and the chapter's bibliography. The hidden selectivity that continuity editing can achieve is well summarized in a remark of Thom Noble, who edited *Fahrenheit 451* and *Witness:* "What usually happens is that there are maybe seven moments in each scene that are brilliant. But they're all on different takes. My job is to try and get all those seven moments in and yet have it look seamless, so that nobody knows there's a cut in there" (quoted in David Chell, ed., *Moviemakers at Work* [Redmond, WA: Microsoft Press, 1987], pp. 81–82).

Many sources spell out the rules of continuity. See Karel Reisz and Gavin Millar, *The Technique of Film Editing* (New York: Hastings House, 1973); Daniel Arijohn, *A Grammar of the Film Language* (New York: Focal Press, 1978); Edward Dmytryk, *On Screen Directing* (Boston: Focal Press, 1984); and Stuart Bass, "Editing Structures," in *Transitions: Voices on the Craft of Digital Editing* (Birmingham, England: Friends of ED, 2002), pp. 28–39. Our diagram of a hypothetical axis of action has been adapted from Edward Pincus's concise discussion in his *Guide to Filmmaking* (New York: Signet, 1969), pp. 120–25.

For analyses of the continuity style, see Ramond Bellour, "The Obvious and the Code," *Screen* 15, 4 (Winter 1974–75): 7–17; and André Gaudreault, "Detours in Film Narrative: The Development of Cross-Cutting," *Cinema Journal* 19, 1 (Fall 1979): 35–59. Joyce E. Jesionowski presents a detailed study of Griffith's distinctive version of early continuity editing in *Thinking in Pictures: Dramatic Structure in D. W. Griffith's Biograph Films* (Berkeley: University of California Press, 1987). David

Bordwell's *Planet Hong Kong: Popular Cinema and the Art of Entertainment* (Cambridge, MA: Harvard University Press, 2000) considers how Hollywood continuity was used by another national cinema.

Contemporary Editing and Intensified Continuity

Taught in film schools and learned on the job by beginning filmmakers, the principles of continuity editing still dominate cinema around the world. As we suggested on p. 246, however, there have been some changes in the system. Shots tend to be shorter (*Moulin Rouge* contains over 4000) and framed closer to the performers. The medium shots in older filmmaking traditions display the hands and upper body fully, but intensified continuity concentrates on faces, particularly the actor's eyes. Film editor Walter Murch says, "The determining factor for selecting a particular shot is frequently: 'Can you register the expression in the actor's eyes?' If you can't, the editor will tend to use the next closer shot, even though the wider shot may be more than adequate when seen on the big screen."

There's some evidence that today's faster cutting pace and frequent camera movements allow directors to be a bit loose in matching eyelines. In several scenes of *Hulk, Mystic River,* and *Syriana,* the axis of action is crossed, sometimes repeatedly. If viewers aren't confused by these cuts, it's perhaps because the actors don't move around the set very much and so the overall spatial layout remains clear.

For more on intensified continuity, see David Bordwell, *The Way Hollywood Tells It: Story and Style in Modern Movies* (Berkeley: University of California Press, 2006), pp. 117–89.

Alternatives to Continuity Editing

Eisenstein remains the chief source in this area. A highly introspective filmmaker, he bequeathed us a rich set of ideas on the possibilities of non-narrative editing; see the essays in *Selected Works,* vol. 1. For further discussion of editing in *October,* see the essays by Annette Michelson, Noël Carroll, and Rosalind Krauss in the special "Eisenstein/Brakhage" issue of *Artforum* 11, 5 (January 1973): 30–37, 56–65. For a more general view of Eisenstein's editing, see David Bordwell, *The Cinema of Eisenstein* (Cambridge, MA: Harvard University Press, 1993). The writings of another Russian, Dziga Vertov, are also of interest. See Annette Michelson, ed., *Kino-Eye: The Writings of Dziga Vertov* (Berkeley: University of California Press, 1984). On Ozu's manipulation of discontinuities, see David Bordwell, *Ozu and the Poetics of Cinema* (Princeton, N.J.: Princeton University Press, 1988).

Websites

www.editorsguild.com/v2/index.aspx/ A website
supporting *Editors Guild* magazine, with many articles
and interviews discussing editing in current films.

www.uemedia.com/CPC/editorsnet/ Offers articles on
contemporary problems of editing.

www.cinemetrics.lv/ Want to study cutting rhythms in a
movie of your choice? This nifty software allows you to
come up with a profile of editing rates.

Recommended DVD Supplements

Watching people editing is not very exciting, and this
technique usually gets short shrift in DVD supplements.
Each film in the *Lord of the Rings* trilogy, however, has
an "Editorial" section, and *The Fellowship of the Ring* includes an "Editorial Demonstration," juxtaposing the raw
footage from six cameras in an excerpt from the Council
of Elrond scene and showing how sections from each
were fitted together. (An instructive exercise in learning
to notice continuity editing would be to watch the Council of Elrond scene in the film itself with the sound turned
off. Here a complex scene with many characters is
stitched together with numerous correct eyeline matches
and occasional matches on action. Imagine how confusing the characters' conversations could have been if no
attention had been paid to eyeline direction.)

The DVD release of Lodge Kerrigan's *Keane* includes not only the theatrical version but a completely re-
cut version of the film by producer Steven Soderberg.
Soderberg calls his cut his "commentary track" for the
disc.

In "Tell Us What You See," the camera operator for
A Hard Day's Night discusses continuity of screen direction, and in "Every Head She's Had the Pleasure to
Know," the film's hairdresser talks about having to keep
hair length consistent for continuity.

"15-Minute Film School with Robert Rodriguez,"
one of the *Sin City* supplements, provides a clear instance
of the Kuleshov effect in use. Although Rodriguez does
not use that term, he demonstrates how he could cut together shots of characters interacting with each other via
eyeline matches even though several of the actors never
worked together during the filming.

A brief section of *Toy Story*'s supplements entitled
"Layout Tricks" demonstrates how continuity editing
principles are adhered to in animation as well as live-
action filming. In a shot/reverse-shot sequence involving
Buzz and Woody, the filmmakers diagram (as we do on
p. 235) where a camera can be placed to maintain the axis
of action (or "stage line," as it is termed here). The segment also shows how a camera movement can be used to
shift the axis of action just before an important character
enters the scene.

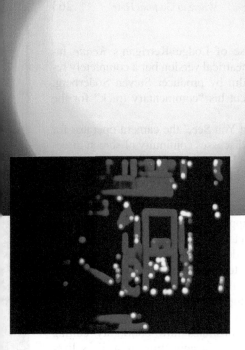

10

Documentary, Experimental, and Animated Films

Some of the most basic types of films line up as distinct alternatives. We commonly distinguish documentary from fiction, experimental films from mainstream fare, and animation from live-action filmmaking. In all these cases, we make assumptions about how the material to be filmed was chosen or arranged, how the filming was done, and how the filmmakers intended the finished work to affect the spectator. Chapter 3, on narrative form, drew its examples principally from fictional, live-action cinema. Now we'll explore these other important types of films.

Documentary

Before we see a film, we nearly always have some sense whether it is a documentary or a piece of fiction. Moviegoers entering theaters to view *March of the Penguins* expected to see real birds in nature, not wisecracking caricatures like the penguins in *Madagascar.*

What Is a Documentary?

What justifies our assumption that a film is a documentary? For one thing, a documentary typically comes to us identified as such—by its title, publicity, press coverage, word of mouth, and subject matter. This labeling leads us to expect that the persons, places, and events shown to us exist and that the information presented about them will be trustworthy.

Every documentary aims to present factual information about the world, but the ways in which this can be done are just as varied as for fiction films. In some cases, the filmmakers are able to record events as they actually occur. For example, in making *Primary,* an account of John Kennedy and Hubert Humphrey campaigning for the 1960 Democratic presidential nomination, the camera operator and sound recordist were able to closely follow the candidates through crowds at rallies (5.134). But a documentary may convey information in other ways as well. The filmmaker might supply charts, maps, or other visual aids. In addition, the documentary filmmaker may stage certain events for the camera to record.

It's worth pausing on this last point. Some viewers tend to suspect that a documentary is unreliable if it manipulates the events that are filmed. It is true that, very often, the documentary filmmaker records an event without scripting or staging it. For example, in interviewing an eyewitness, the documentarist typically controls where the camera is placed, what is in focus, and so on; the filmmaker likewise controls the final editing of the images. But the filmmaker doesn't tell the witness what to say or how to act. The filmmaker may also have no choice about setting or lighting.

Still, both viewers and filmmakers regard some staging as legitimate in a documentary if the staging serves the larger purpose of presenting information. Suppose you are filming a farmer's daily routines. You might ask him or her to walk toward a field in order to frame a shot showing the whole farm. Similarly, the cameraman who is the central figure in Dziga Vertov's documentary *Man with a Movie Camera* is clearly performing for Vertov's camera (**10.1**).

In some cases, staging may intensify the documentary value of the film. Humphrey Jennings made *Fires Were Started* during the German bombardment of London during World War II. Unable to film during the air raids, Jennings found a group of bombed-out buildings and set them afire. He then filmed the fire patrol battling the blaze (**10.2**). Although the event was staged, the actual firefighters who took part judged it an authentic depiction of the challenges they faced under real bombing. Similarly, after Allied troops liberated the Auschwitz concentration camp near the end of World War II, a newsreel cameraman assembled a group of children and had them roll up their sleeves to display the prisoner numbers tattooed on their arms. This staging of an action arguably enhanced the film's reliability.

Staging events for the camera, then, need not consign the film to the realm of fiction. Regardless of the details of its production, the documentary film asks us to assume that it presents trustworthy information about its subject. Even if the filmmaker asks the farmer to wait a moment while the camera operator frames the shot, the film suggests that the farmer's morning visit to the field is part of the day's routine, and it's this suggestion that is set forth as reliable.

As a type of film, documentaries present themselves as factually trustworthy. Still, any one documentary may not prove reliable. Throughout film history, many documentaries have been challenged as inaccurate. One controversy involved Michael Moore's *Roger and Me*. The film presents, in sequences ranging from the heartrending to the absurd, the response of the people of Flint, Michigan, to a series of layoffs at General Motors plants during the 1980s. Much of the film shows inept efforts of the local government to revive the town's economy. Ronald Reagan visits, a television evangelist holds a mass rally, and city officials launch expensive new building campaigns, including AutoWorld, an indoor theme park intended to lure tourists to Flint.

No one disputes that all these events took place. The controversy arose when critics claimed that *Roger and Me* leads the audience to believe that the events occurred in the *order* in which they are shown. Ronald Reagan came to Flint in 1980, the TV evangelist in 1982; AutoWorld opened in 1985. These events could not have been responses to the plant closings shown early in the film because the plant closings started in 1986. Moore falsified the actual chronology, critics charged, in order to make the city government look foolish.

Moore's defense is discussed in "Where to Go from Here" at the end of this chapter. The point for our purposes is that his critics accused his film of presenting unreliable information. Even if this charge were true, however, *Roger and Me* would not therefore turn into a fiction film. An unreliable documentary is still a documentary. Just as there are inaccurate and misleading news stories, so there are inaccurate and misleading documentaries.

A documentary may take a stand, state an opinion, or advocate a solution to a problem. As we'll see shortly, documentaries often use rhetoric to persuade an audience. But, again, simply taking a stance does not turn the documentary into fiction. In order to persuade us, the filmmaker marshals evidence, and this evidence

"There are lots of in-between stages from shooting to public projection—developing, printing, editing, commentary, sound effects, music. At each stage the effect of the shot can be changed but the basic content must be in the shot to begin with."

— Joris Ivens, documentary filmmaker

10.1 Although the central figure of *Man with a Movie Camera* is a real cinematographer, his actions were staged.

10.2 A staged blaze in *Fires Were Started*.

10.3 Older documentary footage of protective gear incorporated into *The Atomic Cafe.*

is put forth as being factual and reliable. A documentary may be strongly partisan, but as a documentary, it nonetheless presents itself as providing trustworthy information about its subject.

Types of Documentary

Like fiction films, documentaries have their own genres. One common genre is the *compilation* film, produced by assembling images from archival sources. *The Atomic Cafe* compiles newsreel footage and instructional films to suggest how 1950s American culture reacted to the proliferation of nuclear weapons (**10.3**). The *interview,* or *talking-heads,* documentary records testimony about events or social movements. *Word Is Out* consists largely of interviews with lesbians and gay men discussing their lives.

The *direct-cinema* documentary characteristically records an ongoing event as it happens, with minimal interference by the filmmaker. Direct cinema emerged in the 1950s and 1960s, when portable camera and sound equipment became available and allowed films such as *Primary* to follow an event as it unfolds. For this reason, such documentaries are also known as *cinéma-vérité,* French for "cinema-truth." An example is *Hoop Dreams,* which traces two aspiring basketball players through high school and into college.

Another common type is the *nature* documentary, such as *Microcosmos,* which used magnifying lenses to explore the world of insects. The Imax format has spawned numerous nature documentaries, such as *Everest* and *Galapagos.* With increasingly unobtrusive, lightweight equipment becoming available, the *portrait* documentary has also become prominent in recent years. This type of film centers on scenes from the life of a compelling person. Terry Zwigoff recorded the eccentricities of underground cartoonist Robert Crumb and his family in *Crumb.* In *American Movie,* Chris Smith followed the difficulties of a Milwaukee filmmaker struggling with budgetary problems and amateur actors to make a horror film (**10.4**).

10.4 Filmmaker Mark Borchardt and his friend Mike (on left) freely discussed their lives and projects with Chris Smith for *American Movie.*

Very often a documentary pursues several of these options at once. A film may mix archival footage, interviews, and material shot on the fly, as do *Fahrenheit 9/11, The Fog of War,* and *In the Year of the Pig.* This *synthetic* documentary format is also common in television journalism.

The Boundaries Between Documentary and Fiction

By contrast with documentary, we assume that a fictional film presents imaginary beings, places, or events. We take it for granted that Don Vito Corleone and his family never existed, and that their activities, as depicted in *The Godfather,* never took place. Bambi's mother did not really get shot by a hunter because Bambi, his mother, and their forest companions are imaginary.

If a film is fictional, that doesn't mean that it's completely unrelated to actuality. For one thing, not everything shown or implied by a fiction film need be imaginary. *The Godfather* alludes to World War II and the building of Las Vegas, both historical events; it takes place in New York City and in Sicily, both real locales. Nonetheless, the characters and their activities remain fictional, with history and geography providing a context for the made-up elements.

Fictional films are tied to actuality in another way: they often comment on the real world. *Dave,* about an imaginary U.S. president and his corrupt administration, criticizes contemporary political conduct. In 1943, some viewers took Carl Dreyer's *Day of Wrath,* a film about witch-hunts and prejudice in 17th-century Denmark, as a covert protest against the Nazis currently occupying the country. Through theme, subject, characterization, and other means, a fictional film can directly or obliquely present ideas about the world outside the film.

Sometimes our response to a fictional film is shaped by our assumptions about how it was made. The typical fictional film stages all or nearly all its events; they are designed, planned, rehearsed, filmed, and refilmed. The studio mode of production is well suited to creating fiction films, since it allows stories to be scripted and action to be staged until what is captured on film satisfies the decision makers. Similarly, in a fictional film, the characters are portrayed by actors, not photographed directly (as in a documentary). The camera films not Vito Corleone but Marlon Brando portraying the Don.

This assumption about how the film was made typically comes into play when we consider historical films or biographies. *Apollo 13* and *Schindler's List* base themselves on actual events, while *Malcolm X, Walk the Line, Nixon,* and other *biopics* trace episodes in the lives of people who really existed. Are these documentaries or fictional films? In practice, most such films add purely make-believe characters, speeches, or actions. But even if the films did not tamper with the record in this way, they would remain fictional according to our assumptions about how they were produced. Their events are wholly staged, and the historical agents are portrayed through actors' performances. In David Lynch's *The Straight Story,* the person photographed is actor Richard Farnsworth, not Alvin Straight himself. Like plays or novels based on real-life events, historical and biographical movies convey ideas about history by means of fictional portrayal.

Sometimes, however, the ways in which the images and sounds were produced will not distinguish sharply between a fiction film and a documentary. Documentaries may include shots of prearranged or staged events, while fictions can incorporate unstaged material. Some fictional films include newsreel footage to bolster their stories. Early in *The Road Warrior,* a sequence of shots from documentaries suggests an apocalyptic war that precedes the main story. Some filmmakers have made fictional films almost completely out of documentary footage. Craig Baldwin's *Tribulation 99: Alien Anomalies Under America* draws extensively on newsreel footage to present a conspiracy involving space aliens living within the earth and controlling international politics. As with documentary, the overall *purpose and point* of the fictional film—to present imaginary actions and events—govern how we will take even documentary footage seen within it.

As you might expect, filmmakers have sometimes sought to blur the lines separating documentary and fiction. A notorious example is Mitchell Block's *No Lies,* which purports to present an interview with a woman who has been raped. Audiences are typically disturbed by the woman's emotional account and by the callousness of the offscreen filmmaker questioning her. A final title, however, reveals that the film was scripted and that the woman was an actor. Part of Block's purpose was to show how the look and sound of *cinéma-vérité* documentary can elicit viewers' uncritical belief in what they are shown.

Most fake documentaries—a genre often referred to as *mockumentaries*—are not this serious. Often mock documentaries imitate the conventions of documentaries but do not try to fool audiences into thinking that they portray actual people or events. A classic case is Rob Reiner's *This Is Spinal Tap,* which takes the form of a behind-the-scenes documentary about a completely fictional rock band.

A film may fuse documentary and fiction in other ways. For *JFK,* Oliver Stone inserted compilation footage into scenes in which actors played historical figures such as Lee Harvey Oswald. Stone also staged and filmed the assassination of Kennedy in a pseudo-documentary manner. This material was then intercut with genuine archival footage, creating constant uncertainty about what was staged and what was filmed spontaneously. An even more extreme example is *Forrest Gump,* which uses special effects to allow its hero to meet John F. Kennedy, Lyndon Johnson, and Richard Nixon **(10.5)**.

Errol Morris's *The Thin Blue Line,* a documentary investigation into murder, mixes interviews and archival material with episodes performed by actors. The sequences, far from being the jittery reenactments of television true-crime shows, are shot with smooth camera work, dramatic lighting, and vibrant color **(10.6)**. Several of these staged sequences dramatize witnesses' alternative versions of how the crime took place. The result is a film that not only seeks to identify the real killer but also raises questions about how fact and fiction may intermingle. (See pp. 413–419.)

10.5   In *Forrest Gump,* computer-generated imagery allows the hero to meet President Kennedy.

10.6   Carefully composed shots such as this from *The Thin Blue Line* emphasize that some events have been reenacted.

10.45 Maya Deren's *Choreography for Camera* frames and cuts a dancer's movements . . .

Experimental Film

Another basic type of filmmaking is willfully nonconformist. In opposition to dominant, or mainstream, cinema, some filmmakers set out to create films that challenge orthodox notions of what a movie can show and how it can show it. These filmmakers work independently of the studio system, and often they work alone. Their films are hard to classify, but usually they are called *experimental* or *avant-garde.*

Experimental films are made for many reasons. The filmmaker may wish to express personal experiences or viewpoints in ways that would seem eccentric in a mainstream context. In *Mass for the Dakota Sioux,* Bruce Baillie suggests a despair at the failure of America's optimistic vision of history. Su Friedrich's *Damned If You Don't,* a story of a nun who discovers her sexuality, presents the theme of release from religious commitment. Alternatively, the filmmaker may seek to convey a mood or a physical quality (**10.45, 10.46**).

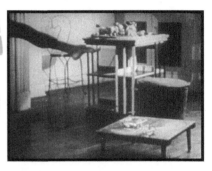

10.46 . . . to suggest graceful passage across different times and places.

The filmmaker may also wish to explore some possibilities of the medium itself. Experimental filmmakers have tinkered with the medium in myriad ways. They have presented cosmic allegories, such as Stan Brakhage's *Dog Star Man,* and highly private japes, as in Ken Jacobs's *Little Stabs at Happiness.* Robert Breer's *Fist Fight* experiments with shots only one or two frames long (6.124); by contrast, the shots in Andy Warhol's *Eat* last until the camera runs out of film. An experimental film might be improvised or built according to mathematical plan. For *Eigazuke (Pickled Film),* Japanese American Sean Morijiro Sunada O'Gara applied pickling agents to negative film and then handprinted the blotchy abstractions onto positive stock.

The experimental filmmaker may tell no story, creating poetic reveries such as Willard Maas's *Geography of the Body* (**10.47**) or pulsating visual collages such as *Ballet mécanique,* which serves as one of our main examples here. Alternatively, the filmmaker may create a fictional story, but it usually challenges the viewer. Yvonne Rainer's *Film About a Woman Who* . . . presents its narrative partly through a series of slides that a group of men and women are watching. At the same time, on the sound track, we hear anonymous voices carrying on a dialogue, but we cannot confidently assign any voice to a particular character. Rainer thus forces us to weigh everything we see and hear on its own terms, outside any involvement with characters (**10.48**).

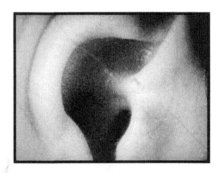

10.47 In *Geography of the Body,* an ear creates an abstract, lyrical composition.

Any sort of footage may be used for an avant-garde film. Images that a documentarist might take as fragments of actuality can be mobilized for quite different purposes (**10.49**). Bruce Conner pulls footage from travelogues and newsreels to create a sweeping image of the destruction of civilization in *A Movie* (pp. 365–370). Within the experimental mode, such scavenged works are often called *found-footage films.*

Experimentalists have also used staging to express distinct feelings or ideas (**10.50**). By superimposing different portions of a kitchen scene from a fiction film, Ivan Galeta's *Two Times in One Space* creates cycles of people splitting or drifting like phantoms. There is avant-garde animation as well, as in Breer's *Fuji* (pp. 375–377) and Red Grooms's *Tappy Toes* (**10.51**).

The freedom available to experimental film is on flamboyant display in Kenneth Anger's *Scorpio Rising.* Anger takes as his subject the motorcycle culture of the 1960s, and he includes scenes of bikers working on their machines, dressing,

"One of the things that goes on in Critical Mass (this is also true of much of the rest of my work and of the work by others I admire) is a process of training the spectator to watch the film."

— Hollis Frampton, experimental filmmaker

10.48   Thanks to Rainer's combination of images, sounds, and captions in *Film About a Woman Who . . .*, the viewer is left free to imagine several possible stories.

reveling, and racing. Alongside footage of bikers glimpsed on the streets or in parties, there are many staged incidents—chiefly around Scorpio, a James Dean figure. Anger also cuts in still photos, comic strips, old movies, and Nazi posters. In addition, each segment is accompanied by a rock-and-roll song that adds an ironic or ominous tone to the images. For example, as one young man fetishistically tunes up his bike, Anger shows the figure of death looming over him **(10.52)**, and on the sound track we hear, "My boyfriend's back . . . and he's coming after you." This sequence links biking to a death wish, an idea that returns in cartoons and other imagery. In such ways, *Scorpio Rising* creates elusive but powerful associations, suggesting the homoerotic dimensions of bike culture, comparing its rituals to fascism and Christianity, and evoking the possibility that people often model their behavior on images supplied by mass media.

Impossible to define in a capsule formula, avant-garde cinema is recognizable by its efforts at self-expression or experimentation outside mainstream cinema. Yet the boundary lines can be breached. Techniques associated with the avant-garde have been deployed in music videos by Michel Gondry and Chris Cunningham. In fact, Conner, Anger, Derek Jarman, and other experimentalists were early pioneers of music video. And mainstream features have been continually drawing on the avant-garde for ideas and techniques. Over the history of film, the basic modes have cross-fertilized each other constantly.

Types of Form in Experimental Films

Like documentaries, experimental films sometimes use narrative form. James Sibley Watson, Jr., and Melville Webber's 1928 film *The Fall of the House of Usher* evokes the atmosphere of the Edgar Allan Poe story through expressionistic sets and lighting. Occasionally, we find an experimental film organized by categories, as in Peter Greenaway's *The Falls,* a mockumentary tracing, in alphabetical order, information about a disparate group of people named Fall. Yet other types of form are characteristic of experimental films: abstract form and associational form.

Abstract Form

When we watch a film that tells a story, or surveys categories, or makes an argument, we usually pay little attention to the sheer pictorial qualities of the shots. Yet it is possible to organize an entire film around colors, shapes, sizes, and movements in the images.

How? Consider *Railroad Turnbridge,* by the sculptor Richard Serra. A turnbridge allows a section of railroad tracks to swivel on a central column, clearing space for tall boats passing along the river. Serra set up a camera at the center of a turnbridge and filmed the bridge's movement. The result onscreen is surprising. The bridge is swiveling, but because the camera is anchored to it, the crossed girders and powerful uprights seem monumentally static, and the landscape rotates majestically **(10.53)**. There is no argument, no survey of categories. A narrative film might have used the bridge for an exciting chase or fight, but Serra invites us to contemplate the bridge as a geometrical sculpture, all grids and angles, in relation to the curves and sweeps of nature beyond. Serra asks us to notice and enjoy the slowly changing pictorial qualities of line, shape, tonalities, and movement.

Of course, all films contain these qualities. We have seen how the lyrical beauty of the river and lake shots in *The River* functions to create parallels, and the rhythm of its musical score enhances our emotional involvement in the argument being made. But in *The River*, an abstract pattern becomes a means to an end, always subordinate to the rhetorical purposes of the film. It is not organized around abstract qualities but rather emphasizes such qualities only occasionally. In **abstract form**, the *whole* film's system will be determined by such qualities.

Abstract films are often organized in a way that we might call *theme and variations*. This term usually applies to music, where a melody or other type of motif is introduced, and then a series of different versions of that same melody follows—often with such extreme differences of key and rhythm that the original melody becomes difficult to recognize. An abstract film's form may work in a similar fashion. An introductory section will typically show us the kinds of relationships the film will use as its basic material. Then other segments will go on to present similar kinds of relationships but with changes. The changes may be slight, depending on our noticing that the similarities are still greater than the differences. But abstract films also usually depend on building up greater and greater differences from the introductory material. Thus we may find considerable contrast coming into the film, and sudden differences can help us to sense when a new segment has started. If the film's formal organization has been created with care, the similarities and differences will not be random. There will be some underlying principle that runs through the film.

The theme-and-variations principle is clearly evident in J. J. Murphy's *Print Generation.* Murphy selected 60 shots from home movies, then rephotographed them over and over on a contact printer. Each succeeding duplication lost photographic quality, until the final images became unrecognizable. *Print Generation* repeats the footage 25 times, starting with the most abstract images and moving to the most recognizable ones. Then the process is reversed, and the images gradually move back toward abstraction (**10.54, 10.55**). On the sound track, the progression is exactly the opposite. Murphy rerecorded the sound 25 times, but the film begins with the most clearly audible version. As the image clarifies, the sound deteriorates; as the image slips back into abstraction, the sound clarifies. Part of the fascination of this experimental film derives from seeing blobs and sparkles of abstract color become slowly defined as people and landscapes before passing back into abstraction. The film also teases us to discover its overall formal pattern.

As *Railroad Turnbridge* and *Print Generation* indicate, by calling a film's form abstract, we do not mean that the film has no recognizable objects in it. It is true that many abstract films use pure shapes and colors, created by the filmmaker by drawing, cutting out pieces of colored paper, animating clay shapes, and the like. There is an alternative approach, however, and that is to use real objects and to isolate them from their everyday context in such a way that their abstract qualities come forward. After all, shapes, colors, rhythmic movements, and every abstract quality that the filmmaker uses exist both in nature and in human-made objects. Markings on animals, bird songs, cloud formations, and other such natural phenomena often attract us because they seem beautiful or striking—qualities similar to those that we look for in artworks. Moreover, even those objects that we create for very practical and mundane uses may have pleasing contours or textures. Chairs are made to sit on, but we will usually try to furnish our home with chairs that also look attractive to us.

Because abstract qualities are common, experimental filmmakers often start by photographing real objects. But, since the filmmakers then juxtapose the images to create relations of shape, color, and so on, the film is still using abstract organization in spite of the fact that we can still recognize the object as a bird, a face, or a spoon. And, because the abstract qualities in films are shared with real objects, such films call on skills we use in everyday life. Normally, we use our ability to recognize shapes and colors in practical ways, as when we drive and have to interpret traffic signs and lights quickly. But, in watching an abstract film, we don't need to use the shapes, colors, or repetitions that we see and hear for practical purposes. Consequently, we can notice them more fully and see relationships that we would seldom bother to look for during the practical activities of everyday life. In a film, these abstract qualities become interesting for their own sake.

This impractical interest has led some critics and viewers to think of abstract films as frivolous. Critics may call them "art for art's sake," since all they seem to

> "Thematic interpretation comes from literature: it's been carried over to conventional narrative films, but it shouldn't be grafted onto experimental films, which are often a reaction against such conventions."
>
> — J. J. Murphy, experimental filmmaker

10.49 Gianfranco Baruchello's *La Verifica inserta* scavenges frames from old features to create a flicker film, here juxtaposing shots including telephones.

10.50   James Broughton's *Mother's Day* offers static pictures of adults playing children's games.

10.51   Pop-art painter Red Grooms animates cut-out figures to create the cheerful experimental film *Tappy Toes*.

10.52   Death imagery in *Scorpio Rising*.

10.53   The slowly changing background obliges the viewer to notice the symmetrical geometry of the bridge's design in *Railroad Turnbridge*.

10.54   Theme and variations in *Print Generation*: In earlier portions of the film, each one-second shot is more or less identifiable.

do is present us with a series of interesting patterns. Yet in doing so, such films often make us more aware of such patterns, and we may be better able to notice them in the everyday world as well. No one who has watched *Railroad Turnbridge* can see bridges in quite the same way afterward. In talking about abstract films, we might amend the phrase to "art for life's sake"—for such films enhance our lives as much as do the films of other formal types.

An Example of Abstract Form: *Ballet mécanique*   *Ballet mécanique* ("Mechanical Ballet"), one of the earliest abstract films, was also one of the most influential. It remains a highly enjoyable avant-garde film and a classic example of how mundane objects can be transformed when their abstract qualities are used as the basis for a film's form.

Two filmmakers collaborated on *Ballet mécanique* during 1923–1924. They were Dudley Murphy, a young American journalist and aspiring film producer, and Fernand Léger, a major French painter. Léger had developed his own distinctive version of Cubism in his paintings, often using stylized machine parts. His interest in machines transferred well into the cinema, and it contributed to the central formal principles of *Ballet mécanique*.

This title suggests the paradox the filmmakers employ in creating their film's thematic material and variations. We expect a ballet to be flowing, with human dancers performing it. A classical ballet seems the opposite of a machine's movements, yet the film creates a mechanical dance. Relatively few of the many objects we see in the film are actually machines; it mostly uses hats, faces, bottles, kitchen utensils and the like. But through juxtaposition with machines and through visual and temporal rhythms, we are cued to see even a woman's moving eyes and mouth as being like machine parts.

Film style plays a crucial role in most films using abstract form. Indeed, we often refer to the emphasis on abstract qualities of objects as *stylization*. In keeping with its overall formal design, *Ballet mécanique* uses film techniques to stress the geometric qualities of ordinary things. Close framing, masks, unusual camera angles, and neutral backgrounds isolate objects and emphasize their shapes and textures (**10.56**). This stylization enables the film to reverse our normal expectations about the nature of movement, making objects dance and turning human action into mechanical gestures.

We cannot segment *Ballet mécanique* by tracing its arguments or dividing it into scenes of narrative action. Rather, we must look for changes in abstract qualities being used at different points in the film. Going by this principle, we can find nine segments in *Ballet mécanique*:

C.   A credits sequence with a stylized, animated figure of Charlie Chaplin introducing the film's title (The word "Charlot" in this introduction is Chaplin's character's name in France.)

1. The introduction of the film's rhythmic elements.

2. A treatment of objects viewed through prisms.

3. Rhythmic movements.

4. A comparison of people and machines.

5. Rhythmic movements of intertitles and pictures.

6. More rhythmic movements, mostly of circular objects.

7. Quick dances of objects.

8. A return to Charlot and the opening elements.

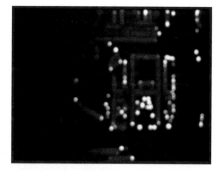

10.55 After many generations of reprinting, the same image becomes abstract, with hot highlights remaining. The color is biased toward red because that is the last layer of the emulsion to fade in rephotography.

Ballet mécanique uses the theme-and-variations approach in a complex way, introducing many individual motifs in rapid succession, then bringing them back at intervals and in different combinations. There is a definite pattern of development built from elements of the earlier segments. Each new segment picks up on a limited number of the abstract qualities from the previous one and plays with these for a while. The final segments use elements from early in the film once again, and the ending strongly echoes the opening. The film throws a great deal of material at us in a short time, and we must actively seek to make connections among motifs if we are to perceive the film's repetitions and variations.

As suggested previously, the introductory portion of an abstract film usually gives us strong cues as to what we can expect to see developed later. *Ballet mécanique*'s animated Chaplin begins this process **(10.57)**. Already we have the human figure as an object.

Segment 1 surprises us by beginning with a woman swinging in a garden **(10.58)**. Yet the film's title may lead us to notice the regular rhythm of the swinging and the puppetlike gestures as the woman repeatedly lifts her eyes and head, then lowers them, a fixed smile on her face. Certain abstract qualities already have become prominent. Suddenly, a rapid succession of images appears, passing too quickly for us to do any more than glimpse a hat, bottles, an abstract white triangle, and other objects. Next a woman's mouth appears, smiling, then not smiling, then smiling again. The hat returns, then the smiling mouth again, then some spinning gears, then a shiny ball circles close to the camera. Next we see the woman in the swing, and the camera moves back and forth with her—but now she is upside down **(10.59)**. This segment ends with the shiny ball, now swinging back and forth directly toward the camera, and we are invited to compare its movement with that of the woman in the swing. We are thus confirmed in our expectation that she is not a character but an object, like the bottle or the shiny ball. The same is true of that smiling mouth, which does not suggest an emotion as much as a regularly changing shape. Shapes of objects (a round hat, vertical bottles), direction of movement (the swing, the shiny ball), textures (the shininess of both the ball and the bottles), and the rhythms of the objects' movements and the changes from object to object will be qualities that the film calls to our attention.

10.56 A horse collar in *Ballet mécanique.*

10.57 In *Ballet mécanique,* the figure of Chaplin is highly abstract—recognizably human but also made up of simple shapes that move in a jerky fashion.

With these expectations set up in the short introductory section, the film goes on to vary its elements. Segment 2 sticks fairly closely to the elements just introduced by beginning with another view of the shiny ball, now seen through a prism. There follow other shots of household objects, similar to the ball in that they are also shiny and are seen through a prism **(10.60)**. Here is a good example of how a mundane object can be taken out of its everyday context and its abstract qualities used to create formal relations.

In the middle of the series of prism shots, we see a rapid burst of shots, alternating a white circle and a white triangle. This is yet another motif that will return at intervals, with variations. In a sense, these shapes, which are not recognizable objects, contrast with the kitchen utensils of the other shots. But they also invite us to make comparisons: the pot lid is also round whereas the prismatic facets are somewhat triangular. During the rest of segment 2, we see more prism shots, interspersed

10.58   The opening shot of *Ballet mécanique*'s first segment.

10.59   *Ballet mécanique.*

10.60   In *Ballet mécanique*, a prism shot is recognizable as a pot lid, its round shape picking up that of both the ball and the hat of the previous segment.

10.61   A masked shot in *Ballet mécanique.*

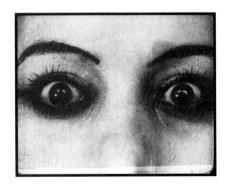

10.62   *Ballet mécanique:* a shot of a woman with open eyes.

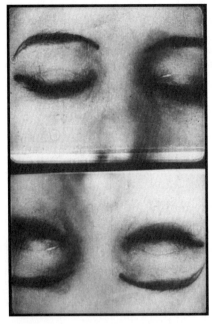

10.63   By the last frame of the same shot, her eyes are closed, and the first frame of the next shows her upside down.

with another rapid series of circles and triangles, and also with views of a woman's eyes opening and closing, a woman's eyes partially masked off by dark shapes (**10.61**), and finally the smiling/unsmiling mouth from segment 1.

Segment 2 has further confirmed our expectations that the film will concentrate on comparisons of shapes, rhythms, or textures. We also begin to see a pattern of surprising interruptions of the segments with brief bursts of short shots. In segment 1, interruptions were created by shots alternating objects and a single triangle. Now we have twice seen a circle and triangle alternate. The rhythm of editing is as important as the rhythm of movement within individual shots.

Already the film has established editing as a major tool for creating abstract relationships. *Ballet mécanique* provides a good example of how filmmakers may work outside the continuity editing system and create dynamic patterns of shots. One of the film's funniest moments comes in segment 2 and depends on a precise graphic match. We see an extreme close-up of a woman's wide-open eyes (**10.62**). She closes them, leaving her eyeliner and brows as dark crescents against her white skin (**10.63**). A cut presents us with the same composition, now upside down (10.63). The eyes and brows are in nearly identical positions, but reversed. When the eyes pop open (**10.64**), we're surprised to find their positions switched; the match is nearly indiscernible. The surprise is enhanced by a quick cutting rate that doesn't allow us to examine the shots closely. Amusing touches like this occur throughout *Ballet mécanique* and make it as enjoyable to watch today as it must have been when it was first shown 80 years ago.

Now that its basic patterns are well established, the film begins to introduce greater variations in order to complicate and sometimes overturn our expectations. Segment 3 begins with shots of rows of platelike discs, alternating with spinning shapes reminiscent of a fairground game wheel. Will round shapes and movements provide the main principle of development in this segment? Suddenly, the camera is plunging down a twisting fairground slide. We see elements such as marching

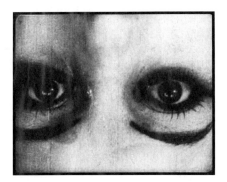

10.64   Later in the second shot, she opens her eyes.

10.65   In *Ballet mécanique,* a strongly horizontal composition is contrasted with . . .

10.66   . . . a strongly vertical one.

feet, cars going over the camera, and rapid shots of a carnival ride's cars spinning past. Here different rhythms succeed one another, and common shape seems less important. Relatively few of the elements from segments 1 and 2 return. We do not see the parts of the woman's face, and many of the objects are new ones, seen out of doors. Yet, after the carnival cars, we see a relatively lengthy shot of a spinning, shiny object—not in a prism view but at least recalling the image of the kitchen utensils seen earlier. The segment ends with the familiar rapid alternation of circle and triangle.

Segment 4 gives us the film's most explicit comparison of humans and machines. We first see a carnival slide from above, picking up on an element from segment 3 (though here the camera does not move down the slide). The slide stretches horizontally across the screen, and in quick succession a man's silhouette whizzes down it four times **(10.65)**. This may seem a continuation of segment 3's concentration on rhythm, but next we see a machine part, strongly vertical on the screen **(10.66)**, with a piston moving up and down rhythmically. Again we see similarities—a tubelike object with another object moving along it—and differences—the compositions use opposing directions, and the four movements of the man are shown in different shots, while the camera holds as the piston moves up and down within one shot. More shots compare the slide and machine parts, ending with one machine seen through a prism.

The familiar alternating circle and triangle return, but with differences: now the triangle is sometimes upside down, and each shape remains on the screen slightly longer. The segment continues with more spinning shiny objects and machine parts; then it reintroduces the motif of the woman's masked eye (similar to 10.61)**.** Now the motions of this eye are compared to machine parts.

Segment 4 closes with one of *Ballet mécanique*'s most famous and daring moments. After a shot of a rotating machine part **(10.67)**, we see 7 identically repeated shots of a laundry woman climbing a stair and gesturing **(10.68)**. The segment returns to the smiling mouth, then gives us 11 more repetitions of the same shot of the laundry woman, a shot of a large piston, and 5 more repetitions of the laundry woman shot. This insistent repetition makes the woman's movements as precise as those of the machine. Even though she is seen in a real place, we cannot see her as a character but must concentrate on her movements' rhythms. (The filmmakers have taken advantage of the cinema's own mechanical ability to multiply the same image.) Segment 4 is quite different from earlier ones, but it does bring back motifs: The prism recurs briefly (from segment 2), spinning shiny objects recall those of segment 3, and the woman's eyes and mouth (segments 1 and 2) return, having been absent from segment 3.

Segment 4 has been the culmination of the film's comparison of mechanical objects with people. Now segment 5 introduces a strong contrast by concentrating on printed intertitles. Unlike other segments, this one begins with a black screen,

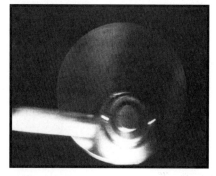

10.67   *Ballet mécanique* cuts from a machine part . . .

10.68   . . . to mechanical repetitions of a woman's movements.

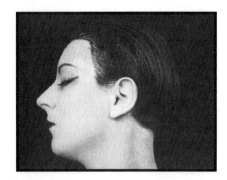

10.69 *Ballet mécanique*'s series of circular shapes begins with a woman's head, eyes closed, turning . . .

10.70 . . . after which we see a statue swing toward and away from the camera.

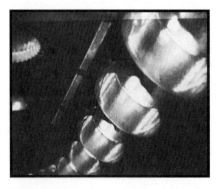

10.71 *Ballet mécanique:* a brief shot of kitchen utensils.

which is gradually revealed to be a dark card on which a white zero is painted. We see this first as a prismed shot (once again recalling segment 2). An unprismed view of the zero shows it shrinking.

Unexpectedly, an intertitle appears: "ON A VOLÉ UN COLLIER DE PERLES DE 5 MILLIONS" ("A pearl necklace worth 5 million has been stolen"). In a narrative film, this might give us story information, but the filmmakers use the printed language as one more visual motif for rhythmic variation. There follows a series of quick shots, with large zeros, sometimes one, sometimes three, appearing and disappearing, shrinking and growing. Parts of the intertitle appear in isolation ("on a volé"), participating in this dance of letters. The film plays with an ambiguity: is the zero really an "0," the first letter of the sentence, or is it part of the number 5,000,000, or is it a stylized representation of the pearl necklace itself? Beyond this sort of play with a visual pun, the zero recalls and varies the circle motif that has been so prominent in the film.

More punning occurs as the zero gives way to a picture of a horse collar—which resembles the zero visually but also refers to the word *collier* (which in French can mean either "necklace" or "collar"). Editing makes the collar bob about in its own little dance (10.56) and alternate with moving zeros and parts of the intertitle sentence, sometimes printed backward—to emphasize their graphic, rather than informative, function. This segment has been very different from earlier ones, but even here a couple of motifs are repeated. Just before the horse collar is introduced, we see the masked woman's eye briefly, and, in the course of the rapid flashes of intertitles, one tiny shot of a machine part is inserted.

After this point, the film begins to move toward variations that are closer to the elements of the opening segments. Segment 6 shows us rhythmic movements involving mostly circular shapes (**10.69, 10.70**). Once again the comparison of person and object comes forward. An abstract circular shape grows, cueing us to watch for the recurrence of this shape. A woman's face appears in a prismed view; she passes a piece of cardboard with holes cut in it before her face, with her expression continually changing in a mechanical fashion. We see the circles and triangles alternate again, but this time these shapes are presented in four different sizes. A quick series of shots of rows of shiny kitchen utensils follows (**10.71**), with short bursts of black film interspersed. This blackness picks up and varies the dark backgrounds of the intertitles in segment 5, and the shiny pots and other utensils reintroduce a motif that has appeared in every segment *except* 5. The motif of rows of objects had come in segment 3, while the swinging motion of the utensils in many of these shots echoes the swinging of the woman and the shiny ball from way back in segment 1. With this sequence and the next segment, the film's development is turning back toward its beginning.

Segment 7 begins with a shot of a display window (**10.72**). The circle motif returns, leading into a set of dances that vary key motifs. Very rapid editing makes a pair of mannequin legs dance (**10.73**); then the legs start to spin within the shots. The shiny ball motif returns, but now two balls spin in opposite directions. Then a hat and a shoe alternate quickly (**10.74**), and the editing creates a startlingly abstract effect. At first, we see the different shapes distinctly, but as the brief shots continue to alternate, we notice variations. The hat changes position, and sometimes the shoe points in one direction, sometimes the other. The cutting rhythm accelerates, and the shots become so short that we see only a single white object pulsating, morphing from circle to lozenge and back again. The filmmakers use the graphic contrasts they've created to make us aware of apparent motion, our tendency to see movement in a series of slightly different still pictures. This is one process that makes cinema itself possible. (See Chapter 1.)

After the shoe-and-hat duet, more shots of the woman follow, again cut to make her face execute a series of artificial shifts. Two slightly different views of a woman's face quickly alternate, inducing us to see the head as nodding (**10.75**). Finally, quick shots of bottles make them seem to change position in a dancelike rhythm. Interestingly, the motifs used in segment 7 come primarily from segments 1 and 2 (the shiny balls, hat, bottles) and from segment 6 (the prismed face, the growing circle). Here, where the mechanical ballet becomes most explicit, the film draws together elements from its beginning, and from the previous segment, where the recapitulation of the earlier segments had begun. Segment 7 avoids motifs from the center of the film—segments 3–5—and thus gives us a sense both that the film is continuing to develop and that it is coming full circle.

The final segment makes this return more obvious by showing us the Chaplin figure again. Now its movements are even less human, and at the end, most of its parts seem to fall away, leaving the head alone on the screen. The spinning head may remind us of the woman's profile (10.69) seen earlier. But the film is not quite over. Its last shot brings back the woman from the swing in segment 1, now standing in the same garden smelling a flower and looking around. Seen in another context, her gestures might seem ordinary to us **(10.76)**. But by now, the film has trained us sufficiently for us to make the connection between this shot and what has preceded it. Our expectations have been so strongly geared to seeing rhythmic, mechanical movement that we will probably see her smiles and head gestures as *unnatural*, like other motifs we have seen in the film. Léger and Murphy end their abstract film by emphasizing how much they have altered our perception of ordinary objects and people.

Associational Form

Many experimental films draw on a poetic series of transitions that create what we may term **associational form**. Associational formal systems suggest ideas and expressive qualities by grouping images that may not have any immediate logical connection. But the very fact that the images and sounds are juxtaposed prods us to look for some connection—an *association* that binds them together.

Godfrey Reggio's *Koyaanisqatsi* is a clear example of associational form. The film is built out of shots of widely different things—airplanes and buttes, subways and clouds, rockets and pedestrians. At one point, rows of frankfurters are pumped out of a machine and fed onto an assembly line. Reggio then cuts to fast-motion shots of commuters riding escalators. The juxtaposition has no narrative connection, and the pictorial qualities are not as strongly stressed as they would be in *Ballet mécanique.* Instead, the shots evoke the idea of impersonal, routine sameness, perhaps suggesting that modern life makes people into standardized units. The filmmaker has created an association among unlike things.

Koyaanisqatsi illustrates the unique qualities of associational form. The film surely presents a process, but it does not tell a story in the manner of narrative filmmaking. It offers no continuing characters, no specific causal connections, and no temporal order among the scenes. The film has a point, perhaps several, but it doesn't attempt to persuade us of it through an argument, giving reasons and offering evidence to lead us to a conclusion. There is no voice-over narrator as in *The River* to define problems and marshall evidence. Nor does the film explore a clear-cut set of categories. It centers on majestic nature and destructive technology, very loose and open-ended ideas. But *Koyaanisqatsi* is not purely a pictorial exercise either, in the manner of abstract form. The connections we make among its images sometimes involve visual qualities, but these qualities are associated with broader concepts and emotions.

This process is somewhat comparable to the techniques of metaphor and simile used in lyric poetry. When the poet Robert Burns says, "My love is like a red, red rose," we do not leap to the conclusion that his love is prickly to the touch, bright red, or vulnerable to aphids. Rather, we look for the possible conceptual links: her beauty is the most likely reason for the comparison.

A similar process goes on in associational films. Here the imagery and the metaphorical connections that poetry conveys through language are presented in a

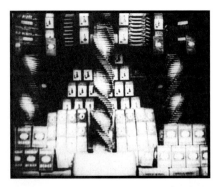

10.72 In *Ballet mécanique,* spiral shapes seem to freeze the gyrating motions that have made up so much of the film.

10.73 In *Ballet mécanique,* very short shots make mannequin legs "dance."

10.74   Shapes create graphic contrast in *Ballet mécanique.*

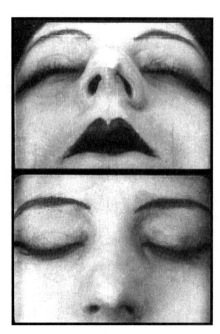

10.75   In *Ballet mécanique,* slight changes of composition make a face "nod."

10.76   The final shot of *Ballet mécanique.*

more direct fashion. A filmmaker could film a woman he loved in a garden and suggest by visual juxtaposition that she is like the flowers that surround her. (Indeed, this might be an implicit meaning that viewers could assign to *Ballet mécanique*'s last shot, if it were taken out of context.)

The imagery used in associational form may range from the conventional to the strikingly original, and the conceptual connections can be readily apparent or downright mystifying. These possibilities are not necessarily linked: A highly original juxtaposition might have an obvious emotional or conceptual implication. Again, poetry offers examples. Many religious, patriotic, romantic, and laudatory poems use strings of images to create an expressive tone. In "America the Beautiful," the images of "spacious skies," "purple mountains' majesty," and "fruited plain" add up to suggest the patriotic fervor expressed in the chorus, "God shed his grace on thee."

Another poem might be more elusive in its effect, giving us less explicit statements of the associative qualities of its imagery. The Japanese poetic form called *haiku* usually juxtaposes two images in a brief three-line form, in order to create an immediate emotion in the reader. Here, for example, is a haiku by Bashō:

> The eleventh moon—
> Storks listlessly
> Standing in a row

Bashō's images are somewhat cryptic and the purpose for connecting them somewhat mysterious. Yet, if we are willing to fill in with our imaginations, as one is supposed to do with haiku, the effect should be a mood, evoking autumnal stillness with perhaps a trace of melancholy. This tone isn't present in either the moon or the storks but results from the juxtaposition of the two images.

So far we have looked at associational form working at a fairly small-scale level: the side-by-side juxtaposition of images. Associational form also creates larger-scale patterns that can organize an entire film. Yet because associational formal systems are unlimited in their subjects and means of organization, it's impossible to define a conventional set of parts into which an associational film will fall. Some films will show us a series of amusing images, while others may offer us frightening ones. Still, we can make a start at understanding associational form by noticing that it usually accords with a few general principles.

First, the filmmaker typically groups images together in larger sets, each of which creates a distinct, unified part of the film. Each group of images can then contrast with other groups of images. This principle of grouping is also seen in abstract form, as our *Ballet mécanique* analysis shows. Second, as in other types of form, the film uses repeated motifs to reinforce associational connections. Third, associational form strongly invites interpretation, the assigning of general meanings to the film, as in the environmentalist implications of *Koyaanisqatsi*.

The associational small-scale connections, the distinct large-scale parts, the repeated motifs, the cues for interpretation—all these factors indicate that associational organization puts demands on the viewer. This is why so many filmmakers seeking to push the boundaries of form use associational patterns. Although associational form may use striking, original, even puzzling, juxtapositions, it may still elicit a fairly familiar emotion or idea. The explicit point of *Koyaanisqatsi* is not particularly subtle or novel. Here, as in many associational films, the purpose is to make a familiar emotion or concept vivid by means of new imagery and fresh juxtapositions.

Other associational films are more complex and evocative. The filmmaker will not necessarily give us obvious cues to the appropriate expressive qualities or concepts. He or she may simply create a series of unusual and striking combinations and leave it up to us to tease out their relations. Kenneth Anger's *Scorpio Rising,* for instance, explicitly associates motorcycle gangs with traditional religious groups and with Nazi violence, but it also suggests, more elusively, that gang regalia and rituals have homoerotic aspects. Like other sorts of film form, associational form can offer implicit as well as more explicit meanings.

An Example of Associational Form: A Movie   Bruce Conner's film *A Movie* illustrates how associational form can confront us with evocative and mysterious juxtapositions, yet can at the same time create a coherent film that has an intense impact on the viewer.

Conner made *A Movie,* his first film, in 1958. Like Léger, he worked in the visual and plastic arts and was noted for his *assemblage* pieces—collages built up of miscellaneous found objects. Conner takes a comparable approach to filmmaking. He typically uses footage from old newsreels, Hollywood movies, soft-core pornography, and the like. By working in the found-footage genre, Conner can juxtapose two shots from widely different sources. When we see the two shots together, we will strive to find some connection between them. From a series of juxtapositions, our activity can create an overall emotion or concept.

A Movie uses a musical accompaniment that helps establish these emotions and ideas. As with the images, Conner chose music that already existed: three portions of Respighi's well-known tone poem *The Pines of Rome.* The music is important to the film's form, since it has distinct sections. Moreover, the overall tone of each segment is different, corresponding to the music. The beginning of what we'll identify as segment 3, showing women carrying totems, the crash of the Hindenburg dirigible, and some daring acrobats, gains its ominous effect largely from the eerie score. Likewise, the driving music accompanying segment 4 sweeps a string of horrendous disasters into one plunging apocalyptic rush. Conner's use of *The Pines of Rome* shows vividly how associational form can create both general ideas and strong emotional effects.

We can break *A Movie* into four large-scale segments. Each segment consists of related images, marked off from other segments by a shared expressive idea and by a distinct musical accompaniment.

1. An introductory portion with the film's title and director's name and projectionists' markings.

2. Quick, dynamic music with images of moving animals and vehicles on land.

3. A more mysterious, tense section stressing precariously balanced objects in air and water.

4. Frightening images of disaster and war interspersed with more lyrical, mysterious scenes.

In only 12 minutes, *A Movie* leads us through a range of emotionally charged ideas and qualities. It also creates a distinct developmental thread. In segments 2–4, many shots emphasize accidents or aggressive actions, and while some of these seem funny or trivial at first, they gradually accumulate and become more serious. By segment 4, a series of war scenes and natural disasters presents practically an apocalyptic vision. *A Movie*'s tone finally eases in its closing underwater scenes.

Segment 1   This segment does far more than give us the title and the filmmaker's name, and for that reason, we have numbered it as the first segment rather than separating it off as a credits sequence. At first, we see blank black leader, over which the quick opening of *The Pines of Rome* begins. This stresses the importance of the music in the film, since we hear it before seeing any images. Then the words "Bruce Conner" appear, remaining on the screen for many seconds. Because we do not need that much time to read the name, we may begin to sense that the film will playfully thwart our expectations.

After the name, we see more black leader, then white leader, then a quick flicker effect rapidly alternating two frames of the word "A" with a blank white leader, and finally the word "Movie." The word "By" appears, with more white frames, then "Bruce Conner," as before. Now a black leader appears, with markings that usually appear on the first portion of the film strip but that are seldom projected on the screen for the audience to see: splice cues, dots, and other signs. Then, suddenly, "End of Part Four" flashes on the screen.

We might think that Conner is simply playing with the graphic qualities of titles and leader marks, as Léger and Murphy did in segment 5 of *Ballet mécanique* with its dance of intertitles and zeros. But here Conner uses graphics with conventional meanings: Leaders and credits usually signal the beginning, while "End of Part Four" implies we have already seen a considerable part of the film. Once again *A Movie* signals us that it will not be an ordinary film—not one in which the parts follow in logical order. We must expect odd juxtapositions. Moreover, the flicker and leader markings stress the physical qualities of the film medium itself. The title *A Movie* reinforces this reference to the medium, cueing us to watch this assemblage of shots *as* bits of film.

The opening continues with a countdown leader, beginning with "12" and flashing other numbers at one-second intervals—again, more signals to the projectionist, but seldom seen by the audience. Is *this* the beginning, then? But after "4," we are startled to see the film's first moving image: a "nudie" shot of a woman taking off her stockings. The shot is very worn, with lines and scratches, and we surmise that Conner scavenged it from an old stag film. Here *A Movie* helps us to focus our expectations by suggesting that it will involve more found footage of this type. After the nude shot, the countdown leader continues to "1," then the words "The End" appear. Another joke: this is the end of the leader, not of the film. Yet even this is untrue, since more leader appears, with "Movie" backward, more projectionists' signals, and a repeating number "1" that flickers in time to the music's quick tempo, then goes to black.

Segment 2   Although the music runs continuously over the transition, in segment 2, we begin to see a very different kind of image. A series of 12 shots shows us mounted Indians sitting on a hill, then chasing a fleeing wagon train, with Hopalong Cassidy recognizable as one of the cowboys. More old film footage follows, this time a clip suggesting a story situation that will continue from shot to shot: a fight between Indians and settlers. But Conner shows us this scene only to refer

"Part of the creation of the sequence you're thinking about happened during the process of collecting film. I snip out small parts of films and collect them on a larger reel. Sometimes when I tail-end one bit of the film onto another, I'll find a relationship that I would have never thought about consciously—because it doesn't create a logical continuity, or it doesn't fit my concept of how to edit a film."

— Bruce Conner, experimental filmmaker

briefly to the conventional kind of movie he is *not* making (**10.77, 10.78**). The association here seems clear enough; we move from horses to more horses, all in rapid motion. The next change, moving toward imagery of cavalry, confirms this association among horse-drawn vehicles.

There follows a shaky shot of a charging elephant. Now we must stretch our associations to account for this: maybe the link is through a series of rapidly moving animals? This seems safe enough to assume, as we see two more shots of horses' running legs. But the next shot shows a speeding locomotive's wheels. We must generalize the terms of the association still further—the rapid motion of animals and vehicles on land. (The "on land" idea may not seem important at this point, but it will become significant in contrast to the later segments, which often emphasize air and water.) The next series of shots, repeating these motifs and introducing a military tank, seems to confirm this overall idea of rushing movement.

Conner's editing creates the effect of one rushing mass of activity by a simple convention: common screen direction. The animals and vehicles move from left to right, or come directly at the camera, creating shots that cut together in traditional continuity (10.77, 10.78). The effect is to suggest a colossal rush toward a single target. The impossibility of this juxtaposition is amusing, but it also suggests that humans, animals, and machines are caught up in an energetic planetary race—but toward what? The urgency of this sequence is heightened by graphic matches on objects hurtling out at the viewer (**10.79, 10.80**).

This sense of rapid activity continues into the later part of segment 2, which moves from the tank to a series of shots of race cars speeding around tracks. Since these shots initially confirm our expectations about moving animals and vehicles, they are less challenging to us—at first. Then one race car crashes, followed by two other similar crashes; and the segment ends with the long, spectacular fall of an old-fashioned car off a cliff. The sense of movement has become less funny and exhilarating, more uncontrolled and frightening. The tone of amusement has shifted toward one based on shock and horror in the face of so much devastation. Again, this effect is created by tight coordination of cutting, music, and movement in the frame. For instance, the frenzied buildup in the musical score accompanies the string of race car crashes. Blaring, dissonant phrases begin to punctuate the music at regular intervals, and Conner's editing times each one to coincide with a car crash. The manic energy of the tumultuous race has turned reckless and self-destructive.

During the crashes, the music has built up to a frenzied climax, and it cuts off abruptly as a "The End" title flashes on the screen. This parody of the ending of a conventional film suggests that the crashes have resulted from all that rushing motion earlier in the segment. At this point, we might begin to sense that there has been an underlying tone of aggression and danger from the start: the attacking Indians, the cavalry, the charging elephant, the tank, and so on. This element will be intensified in segments 3 and 4.

Segment 3   More black leader continues the transition set up by the "The End" title, and there is a pause before the music of segment 3 begins. (As at the film's opening, it plays at first over the darkness.) But this time the music is slow, bleak, and slightly ominous. The "Movie" title and more black leader move us into a series of shots very different from those of segment 2. Two Polynesian women carry large, totemlike objects on their heads. Leader and a title interrupt once more, introducing a short series of shots of a large dirigible in flight (**10.81**) and of an acrobat couple performing on a small platform and tightrope high above a street (**10.82**). If the women and the dirigible are associated through balancing, the dirigible is linked to the acrobats not only by that but also by an emphasis on heights and danger. This portion of the segment ends with a shot of a small plane plunging downward through fleecy clouds, as if, having lost its balance, it is falling. Slow, sinister music has cued us how to react to these floating and falling objects; without the music, we might take

10.77   In *A Movie,* from a shot of galloping horses pulling a wagon, Conner cuts to . . .

10.78   . . . similar horses, but now pulling a fire engine on a city street.

10.79   A graphic match in *A Movie* links wagon . . .

10.80   . . . and tank.

10.81   *A Movie:* images of heights . . .

10.82   . . . and danger.

10.83   An inexplicably grotesque image from *A Movie.*

10.84   In this puzzling shot from *A Movie,* Roosevelt speaks vigorously, seemingly angry, with bared teeth.

them to be lyrical, but in context, they suggest a vague threat. This passage ends with more titles: "A," "Movie," "By," and "Bruce Conner," followed by black leader.

The next part of the segment begins with an apparent incongruity between music and image. A series of shots shows parts of a submarine, including an officer looking through a periscope (6.38). The next shot seems to suggest that he sees a bikini-clad woman (6.39). This shot picks up the stag film motif from segment 1 and points out the paradox of this juxtaposition. We know the shots of the officer and the woman come from different films—yet, at the same time, we cannot help but interpret the shots as showing him looking at her, and thus we find the moment comic. As earlier parts of the film reminded us of endless credit sequences, perhaps this makes fun of point-of-view editing and the Kuleshov effect.

The same principle underlies the next shots, as the officer orders a torpedo fired, and we see it seeming to race toward the woman, creating a sexual pun. This, too, is funny, as is the atomic-bomb orgasm that seems to result. But, as in the first segment, there is an overtone of threat and aggression—now specifically sexual aggression—in these images. They move quickly from humor to disaster as additional mushroom cloud shots undercut the joke. Moreover, the music that plays through the submarine–woman series is slow, quiet, and ethereal—*not* appropriate to the erotic joke, but more suited to the images of the bomb blasts.

This music carries us into a series of shots of waves and wavelike movements that seem to result from the bomb: a ship engulfed by fog or smoke, surfers and rowing teams battered by heavy waves, water-skiers and motorboaters falling during stunts. During this, the music's ethereal quality gives way to a slow melody with a dynamic tempo, played on low stringed instruments; this creates a more ominous tone. The first accidents seem trivial, as when water-skiers fall over. But gradually things become more disturbing. A motorboat driver plows into a pile of debris and is hurled out.

Abruptly, people are seen riding odd bicycles **(10.83)**. The move from the boat to the bikes takes us briefly away from the accident series to a string of shots showing people deliberately doing things that look grotesque. Additional shots show motorcyclists riding through mud and water, and a plane, trying to land on a lake and flipping over.

The whole segment has developed steadily, introducing tension at the beginning and then juxtaposing the humorous (the submarine–woman scene) with the disastrous (the bomb) and trivial accidents with grotesque actions. The sequence ends in an odd way: black leader appears after the plane crash, with the music building up toward a climax. This is followed by a close view of Theodore Roosevelt speaking vigorously, seemingly angry, with bared teeth **(10.84)**. Immediately, there follows a shot of a collapsing suspension bridge, with the music swelling up as the pieces fall **(10.85)** and then fading down. Although these shots are difficult to interpret, the association of human-caused disasters with one of America's most belligerent presidents would seem to link even the toppling bridge to human, especially political, aggression.

Segment 4   Once more *A Movie* marks off its segments clearly, with black leader again accompanying the opening of the third portion of *The Pines of Rome.* An eerie gong and low, slow chords create a distinctly ominous mood. Segments 2 and 3 both built up toward accidents and disasters. Now segment 4 begins with a series of images of military planes being shot out of the sky and firing on the ground, followed by a series of explosions against a dark sky.

Yet the next passage juxtaposes shots of disasters with some shots that are inexplicable in this context. All the images of planes and explosions seem associated with war and disaster. Now we see two planes flying past an Egyptian pyramid **(10.86)**. As with so many of the earlier juxtapositions, we must abruptly switch our assumptions about how these shots relate to one another, since now we see *nonmilitary* planes. But immediately, two shots of an erupting volcano appear. Clearly, the connection between them and the previous shot is mainly created by the pictorial similarity of mountains and pyramids. Are we back to disasters again? Seemingly not, for we next see an elaborate church ceremony, and all our expectations are thwarted. But the disaster motif returns as strongly as ever: the burning dirigible *Hindenburg,* tanks, more race car crashes, and tumbling bodies.

All these images create tension, but the next shots we see are of people parachuting from a plane. Interestingly, this action is not threatening, and the people here are not hurt. Yet in the context of the earlier accidents, and because of the ominous music, we have begun to expect some sort of disaster as the likeliest subject of each shot. Now even these innocent actions seem threatening and again may be seen as linked to military and political aggression.

10.85   A collapsing bridge in *A Movie.*

The next series of shots is equally innocent in itself but takes on mysterious and ominous overtones as part of the overall segment. We see a burning balloon floating to earth, reminding us of the floating dirigible and *Hindenburg* footage. Shots of palm trees, cattle, and other images follow, suggesting some idyllic Middle Eastern or African setting **(10.87).** This brief respite, however, leads into one of the film's eeriest and most striking moments: three shots of a suspension bridge writhing and buckling as if shaken by a giant hand **(10.88).** This is followed by the most intense disaster images in the whole film, including the burning *Hindenburg:* a sinking ship **(10.89),** a firing-squad execution, bodies hanging on a scaffold, dead soldiers, and a mushroom cloud. A shot of a dead elephant and hunters introduces a brief series of shots of suffering Africans. The music has built up during this, becoming steadily less ominous and more triumphant with fanfares of brass instruments.

10.86   *A Movie.*

After the climactic series of disaster shots, the tone shifts one more time. A relatively lengthy series of underwater shots follows a scuba diver. He explores a sunken wreck encrusted with barnacles **(10.90).** It recalls the disasters just witnessed, especially the sinking ship (10.89). The music builds to a triumphant climax as the diver swims into the ship's interior. The film ends on a long-held musical chord over more black leader and a final shot looking up toward the surface of the sea. Ironically, there is no "The End" title at this point.

A Movie has taken us through its disparate footage almost entirely by means of association. There is no argument about why we should find these images disturbing or why we should link volcanoes and earthquakes to sexual or military aggression. There are no categorical similarities between many of the things juxtaposed and no story told about them. Occasionally, Conner does use abstract qualities to compare objects, but this is only a small-scale strategy, not one that organizes the whole film.

10.87   A brief moment of peace in *A Movie.*

In building its associations, *A Movie* uses the familiar formal principles of repetition and variation. Even though the images come from different films, certain elements are repeated, as with the series of horse shots in segment 1 or the different airplanes. These repetitions form motifs that help unify the whole film.

Moreover, these motifs return in a distinct pattern. We have seen how the titles and leader of the opening come back in some way in all the segments and how the "nudie" shot of segment 1 is similar to the one used with the submarine footage in segment 3. Interestingly, not a single motif that appears in segment 2 returns in segment 3, creating a strong contrast between the two. But then segment 4 picks up and varies many of the motifs of both 2 and 3. As in so many films, the ending thus seems to develop and return to earlier portions. The dead elephant, the tanks, and the race cars all hark back to the frantic race of segment 2, while the tribal people, the *Hindenburg* disaster, the planes, the ships, and the bridge collapse all continue motifs begun in 3. The juxtapositions that have obvious links play on repetition, while startling and obscure ones create contrast. Thus Conner has created a unified work from what would seem to be a disunified mass of footage.

10.88   *A Movie:* a frightening image of a buckling bridge.

The pattern of development is also strikingly unified. Segment 1 is primarily amusing, and a sense of play and exhilaration also carries through most of

10.89   *A Movie:* more disasters as a ship sinks.

10.90   A *Movie:* the diver in the final scene.

segment 2, up to the car crashes. But we have seen that the subjects of all the shots in segment 2 could also suggest aggression and violence, and they all relate in some way to the disasters to come. Segment 3 makes this more explicit but uses some humor and playfulness as well. By segment 4, the mixture of tones has largely disappeared, and an intensifying sense of tension and doom replaces it. Now even odd or neutral events seem ominous.

Unlike the more clear-cut *Koyaanisqatsi, A Movie* withholds explicit meanings. Still, *A Movie*'s constantly shifting associations invite us to reflect on a range of implicit meanings. From one standpoint, the film can be interpreted as presenting the devastating consequences of unbridled aggressive energy. The horrors of the modern world—warfare and the hydrogen bomb—are linked with more trivial pastimes, such as sports and risky stunts. We are asked to reflect on whether both may spring from the same impulse, perhaps a kind of death wish. This impulse may, in turn, be tied to sexual drives (the pornographic motif) and political repression (the recurring images of people in developing countries).

Another interpretation might see the film as commenting on how cinema itself stirs our emotions through sex, violence, and exotic spectacle. In this sense, *A Movie* is "a movie" like any other, with the important difference that its thrills and disasters are actual parts of our world.

What of the ending? The scuba diver epilogue also offers a wide range of implicit meanings. It returns to the beginning in a formal sense: along with the Hopalong Cassidy segment, it is the longest continuous action we get. It might offer a kind of hope, perhaps an escape from the world's horrors. Or the images may suggest humankind's final death. After despoiling the planet, the human can only return to the primeval sea. Like much of *A Movie,* the ending is ambiguous, saying little but suggesting much. Certainly, we can say that it serves to relax the tension aroused by the mounting disasters. In this respect, it demonstrates the power of an associational formal system: its ability to guide our emotions and to arouse our thinking simply by juxtaposing different images and sounds.

PART SIX

FILM HISTORY

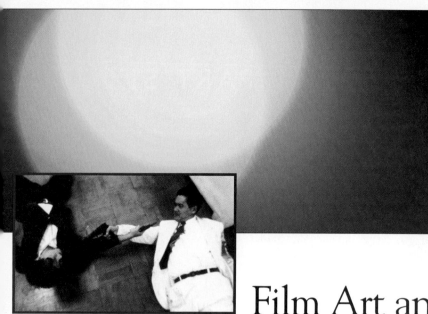

Film Art and Film History

"N ot everything is possible at all times." This aphorism of art historian Heinrich Wölfflin might serve as a slogan for our final chapter. So far, our survey of film art has examined various formal and stylistic possibilities, and we've drawn our examples from the entire range of film history. But film forms and techniques don't exist in a timeless realm, equally accessible to all filmmakers. In particular historical circumstances, certain possibilities are present while others are not. Griffith could not make films as Godard does, nor could Godard make films as Griffith did. This chapter asks, What are some ways in which film art has been treated in particular historical contexts?

These contexts will be defined, first by period and then by nation. Although there are other equally good tools for tracing change, period and nation remain useful ways of organizing historical problems. Second, in some of our cases, we'll look for what are typically called *film movements*. A film movement consists of two elements:

1. Films that are produced within a particular period and/or nation and that share significant traits of style and form

2. Filmmakers who operate within a common production structure and who share certain assumptions about filmmaking

There are other ways of defining a historical context (for example, biographical study, genre study), but the category of *movement* corresponds most closely to the emphasis of this book. The concepts of formal and stylistic systems permit us to compare films within a movement and to contrast them with films of other movements.

Our range of choice will be narrowed still further. We're concerned with Hollywood and selected alternatives. We'll trace the development of the commercial narrative cinema while contrasting it to other approaches to style and form.

Since a film movement consists of not only films but also the activities of specific filmmakers, we must go beyond noting stylistic and formal qualities. For each period and nation, we'll also sketch relevant factors that affect the cinema. These factors include the state of the film industry, artistic theories held by the filmmakers themselves, pertinent technological features, and cultural and economic elements. These factors necessarily help explain how a particular movement began, what shaped its development, and what affected its decline. This material will also provide a context for particular films we've already discussed; for example, the following section on early cinema situates Lumière and Méliès in their period.

Needless to say, what follows is drastically incomplete. The writing of serious film history is in its early stages, and we must often rely on secondary sources that will eventually be superseded. This chapter reflects only current states of knowledge; there are doubtless important films, filmmakers, and movements that await discovery. Moreover, there are many unfortunate omissions. Important filmmakers who don't relate to a movement (for example, Tati, Bresson, and Kurosawa) are absent, as are certain important film movements, such as French populist cinema of the 1930s and Brazil's Cinema Nôvo movement of the early 1960s. What follows simply seeks to show how certain possibilities of film form and style were explored within a few typical and well-known historical periods.

Early Cinema (1893–1903)

In order to create the illusion of movement, still pictures must appear in rapid succession. To prepare them and display them at the right rate, certain technologies are necessary. Most basically, there must be a way of recording a long series of images on some sort of support. In principle, one could simply draw a string of images on a strip of paper or a disc. But photography offered the cheapest and most efficient way to generate the thousands of images needed for a reasonably lengthy display. Thus the invention of photography in 1826 launched a series of discoveries that made cinema possible.

Early photographs required lengthy exposures (initially hours, later minutes) for a single image; this made photographed motion pictures, which need 12 or more frames per second, impossible. Faster exposures, of about $1/25$ second, became possible by the 1870s, but only on glass plates. Glass plates weren't usable for motion pictures since there was no practical way to move them through a camera or projector. In 1878, Eadweard Muybridge, an American photographer, did make a series of photographs of a running horse by using a series of cameras with glass plate film and fast exposure, but he was primarily interested in freezing phases of an action, not re-creating the movement by projecting the images in succession.

In 1882, another scientist interested in analyzing animal movement, the Frenchman Étienne-Jules Marey, invented a camera that recorded 12 separate images on the edge of a revolving disc of film on glass. This constituted a step toward the motion picture camera. In 1888, Marey built the first camera to use a strip of flexible film, this time on paper. Again, the purpose was only to break down movement into a series of stills, and the movements photographed lasted a second or less.

In 1889, George Eastman introduced a crude flexible film base, celluloid. Once this base was improved and camera mechanisms had been devised to draw the film past the lens and expose it to light, the creation of long strips of frames became possible.

Projectors had existed for many years and had been used to show slides and other shadow entertainments. These magic lanterns were modified by the addition of shutters, cranks, and other devices to become early motion picture projectors.

One final device was needed if films were to be projected. Since the film stops briefly while the light shines through each individual frame, there had to be a mechanism to create an *intermittent* motion of the film. Marey used a Maltese cross gear on his 1888 camera, and this became a standard part of early cameras and projectors.

The combination of a flexible and transparent film base, a fast exposure time, a mechanism to pull the film through the camera, an intermittent device to stop the film, and a shutter to block off light was achieved by the early 1890s. After several

12.1   The Kinetoscope held film in a continuous loop threaded around a series of bobbins.

12.2   Placing a magic lantern behind the Lumière camera turned it into a projector.

years, inventors working independently in many countries had developed different film cameras and projection devices. The two most important firms were the Edison Manufacturing Company in America, owned by inventor Thomas A. Edison, and Lumière Frères in France, the family firm of Louis and Auguste Lumière.

By 1893, Thomas A. Edison's assistant, W.K.L. Dickson, had developed a camera that made short 35mm films. Interested in exploiting these films as a novelty, Edison hoped to combine them with his phonograph to show sound movies. He had Dickson develop a peep-show machine, the *Kinetoscope* (**12.1**), to display these films to individual viewers.

Since Edison believed that movies were a passing fad, he did not develop a system to project films onto a screen. This was left to the Lumière brothers. They invented their own camera independently; it exposed a short roll of 35mm film and also served as a projector (**12.2**). On December 28, 1895, the Lumière brothers held one of the first public showings of motion pictures projected on a screen, at the Grand Café in Paris.

There had been several earlier public screenings, including one on November 1 of the same year, by the German inventor Max Skladanowsky. But Skladanowsky's bulky machine required two strips of wide-gauge film running simultaneously and hence had less influence on the subsequent technological development of the cinema. Although the Lumières didn't wholly invent cinema, they largely determined the specific form the new medium was to take. Edison himself was soon to abandon Kinetoscopes and form his own production company to make films for theaters.

The first films were extremely simple in form and style. They usually consisted of a single shot framing an action, usually at long-shot distance. In the first film studio, Edison's Black Maria (**12.3**), vaudeville entertainers, famous sports figures, and celebrities (for example, Annie Oakley) performed for the camera. A hinged portion of the roof opened to admit a patch of sunlight, and the entire building turned on a circular rail (visible in 12.3) to follow the sun's motion. The Lumières, however, took their cameras out to parks, gardens, beaches, and other public places to film everyday activities or news events, as in their *Arrival of a Train at La Ciotat* (5.61).

Until about 1903, most films showed scenic places or noteworthy events, but narrative form also entered the cinema from the beginning. Edison staged comic

12.3   The hinged portion of the Black Maria's roof, at the center, swung open for filming.

scenes, such as one copyrighted 1893 in which a drunken man struggles briefly with a policeman. The Lumières made a popular short *L'Arroseur arrosé* (*The Waterer Watered*, 1895), also a comic scene, in which a boy tricks a gardener into squirting himself with a hose (4.7).

After the initial success of the new medium, filmmakers had to find more complex or interesting formal properties to keep the public's interest. The Lumières sent camera operators all over the world to show films and to photograph important events and exotic locales. But after making a huge number of films in their first few years, the Lumières reduced their output, and they ceased filmmaking altogether in 1905.

In 1896, Georges Méliès purchased a projector from the British inventor Robert William Paul and soon built a camera based on the same mechanism. Méliès's first films resembled the Lumières' shots of everyday activities. But as we have seen (pp. 113–115), Méliès was also a magician, and he discovered the possibilities of simple special effects. In 1897, Méliès built his own studio. Unlike Edison's Black Maria, Méliès's studio was glass-sided like a greenhouse, so that the studio did not have to move with the sun (**12.4**).

Méliès also began to build elaborate settings to create fantasy worlds within which his magical transformations could occur. We have already seen how Méliès thereby became the first master of mise-en-scene technique (4.3–4.6). From the simple filming of a magician performing a trick or two in a traditional stage setting, Méliès progressed to longer narratives with a series of tableaux. Each consisted of one shot, except when the transformations occurred. These were created by cuts designed to be imperceptible on the screen. He also adapted old stories, such as *Cinderella* (1899), or wrote his own. All these factors made Méliès's films extremely popular and widely imitated.

During this early period, films circulated freely from country to country. The French phonograph company Pathé Frères moved increasingly to filmmaking from 1901 on, establishing production and distribution branches in many countries. Soon it was the largest film concern in the world, a position it retained until 1914, when the beginning of World War I forced it to cut back production. In England, several entrepreneurs managed to invent or obtain their own filmmaking equipment and made scenics, narratives, and trick films from 1895 into the early years of the 20th century.

> "In conjuring you work under the attentive gaze of the public, who never fail to spot a suspicious movement. You are alone, their eyes never leave you. Failure would not be tolerated. . . . While in the cinema . . . you can do your confecting quietly, far from those profane gazes, and you can do things thirty-six times if necessary until they are right. This allows you to travel further in the domain of the marvellous."
>
> — George Méliès, magician and filmmaker

12.4 Méliès's glass-sided studio admitted sunlight from a variety of directions.

12.5 G. Albert Smith's *Santa Claus* (1898).

Members of the Brighton School (primarily G. Albert Smith and James Williamson), as well as others like Cecil Hepworth, shot their films on location or in simple open-air studios (as in **12.5**). Their innovative films circulated abroad and influenced other filmmakers. Pioneers in other countries invented or bought equipment and were soon making their own films of everyday scenes or fantasy transformations.

From about 1904 on, narrative form became the most prominent type of filmmaking in the commercial industry, and the worldwide popularity of cinema continued to grow. French, Italian, and American films dominated world markets. Later, World War I was to restrict the free flow of films from country to country, and Hollywood emerged as the dominant industrial force in world film production, contributing to the creation of distinct differences in the formal traits of individual national cinemas.

The Development of the Classical Hollywood Cinema (1908–1927)

Edison was determined to exploit the money-making potential of his company's invention. He tried to force competing filmmakers out of business by bringing patent-violation suits against them. One other company, American Mutoscope & Biograph, managed to survive by inventing cameras that differed from Edison's patents. Other firms kept operating while Edison fought them in court. In 1908, Edison cooperated with Biograph to bring these other companies under control by forming the Motion Picture Patents Company (MPPC), a group of 10 firms based primarily in Chicago, New York, and New Jersey. Edison and Biograph were the only stockholders and patent owners. They licensed other members to make, distribute, and exhibit films.

The MPPC never succeeded in eliminating its competition. Numerous independent companies were established throughout this period. Biograph's most important director from 1908 on, D. W. Griffith, formed his own company in 1913, as did other filmmakers. The United States government brought suit against the MPPC in 1912; in 1915, it was declared a monopoly.

Around 1910, film companies began to move permanently to California. Some historians claim that the independent companies fled west to avoid the harassment of the MPPC, but some MPPC companies also made the move. Among the advantages of Hollywood were the climate, which permitted shooting year-round, and the great variety of terrains—mountains, ocean, desert, city—available for location shooting. Soon Hollywood and other small towns on the outskirts of Los Angeles played host to film production.

The demand for films was so great that no single studio could meet it. This was one of the factors that had led Edison to accept the existence of a group of other companies, although he tried to control them through his licensing procedure. Before 1920, the American industry assumed the structure that would continue for decades: a few large studios with individual artists under contract and a peripheral group of small independent producers. In Hollywood, the studios developed a factory system, with each production under the control of the producer, who usually did not work on the actual making of the films. Even an independent director such as Buster Keaton, with his own studio, had a business manager and distributed his films through larger companies, first Metro and then United Artists.

Gradually, through the 1910s and 1920s, the smaller studios merged to form the large firms that still exist today. Famous Players joined with Jesse L. Lasky and then formed a distribution wing, Paramount. By the late 1920s, most of the major companies—MGM (a merger of Metro, Goldwyn, and Mayer), Fox Film Corporation (merged with 20th Century in 1935), Warner Bros., Universal, and Paramount—had been created. Though in competition with one another, these studios tended to cooperate to a degree, realizing that no one firm could satisfy the market.

"The cinema knows so well how to tell a story that perhaps there is an impression that it has always known how."

— André Gaudreault, film historian

Within this system of mass-production studios, the American cinema became definitively oriented toward narrative form. Early films had consisted primarily of tableaux or vaudeville skits (12.5). One of Edison's directors, Edwin S. Porter, made some of the first films to use principles of narrative continuity and development. Among these was *The Life of an American Fireman* (1903), which showed the race of the firefighters to rescue a mother and a child from a burning house. Although this film used several important classical narrative elements (a fireman's premonition of the disaster, a series of shots of the horse-drawn engine racing to the house), it still had not worked out the logic of temporal relations in cutting. Thus we see the rescue of a mother and her child twice, from both inside and outside the house. Porter had not realized the possibility of intercutting the two locales within the action or matching on action to convey narrative information to the audience.

In 1903, Porter made *The Great Train Robbery,* in some ways a prototype for the classical American film. Here the action develops with a clear linearity of time, space, and logic. We follow each stage of the robbery (**12.6**), the pursuit, and the final defeat of the robbers. In 1905, Porter also created a simple parallel narrative in *The Kleptomaniac,* contrasting the fates of a rich woman and a starving woman who are both caught stealing.

British filmmakers were working along similar lines. Indeed, many historians now believe that Porter derived some of his editing techniques from films such as James Williamson's *Fire!* (1901) and G. A. Smith's *Mary Jane's Mishap* (1903). The most famous British film of this era was Lewin Fitzhamon's 1905 film *Rescued by Rover* (produced by a major British firm, Cecil Hepworth), which treated a kidnapping in a linear fashion similar to that of *The Great Train Robbery.* After the kidnapping, we see each stage of Rover's journey to find the child, his return to fetch the child's father, and their retracing of the route to the kidnapper's lair. All the shots along the route maintain consistent screen direction, so that the geography of the action is completely intelligible (**12.7, 12.8**).

In 1908, D. W. Griffith began his directing career. Over the next five years, he would make hundreds of one- and two-reelers (running about 15 and 30 minutes, respectively). These films created relatively complex narratives in short spans. Griffith certainly didn't invent all the devices with which he has been credited, but he did give many techniques strong narrative motivation. For example, a few other filmmakers had used simple last-minute rescues with crosscutting between the rescuers and victims, but Griffith developed and popularized this technique (6.103–6.106). By the time he made *The Birth of a Nation* (1915) and *Intolerance* (1916), Griffith was creating lengthy sequences by cutting among several different locales. During the early teens, he also directed his actors in an unusual way, concentrating on subtle changes in facial expression (4.32). To catch such nuances, he set up his camera closer than did many of his contemporaries, framing his actors in medium long shot or medium shot. Griffith's films were widely influential. In addition, his dynamic, rapid editing in the final chase scenes of *Intolerance* was to have a considerable impact on the Soviet Montage style of the 1920s.

The refinement of narratively motivated cutting occurs in the work of a number of important filmmakers of the period. One of these was Thomas H. Ince, a producer and director responsible for many films between 1910 and the end of World War I. He devised a unit system, whereby a single producer could oversee the making of several films at once. He also called for tight narratives, with no digressions or loose ends. *Civilization* (1915) and *The Italian* (1915) are good examples of films directed or supervised by Ince. He also supervised the popular Westerns of William S. Hart (p. 328), who directed many of his own films.

Another prolific filmmaker of this period (and later years as well) was Cecil B. De Mille. Not yet engaged in the creation of historical epics, De Mille made a series of feature-length dramas and comedies. His *The Cheat* (1915) reflects important changes occurring in the studio style between 1914 and 1917. During that

12.6   The robbers in the telegraph office in *The Great Train Robbery,* preparing to board the train seen through the window.

12.7   In *Rescued by Rover,* the heroic dog leads his master along a street from the right rear moving toward the left foreground . . .

12.8   . . . and the pair is moving from right to left as they reach their destination.

period, the glass-roofed studios of the earlier period began to give way to studios dependent on artificial lighting rather than mixed daylight and electric lighting. *The Cheat* used spectacular effects of chiaroscuro, with only one or two bright sources of light and no fill light. According to legend, De Mille justified this effect to nervous exhibitors as *Rembrandt lighting.* This so-called Rembrandt, or *north,* lighting was to become part of the classical repertoire of lighting techniques. *The Cheat* also greatly impressed the French Impressionist filmmakers, who occasionally used similar stark lighting effects.

Like many American films of the teens, *The Cheat* also uses a linear pattern of narrative. The first scene **(12.9)** introduces the hard lighting but also quickly establishes the Japanese businessman as a ruthless collector of objects; we see him burning his brand onto a small statue. The initial action motivates a later scene in which the businessman brands the heroine, who has fallen into his power by borrowing money from him **(12.10)**. *The Cheat* was evidence of the growing formal complexity of the Hollywood film.

The period 1909–1917 saw the development of the basic continuity principles. Eyeline matches occur with increasing frequency from 1910 on. The match on action developed at about the same time and was in common use by 1916. It appears in such Douglas Fairbanks films as *The Americano* (1916) and *Wild and Woolly* (1917). Shot/reverse shot was used only occasionally between 1911 and 1915, but it became widespread by 1916–1917; instances occur in such films as De Mille's *The Cheat* (1915), Hart's Western *The Narrow Trail* (1917), and Griffith's *A Romance of Happy Valley* (1919). During this period, films rarely violated the axis-of-action rule in using these techniques.

By the 1920s, the continuity system had become a standardized style that directors in the Hollywood studios used almost automatically to create coherent spatial and temporal relations within narratives. A match on action could provide a cut to a closer view in a scene **(12.11, 12.12)**. A three-way conversation around a table would no longer be handled in a single frontal shot. Note the clear spatial relations in **12.13–12.17**, shots from *Are Parents People?* (Malcolm St. Clair, 1925). At the time, screen direction was usually respected, as in this case. When an awkward match might have resulted from the joining of two shots, the filmmakers could cover it by inserting a dialogue title.

Keaton's *Our Hospitality* (1923), which we examined in Chapter 4, provides another example of a classical narrative. Keaton's mastery of classical form and style are evident in the carefully motivated recurrences of the various narrative elements and in the straightforward causal development from the death of Willie McKay's father in the feud to Willie's final resolution of the feud.

By the end of the silent era, in the late 1920s, the classical Hollywood cinema had developed into a sophisticated movement, but the Hollywood product was remarkably standardized. All of the major studios used the same production system,

"That evening I tried to increase my knowledge of motion-picture technique by going to the movies. I sat with a stop watch and notebook and tried to estimate the number of cuts or scenes in a thousand-foot reel, the length of individual scenes, the distance of the subject from the camera, and various other technical details."

— King Vidor, director, recalling the night before he began directing his first film, c. 1912

12.9   The opening scene of *The Cheat* introduces the branding motif . . .

12.10   . . . that returns later when the villain brands the heroine.

12.11   In Fred Niblo's *The Three Musketeers* (1921), a long shot of the group leads to . . .

12.12   . . . a cut-in to the central character, played by Douglas Fairbanks.

12.13 In an establishing shot from *Are Parents People?* the daughter sits down at the table.

12.14 In the medium shot she looks leftward toward her father . . .

12.15 . . . who looks rightward at her in the reverse shot.

with a similar division of labor at each. Independent production was less important. Some independent firms made low-budget films, often Westerns, for small and rural theaters. Even powerful Hollywood stars and producers had trouble remaining independent. Keaton gave up his small studio in 1928 to go to MGM under contract; there his career declined, partly because of the incompatibility of his old working methods with the rigid production patterns of the huge studio. Griffith, Mary Pickford, Fairbanks, and Charles Chaplin were better off. Forming a distributing corporation of their own, United Artists, in 1919, they were able to continue independent production at small companies under their umbrella corporation, though Griffith's company soon failed, and the careers of Fairbanks and Pickford declined soon after the introduction of sound.

There were alternative kinds of films being made during the silent era—most of them in other countries. After examining these alternative movements, we'll return to consider the classical Hollywood cinema after the coming of sound.

12.16 The daughter then turns to look to the right at her mother . . .

12.17 . . . who also returns her gaze in reverse shot.

German Expressionism (1919–1926)

At the start of World War I, the output of the German film industry was relatively small, though some impressive pictures had been made there. Germany's 2000 movie theaters were playing mostly French, American, Italian, and Danish films. Although America and France banned German films from their screens immediately, Germany was not even in a solid enough position to ban French and American films, for then the theaters would have had little to show.

To combat imported competition, as well as to create its own propaganda films, the German government began to support the film industry. In 1916, film imports were banned except from neutral Denmark. Production increased rapidly; from a dozen small companies in 1911, the number grew to 131 by 1918. But government policy encouraged these companies to band together into cartels.

The war was unpopular with many in Germany, and rebellious tendencies increased after the success of the Russian Revolution in 1917. Widespread strikes and antiwar petitions were organized during the winter of 1916–1917. To promote pro-war films, the government, the Deutsche Bank, and large industrial concerns combined several small film firms to create the large company UFA (short for Universum Film Aktiengesellschaft) in late 1917. Backed by these essentially conservative interests, UFA was a move toward control of not only the German market but the postwar international market as well.

With this huge financial backing, UFA was able to gather superb technicians and build the best-equipped studios in Europe. These studios later attracted foreign filmmakers, including the young Alfred Hitchcock. During the 1920s, Germany coproduced many films with companies in other countries, thus helping to spread German stylistic influence abroad.

12.18   *Madame Dubarry:* a crowd scene in the Tribunal of the French Revolution.

"Everything is composition; any image whatsoever could be stopped on the screen and would be a marvellously balanced painting of forms and lights. Also, it is one of the films which leaves in our memories the clearest visions—precise and of a slightly static beauty. But even more than painting, it is animated architecture."

— François Berge, French critic, on Fritz Lang's
The Nibelungen

12.19   The heroine's flamboyantly Expressionistic bedroom in Robert Wiene's *Genuine.* As she leans backwards, she blends with the curved, spiky shapes behind her.

In late 1918, with the end of the war, the need for overt militarist propaganda disappeared. Although mainstream dramas and comedies continued to be made, the German film industry concentrated on three genres. One was the internationally popular adventure serial, featuring spy rings, clever detectives, or exotic settings. Another was a brief sex exploitation cycle, which dealt "educationally" with such topics as homosexuality and prostitution. Also, UFA set out to copy the popular Italian historical epics of the prewar period.

This last type of film proved financially successful. In spite of continued bans on and prejudice against German films in America, England, and France, UFA finally was able to break into the international market. In September 1919, Ernst Lubitsch's *Madame Dubarry,* an epic of the French Revolution (**12.18**), inaugurated the magnificent UFA Palast theater in Berlin. This film helped reopen the world film market to Germany. Released as *Passion* in the United States, this film was extremely popular. It was not enthusiastically received in France, where its premiere was considerably delayed by charges that it was anti-French propaganda. But it did well in most markets, and other Lubitsch historical films were soon exported. In 1923, he became the first German director to be hired by Hollywood.

Some small companies briefly remained independent. Among these was Erich Pommer's Decla (later Decla-Bioscop). In 1919, the firm undertook to produce an unconventional script by two unknowns, Carl Mayer and Hans Janowitz. These young writers wanted the film to be made in an unusually stylized way. The three designers assigned to the film—Hermann Warm, Walter Reimann, and Walter Röhrig—suggested that it be done in an Expressionist style. As an avant-garde movement, Expressionism had first been important in painting (starting about 1910) and had been quickly taken up in theater, then in literature and architecture. Now company officials consented to try it in the cinema, apparently believing that this might be a selling point in the international market.

This belief was vindicated when the inexpensive film *The Cabinet of Dr. Caligari* (1920) created a sensation in Berlin and then in the United States, France, and other countries. Because of its success, other films in the Expressionist style soon followed. The result was a stylistic movement in cinema that lasted several years.

The success of *Caligari* and other Expressionist films kept Germany's avant-garde directors largely within the industry. A few experimental filmmakers made abstract films, like Viking Eggeling's *Diagonal-symphonie* (1923), or Dada films influenced by the international art movement, like Hans Richter's *Ghosts Before Breakfast* (1928). Big firms such as UFA (which absorbed Decla-Bioscop in 1921), as well as smaller companies, invested in Expressionist films because these films could compete with those of America. Indeed, by the mid-1920s, the most prominent German films were widely regarded as among the best in the world.

The first film of the movement, *Caligari,* is also one of the most typical examples. One of its designers, Warm, claimed, "The film image must become graphic art." *Caligari,* with its extreme stylization, was indeed like a moving Expressionist painting or woodcut print. In contrast to French Impressionism, which bases its style primarily on cinematography and editing, German Expressionism depends heavily on mise-en-scene. Shapes are distorted and exaggerated unrealistically for expressive purposes (4.2). Actors often wear heavy makeup and move in jerky or slow, sinuous patterns. Most important, all of the elements of the mise-en-scene interact graphically to create an overall composition. Characters do not simply exist within a setting but rather form visual elements that merge with the setting (**12.19**). We have already seen an example of this in 4.103, where the character Cesare collapses in a stylized forest, his body and outstretched arms echoing the shapes of the trees' trunks and branches.

In *Caligari,* the Expressionist stylization functions to convey the distorted viewpoint of a madman. We see the world as the hero does. This narrative function of the settings becomes explicit at one point, when the hero enters an asylum in his pursuit of Caligari. As he pauses to look around, he stands at the center of a pattern of radiating black-and-white lines that run across the floor and up the walls (**12.20**). The world of the film is literally a projection of the hero's vision.

Later, as Expressionism became an accepted style, filmmakers didn't motivate Expressionist style as the narrative point of view of mad characters. Instead, Expressionism often functioned to create stylized situations for fantasy and horror stories (as with *Waxworks,* 1924, and *Nosferatu,* 1922; see 9.15) or historical epics (as with *The Nibelungen,* 1923–1924). Expressionist films depended greatly on their designers. In the German studios, a film's designer received a relatively high salary and was often mentioned prominently in the advertisements.

A combination of circumstances led to the disappearance of the movement. The rampant inflation of the early 1920s in Germany actually favored Expressionist filmmaking, partly by making it easy for German exporters to sell their films cheaply abroad. Inflation discouraged imports, however, for the tumbling exchange rate of the mark made foreign purchases prohibitively expensive. But in 1924, the U.S. Dawes Plan helped to stabilize the German economy, and foreign films came in more frequently, offering a degree of competition unknown in Germany for nearly a decade. Expressionist film budgets, however, were climbing. The last major films of the movement, F. W. Murnau's *Faust* (1926) and Fritz Lang's *Metropolis* (1927), were costly epics that helped drive UFA deeper into financial difficulty, leading Erich Pommer to quit and try his luck briefly in America (**12.21**). Other personnel were lured away to Hollywood as well. Murnau left after finishing *Faust,* his last German film. Major actors (such as Conrad Veidt and Emil Jannings) and cinematographers (such as Karl Freund) went to Hollywood as well. Lang stayed on, but after the criticisms of *Metropolis*'s extravagance on its release, he formed his own production company and turned to other styles in his later German films. At the beginning of the Nazi regime in 1933, he too left the country.

Trying to counter the stiffer competition from imported Hollywood films after 1924, the Germans also began to imitate the American product. The resulting films, though sometimes impressive, diluted the unique qualities of the Expressionist style. Thus, by 1927, Expressionism as a movement had died out. But as Georges Sadoul has pointed out, an expressionist (spelled with a small "e" to distinguish it from the Expressionist movement proper) tendency lingered on in many of the German films of the late 1920s and even into such 1930s films as Lang's *M* (1930; see **12.22**) and *Testament of Dr. Mabuse* (1932). And because so many of the German filmmakers came to the United States, Hollywood films also displayed

12.20   The insane asylum set of *The Cabinet of Dr. Caligari.*

12.21   *Metropolis* contained many large, Expressionistic sets, including this garden, with pillars that appear to be made of melting clay.

12.22   In *M,* reflections and a display of knives in a shop window create a semi-abstract composition that mirrors the murderer's obsession.

expressionist tendencies. Horror films, such as *Son of Frankenstein* (1939), and films noirs have strong expressionist touches in their settings and lighting. Although the German movement lasted only about seven years, expressionism has never entirely died out as a trend in film style.

French Impressionism and Surrealism (1918–1930)

During the silent era, a number of film movements in France posed major alternatives to classical Hollywood narrative form. Some of these alternatives—abstract cinema, Dada filmmaking—are not specifically French and constituted instead a part of the growing international avant-garde. But two alternatives to the American mode remained quite localized. Impressionism was an avant-garde style that operated largely within the film industry. Most of the Impressionist filmmakers started out working for major French companies, and some of their avant-garde works proved financially successful. In the mid-1920s, most formed their own independent companies but remained within the mainstream commercial industry by renting studio facilities and releasing their films through established firms. The other alternative movement, Surrealism, lay largely outside the film industry. Allied with the Surrealist movement in other arts, these filmmakers relied on their own means and private patronage. France in the 1920s offers a striking instance of how different film movements may coexist at the same time and place.

Impressionism

World War I struck a serious blow to the French film industry. Personnel were conscripted, many film studios were shifted to wartime uses, and much export was halted. Yet the two major firms, Pathé Frères and Léon Gaumont, also controlled circuits of theaters. They needed to fill vacant screens, and so in 1915, American films began increasingly to flood into France. Represented by Pearl White, Douglas Fairbanks, Chaplin and Ince films, De Mille's *The Cheat,* and William S. Hart (affectionately named "Rio Jim" by the French), the Hollywood cinema dominated the market by the end of 1917. After the war, French filmmaking never fully recovered: In the 1920s, French audiences saw eight times more Hollywood footage than domestic footage. The film industry tried in several ways to recapture the market, mostly through imitation of Hollywood production methods and genres. Artistically, however, the most significant move was the firms' encouragement of younger French directors: Abel Gance, Louis Delluc, Germaine Dulac, Marcel L'Herbier, and Jean Epstein.

These directors differed from their predecessors. The previous generation had regarded filmmaking as a commercial craft, but the younger filmmakers wrote essays proclaiming cinema was an art comparable to poetry, painting, and music. Cinema should, they said, be purely itself and should not borrow from the theater or literature. Impressed by the verve and energy of the American cinema, the young theorists compared Chaplin to Nijinsky and the films of Rio Jim to *The Song of Roland.* Cinema should, above all, be (like music) an occasion for the artist to express feelings. Gance, Delluc, Dulac, L'Herbier, Epstein, and other, more tangential members of the movement sought to put this aesthetic into practice as filmmakers.

Between 1918 and 1928, in a series of extraordinary films, the younger directors experimented with cinema in ways that posed an alternative to the dominant Hollywood formal principles. Given the centrality of emotion in their aesthetic, it is no wonder that the intimate psychological narrative dominated their filmmaking practice. The interactions of a few characters, usually a love triangle (as in Delluc's *L'Inondation,* 1924; Epstein's *Coeur fidèle,* 1923, and *La Belle nivernaise,*

1923; and Gance's *La Dixième symphonie*, 1918, would serve as the basis for the filmmaker's exploration of fleeting moods and shifting sensations.

As in the Hollywood cinema, psychological causes were paramount, but the school gained the name Impressionist because of its interest in giving narration considerable psychological depth, revealing the play of a character's consciousness. The interest falls not on external physical behavior but on *inner* action. To a degree unprecedented in international filmmaking, Impressionist films manipulate plot time and subjectivity. To depict memories, flashbacks are common; sometimes the bulk of a film will be one flashback or a series of them. Even more striking is the films' insistence on registering characters' dreams, fantasies, and mental states. Dulac's *The Smiling Mme. Beudet* (1923) consists almost entirely of the main character's fantasy life, her imaginary escape from a dull marriage. Despite its epic length (over five hours), Gance's *La Roue* (1922) rests essentially on the erotic relations among only four people, and the director seeks to trace the development of each character's feelings in great detail. Impressionism's emphasis on personal emotion gives the films' narratives an intensely psychological focus.

The Impressionist movement earned its name as well for its use of film style. The filmmakers experimented with ways of rendering mental states by means of cinematography and editing. In Impressionist films, irises, masks, and superimpositions function as traces of characters' thoughts and feelings **(12.23)**. In *La Roue*, the image of Norma is superimposed over the smoke from a locomotive, representing the fantasy of the engine driver, who is in love with her.

To intensify the subjectivity, the Impressionists' cinematography and editing present characters' perceptual experience, their optical impressions. These films use a great deal of point-of-view cutting, showing a shot of a character looking at something, then a shot of that thing, from an angle and distance replicating the character's vantage point. When a character in an Impressionist film gets drunk or dizzy, the filmmaker renders that experience through distorted or filtered shots or vertiginous camera movements. In **12.24**, from L'Herbier's *El Dorado* (1920), a man is drinking in a cabaret.

The Impressionists also experimented with pronounced rhythmic editing to suggest the pace of an experience as a character feels it, moment by moment. During scenes of violence or emotional turmoil, the rhythm accelerates—the shots get shorter and shorter, building to a climax, sometimes with shots only a few frames long. In *La Roue*, a train crash is presented in accelerating shots ranging from 13 frames down to 2, and a man's last thoughts before he falls from a cliff are rendered in a blur of many single-frame shots (the first known use of such rapid editing). In *Coeur fidèle*, lovers at a fair ride in whirling swings, and Epstein presents their giddiness in a series of shots 4 frames, then 2 frames, long. Several Impressionist films use a dance to motivate a markedly accelerated cutting rhythm. More generally, the comparison of cinema to music encouraged the Impressionists to explore rhythmic editing. In such ways, subjective shooting and editing patterns function within Impressionist films to reinforce the narrative treatment of psychological states.

Impressionist form created certain demands on film technology. Gance, the boldest innovator in this respect, used his epic *Napoléon* (1927) as a chance to try new lenses (even a 275mm telephoto), multiple frame images (called Polyvision), and widescreen ratio (the celebrated triptychs; see 5.63). The most influential Impressionist technological innovation was the development of new means of frame mobility. If the camera was to represent a character's eyes, it should be able to move with the ease of a person. Impressionists strapped their cameras to cars, carousels, and locomotives. For Gance's *Napoléon*, the camera manufacturer Debrie perfected a handheld model that let the operator move on roller skates. Gance lashed the machine to wheels, cables, pendulums, and bobsleds. In *L'Argent* (1928), L'Herbier had his camera gliding through huge rooms and even plummeting straight down toward the crowd from the dome of the Paris stock exchange **(12.25)**.

> "Another period arrived, that of the psychological and impressionist film. It would seem stupid to place a character in a given situation without penetrating into the secret realm of his inner life, and the actor's performance is explained by the play of thoughts and of visualized sensations."
>
> — Germaine Dulac, director

12.23   In *Coeur fidèle*, the heroine looks out a window, and a superimposition of the foul jetsam of the waterfront conveys her dejection at working as a barmaid in a dockside tavern.

12.24   In *El Dorado*, a man's tipsiness is conveyed by means of a curved mirror that stretches his body sideways.

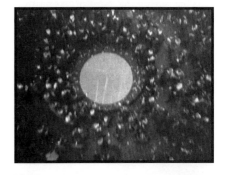

12.25   In *L'Argent*, the camera drops toward the floor of the stock exchange in an effort to convey the traders's frenzied excitement.

Such formal, stylistic, and technological innovations had given French film-makers the hope that their films could win the popularity granted to Hollywood's product. During the 1920s, the Impressionists operated somewhat independently; they formed their own production companies and leased studio facilities from Pathé and Gaumont in exchange for distribution rights. Some Impressionist films did prove moderately popular with French audiences. But by 1929, most foreign audiences had not taken to Impressionism; its experimentation was attuned to elite tastes. Moreover, although production costs were rising, Impressionists such as Gance and L'Herbier became even more free-spending. As a result, filmmakers' companies either went out of business or were absorbed by the big firms. Two behemoth productions of the decade, *Napoléon* and *L'Argent,* failed and were reedited by the producers; they were among the last Impressionist films released. With the arrival of the sound film, the French film industry tightened its belt and had no money to risk on experiments.

Impressionism as a distinct movement may be said to have ceased by 1929. But the influences of Impressionist form—the psychological narrative, subjective camera work, and editing—were more long-lived. They continued to operate, for example, in the work of Alfred Hitchcock and Maya Deren, in Hollywood montage sequences, and in certain American genres and styles (the horror film, film noir).

Surrealism

Whereas the French Impressionist filmmakers worked within the commercial film industry, the Surrealist filmmakers relied on private patronage and screened their work in small artists' gatherings. Such isolation is hardly surprising, since Surrealist cinema was a more radical movement, producing films that perplexed and shocked most audiences.

Surrealist cinema was directly linked to Surrealism in literature and painting. According to its spokesperson, André Breton, "Surrealism [was] based on the belief in the superior reality of certain forms of association, heretofore neglected, in the omnipotence of dreams, in the undirected play of thought." Influenced by Freudian psychology, Surrealist art sought to register the hidden currents of the unconscious, "in the absence of any control exercised by reason, and beyond any aesthetic and moral preoccupation."

Automatic writing and painting, the search for bizarre or evocative imagery, the deliberate avoidance of rationally explicable form or style—these became features of Surrealism as it developed in the period 1924–1929. From the start, the Surrealists were attracted to the cinema, especially admiring films that presented untamed desire or the fantastic and marvelous (for example, slapstick comedies, *Nosferatu,* and serials about mysterious supercriminals). In due time, painters such as Man Ray and Salvador Dalí and writers such as Antonin Artaud began dabbling in cinema, while the young Spaniard Luis Buñuel, drawn to Surrealism, became its most famous filmmaker.

Surrealist cinema is overtly anti-narrative, attacking causality itself. If rationality is to be fought, causal connections among events must be dissolved, as in *The Seashell and the Clergyman* (1928; scripted by Artaud, filmed by the Impressionist Germaine Dulac; see **(12.26)**. In Dalí and Buñuel's *Un Chien andalou* (*An Andalusian Dog,* 1928) the hero drags two pianos, stuffed with dead donkeys, across a parlor. In Buñuel's *L'Age d'or* (1930), a woman begins obsessively sucking the toes of a statue.

Many Surrealist films tease us to find a narrative logic that is simply absent. Causality is as evasive as in a dream. Instead, we find events juxtaposed for their disturbing effect. The hero gratuitously shoots a child (*L'Age d'or*), a woman closes her eyes only to reveal eyes painted on her eyelids (Ray's *Emak Bakia,* 1927), and—most famous of all—a man strops a razor and deliberately slits the eyeball of an unprotesting woman (*Un Chien andalou,* **12.27**). An Impressionist film would

12.26 *The Seashell and the Clergyman:* the clergyman's distorted view of a threatening military officer, inexplicably dressed in baby's clothes.

12.27 The shocking eye-slitting scene in *Un chien andalou.*

motivate such events as a character's dreams or hallucinations, but in these films, character psychology is all but nonexistent. Sexual desire and ecstasy, violence, blasphemy, and bizarre humor furnish events that Surrealist film form employs with a disregard for conventional narrative principles. The hope was that the free form of the film would arouse the deepest impulses of the viewer. Buñuel called *Un Chien andalou* "a passionate call to murder."

The style of Surrealist cinema is eclectic. Mise-en-scene is often influenced by Surrealist painting. The ants in *Un Chien andalou* come from Dalí's pictures; the pillars and city squares of *The Seashell and the Clergyman* hark back to the Italian painter Giorgio de Chirico. Surrealist editing is an amalgam of some Impressionist devices (many dissolves and superimpositions) and some devices of the dominant cinema. The shocking eyeball slitting at the start of *Un Chien andalou* relies on some principles of continuity editing (and indeed on the Kuleshov effect). However, discontinuous editing is also commonly used to fracture any organized temporal-spatial coherence. In *Un Chien andalou*, the heroine locks the man out of a room only to turn to find him inexplicably behind her. On the whole, Surrealist film style refused to canonize any particular devices, since that would order and rationalize what had to be an "undirected play of thought."

The fortunes of Surrealist cinema shifted with changes in the art movement as a whole. By late 1929, when Breton joined the Communist Party, Surrealists were embroiled in internal dissension about whether communism was a political equivalent of Surrealism. Buñuel left France for a brief stay in Hollywood and then returned to Spain. The chief patron of Surrealist filmmaking, the Vicomte de Noailles, supported Jean Vigo's *Zéro de Conduite* (1933), a film of Surrealist ambitions, but then stopped sponsoring the avant-garde. Thus, as a unified movement, French Surrealism was no longer viable after 1930. Individual Surrealists continued to work, however. The most famous was Buñuel, who continued to work in his own brand of the Surrealist style for 50 years. His later films, such as *Belle de Jour* (1967) and *The Discreet Charm of the Bourgeoisie* (1972), continue the Surrealist tradition.

Soviet Montage (1924–1930)

Following the Russian Revolution in October 1917, the new Soviet government faced the difficult task of controlling all sectors of life. Like other industries, the film production and distribution systems took years to build up a substantial output that could serve the aims of the new government.

During World War I, there were a number of private production companies operating in Moscow and Petersburg. With most imports cut off, these companies did quite well making films for the domestic market. The most distinctive Russian films made during the mid-1910s were slow-paced melodramas that concentrated on bravura performances by actors playing characters caught in extremely emotional situations. Such films showcased the talents of Ivan Mozhukin and other popular stars (**12.28**) and were aimed mainly at the large Russian audience, seldom being seen abroad.

These film companies resisted the move made directly after the Revolution to nationalize all private property. They simply refused to supply films to theaters operating under the control of the government. In July 1918, the government's film subsection of the State Commission of Education put strict controls on the existing supplies of raw film stock. As a result, producers began hoarding their stock; the largest firms took all the equipment they could and fled to other countries. Some companies made films commissioned by the government, while hoping that the Reds would lose the Civil War and that things would return to pre-Revolutionary conditions.

In the face of shortages of equipment and difficult living conditions, a few young filmmakers made tentative moves that would result in the development of a national cinema movement. Dziga Vertov began working on documentary footage of the war; at age 20, he was placed in charge of all newsreels. Lev Kuleshov, teaching

12.28 In Yakov Protazanov's 1916 *The Queen of Spades*, the gambling addicted hero, played by Mozhukin, imagines himself winning at cards, with his vision superimposed at the right.

in the newly founded State School on Cinema Art, performed a series of experiments by editing footage from different sources into a whole that creates an impression of continuity. Kuleshov was perhaps the most conservative of the young Soviet film-makers, since he was basically trying to systematize principles of editing similar to the continuity practices of the classical Hollywood cinema (pp. 227–228). Thus, even before they were able to make films, Kuleshov and his young pupils were working at the first film school in the world and writing theoretical essays on the new art form. This grounding in theory would be the basis of the Montage style.

In 1920, Sergei Eisenstein worked briefly in a train carrying propaganda to the troops in the Civil War. He returned that year to Moscow to stage plays in a work-ers' theater. In May 1920, Vsevolod Pudovkin made his acting debut in a play pre-sented by Kuleshov's State Film School. He had been inspired to go into filmmaking by seeing Griffith's *Intolerance,* which was first shown widely in Rus-sia in 1919. American films, particularly those of D. W. Griffith, Douglas Fair-banks, and Mary Pickford, which kept circulating to fill the void left by the low output of new Soviet productions, were a tremendous influence on the filmmakers of the emerging Soviet movement.

None of the important filmmakers of the Montage style was a veteran of the pre-Revolutionary industry. All came from other fields (for example, Eisenstein from engineering and Pudovkin from chemistry) and discovered the cinema in the midst of the Revolution's ferment. The Czarist-era filmmakers who remained active in the USSR in the 1920s tended to stick to older traditions. One popular director of the Czarist period, Yakov Protazanov, went abroad briefly after the Revolution but returned to continue making films whose style and form owed almost nothing to the theory and practice of the new filmmakers.

Protazanov's return coincided with a general loosening of government restric-tions on private enterprise. In 1921, the country was facing tremendous problems, including a widespread famine. In order to facilitate the production and distribution of goods, Lenin instituted the New Economic Policy (NEP), which for several years permitted private management of business. For film, the NEP meant a sudden reap-pearance of film stock and equipment belonging to the producers who had not em-igrated. Slowly, Soviet production began to grow as private firms made more films. The government attempted, with little success, to control the film industry by cre-ating a central distribution company, Goskino, in 1922.

"Of all the arts, for us the cinema is the most important," Lenin stated in 1922. Since Lenin saw film as a powerful tool for education, the first films encouraged by the government were documentaries and newsreels such as Vertov's newsreel series *Kino-Pravda,* which began in May 1922. Fictional films were also being made from 1917 on, but it was not until 1923 that a Georgian feature, *Red Imps,* became the first Soviet film to compete successfully with the foreign films predominant on So-viet screens. (And not until 1927 did the Soviet industry's income from its own films top that of the films it imported.)

The Soviet Montage style displayed tentative beginnings in 1924, with Kuleshov's class from the State Film School presenting *The Extraordinary Adven-tures of Mr. West in the Land of the Bolsheviks* **(12.29)**. This delightful film, along with Kuleshov's next film, *The Death Ray* (1925), showed that Soviet directors could apply Montage principles and come up with amusing satires or exciting ad-ventures as entertaining as the Hollywood product.

Eisenstein's first feature, *Strike,* was released early in 1925 and initiated the movement proper. His second, *Potemkin,* premiered later in 1925, was successful abroad and drew the attention of other countries to the new movement. In the next few years, Eisenstein, Pudovkin, Vertov, and the Ukrainian Alexander Dovzhenko created a series of films that are classics of the Montage style.

In their writings and films, these directors championed the powers of editing. Until the late 1910s, most Russian fiction films had based their scenes around lengthy, fairly distant shots that captured the actors' performances. Analytical edit-

12.29   *The Extraordinary Adventures of Mr. West in the Land of the Bolsheviks:* a gang of thieves terrifies the naive American, Mr. West, by presenting him with clichéd caricatures of fierce Soviet revolutionaries.

"Everyone who has had in his hands a piece of film to be edited knows by experience how neutral it remains, even though a part of a planned sequence, until it is joined with another piece, when it suddenly acquires and conveys a sharper and quite different meaning than that planned for it at the time of filming."

— Sergei Eisenstein, director

ing was rare. But films from Hollywood and from the French Impressionist film-makers told their stories through fast cutting, including frequent close framings. Inspired by these imports, the young Soviet directors declared that a film's power arose from the combination of shots. Montage seemed to be the way forward for modern cinema.

Not all of the young theoreticians agreed on exactly what the Montage approach to editing should be. Pudovkin, for example, believed that shots were like bricks, to be joined together to build a sequence. Eisenstein disagreed, saying that the maximum effect would be gained if the shots did not fit together perfectly, if they created a jolt for the spectator. Many filmmakers in the montage movement followed this approach (**12.30**). Eisenstein also favored juxtaposing shots in order to create a concept, as we have already seen with his use of conceptual editing in *October* (pp. 257–260). Vertov disagreed with both theorists, favoring a cinema-eye approach to recording and shaping documentary reality (pp. 410–413).

Pudovkin's *Storm over Asia* makes use of conceptual editing similar to that of Eisenstein's *October.* Shots of a military officer and his wife being dressed in their accessories are intercut with shots of the preparation at the temple (**12.31–12.34**). Pudovkin's parallel montage points up the absurdity of both rituals.

The Montagists' approach to narrative form set them apart from the cinemas of other countries. Soviet narrative films tended to downplay character psychology as a cause; instead, social forces provided the major causes. Characters were interesting for the way these social causes affected their lives. As a result, films of the Soviet Montage movement did not always have a single protagonist. Social groups could form a collective hero, as in several of Eisenstein's films. In keeping with this downplaying of individual personalities, Soviet filmmakers often avoided well-known actors, preferring to cast parts by searching out nonactors. This practice was called **typage**, since the filmmakers would often choose an individual whose appearance seemed at once to convey the type of character he or she was to play. Except for the hero, Pudovkin used nonactors to play all of the Mongols in *Storm over Asia.*

By the end of the 1920s, each of the major directors of this movement had made about four important films. The decline of the movement was not caused primarily by industrial and economic factors as in Germany and France. Instead, the government strongly discouraged the use of the Montage style. By the late 1920s, Vertov, Eisenstein, and Dovzhenko were being criticized for their excessively formal and esoteric approaches. In 1929, Eisenstein went to Hollywood to study the new technique of sound; by the time he returned in 1932, the attitude of the film industry had changed. While he was away, a few filmmakers carried their Montage experiments into sound cinema in the early 1930s. But the Soviet authorities, under Stalin's direction, encouraged filmmakers to create simple films that would be readily understandable to all audiences. Stylistic experimentation or nonrealistic subject matter was often criticized or censored.

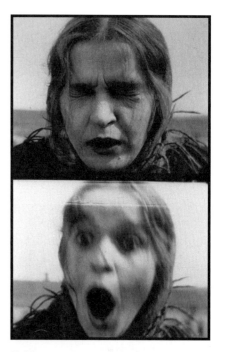

12.30 In *House on Trubnoi Square,* Montage director Boris Barnet uses a jump cut to convey the heroine's sudden realization that a streetcar is headed straight for her.

12.31 In *Storm over Asia,* after a medium close-up of an elaborate piece of jewelry being lowered over the head of a priest, there is a cut . . .

12.32 . . . to a close-up of a servant placing a necklace around the neck of the officer's wife . . .

12.33 . . . then a cut back to a large headdress being positioned on a priest's head . . .

12.34 . . . juxtaposed with a close-up of a tiara being set on the wife's head.

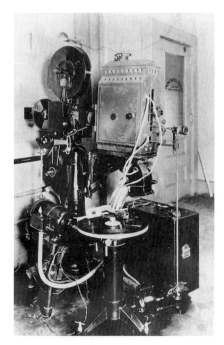

12.35 An early projector with a turntable (lower center) attached.

This trend culminated in 1934, when the government instituted a new artistic policy called Socialist Realism. This policy dictated that all artworks must depict revolutionary development while being firmly grounded in realism. The great Soviet directors continued to make films, occasionally masterpieces, but the Montage experiments of the 1920s had to be discarded or modified. Eisenstein managed to continue his work on Montage but occasionally incurred the wrath of the authorities up until his death in 1948. As a movement, the Soviet Montage style can be said to have ended by 1933, with the release of such films as Vertov's *Enthusiasm* (1931) and Pudovkin's *Deserter* (1933).

The Classical Hollywood Cinema After the Coming of Sound

The introduction of sound technology came about through the efforts of Hollywood firms to widen their power. During the mid-1920s, Warner Bros. was expanding its facilities and holdings. One of these expansions was the investment in a sound system using records in synchronization with film images **(12.35)**.

By releasing *Don Juan* (1926) with orchestral accompaniment and sound effects on disc, along with a series of vaudeville shorts with singing and talking, Warner Bros. began to popularize the idea of sound films. In 1927, *The Jazz Singer* (a part-talkie with some scenes accompanied only by music) was a tremendous success, and the Warner Bros. investment began to pay off.

The success of *Don Juan, The Jazz Singer,* and the shorts convinced other studios that sound contributed to profitable filmmaking. Unlike the early period of filmmaking and the Motion Picture Patents Company, there was now no fierce competition within the industry. Instead, firms realized that whatever sound system the studios finally adopted, it would have to be compatible with the projection machinery of any theater. Eventually, a sound-on-film rather than a sound-on-disc system became the standard and continues so to the present. (That is, as we saw in Chapter 1, the sound track is printed on the strip of film alongside the image.) By 1930, most theaters in America were wired for sound.

For a few years, sound created a setback for Hollywood film style. The camera had to be put inside a sound booth so that its motor noise would not be picked up by the microphone. The components of a dialogue scene in a 1928 MGM film can be seen in **12.36**. The camera operator can hear only through his earphones, and the camera cannot move except for short pans to reframe. The bulky microphone, on the table at the right, also did not move. The actors had to stay within a limited space if their speech was to register on the track. The result of such restrictions was a brief period of static films resembling stage plays.

Still, from the very beginning of sound filming, solutions were found for these problems. Sometimes several cameras, all in soundproof booths, would record the scene from different angles simultaneously. The resulting footage could be cut together to provide a standard continuity editing pattern in a scene, with all the sound synchronized. The whole camera booth might be mounted on wheels to create camera movements, or a scene might be shot silent and a sound track added later. Early sound films such as Rouben Mamoulian's *Applause* (1929) demonstrate that the camera soon regained a great flexibility of movement. Later, smaller cases, enclosing only the camera body, replaced the cumbersome booths. These *blimps* **(12.37)** permitted cinematographers to place the camera on movable supports. Similarly, microphones mounted on booms and hanging over the heads of the actors could also follow moving action without a loss of recording quality.

Once camera movement and subject movement were restored to sound films, filmmakers continued to use many of the stylistic characteristics developed in Hollywood during the silent period. Diegetic sound provided a powerful addition to the system of continuity editing. A line of dialogue could continue over a cut, creating smooth temporal continuity. (See pp. 270–272.)

12.36　A posed publicity still demonstrated the limitations of early sound filming.

12.37　A blimped camera during the early 1930s allowed the camera tripod to be placed on a rolling dolly.

Within the overall tradition of continuity style and classical narrative form, each of the large studios developed a distinctive approach of its own. Thus MGM, for example, became the prestige studio, with a huge number of stars and technicians under long-term contract. MGM lavished money on settings, costumes, and special effects, as in *The Good Earth* (1937), with its locust attack, and *San Francisco* (1936), in which the great earthquake is spectacularly re-created. Warner Bros., in spite of its success with sound, was still a relatively small studio and specialized in less expensive genre pictures. Its series of gangster films (*Little Caesar, Public Enemy*) and musicals (*42nd Street, Gold Diggers of 1933, Dames*) were among the studio's most successful products. Even lower on the ladder of prestige was Universal, which depended on imaginative filmmaking rather than established stars or expensive sets in its atmospheric horror films, such as *Frankenstein* (1931) and *The Old Dark House* (1932; **12.38**).

One major genre, the musical, became possible only with the introduction of sound. Indeed, the original intention of the Warners when they began their investment in sound equipment was to circulate vaudeville acts on film. The form of most musicals involved separate numbers inserted into a linear narrative, although a few revue musicals simply strung together a series of numbers with little or no connecting narrative. One of the major studios, RKO, made a series of musicals starring Fred Astaire and Ginger Rogers: *Swing Time* (George Stevens, 1936) illustrates how a musical can be a classically constructed narrative (see pp. 334–335).

During the 1930s, color film stocks became widely used for the first time. In the 1920s, a small number of films had Technicolor sequences, but the process was crude, using only two colors in combination to create all other hues. The result tended to emphasize greenish-blue and pink tones; it was also too costly to use extensively (**12.39**). By the early 1930s, however, Technicolor had been improved. It now used three primary colors and thus could reproduce a large range of hues. Though still expensive, it was soon proved to add hugely to the appeal of many films. After *Becky Sharp* (1935), the first feature-length film to use the new Technicolor, and *The Trail of the Lonesome Pine* (1936), studios began using Technicolor extensively. The Technicolor process was used until the early 1970s. (For a variety of examples of Technicolor, running from the 1940s to the 1960s, see 4.41–4.43, 4.77, 4.131, 5.5, and 5.47.)

Technicolor needed a great deal of light on the set, and the light had to favor certain hues. Thus brighter lights specifically designed for color filmmaking were introduced. Some cinematographers began to use the new lights for black-and-white filming. These brighter lights, combined with faster film stocks, made it easier to achieve greater depth of field with more light and a smaller aperture. Many cinematographers stuck to the standard soft-focus style of the 1920s and 1930s, but

12.38 Heavy shadows, spiky shapes, and eccentric performances mixed a menacing atmosphere with a touch of humor in *The Old Dark Horse.*

12.39 *Under a Texas Moon* (1930): typical two-strip Technicolor, with mostly orange and green hues.

others began to experiment. By the late 1930s, there was a definite trend toward a deep-focus style.

Mervyn Leroy's *Anthony Adverse* (1936), Alfred L. Werker's *The Adventures of Sherlock Holmes* (1939), and the Sam Wood–William Cameron Menzies *Our Town* (1940) all used deep focus to a considerable degree. But it was *Citizen Kane* that in 1941 brought deep focus strongly to the attention of spectators and film-makers alike. Welles's compositions placed the foreground figures close to the camera and the background figures deep in the space of the shot (5.39). In some cases, the apparently deep-focus image was achieved through matte work and rear projection. Overall, *Citizen Kane* helped make the tendency toward deep focus a major part of classical Hollywood style in the next decade. Many films using the technique soon appeared. *Citizen Kane*'s cinematographer, Gregg Toland, worked on some of them, such as *The Little Foxes* (**12.40**).

12.40   William Wyler stages in depth in *The Little Foxes.*

The light necessary for deep focus also tended to lend a hard-edge appearance to objects. Gauzy effects were largely eliminated, and much 1940s cinema became visually quite distinct from that of the 1930s. But the insistence on the clear narrative functioning of all these techniques remained strong. The classical Hollywood narrative modified itself over the years but did not change radically.

Italian Neorealism (1942–1951)

There is no definitive source for the term *Neorealism,* but it first appeared in the early 1940s in the writings of Italian critics. From one perspective, the term represented a younger generation's desire to break free of the conventions of ordinary Italian cinema. Under Mussolini, the motion picture industry had created colossal historical epics and sentimental upper-class melodramas (nicknamed *white-telephone films*), and many critics felt these to be artificial and decadent. A new realism was needed. Some critics found it in French films of the 1930s, especially works by Jean Renoir. Other critics turned closer to home to praise films like Luchino Visconti's *Ossessione* (1942).

Today most historians believe that Neorealist filmmaking was not a complete break with Italian cinema under Mussolini. Pseudo-documentaries such as Roberto Rossellini's *White Ship* (1941), even though propagandistic, prepared the way for more forthright handling of contemporary events. Other current trends, such as regional dialect comedy and urban melodrama, encouraged directors and scriptwriters to turn toward realism. Overall, spurred by both foreign influences and indigenous traditions, the postwar period saw several filmmakers beginning to work with the goal of revealing contemporary social conditions. This trend became known as the Neorealist movement.

Economic, political, and cultural factors helped Neorealism survive. Nearly all the major Neorealists—Rossellini, Vittorio De Sica, Visconti, and others—came to the movement as experienced filmmakers. They knew one another, frequently shared scriptwriters and personnel, and gained public attention in the journals *Cinema* and *Bianco e Nero.* Before 1948, the Neorealist movement had enough friends in the government to be relatively free of censorship. There was even a correspondence between Neorealism and an Italian literary movement of the same period modeled on the *verismo* of the previous century. The result was an array of Italian films that gained worldwide recognition: Visconti's *La Terra Trema* (1947); Rossellini's *Rome Open City* (1945), *Paisan* (1946), and *Germany Year Zero* (1947); De Sica's *Shoeshine* (1946) and *Bicycle Thieves* (1948).

Neorealism created a somewhat distinctive approach to film style. By 1945, the fighting had destroyed most of Cinecittà, the large Roman studio complex, so sets were in short supply and sound equipment was rare. As a result, Neorealist mise-en-scene relied on actual locales, and its photographic work tended toward the raw roughness of documentaries. Rossellini has told of buying bits of negative stock

12.41   Shooting in the streets for the death of Pina in *Rome Open City*: Francesco is thrown into a truck by Nazi soldiers. . .

12.42   . . . Pina breaks through the guards . . .

12.43   . . . and a rough, bumpy shot taken from the truck shows her running after it.

12.44   One of the magnificent landscapes in depth in *La Terra Trema*.

12.45   In *Bicycle Thieves*, the hero takes shelter along with a group of priests during a rain shower. The incident doesn't affect the plot and seems as casual as any moment in daily life.

from street photographers, so that much of *Rome Open City* was shot on film with varying photographic qualities.

Shooting on the streets and in private buildings made Italian camera operators adept at cinematography that often avoided the three-point lighting system of Hollywood (4.36). Although Neorealist films often featured famous stage or film actors, they also made use of nonactors, recruited for their realistic looks or behavior. For the adult "star" of *Bicycle Thieves*, De Sica chose a factory worker: "The way he moved, the way he sat down, his gestures with those hands of a working man and not of an actor . . . everything about him was perfect." The Italian cinema had a long tradition of dubbing, and the ability to postsynchronize dialogue permitted the filmmakers to work on location with smaller crews and to move the camera freely. With a degree of improvisational freedom in the acting and setting went a certain flexibility of framing, well displayed in the death of Pina in *Rome Open City* (**12.41–12.43**), the final sequence of *Germany Year Zero,* and *La Terra Trema* (**12.44**). The tracking shots through the open-air bicycle market in *Bicycle Thieves* illustrate the possibilities that the Neorealist director found in returning to location filming.

Perhaps even more influential was the Neorealist sense of narrative form. Reacting against the intricately plotted white-telephone dramas, the Neorealists tended to loosen up narrative relations. The earliest major films of the movement, such as *Ossessione, Rome Open City,* and *Shoeshine,* contain relatively conventionally organized plots (albeit with unhappy endings). But the most formally innovative Neorealist films allow the intrusion of noncausally motivated details (**12.45**). Although the causes of characters' actions are usually seen as concretely economic and political (poverty, unemployment, exploitation), the effects are often fragmentary and inconclusive. Rossellini's *Paisan* is frankly episodic, presenting six anecdotes of life in Italy during the Allied invasion; often we are not told the outcome of an event, the consequence of a cause.

The ambiguity of Neorealist films is also a product of narration that refuses to yield an omniscient knowledge of events. The film seems to admit that the totality of reality is simply unknowable. This is especially evident in the films' endings. *Bicycle Thieves* concludes with the worker and his son wandering down the street, their stolen bicycle still missing, their future uncertain. Although ending with the defeat of the Sicilian fishermen's revolt against the merchants, *La Terra Trema* does not cancel the possibility that a later revolt will succeed. Neorealism's tendency toward slice-of-life plot construction gave many films of the movement an open-ended quality quite opposed to the narrative closure of the Hollywood cinema.

As economic and cultural forces had sustained the Neorealist movement, so they helped bring it to an end. When Italy began to prosper after the war, the government looked askance at films so critical of contemporary society. After 1949, censorship and state pressures began to constrain the movement. Large-scale Italian film production began to reappear, and Neorealism no longer had the freedom of the small production company. In addition, the Neorealist directors, now famous, began to pursue more individualized concerns: Rossellini's investigation of Christian humanism and Western history, De Sica's sentimental romances, and Visconti's examination of upper-class milieus. Most historians date the end of the Neorealist movement with the public attacks on De Sica's *Umberto D* (1951). Nevertheless, Neorealist elements are still quite visible in the early works of Federico Fellini (*I. Vitelloni*, 1954, is a good example) and Michelangelo Antonioni (*Cronaca di un amore*, 1951); both directors had worked on Neorealist films. The movement exercised a strong influence on individual filmmakers such as Ermanno Olmi and Satyajit Ray and on groups such as the French New Wave.

> "The sentiment of [Bicycle Thieves] is expressed overtly. The feelings invoked are a natural consequence of the themes of the story and the point of view it is told from. It is a politically committed film, fueled by a quiet but burning passion. But it never lectures. It observes rather than explains."
>
> — Sally Potter, director, *Orlando*

The French New Wave (1959–1964)

The late 1950s and early 1960s saw the rise of a new generation of filmmakers around the world. In country after country, there emerged directors born before World War II but grown to adulthood in the postwar era of reconstruction and rising prosperity. Japan, Canada, England, Italy, Spain, Brazil, and the United States all had their new waves or young cinema groups—some trained in film schools, many allied with specialized film magazines, most in revolt against their elders in the industry. The most influential of these groups appeared in France.

In the mid-1950s, a group of young men who wrote for the Paris film journal *Cahiers du cinéma* made a habit of attacking the most artistically respected French filmmakers of the day. "I consider an adaptation of value," wrote François Truffaut, "only when written by a *man of the cinema*. Aurenche and Bost [the leading scriptwriters of the time] are essentially literary men and I reproach them here for being contemptuous of the cinema by underestimating it." Addressing 21 major directors, Jean-Luc Godard asserted, "Your camera movements are ugly because your subjects are bad, your casts act badly because your dialogue is worthless; in a word, you don't know how to create cinema because you no longer even know what it is." Truffaut and Godard, along with Claude Chabrol, Eric Rohmer, and Jacques Rivette, also praised directors considered somewhat outdated (Jean Renoir, Max Ophuls) or eccentric (Robert Bresson, Jacques Tati).

More important, the young men saw no contradiction in rejecting the French filmmaking establishment while loving blatantly commercial Hollywood. The young rebels of *Cahiers* claimed that in the works of certain directors—certain *auteurs* (authors)—artistry existed in the American cinema. An **auteur** usually did not literally write scripts but managed nonetheless to stamp his or her personality on studio products, transcending the constraints of Hollywood's standardized system. Howard Hawks, Otto Preminger, Samuel Fuller, Vincente Minnelli, Nicholas Ray, Alfred Hitchcock—these were more than craftsmen. Each person's total output constituted a coherent world. Truffaut quoted Giraudoux, "There are no works, there are only auteurs." Godard remarked later, "We won the day in having it acknowledged in principle that a film by Hitchcock, for example, is as important as a book by Aragon. Film auteurs, thanks to us, have finally entered the history of art." And indeed, many of the Hollywood directors these critics and filmmakers championed have become recognized as great artists.

Writing criticism didn't satisfy these young men. They itched to make movies. Borrowing money from friends and filming on location, each started to shoot short films. By 1959, they had become a force to be reckoned with. In that year, Rivette filmed *Paris nous appartient* (*Paris Belongs to Us*); Godard made *À Bout de souffle* (*Breathless*); Chabrol made his second feature, *Les Cousins;* and in April Truffaut's *Les Quatre cent coups* (*The 400 Blows*) won the Grand Prize at the Cannes Festival.

The novelty and youthful vigor of these directors led journalists to nickname them *la nouvelle vague*—the *New Wave*. Their output was staggering. All told, the five central directors made 32 feature films between 1959 and 1966; Godard and Chabrol made 11 apiece. So many films must of course be highly disparate, but

> "We were all critics before beginning to make films, and I loved all kinds of cinema—the Russians, the Americans, the neorealists. It was the cinema that made us—or me, at least—want to make films. I knew nothing of life except through the cinema."
>
> — Jean-Luc Godard, director

12.46 *Les Bonnes femmes*: While a serial killer stalks them, two of the heroines kill time at work. Like many New Wave directors, Claude Chabrol followed the Neorealists in shooting on locations like this drab appliance shop.

12.47   In *Vivre sa vie,* a clip from Dreyer's *The Passion of Joan of Arc* . . .

12.48   . . . helps dramatize the heroine's feelings as she watches it.

there are enough similarities for us to identify a broadly distinctive New Wave approach to style and form.

The most obviously revolutionary quality of the New Wave films was their casual look. To proponents of the carefully polished French *cinema of quality,* the young directors must have seemed hopelessly sloppy. The New Wave directors had admired the Neorealists (especially Rossellini) and, in opposition to studio filmmaking, took as their mise-en-scene actual locales in and around Paris. Shooting on location became the norm **(12.46)**. Similarly, glossy studio lighting was replaced by available light and simple supplemental sources. Few postwar French films would have shown the dim, grimy apartments and corridors featured in *Paris Belongs to Us*.

Cinematography changed, too. The New Wave camera moves a great deal, panning and tracking to follow characters or trace out relations within a locale. Furthermore, shooting cheaply on location demanded flexible, portable equipment. Fortunately, Eclair had recently developed a lightweight camera that could be handheld. (That the Eclair had been used primarily for documentary work accorded perfectly with the realistic mise-en-scene of the New Wave.) New Wave films were intoxicated with the new freedom offered by the handheld camera. In *The 400 Blows,* the camera explores a cramped apartment and rides a carnival centrifuge. In *Breathless,* the cinematographer held the camera while seated in a wheelchair to follow the hero along a complex path in a travel agency's office (11.36).

One of the most salient features of New Wave films is their casual humor. These young men deliberately played with the medium. In Godard's *Band of Outsiders,* the three main characters resolve to be silent for a minute, and Godard dutifully shuts off *all* the sound. In Truffaut's *Shoot the Piano Player,* a character swears that he's not lying: "May my mother drop dead if I'm not telling the truth." Cut to a shot of an old lady keeling over. But most often the humor lies in esoteric references to other films, Hollywood or European. There are homages to admired auteurs: Godard characters allude to *Johnny Guitar* (Ray), *Some Came Running* (Minnelli), and "Arizona Jim" (from Renoir's *Crime of M. Lange*). In *Les Carabiniers,* Godard parodies Lumière, and in *Vivre sa vie,* he visually quotes *La Passion de Jeanne d'Arc.* **(12.47, 12.48)**. Hitchcock is frequently cited in Chabrol's films, and Truffaut's *Les Mistons* re-creates a shot from a Lumière short. Such homages even became in-jokes, as when New Wave actors Jean-Claude Brialy and Jeanne Moreau walk on in *The 400 Blows* or when a Godard character mentions "Arizona Jules" (combining names from *The Crime of M. Lange* and *Jules and Jim*). Such gags, the New Wave directors felt, took some of the solemnity out of filmmaking and film viewing.

New Wave films also pushed further the Neorealist experimentation with plot construction. In general, causal connections became quite loose. Is there actually a political conspiracy going on in *Paris Belongs to Us?* Why is Nana shot at the end of *Vivre sa vie?* In *Shoot the Piano Player,* the first sequence consists mainly of a conversation between the hero's brother and a man he accidentally meets on the street; the latter tells of his marital problems at some length, even though he has nothing to do with the film's narrative.

Moreover, the films often lack goal-oriented protagonists. The heroes may drift aimlessly, engage in actions on the spur of the moment, spend their time talking and drinking in a café or going to movies. New Wave narratives often introduce startling shifts in tone, jolting our expectations. When two gangsters kidnap the hero and his girlfriend in *Shoot the Piano Player,* the whole group begins a comic discussion of sex. Discontinuous editing further disturbs narrative continuity; this tendency reaches its limit in Godard's jump cuts (6.136, 6.137, 11.39, 11.40).

Perhaps most important, the New Wave film typically ends ambiguously. We have seen this already in *Breathless* (p. 399). Antoine in *The 400 Blows* reaches the sea in the last shot, but as he moves forward, Truffaut zooms in and freezes the frame, ending the film with the question of where Antoine will go from there (3.8). In Chabrol's *Les Bonnes Femmes* and *Ophelia,* in Rivette's *Paris Belongs to Us,* and in nearly all the work of Godard and Truffaut in this period, the looseness of the causal chain leads to endings that remain defiantly open and uncertain.

Despite the demands that the films placed on the viewer and despite the critical rampages of the filmmakers, the French film industry wasn't hostile to the New Wave. The decade 1947–1957 had been good to film production: The government supported the industry through enforced quotas, banks had invested heavily, and there was a flourishing business of international coproductions. But in 1957, cinema attendance fell off drastically, chiefly because television became more widespread. By 1959, the industry was in a crisis. The independent financing of low-budget films seemed to offer a good solution. New Wave directors shot films much more quickly and cheaply than did reigning directors. Moreover, the young directors helped one another out and thus reduced the financial risk of the established companies. Thus the French industry supported the New Wave through distribution, exhibition, and eventually production.

Indeed, it is possible to argue that by 1964, although each New Wave director had his or her own production company, the group had become absorbed into the film industry. Godard made *Le Mépris (Contempt,* 1963) for a major commercial producer, Carlo Ponti; Truffaut made *Fahrenheit 451* (1966) in England for Universal; and Chabrol began turning out parodies of James Bond thrillers.

Dating the exact end of the movement is difficult, but most historians select 1964, when the characteristic New Wave form and style had already become diffused and imitated (by, for instance, Tony Richardson in his 1963 English film *Tom Jones*). Certainly, after 1968, the political upheavals in France drastically altered the personal relations among the directors. Chabrol, Truffaut, and Rohmer became firmly entrenched in the French film industry, whereas Godard set up an experimental film and video studio in Switzerland, and Rivette began to create narratives of staggering complexity and length (such as *Out One,* originally about 12 hours long). By the mid-1980s, Truffaut had died, Chabrol's films were often unseen outside France, and Rivette's output had become esoteric. Rohmer retained international attention with his ironic tales of love and self-deception among the upper-middle class (*Pauline at the Beach* [1982] and *Full Moon over Paris* [1984]). Godard continued to attract notoriety with such films as *Passion* (1981) and his controversial retelling of the Old and New Testaments, *Hail Mary* (1983). In 1990, he released an elegant, enigmatic film ironically entitled *Nouvelle vague,* one that bears little relationship to the original tendency. In retrospect, the New Wave not only offered several original and valuable films but also demonstrated that renewal in the film industry could come from talented, aggressive young people inspired in large part by the sheer love of cinema.

The New Hollywood and Independent Filmmaking

Midway through the 1960s, the Hollywood industry seemed very healthy, with blockbusters such as *The Sound of Music* (1965) and *Dr. Zhivago* (1965) yielding huge profits. But soon problems arose. Expensive studio projects failed miserably. Television networks, which had paid high prices to broadcast films after theatrical release, stopped bidding for pictures. American movie attendance flattened out at around 1 billion tickets per year (a figure that, despite home video, remained constant until the early 1990s). By 1969, Hollywood companies were losing over $200 million annually.

Producers fought back. One strategy was to produce counterculture-flavored films aimed at young people. The most popular and influential were Dennis Hopper's low-budget *Easy Rider* (1969) and Robert Altman's *M*A*S*H* (1970). By and large, however, other "youthpix" about campus revolution and unorthodox lifestyles proved disappointing at the box office. What did help lift the industry's fortunes were films aimed squarely at broader audiences. The most successful were Francis Ford Coppola's *The Godfather* (1972); William Friedkin's *The Exorcist* (1973); Steven Spielberg's *Jaws* (1975) and *Close Encounters of the Third Kind* (1977); John Carpenter's *Halloween* (1978); and George Lucas's *American Graffiti* (1973), *Star Wars* (1977), and *The Empire Strikes Back* (1980). In addition, films by Brian De Palma (*Obsession,* 1976) and Martin Scorsese (*Taxi Driver,* 1976; *Raging Bull,* 1980) attracted critical praise.

These and other directors came to be known as the movie brats. Instead of coming up through the ranks of the studio system, most had gone to film schools. At New York University, the University of Southern California, and the University of California at Los Angeles, they had not only mastered the mechanics of production but also learned about film aesthetics and history. Unlike earlier Hollywood directors, the movie brats often had an encyclopedic knowledge of great movies and directors. Even those who did not attend film school were admirers of the classical Hollywood tradition.

As had been the case with the French New Wave, these film-buff directors produced some personal, highly self-conscious films. The movie brats worked in traditional genres, but they also tried to give them an autobiographical coloring. Thus *American Graffiti* was not only a teenage musical but also Lucas's reflection on growing up in California in the 1960s. Martin Scorsese drew on his youth in New York's Little Italy for his crime drama *Mean Streets* (1973; **12.49**). Coppola imbued both *Godfather* films with a vivacious and melancholy sense of the intense bonds within the Italian American family. Paul Schrader poured his own obsessions with violence and sexuality into his scripts for *Taxi Driver* and *Raging Bull* and the films he directed, such as *Hard Core* (1979).

Since movies had been a major part of the young directors' lives, many films of the New Hollywood were based on the old Hollywood. De Palma's films

12.49 *Mean Streets*: Scorsese uses depth staging and deep focus for the famous "Mook" confrontation.

borrowed heavily from Hitchcock, with *Dressed to Kill* (1980) an overt redoing of *Psycho*. Peter Bogdanovich's *What's Up, Doc?* (1972) was an updating of screwball comedy, with particular reference to Howard Hawks's *Bringing Up Baby*. Carpenter's *Assault on Precinct 13* (1976) derived partly from Hawks's *Rio Bravo;* the editing is credited to "John T. Chance," the character played by John Wayne in Hawks's Western.

At the same time, many directors admired the European tradition, with Scorsese drawn to the visual splendor of Luchino Visconti and British director Michael Powell. Some directors dreamed of making complex art films in the European mold. The best-known effort is probably Coppola's *The Conversation* (1974), a mystery-story reworking of Antonioni's *Blow-Up* (1966) that plays ambiguously between reality and hallucination (pp. 170, 172).

Robert Altman and Woody Allen, in quite different ways, displayed creative attitudes fed by European cinema. Altman's *Three Women* (1977) and Allen's *Interiors* (1978), for example, owed a good deal to Ingmar Bergman's work. More influential were their innovations on other fronts. Allen revived the American comedy of manners in *Annie Hall* (1977), *Manhattan* (1979), *Hannah and Her Sisters* (1985). Altman's *McCabe and Mrs. Miller* (1971) and *The Long Goodbye* (1973) displayed rough-edged performances, dense soundtracks, and a disrespectful approach to genre. His *Nashville* (1975) built its plot out of the casual encounters among two dozen characters, none of whom is singled out as the protagonist. Altman has explored this narrative form throughout his career, notably in *A Wedding* (1978), *Short Cuts* (1993), and *A Prairie Home Companion* (2006). Such network-based plotting became a common option for independent films such as *Magnolia* (1999), *Crash* (2005), and *Me and You and Everyone We Know* (2005).

Altman and Allen were of a slightly older generation, but many movie brats proved to be the most continuously successful directors of the era. Lucas and Spielberg became powerful producers, working together on the Indiana Jones series and personifying Hollywood's new generation. Coppola failed to sustain his own studio, but he remained an important director. Scorsese's reputation rose steadily: By the end of the 1980s, he was the most critically acclaimed living American filmmaker.

During the 1980s, fresh talents won recognition, creating a New New Hollywood. Many of the biggest hits of the decade continued to come from Lucas and Spielberg, but other, somewhat younger directors were successful: James Cameron (*The Terminator,* 1984; *Terminator 2: Judgment Day,* 1991), Tim Burton (*Beetlejuice,* 1988; *Batman,* 1989), and Robert Zemeckis (*Back to the Future,* 1985; *Who Framed Roger Rabbit,* 1988). Many of the successful films of the 1990s came from directors from both these successive waves of the Hollywood renaissance: Spielberg's *Jurassic Park* (1993), De Palma's *Mission: Impossible* (1996), and Lucas's *The Phantom Empire* (1999), as well as Zemeckis's *Forrest Gump* (1994), Cameron's *Titanic* (1997), and Burton's *Sleepy Hollow* (1999).

The resurgence of mainstream film was also fed by filmmakers from outside Hollywood. Many directors came from abroad—from Britain (Tony and Ridley Scott), Australia (Peter Weir, Fred Schepisi), Germany (Wolfgang Peterson), the Netherlands (Paul Verhoeven), and Finland (Rennie Harlin). During the 1980s and 1990s, more women filmmakers also became commercially successful, such as Amy Heckerling (*Fast Times at Ridgemont High,* 1982; *Look Who's Talking,* 1990), Martha Coolidge (*Valley Girl,* 1983; *Rambling Rose,* 1991), and Penelope Spheeris (*Wayne's World,* 1992).

Several directors from independent film managed to shift into the mainstream, making medium-budget pictures with widely known stars. David Lynch moved from the midnight movie *Eraserhead* (1978) to the cult classic *Blue Velvet* (1986), while Canadian David Cronenberg, a specialist in low-budget horror films such as *Shivers* (1975), won wider recognition with *The Dead Zone* (1983; **12.50**) and *The Fly* (1986). The New New Hollywood also absorbed some minority directors from

"I love the idea of not being an independent filmmaker. I've liked working within the system. And I've admired a lot of the older directors who were sort of 'directors for hire.' Like Victor Fleming was in a contract all those years to Metro and Selznick and Mayer . . . he made Captains Courageous. *And you know, his most famous films:* Wizard of Oz *and* Gone with the Wind.*"*

— Steven Spielberg, producer/director

independent film. Wayne Wang was the most successful Asian American filmmaker (*Chan Is Missing,* 1982; *Smoke,* 1995). Spike Lee (*She's Gotta Have It,* 1986; *Malcolm X,* 1992) led the way for young African American directors such as Reginald Hudlin (*House Party,* 1990), John Singleton (*Boyz N the Hood,* 1991), Mario van Peebles (*New Jack City,* 1991), and Allen and Albert Hughes (*Menace II Society,* 1993).

Still other directors remained independent and more or less marginal to the studios. In *Stranger Than Paradise* (1984) and *Down by Law* (1986), Jim Jarmusch presented quirky, decentered narratives peopled by drifting losers **(12.51)**. Allison Anders treated the contemporary experiences of disaffected young women, either in small towns (*Gas Food Lodging,* 1992) or city centers (*Mi Vida Loca,* 1994). Leslie Harris's *Just Another Girl on the IRT* (1994; 1.33) likewise focused on the problems of urban women of color.

Stylistically, no single coherent film movement emerged during the 1970s and 1980s. The most mainstream of the young directors continued the tradition of classical American cinema. Continuity editing remained the norm, with clear signals for time shifts and new plot developments. Some directors embellished Hollywood's traditional storytelling strategies with new or revived visual techniques. In films from *Jaws* onward, Spielberg used deep-focus techniques reminiscent of *Citizen Kane* (5.39, **12.52**). Lucas developed motion-control techniques for filming miniatures for *Star Wars,* and his firm Industrial Light and Magic (ILM) became the leader in new special-effects technology. With the aid of ILM, Zemeckis astutely exploited digital imaging for *Forrest Gump* (10.5). Spielberg and Lucas also led the move toward digital sound and high-quality theater reproduction technology.

Less well funded Hollywood filmmaking cultivated more flamboyant styles. Scorsese's *Taxi Driver, Raging Bull* (pp. 426–430), and *The Age of Innocence* (1993) use camera movement and slow motion to extend the emotional impact of a scene. De Palma has been an even more outrageous stylist; his films flaunt long takes, startling overhead compositions, and split-screen devices. Coppola has experimented with fast-motion black-and-white in *Rumble Fish* (1983), phone conversations handled in the foreground and background of a single shot (*Tucker,* 1988), and old-fashioned special effects to lend a period mood to *Bram Stoker's Dracula* (1993).

Several of the newer entrants into Hollywood enriched mainstream conventions of genre, narrative, and style. We have already seen one example of this

12.50   *The Dead Zone:* The hero, a psychic possessed by visions of future events, imagines a fire.

12.51   Eva and Willie, the listless protagonists of *Stranger Than Paradise.* "These characters," Jarmusch explains, "move through the world of the film in a kind of random, aimless way, like looking for the next card game or something."

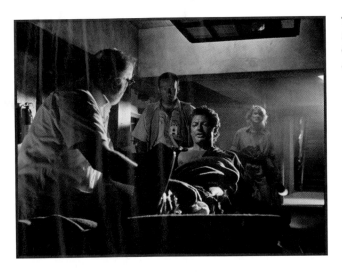

12.52 In *Jurassic Park* Spielberg harks back to Orson Welles's use of depth compositions.

12.53 *The Joy Luck Club.*

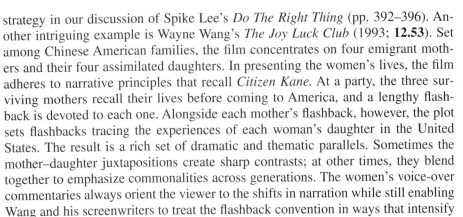

12.54 Wide-angle tracking shots follow crawling babies along the floor and under furniture in *Raising Arizona*.

strategy in our discussion of Spike Lee's *Do The Right Thing* (pp. 392–396). Another intriguing example is Wayne Wang's *The Joy Luck Club* (1993; **12.53**). Set among Chinese American families, the film concentrates on four emigrant mothers and their four assimilated daughters. In presenting the women's lives, the film adheres to narrative principles that recall *Citizen Kane*. At a party, the three surviving mothers recall their lives before coming to America, and a lengthy flashback is devoted to each one. Alongside each mother's flashback, however, the plot sets flashbacks tracing the experiences of each woman's daughter in the United States. The result is a rich set of dramatic and thematic parallels. Sometimes the mother–daughter juxtapositions create sharp contrasts; at other times, they blend together to emphasize commonalities across generations. The women's voice-over commentaries always orient the viewer to the shifts in narration while still enabling Wang and his screenwriters to treat the flashback convention in ways that intensify the emotional effect.

A similar effort to revise conventions pervades the work of other independent directors. The brothers Joel and Ethan Coen treat each film as a pretext for exploring cinema's expressive resources. In *Raising Arizona* (1987), high-speed tracking shots combine with distorting wide-angle close-ups to create comic-book exaggerations **(12.54)**. A somewhat similar approach is taken in Gregg Araki's gay road picture *The Living End* (1992). In films such as *Trust* (1991), Hal Hartley mutes a melodramatic plot through slow pacing, brooding close-ups, and dynamic foreground/background compositions **(12.55)**.

Independent directors of the 1980s and 1990s have also experimented with narrative construction. The Coens' *Barton Fink* (1991) passes unnoticeably from a satiric portrait of 1930s Hollywood into a hallucinatory fantasy. Quentin Tarantino's *Reservoir Dogs* (1993) and *Pulp Fiction* (1994) juggle story and plot time in ways that recall the complex flashbacks of the 1940s. Unlike the flashbacks in *The Joy Luck Club,* moreover, the switches are not motivated as characters' memories; the audience is forced to puzzle out the purposes served by the time shifts. In *Daughters of the Dust* (1991), Julie Dash incorporates the rich Gullah dialect and explores a complex time scheme that seeks to fuse present and future. In one scene, optical effects give the characters a glimpse of a child who is as yet unborn.

So, while in the 1980s and 1990s younger studio directors adapted classical conventions to modern tastes, an energetic independent film tradition began pushing the envelope. By the end of the 1990s, the two trends were merging in surprising ways. As independent films began to win larger audiences, major studios eagerly acquired distribution companies such as Miramax and October Films. Much media journalism fostered the impression that Hollywood was becoming subverted by independent filmmaking, but in fact, more and more, the major studios

12.55 In *Trust,* a melodramatic scene between mother and daughter is intensified through deep-space staging and a tight close-up.

12.56 An ambiguous image that recurs throughout *The Limey:* it may be construed either as a flashback to the protagonist's trip to the United States or as a flash-forward to his trip back to Britain, presented in the final scene.

controlled audiences' access to formerly independent productions. The Sundance Film Festival, founded as a forum for the off-Hollywood scene, came to be treated as a talent market by the studios, which often bought films in order to line up the filmmaker for more mainstream projects. Thus after Kevin Smith found success with *Clerks* (1994), he directed *Mallrats* (1995), a tame twenty-something comedy for Universal. Robert Rodriguez's similarly microbudgeted *El Mariachi* (1992) proved a hit, so he was hired to remake it as an all-out action picture starring Antonio Banderas (*Desperado,* 1995).

Yet sometimes the big-budget films of independent filmmakers conveyed a distinctly experimental attitude. Kevin Smith used the star-filled *Dogma* (1999) to question Catholic doctrine. David O. Russell, who had worked his way into the system with off-kilter comedies (*Spanking the Monkey,* 1994; *Flirting with Disaster,* 1996), made *Three Kings* (1999), an action picture that criticized Gulf War policies and that reveled in a flamboyant, digital-era style. Following in the path of *Pulp Fiction,* studio pictures began to play more boldly with narrative form. A genre thriller such as *The Sixth Sense* (1999) encouraged viewers to see it twice in order to detect how the narration had misled them. Stories might be told through complicated flashbacks, as in Steven Soderbergh's *The Limey* (**12.56**). (See also box, pp. 83–85.) A film might reveal that one character was the imaginary creation of another (David Fincher's *Fight Club,* 1999) or that a person could crawl into another's brain (Spike Jonze's *Being John Malkovich,* 1999), or that the external world was merely an illusion produced by sophisticated software (the Wachowski brothers' *The Matrix,* 1999). In their willingness to experiment with ambiguous and teasing modes of narration, many American studio films began rivaling their overseas counterparts such as *Breaking the Waves* (1996), *Sliding Doors* (1998), and *Run Lola Run* (1998).

At the start of the new century, many of the most thrilling Hollywood films were being created by a robust new generation, born in the 1960s and 1970s and brought up on videotape, video games, and the Internet. Like their predecessors, these directors were reshaping the formal and stylistic conventions of the classical cinema while also making their innovations accessible to a broad audience.

Contemporary Hong Kong Cinema

While the New Hollywood directors were revamping American films, a young generation of directors in Hong Kong found footing in their industry and recast its traditional genres and creative methods. The result was not exactly a unified film movement, but a local cinema with a robust identity. Hong Kong's innovations in cinematic style and storytelling vigorously influenced world filmmaking well into the twenty-first century.

Hong Kong produced films in the silent era and during the 1930s, although World War II halted production. When the industry revived in the 1950s, the most powerful studio was Shaw Brothers. Shaws owned theaters throughout East Asia and used Hong Kong as a production base for films in several languages, chiefly Mandarin Chinese. Shaws made films in many genres, but among its biggest successes were dynamic, gory swordfighting films (*wuxia pian,* or "tales of martial chivalry"). In the 1970s, another studio, Golden Harvest, triumphed with kung-fu films starring Bruce Lee. Although Lee completed only four martial-arts films before his death in 1973, he brought Hong Kong cinema to worldwide attention and forever identified it with films of acrobatic and violent action.

Several major directors worked in this period. Most famous is King Hu, who started as a Shaws director. In films like *Dragon Gate Inn* (1967) and *The Valiant Ones* (1975; 5.69), Hu reinvigorated the *wuxia pian* through graceful airborne swordplay and inventive cutting. Chang Cheh, another Shaws director, turned the swordplay film toward violent male melodrama (such as *The One-Armed Swordsman,* 1967) before specializing in flamboyant kung-fu films such as *Crippled*

Avengers (also called *Mortal Combat,* 1978). Neither King Hu nor Chang Cheh was a practitioner of martial arts, but Lau Kar-leung was a fight choreographer before becoming a full-fledged director. Lau created a string of inventive films (such as *36th Chamber of Shaolin,* 1978, and *The Eight-Diagram Pole Fighter,* 1983) that showcased a range of dazzling marital-arts techniques.

By the early 1980s, traditional kung-fu was fading in popularity, and Shaws turned from moviemaking to its lucrative television business. At the same time, a new generation of directors came forward. One group had little formal education but had grown up in the film industry, working as stuntmen and martial artists. Among those who became directors were choreographers Yuen Wo-ping and Yuen Kuei (*Yes, Madam!,* 1985). Sammo Hung choreographed, directed, and starred in many lively action films (such as *Eastern Condors,* 1987).

The most famous graduate of the studio system was Jackie Chan, who labored as a copy of Bruce Lee before finding his feet in comic kung-fu. With *Drunken Master* (1978, directed by Yuen Wo-ping), he became a star throughout Asia and gained the power to direct his own films. In the early 1980s, Chan and his colleagues realized that kung-fu could be incorporated into Hollywoodish action-adventure movies. Chan made the historical adventure *Project A* (1983, also starring Hung) and the contemporary cop drama *Police Story* (1985). These and others were huge hits across Asia, partly because of Chan's lovably goofy star persona, partly because of his ingenious and dangerous action scenes (6.49–6.51).

Another group of directors had more formal training, with many attending film schools in the United States or Britain. When Ann Hui, Allen Fong, and others returned to Hong Kong, they found work in television before moving on to feature filmmaking. For a time, they constituted a local art cinema, attracting attention at festivals with such films as Hui's *Boat People* (1982). But most of this group gravitated toward independent companies turning out comedies, dramas, and action films. Tsui Hark was the leader of this trend. As both director and producer Tsui revived and reworked a range of genres: swordplay fantasy (*Zu: Warriors of the Magic Mountain,* 1979), romantic comedy (*Shanghai Blues,* 1984), historical adventure (*Peking Opera Blues,* 1986; **12.57**), supernatural romance (*A Chinese Ghost Story,* 1987, directed by Ching Siu-tung), and classic kung-fu (*Once upon a Time in China,* 1990).

Seeing the success that modern cops-and-crooks films were then enjoying, Tsui partnered with John Woo on *A Better Tomorrow* (1986), a remake of a 1960s movie (**12.58**). Woo was something of an in-between figure, having been a successful studio comedy director during the 1970s. With Tsui as producer, *A Better Tomorrow* became Woo's comeback effort, one of the most successful Hong Kong films of the

12.57 Rapid movements into and out of the frame are characteristic of Hong Kong film style. In this shot from *Peking Opera Blues*, the sheriff and his captive rise into the foreground as the three heroines watch from the rear.

12.58 John Woo's debt to the Western: A striking long shot as a hero walks to meet his fate in *A Better Tomorrow*.

12.59   Cop and hitman as blood brothers in *The Killer.*

12.60   Stylized blocks of light for *The Longest Nite* (Patrick Yau, Johnnie To, 1998).

1980s and a star-making vehicle for the charismatic Chow Yun-fat. Hark, Woo, and Chow teamed again for a sequel and for the film that made Woo famous in the West, *The Killer* (1989), a lush and baroque story of the unexpected alliance between a hitman and a detective **(12.59)**.

Hong Kong cinema of the 1980s and early 1990s surged with almost reckless energy. The rushed production schedules didn't allow much time to prepare scripts, so the plots, borrowing freely from Chinese legend and Hollywood genres, tended to be less tightly unified than those in U.S. films. They avoided tight linkage of cause and effect in favor of a more casual, episodic construction—not, as in Italian Neorealism, to suggest the randomness of everyday life but rather to permit chases and fights to be inserted easily. While action sequences were meticulously choreographed, connecting scenes were often improvised and shot quickly. Similarly, the kung-fu films had often bounced between pathos and almost silly comedy, and this tendency to mix tones continued through the 1980s. In *A Better Tomorrow,* for example, Tsui Hark appears in a slapstick interlude involving a cello. Again, because of rushed shooting, the plots often end abruptly, with a big action set-piece but little in the nature of a mood-setting epilogue. One of Tsui's innovations was to provide more satisfying conclusions, as in the lilting railroad station finale of *Shanghai Blues.*

At the level of visual style, Hong Kong directors brought the action film to a new pitch of excitement. Gunmen (and gunwomen) leaped and fired in slow motion, hovering in midair like 1970s swordfighters and kung-fu warriors. John Woo, who had been an assistant director for Chang Cheh, pushed such shots to extravagant limits. Directors also developed florid color designs, with rich reds, blues, and yellows glowing out of smoky nightclubs or narrow alleyways. Well into the 1990s, unrealistically tinted mood lighting was a trademark of Hong Kong cinema **(12.60)**.

Above all, everything was sacrificed to constant motion; even in dialogue scenes, the camera or the characters seldom stood still.

Aiming to energize the viewer, the new action directors built on the innovations of King Hu and his contemporaries. They developed a staccato cutting technique based on the tempo of martial-arts routines and Peking Opera displays, alternating rapid movement with sudden pauses. If shot composition was kept simple, an action could be cut to flow across shots very rapidly, while another cut could accentuate a moment of stillness (**12.61–12.63**). Most Hong Kong directors were unaware of the Soviet Montage movement, but in their efforts to arouse viewers kinesthetically through expressive movement and editing, they were reviving ideas of concern to 1920s filmmakers.

The 1990s brought the golden age of Hong Kong action cinema to a close. Jackie Chan, John Woo, Chow Yun-fat, Sammo Hung, and action star Jet Li began working in Hollywood, with Yuen Wo-ping designing the action choreography for *The Matrix* (1999) and *Crouching Tiger, Hidden Dragon* (2000). A recession after Hong Kong's 1997 handover to China depressed the local film industry. As Hollywood began imitating Hong Kong movies (as in *The Replacement Killers,* 1998), local audiences developed a taste for U.S. films. At the same time, the art-cinema wing became more ambitious, and festivals rewarded the offbeat works of Wong Kar-wai (see the analysis of *Chungking Express,* pp. 405–410). The action tradition was maintained by only a few directors such as Johnnie To, whose laconic film noir *The Mission* (1999) brought a leanness and pictorial abstraction to the gangster genre.

12.61   Crisp editing in *Yes, Madam!* In a shot only 7 frames long, Michele Yeoh swings swiftly . . .

12.62   . . . to knock the villain spinning (15 frames) . . .

12.63   . . . before she drops smoothly into a relaxed posture on the rail (17 frames).

Where to Go from Here

General

Allen, Robert C., and Douglas Gomery. *Film History: Theory and Practice.* New York: Random House, 1985.

Bordwell, David. *On the History of Film Style.* Cambridge, MA: Harvard University Press, 1997.

Gomery, Douglas. *The Hollywood Studio System: A History.* London: BFI Publishing, 2005.

Lanzoni, Rémi Fournier. *French Cinema: From Its Beginnings to the Present.* New York: Continuum, 2002.

Luhr, William, ed. *World Cinema Since 1945.* New York: Ungar, 1987.

Salt, Barry. *Film Style and Technology: History and Analysis,* 2d ed. London: Starword, 1992.

Thompson, Kristin, and David Bordwell. *Film History: An Introduction,* 2d ed. New York: McGraw-Hill, 2003.

Silent Cinema

Abel, Richard, *The Ciné Goes to Town: French Cinema 1896–1914.* Berkeley: University of California Press, 1994.

Allen, Robert C. *Vaudeville and Film, 1895–1915: A Study in Media Interaction.* New York: Arno, 1980.

Brewster, Ben, and Lea Jacobs. *Theatre to Cinema: Stage Pictorialism and the Early Feature Film.* Oxford: Oxford University Press, 1997.

Cherchi Usai, Paolo. *Silent Cinema: An Introduction.* London: British Film Institute, 2000.

Cherchi Usai, Paolo, and Lorenzo Codelli, eds. *Before Caligari: German Cinema, 1895–1920.* Pordenone: Edizioni Biblioteca dell' Immagine, 1990.

Dibbets, Karl, and Bert Hogenkamp, eds. *Film and the First World War.* Amsterdam: Amsterdam University Press, 1995.

Elsaesser, Thomas, ed. *Early Cinema: Space, Frame, Narrative.* London: British Film Institute, 1990.

Fell, John L., ed. *Film Before Griffith.* Berkeley: University of California Press, 1983.

Fullerton, John, ed. *Celebrating 1895: The Centenary of Cinema.* Sydney: John Libbey, 1998.

Grieveson, Lee, and Peter Krämer, eds. *The Silent Cinema Reader.* London: Routledge, 2004.

Gunning, Tom. *D. W. Griffith and the Origins of American Narrative Film: The Early Years at Biograph.* Urbana and Chicago: University of Illinois Press, 1991.

Hammond, Paul. *Marvelous Méliès.* New York: St. Martin's Press, 1975.

Hendricks, Gordon. *The Edison Motion Picture Myth.* Berkeley: University of California Press, 1961.

Leyda, Jay, and Charles Musser, eds. *Before Hollywood: Turn-of-the-Century Film from American Archives.* New York: American Federation of the Arts, 1986.

Musser, Charles. *Before the Nickelodeon: Edwin S. Porter and the Edison Manufacturing Company.* Berkeley: University of California Press, 1991.

———. *The Emergence of Cinema: The American Screen to 1907.* New York: Scribner, 1991.

Pratt, George, ed. *Spellbound in Darkness.* Greenwich, CT: New York Graphic Society, 1973.

Rossell, Deac. *Living Pictures: The Origins of the Movies.* Albany: State University of New York Press, 1998.

Tsivian, Yuri, ed. T*estimoni silenziosi: Film russi 1908–1919.* Pordenone: Edizioni Biblioteca dell'Immagine, 1989. (Bilingual in Italian and English.)

Youngblood, Denise. *The Magic Mirror: Moviemaking in Russia, 1908–1918.* Madison: University of Wisconsin Press, 1999.

Classical Hollywood Cinema (1908–1927)

Balio, Tino, ed. *The American Film Industry,* rev. ed. Madison: University of Wisconsin Press, 1985.

Bordwell, David, Janet Staiger, and Kristin Thompson. *The Classical Hollywood Cinema: Film Style and Mode of Production to 1960.* New York: Columbia University Press, 1985.

Bowser, Eileen. *The Transformation of Cinema, 1907–1915.* New York: Scribner, 1990.

Brownlow, Kevin. *The Parade's Gone By.* New York: Knopf, 1968.

DeBauche, Leslie Midkiff. *Reel Patriotism: The Movies and World War I.* Madison: University of Wisconsin Press, 1997.

Gomery, Douglas. *Shared Pleasures: A History of American Moviegoing.* Madison: University of Wisconsin Press, 1992.

Hampton, Benjamin B. *History of the American Film Industry.* 1931. Reprinted. New York: Dover, 1970.

Keil, Charlie. *Early American Cinema in Transition: Story, Style, and Filmmaking, 1907–1918.* Madison: University of Wisconsin Press, 2001.

Keil, Charlie, and Shelley Stamp, eds. *American Cinema's Transitional Era: Audiences, Institutions, Practices.* Berkeley: University of California Press, 2004.

Koszarski, Richard. *An Evening's Entertainment: The Age of the Silent Feature Picture, 1915–1928.* New York: Scribner, 1990.

Staiger, Janet. *Interpreting Films: Studies in the Historical Reception of American Cinema.* Princeton, NJ: Princeton University Press, 1992.

Vasey, Ruth. *The World According to Hollywood, 1928–1939.* Madison: University of Wisconsin Press, 1997.

German Expressionism

Barlow, John D. *German Expressionist Film.* Boston: Twayne, 1982.

Budd, Mike, ed. *The Cabinet of Dr. Caligari: Texts, Contexts, Histories.* New Brunswick, NJ: Rutgers University Press, 1990.

Eisner, Lotte. *The Haunted Screen.* Berkeley: University of California Press, 1969.

———. *Fritz Lang.* New York: Oxford University Press, 1977.

———. *F. W. Murnau.* Berkeley: University of California Press, 1983.

Kracauer, Siegfried. *From Caligari to Hitler.* Princeton, NJ: Princeton University Press, 1947.

Kreimeier, Klaus. *The UFA Story: A History of Germany's Greatest Film Company 1918–1945.* Trans. by Robert and Rita Kimber. New York: Hill & Wang, 1996.

Myers, Bernard S. *The German Expressionists.* New York: Praeger, 1963.

Robinson, David. *Das Cabinet des Dr. Caligari.* London: British Film Institute, 1997. (In English.)

Scheunemann, Dietrich, ed. *Expressionist Film: New Perspectives.* Rochester, NY: Camden House, 2003.

Selz, Peter. *German Expressionist Painting.* Berkeley: University of California Press, 1957.

Thompson, Kristin. *Herr Lubitsch Goes to Hollywood: German and American Film After World War I.* Amsterdam: Amsterdam University Press, 2005.

Willett, John. *Expressionism.* New York: McGraw-Hill, 1970.

———. *The New Sobriety: Art and Politics in the Weimar Republic, 1917–1933.* London: Thames & Hudson, 1978.

French Impressionism

Abel, Richard. *French Cinema: The First Wave, 1915–1929.* Princeton, NJ: Princeton University Press, 1984.

———. *French Film Theory and Criticism, 1907–1939,* vol. 1. Princeton, NJ: Princeton University Press, 1988.

Brownlow, Kevin. *"Napoleon": Abel Gance's Classic Film.* New York: Knopf, 1983.

Clair, René. *Cinema Yesterday and Today.* New York: Dover, 1972.

King, Norman. *Abel Gance: A Politics of Spectacle.* London: British Film Institute, 1984.

Soviet Montage

Bordwell, David. *The Cinema of Eisenstein.* Cambridge, MA: Harvard University Press, 1993.

Bowlt, John, ed. *Russian Art of the Avant-Garde.* New York: Viking Press, 1973.

Carynnyk, Marco, ed. *Alexander Dovzhenko: Poet as Filmmaker.* Cambridge, MA: MIT Press, 1973.

Eisenstein, S. M. *S. M. Eisenstein: Writings 1922–1934,* Richard Taylor, ed. London: British Film Institute, 1988; *Eisenstein, Volume 2, Towards a Theory of Montage,* Michael Glenny and Richard Taylor, eds. London: British Film Institute, 1991; *Eisenstein Writings 1934–1947,* Richard Taylor, ed. London: British Film Institute, 1996. *Beyond the Stars: The Memoirs of Sergei Eisenstein,* vol. 4, Richard Taylor, ed., William Powell, trans. London: British Film Institute, 1995.

Kepley, Jr., Vance. *In the Service of the State: The Cinema of Alexander Dovzhenko.* Madison: University of Wisconsin Press, 1986.

———. *The End of St. Petersburg.* London: I. B. Tauris, 2003.

Kuleshov, Lev. *Kuleshov on Film.* Ed. and trans. Ronald Levaco. Berkeley: University of California Press, 1974.

Leyda, Jay. *Kino,* 3d ed. Princeton, NJ Princeton University Press, 1983.

Lodder, Christina. *Russian Constructivism.* New Haven, CT: Yale University Press, 1983.

Michelson, Annette, ed. *Kino-Eye: The Writings of Dziga Vertov.* Berkeley: University of California Press, 1984.

Nilsen, Vladimir. *The Cinema as a Graphic Art.* New York: Hill & Wang, 1959.

Petric, Vlada. *Constructivism in Film: The Man with a Movie Camera—A Cinematic Analysis.* London: Cambridge University Press, 1987.

Pudovkin, V. I. *Film Technique and Film Acting.* New York: Grove Press, 1960.

Schnitzer, Luda, Jean Schnitzer, and Marcel Martin, eds. *Cinema and Revolution.* New York: Hill & Wang, 1973.

Taylor, Richard. *The Politics of the Soviet Cinema, 1917–1929.* Cambridge: Cambridge University Press, 1979.

Taylor, Richard, and Ian Christie, eds. *The Film Factory: Russian and Soviet Cinema in Documents, 1896–1939.* Cambridge, Mass.: Harvard University Press, 1988.

———. *Inside the Film Factory: New Approaches to Russian and Soviet Cinema.* London: Routledge, 1991.

Youngblood, Denise. *Soviet Cinema in the Silent Era, 1918–1933.* Ann Arbor, MI: UMI Research Press, 1985.

The Classical Hollywood Cinema After the Coming of Sound

Balio, Tino. *Grand Design: Hollywood as a Modern Business Enterprise, 1930–1939.* New York: Scribner, 1993.

Balio, Tino, ed. *The American Film Industry,* rev. ed. Madison: University of Wisconsin Press, 1985.

———. *Hollywood in the Age of Television.* Boston: Unwin Hyman, 1990.

Bordwell, David, Janet Staiger, and Kristin Thompson. *The Classical Hollywood Cinema: Film Style and Mode of Production to 1960.* New York: Columbia University Press, 1985.

Crafton, Donald. *The Talkies: American Cinema's Transition to Sound 1926–1931.* New York: Scribner, 1997.

Koszarski, Richard, ed. *Hollywood Directors, 1914–1940.* New York: Oxford University Press, 1976.

Maltby, Richard. *Harmless Entertainment: Hollywood and the Ideology of Consensus.* Metuchen, NJ: Scarecrow, 1983.

———. *Hollywood Cinema,* 2nd ed. Oxford: Blackwell, 2003.

Schatz, Thomas. *Boom and Bust: American Cinema in the 1940s.* Berkeley: University of California Press, 1997.

Silver, Alain, and Elizabeth Ward. *Film Noir: An Encyclopedic Reference to the American Style.* Woodstock, NY: Overlook Press, 1979.

Walker, Alexander. *The Shattered Silents: How the Talkies Came to Stay.* New York: Morrow, 1979.

"Widescreen." Issue of *Velvet Light Trap* 21 (Summer 1985).

Italian Neorealism

Armes, Roy. *Patterns of Realism.* New York: A. S. Barnes, 1970.

Bazin, André. "Cinema and Television." *Sight and Sound* 28, 1 (Winter 1958–59): 26–30.

———. *What Is Cinema?* vol. 2. Berkeley: University of California Press, 1971.

Bondanella, Peter. *Italian Cinema from Neorealism to the Present.* New York: Ungar, 1983.

Brunette, Peter. *Roberto Rossellini.* New York: Oxford University Press, 1987.

Leprohon, Pierre. *The Italian Cinema.* New York: Praeger, 1984.

Liehm, Mira. *Passion and Defiance: Film in Italy from 1942 to the Present.* Berkeley: University of California Press, 1984.

Marcus, Millicent. *Italian Film in the Light of Neorealism.* Princeton, NJ: Princeton University Press, 1986.

Overbey, David, ed. *Springtime in Italy: A Reader on Neo-Realism.* London: Talisman, 1978.

Sitney, P. Adams. *Vital Crises in Italian Cinema: Iconography, Stylistics, Politics.* Austin: University of Texas Press, 1995.

The French New Wave

Crisp, Colin. *The Classic French Cinema, 1930–1960.* Bloomington: Indiana University Press, 1994.

Godard, Jean-Luc. *Godard on Godard.* New York: Viking Press, 1972.

Hillier, Jim, ed. *Cahiers du Cinéma: The 1950s: Neo-Realism, Hollywood, New Wave.* Cambridge, MA: Harvard University Press, 1985.

———. *Cahiers du Cinéma: The 1960s: New Wave, New Cinema, Reevaluating Hollywood.* Cambridge, MA: Harvard University Press, 1986.

Insdorf, Annette. *François Truffaut.* New York: William Morrow, 1979.

McCabe, Colin. *Godard: A Portrait of the Artist at Seventy.* New York: Farrar, Straus & Giroux, 2003.

Mussman, Toby, ed. *Jean-Luc Godard.* New York: Dutton, 1968.

Neupert, Richard. *A History of the French New Wave Cinema.* Madison: University of Wisconsin Press, 2002.

Sterritt, David. *The Films of Jean-Luc Godard: Seeing the Invisible.* Cambridge: Cambridge University Press, 1999.

Truffaut, François. *The Films in My Life.* Trans. Leonard Mayhew. New York: Simon & Schuster, 1978.

The New Hollywood and Independent Filmmaking

Andrew, Geoff. *Stranger Than Paradise: Maverick Film-Makers in Recent American Cinema.* London: Prion, 1998.

Bordwell, David. *The Way Hollywood Tells It: Story and Style in Modern Movies.* Berkeley: University of California Press, 2006.

Diawara, Manthia, ed. *Black American Cinema.* New York: Routledge, 1993.

Donahue, Suzanne Mary. *American Film Distribution: The Changing Marketplace.* Ann Arbor, MI: UMI Research Press, 1987.

Fuchs, Cynthia, ed. *Spike Lee Interviews.* Jackson: University Press of Mississippi, 2002.

Goodwin, Michael, and Naomi Wise. *On the Edge: The Life and Times of Francis Coppola.* New York: Morrow, 1989.

King, Geoff. *American Independent Cinema.* Bloomington: Indiana University Press, 2005.

Levy, Emmanuel. *Cinema of Outsiders: The Rise of American Independent Film.* New York: New York University Press, 1999.

Lewis, Jon, ed. *The New American Cinema.* Durham: Duke University Press, 1998.

McBride, Joseph. *Steven Spielberg: A Biography.* New York: Simon & Schuster, 1997.

McGilligan, Patrick. *Robert Altman: Jumping off the Cliff.* New York: St. Martin's Press, 1989.

Neale, Steve, and Murray Smith, eds. *Contemporary Hollywood Cinema.* New York: Routledge, 1998.

Noriega, Chon A. *Chicanos and Film: Representation and Resistance.* Minneapolis: University of Minnesota Press, 1992.

Pye, Michael, and Lynda Myles. *The Movie Brats: How the Film Generation Took Over Hollywood.* New York: Holt, Rinehart & Winston, 1979.

Reid, Mark A. *Redefining Black Film.* Berkeley: University of California Press, 1993.

Thompson, Kristin. *Storytelling in the New Hollywood: Understanding Classical Narrative Technique.* Cambridge, MA: Harvard University Press, 1999.

Welbon, Yvonne. "Calling the Shots: Black Women Directors Take the Helm." *Independent* 15, 2 (March 1992): 18–22.

Contemporary Hong Kong Cinema

Bordwell, David. *Planet Hong Kong: Popular Cinema and the Art of Entertainment.* Cambridge, MA: Harvard University Press, 2000.

Charles, John. *The Hong Kong Filmography, 1977–1997.* Jefferson, NC: McFarland, 2000.

Fu, Poshek, and Desser, David, eds. *The Cinema of Hong Kong: History, Arts, Identity.* Cambridge: Cambridge University Press, 2000.

Logan, Bey. *Hong Kong Action Cinema.* London: Titan Books, 1995.

Teo, Stephen. *Hong Kong Cinema: The Extra Dimensions.* London: British Film Institute, 1997.

Yau, Esther C. M., ed. *At Full Speed: Hong Kong Cinema in a Borderless World.* Minneapolis: University of Minnesota Press, 2001.

Recommended DVDs

Most of the films mentioned in this chapter are available on DVD. (*Rome Open City* was issued under its original American release title, *Open City.*) Kino Video (www.kino.com) and Image Entertainment (www.image-entertainment.com) have brought out many older classics.

Some collections of early films offer an easy way to get a quick overview of a period, filmmaker, or genre. For a brief introduction to the period up to 1913, *Landmarks of Early Film* (1 disc, Image Entertainment) offers 40 shorts. *Edison: The Invention of the Movies* (4 discs, Kino Video and the Museum of Modern Art) collects 140 films from the Thomas A. Edison Company, including *The Great Train Robbery.* It contains interviews with film historians and archivists, as well as program notes and documents. *The Movies Begin: A Treasury of Early Cinema 1894–1913* (5 discs, Kino Video) gathers 133 films arranged thematically: Volume 1, "*The Great Train Robbery* and Other Primary works"; Volume 2, "The European Pioneers" (including films by the Lumières and early British filmmakers); Volume 3, "Experimentation and Discovery" (mostly early British and French films); Volume 4, "The Magic of Méliès"; and Volume 5, "Comedy, Spectacle and New Horizons."

Slapstick Encyclopedia (5 discs, Image Entertainment) surveys the golden age of comedy shorts—the 1910s and early 1920s. *The Harold Lloyd Comedy Collection* (7 discs, New Line) provides an extensive program of films with one of the masters of silent comedy, as well as a disc of bonus material.

A broad range of types of films is collected in *Treasures from American Film Archives: 50 Preserved Films* (4 discs) and *More Treasures from American Film Archives, 1894–1931* (3 discs, Image Entertainment). These include documentaries, home movies, animation, experimental cinema, and fiction films such as D. W. Griffith's 1911 one-reeler *The Lonedale Operator* (illustrating his command of early intercutting) and Ernst Lubitsch's masterpiece of classical continuity filmmaking, *Lady Windermere's Fan* (1925). Each boxed set includes a book of detailed program notes.

RECOMMENDED DVD SUPPLEMENTS

Alien (20th Century Fox Home Entertainment), "Collector's Edition," 2 discs

Amadeus: Director's Cut (Warner Bros.), "Two-Disc Special Edition"

American Graffiti (Universal), "Collector's Edition," 1 disc

Armageddon (The Criterion Collection), 2 discs

Bambi (Disney), "Platinum Edition," 2 discs

Black Narcissus (The Criterion Collection), 1 disc

Butch Cassidy and the Sundance Kid (20th Century Fox), "Special Edition," 1 disc

Charlie and the Chocolate Factory (Warner Bros.), "Two-Disc Deluxe Edition"

Chicken Run (Dreamworks Home Entertainment), "Special Edition," 1 disc

Contempt (The Criterion Collection), 2 discs

Dancer in the Dark (New Line Home Video), 1 disc

The Frighteners (Universal), "Peter Jackson's Director's Cut," 1 disc

The Godfather (Paramount), "The Godfather DVD Collection," 5 discs

The Good, the Bad, and the Ugly (MGM), "Special Edition," 2 discs

A Hard Day's Night (Miramax), 2 discs

The Incredibles (Disney), "Two-Disc Collector's Edition"

Jaws (Universal), "Anniversary Collector's Edition," 1 disc

Jurassic Park (Universal), "Collector's Edition," 1 disc

King Kong (Warner Bros.), "Two-Disc Special Edition"

King Kong: Peter Jackson's Production Diaries (Universal), 2 discs

The Lord of the Rings 3 volumes (New Line Home Entertainment), "Special Extended DVD Edition," 4 discs each

The Magnificent Seven (Metro-Goldwyn-Mayer), "Collector's Edition," 2 discs

Magnolia (New Line Home Video), 2 discs

Master and Commander (20th Century Fox Home Entertainment), "Collector's Edition," 2 discs

Moulin Rouge! (20th Century Fox Home Entertainment), 2 discs

My Fair Lady (Warner Bros.), "Two-Disc Special Edition"

My Own Private Idaho (The Criterion Collection), 2 discs

Norman McLaren: The Collector's Edition (Milestone), 2 discs

North by Northwest (Warner Bros.), 1 disc

Oklahoma! (20th Century Fox Home Entertainment), "50th Anniversary Edition," 2 discs

Pickpocket (The Criterion Collection), 1 disc

Pulp Fiction (Miramax Home Entertainment), "Collector's Edition," 2 discs

Rosemary's Baby (Paramount), 1 disc

Russian Ark (Wellspring), 1 disc

Saturday Night Fever (Paramount), "25th Anniversary DVD Edition," 1 disc

Scream (Dimension Home Video), "The Ultimate Scream Collection," 4 discs

The Searchers (Warner Home Video), "Ultimate Collector's Edition," 2 discs

Seven Men from Now (Paramount), "Special Collector's Edition," 1 disc

The Silence of the Lambs (Metro-Goldwyn-Mayer), "Special Edition," 1 disc

Silverado (Sony Pictures Home Entertainment), 2 discs

Sin City (Dimension), 2 discs

Singin' in the Rain (Warner Bros.), "Two-Disc Special Edition"

Speed (20th Century Fox Home Entertainment), "Five Star Collection," 2 discs

Terminator 2: Judgment Day (Artisan), "Extreme DVD," 2 discs

Titus (20th Century Fox Home Entertinment), 2 discs

Toy Story/Toy Story 2 (Disney/Pixar), "Collector's Edition: The Ultimate Toy Box," 3 discs

20,000 Leagues Under the Sea (Disney), "Special Edition," 2 discs

Wallace & Gromit: The Curse of the Were-Rabbit (DreamWorks), 1 disc

War of the Worlds (2005) (DreamWorks Home Entertainment), "Two-Disc Limited Edition"

abstract form   A type of filmic organization in which the parts relate to one another through repetition and variation of such visual qualities as shape, color, rhythm, and direction of movement.

Academy ratio   The standardized shape of the film frame established by the Academy of Motion Picture Arts and Sciences. In the original ratio, the frame was $1^1/_3$ times as wide as it was high (1.33:1); later the width was normalized at 1.85 times the height (1.85:1).

aerial perspective   A cue for suggesting depth in the image by presenting objects in the distance less distinctly than those in the foreground.

anamorphic lens   A lens for making widescreen films using regular *Academy ratio* frame size. The camera lens takes in a wide field of view and squeezes it onto the frame, and a similar projector lens unsqueezes the image onto a wide theater screen.

angle of framing   The position of the frame in relation to the subject it shows: above it, looking down (a high angle); horizontal, on the same level (a straight-on angle); looking up (a low angle). Also called camera angle.

animation   Any process whereby artificial movement is created by photographing a series of drawings (see also *cel animation*), objects, or computer images one by one. Small changes in position, recorded frame by frame, create the illusion of movement.

aspect ratio   The relationship of the frame's width to its height. The standard *Academy ratio* is currently 1.85:1.

associational form   A type of organization in which the film's parts are juxtaposed to suggest similarities, contrasts, concepts, emotions, and expressive qualities.

asynchronous sound   Sound that is not matched temporally with the movements occurring in the image, as when dialogue is out of synchronization with lip movements.

auteur   The presumed or actual author of a film, usually identified as the director. Also sometimes used in an evaluative sense to distinguish good filmmakers (*auteurs*) from bad ones.

axis of action   In the *continuity editing* system, the imaginary line that passes from side to side through the main actors, defining the spatial relations of all the elements of the scene as being to the right or left. The camera is not supposed to cross the axis at a cut and thus reverse those spatial relations. Also called the 180° line. (See also *180° system*.)

backlighting   Illumination cast onto the figures in the scene from the side opposite the camera, usually creating a thin outline of highlighting on those figures.

boom   A pole upon which a microphone can be suspended above the scene being filmed and that is used to change the microphone's position as the action shifts.

camera angle   See *angle of framing*.

canted framing   A view in which the frame is not level; either the right or the left side is lower than the other, causing objects in the scene to appear slanted out of an upright position.

categorical form   A type of filmic organization in which the parts treat distinct subsets of a topic. For example, a film about the United States might be organized into 50 parts, each devoted to a state.

cel animation   Animation that uses a series of drawings on pieces of celluloid, called *cels* for short. Slight changes between the drawings combine to create an illusion of movement.

CGI   Computer-generated imagery: using digital software systems to create figures, settings, or other material in the frame.

cheat cut   In the *continuity editing* system, a cut that presents continuous time from shot to shot but that mismatches the positions of figures or objects.

cinematography   A general term for all the manipulations of the film strip by the camera in the shooting phase and by the laboratory in the developing phase.

close-up   A framing in which the scale of the object shown is relatively large; most commonly a person's head seen from the neck up, or an object of a comparable size that fills most of the screen.

closure   The degree to which the ending of a narrative film reveals the effects of all the causal events and resolves (or "closes off") all lines of action.

continuity editing   A system of cutting to maintain continuous and clear narrative action. Continuity editing relies on matching screen direction, position, and temporal relations from shot to shot. For specific techniques of continuity editing, see *axis of action, crosscutting, cut-in, establishing shot, eyeline match, match on action, reestablishing shot, screen direction, shot/reverse shot*.

contrast   In cinematography, the difference between the brightest and darkest areas within the frame.

crane shot   A shot with a change in framing accomplished by placing the camera above the subject and moving through the air in any direction.

crosscutting   Editing that alternates shots of two or more lines of action occurring in different places, usually simultaneously.

cut   1. In filmmaking, the joining of two strips of film together with a splice. 2. In the finished film, an instantaneous change from one framing to another. See also *jump cut*.

cut-in   An instantaneous shift from a distant framing to a closer view of some portion of the same space.

deep focus   A use of the camera lens and lighting that keeps objects in both close and distant planes in sharp focus.

deep space   An arrangement of mise-en-scene elements so that there is a considerable distance between the plane closest to the camera and the one farthest away. Any or all of these planes may be in focus. (See *shallow space*.)

depth of field   The measurements of the closest and farthest planes in front of the camera lens between which everything will be in sharp focus. A depth of field from 5 to 16 feet, for example, would mean everything closer than 5 feet and farther than 16 feet would be out of focus.

dialogue overlap   In editing a scene, arranging the cut so that a bit of dialogue coming from shot A is heard under a shot that shows another character or another element in the scene.

diegesis   In a narrative film, the world of the film's story. The diegesis includes events that are presumed to have occurred and actions and spaces not shown onscreen. See also *diegetic sound, nondiegetic insert, nondiegetic sound.*

diegetic sound   Any voice, musical passage, or sound effect presented as originating from a source within the film's world. See also *nondiegetic sound.*

direct sound   Music, noise, and speech recorded from the event at the moment of filming; opposite of *postsynchronization.*

discontinuity editing   Any alternative system of joining shots together using techniques unacceptable within *continuity editing* principles. Possibilities would include mismatching of temporal and spatial relations, violations of the *axis of action*, and concentration on graphic relationships. See also *elliptical editing, graphic match, intellectual montage, jump cut, nondiegetic insert, overlapping editing.*

dissolve   A transition between two shots during which the first image gradually disappears while the second image gradually appears; for a moment the two images blend in *superimposition.*

distance of framing   The apparent distance of the frame from the mise-en-scene elements. Also called camera distance and shot scale. See also *close-up, extreme close-up, extreme long shot, medium close-up, medium shot, plan américain.*

distribution   One of the three branches of the film industry; the process of marketing the film and supplying copies to exhibition venues. See also *exhibition, production.*

dolly   A camera support with wheels, used in making *tracking shots.*

dubbing   The process of replacing part or all of the voices on the sound track in order to correct mistakes or rerecord dialogue. See also *postsynchronization.*

duration   In a narrative film, the aspect of temporal manipulation that involves the time span presented in the *plot* and assumed to operate in the *story.* See also *frequency, order.*

editing   1. In filmmaking, the task of selecting and joining camera takes. 2. In the finished film, the set of techniques that governs the relations among shots.

ellipsis   In a narrative film, the shortening of *plot* duration achieved by omitting some *story* duration. See also *elliptical editing, viewing time.*

elliptical editing   Shot transitions that omit parts of an event, causing an *ellipsis* in plot duration.

establishing shot   A shot, usually involving a distant framing, that shows the spatial relations among the important figures, objects, and setting in a scene.

exhibition   One of the three branches of the film industry; the process of showing the finished film to audiences. See also *distribution, production.*

exposure   The adjustment of the camera mechanism in order to control how much light strikes each frame of film passing through the aperture.

external diegetic sound   Sound represented as coming from a physical source within the story space that we assume characters in the scene also hear. See also *internal diegetic sound.*

extreme close-up   A framing in which the scale of the object shown is very large; most commonly, a small object or a part of the body.

extreme long shot   A framing in which the scale of the object shown is very small; a building, landscape, or crowd of people will fill the screen.

eyeline match   A cut obeying the *axis of action* principle, in which the first shot shows a person looking off in one direction and the second shows a nearby space containing what he or she sees. If the person looks left, the following shot should imply that the looker is offscreen right.

fade   1. *Fade-in:* a dark screen that gradually brightens as a shot appears. 2. *Fade-out:* a shot gradually disappears as the screen darkens. Occasionally, fade-outs brighten to pure white or to a color.

fill light   Illumination from a source less bright than the *key light*, used to soften deep shadows in a scene. See also *three-point lighting.*

film noir   "Dark film," a term applied by French critics to a type of American film, usually in the detective or thriller genres, with low-key lighting and a somber mood.

film stock   The strip of material upon which a series of still photographs is registered; it consists of a clear base coated on one side with a light-sensitive emulsion.

filter   A piece of glass or gelatin placed in front of the camera or printer lens to alter the quality or quantity of light striking the film in the aperture.

flashback   An alteration of story order in which the plot moves back to show events that have taken place earlier than ones already shown.

flash-forward   An alteration of story order in which the plot presentation moves forward to future events and then returns to the present.

focal length   The distance from the center of the lens to the point at which the light rays meet in sharp focus. The focal length determines the perspective relations of the space represented on the flat screen. See also *normal lens, telephoto lens, wide-angle lens.*

focus   The degree to which light rays coming from the same part of an object through different parts of the lens reconverge at the same point on the film frame, creating sharp outlines and distinct textures.

following shot   A shot with framing that shifts to keep a moving figure onscreen.

form   The overall system of relationships among the parts of a film.

frame   A single image on the strip of film. When a series of frames is projected onto a screen in quick succession, an illusion of movement is created.

framing   The use of the edges of the film frame to select and to compose what will be visible onscreen.

frequency   In a narrative film, the aspect of temporal manipulation that involves the number of times any *story* event is shown in the *plot.* See also *duration, order.*

front projection   Composite process whereby footage meant to appear as the background of a shot is projected from the front onto a screen; figures in the foreground are filmed in front of the screen as well. This is the opposite of *rear projection.*

frontal lighting   Illumination directed into the scene from a position near the camera.

frontality   In staging, the positioning of figures so that they face the viewer.

function   The role or effect of any element within the film's form.

gauge   The width of the film strip, measured in millimeters.

genres   Various types of films that audiences and filmmakers recognize by their familiar narrative conventions. Common genres are musical, gangster, and science fiction films.

graphic match   Two successive shots joined so as to create a strong similarity of compositional elements (e.g., color, shape).

hand-held camera   The use of the camera operator's body as a camera support, either holding it by hand or using a harness.

hard lighting   Illumination that creates sharp-edged shadows.

height of framing   The distance of the camera above the ground, regardless of the *angle of framing*.

high-key lighting   Illumination that creates comparatively little contrast between the light and dark areas of the shot. Shadows are fairly transparent and brightened by *fill light*.

ideology   A relatively coherent system of values, beliefs, or ideas shared by some social group and often taken for granted as natural or inherently true.

intellectual montage   The juxtaposition of a series of images to create an abstract idea not present in any one image.

internal diegetic sound   Sound represented as coming from the mind of a character within the story space. Although we and the character can hear it, we assume that the other characters cannot. See also *external diegetic sound*.

interpretation   The viewer's activity of analyzing the implicit and symptomatic meanings suggested in a film. See also *meaning*.

iris   A round, moving *mask* that can close down to end a scene (iris-out) or emphasize a detail, or that can open to begin a scene (iris-in) or to reveal more space around a detail.

jump cut   An elliptical cut that appears to be an interruption of a single shot. Either the figures seem to change instantly against a constant background, or the background changes instantly while the figures remain constant. See also *ellipsis*.

key light   In the three-point lighting system, the brightest illumination coming into the scene. See also *backlighting, fill light, three-point lighting*.

lens   A shaped piece of transparent material (usually glass) with either or both sides curved to gather and focus light rays. Most camera and projector lenses place a series of lenses within a metal tube to form a compound lens.

linearity   In a narrative, the clear motivation of a series of causes and effects that progress without significant digressions, delays, or irrelevant actions.

long shot   A framing in which the scale of the object shown is small; a standing human figure would appear nearly the height of the screen.

long take   A shot that continues for an unusually lengthy time before the transition to the next shot.

low-key lighting   Illumination that creates strong contrast between light and dark areas of the shot, with deep shadows and little *fill light*.

mask   An opaque screen placed in the camera or printer that blocks part of the frame off and changes the shape of the photographed image, leaving part of the frame a solid color. As seen on the screen, most masks are black, although they can be white or colored.

masking   In exhibition, stretches of black fabric that frame the theater scene. Masking can be adjusted according to the *aspect ratio* of the film to be projected.

match on action   A continuity cut that splices two different views of the same action together at the same moment in the movement, making it seem to continue uninterrupted.

matte shot   A type of *process shot* in which different areas of the image (usually actors and setting) are photographed separately and combined in laboratory work.

meaning   1. *Referential meaning*: Allusion to particular items of knowledge outside the film that the viewer is expected to recognize. 2. *Explicit meaning*: Significance presented overtly, usually in language and often near the film's beginning or end. 3. *Implicit meaning*: Significance left tacit, for the viewer to discover upon analysis or reflection. 4. *Symptomatic meaning*: Significance that the film divulges, often against its will, by virtue of its historical or social context.

medium close-up   A framing in which the scale of the object shown is fairly large; a human figure seen from the chest up would fill most of the screen.

medium long shot   A framing at a distance that makes an object about four or five feet high appear to fill most of the screen vertically. See also *plan américain*, the special term for a medium long shot depicting human figures.

medium shot   A framing in which the scale of the object shown is of moderate size; a human figure seen from the waist up would fill most of the screen.

mise-en-scene   All of the elements placed in front of the camera to be photographed: the settings and props, lighting, costumes and makeup, and figure behavior.

mixing   Combining two or more sound tracks by recording them onto a single one.

mobile frame   The effect on the screen of the moving camera, a *zoom lens*, or certain *special effects*; the framing shifts in relation to the scene being photographed. See also *crane shot, pan, tilt, tracking shot*.

monochromatic color design   Color design that emphasizes a narrow set of shades of a single color.

montage   1. A synonym for *editing*. 2. An approach to editing developed by the Soviet filmmakers of the 1920s; it emphasizes dynamic, often discontinuous, relationships between shots and the juxtaposition of images to create ideas not present in either shot by itself. See also *discontinuity editing, intellectual montage*.

montage sequence   A segment of a film that summarizes a topic or compresses a passage of time into brief symbolic or typical images. Frequently *dissolves, fades, superimpositions*, and *wipes* are used to link the images in a montage sequence.

motif   An element in a film that is repeated in a significant way.

motion control   A computerized method of planning and repeating camera movements on miniatures, models, and process work.

motivation   The justification given in the film for the presence of an element. This may be an appeal to the viewer's knowledge of the real world, to genre conventions, to narrative causality, or to a stylistic pattern within the film.

narration   The process through which the *plot* conveys or withholds *story* information. The narration can be more or less restricted to character knowledge and more or less deep in presenting characters' mental perceptions and thoughts.

narrative form   A type of filmic organization in which the parts relate to one another through a series of causally related events taking place in time and space.

nondiegetic insert   A shot or series of shots cut into a sequence, showing objects that are represented as being outside the world of the narrative.

nondiegetic sound   Sound, such as mood music or a narrator's commentary, represented as coming from a source outside the space of the narrative.

nonsimultaneous sound   Diegetic sound that comes from a source in time either earlier or later than the images it accompanies.

normal lens   A lens that shows objects without severely exaggerating or reducing the depth of the scene's planes. In 35mm filming, a normal lens is 35 to 50mm. See also *telephoto lens, wide-angle lens.*

offscreen sound   Simultaneous sound from a source assumed to be in the space of the scene but outside what is visible onscreen.

offscreen space   The six areas blocked from being visible on the screen but still part of the space of the scene: to each side and above and below the frame, behind the set, and behind the camera. See also *space.*

180° system   The continuity approach to editing dictates that the camera should stay on one side of the action to ensure consistent left-right spatial relations between elements from shot to shot. The 180° line is the same as the *axis of action.* See also *continuity editing, screen direction.*

order   In a narrative film, the aspect of temporal manipulation that involves the sequence in which the chronological events of the *story* are arranged in the *plot.* See also *duration, frequency.*

overlap   A cue for suggesting represented depth in the film image by placing objects partly in front of more distant ones.

overlapping editing   Cuts that repeat part or all of an action, thus expanding its viewing time and plot duration.

pan   A camera movement with the camera body turning to the right or left. On the screen, it produces a mobile framing that scans the space horizontally.

pixillation   A form of single-frame animation in which three-dimensional objects, often people, are made to move in staccato bursts through the use of stop-action cinematography.

plan américain   A framing in which the scale of the object shown is moderately small; the human figure seen from the shins to the head would fill most of the screen. This is sometimes referred to as a *medium long shot*, especially when human figures are not shown.

plan-séquence   French term for a scene handled in a single shot, usually a *long take.*

plot   In a narrative film, all the events that are directly presented to us, including their causal relations, chronological order, duration, frequency, and spatial locations. Opposed to *story*, which is the viewer's imaginary construction of all the events in the narrative. See also *duration, ellipsis, frequency, order, viewing time.*

point-of-view shot (POV shot)   A shot taken with the camera placed approximately where the character's eyes would be, showing what the character would see; usually cut in before or after a shot of the character looking.

postsynchronization   The process of adding sound to images after they have been shot and assembled. This can include *dubbing* of voices, as well as inserting diegetic music or sound effects. It is the opposite of *direct sound.*

process shot   Any shot involving rephotography to combine two or more images into one or to create a special effect; also called composite shot. See also *matte shot, rear projection, special effects.*

production   One of the three branches of the film industry; the process of creating the film. See also *distribution, exhibition.*

racking focus   Shifting the area of sharp focus from one plane to another during a shot; the effect on the screen is called rack-focus.

rate   In shooting, the number of frames exposed per second; in projection, the number of frames thrown on the screen per second. If the two are the same, the speed of the action will appear normal, whereas a disparity will create slow or fast motion. The standard rate in sound cinema is 24 frames per second for both shooting and projection.

rear projection   A technique for combining a foreground action with a background action filmed earlier. The foreground is filmed in a studio, against a screen; the background imagery is projected from behind the screen. The opposite of *front projection.*

reestablishing shot   A return to a view of an entire space after a series of closer shots following the *establishing shot.*

reframing   Short panning or tilting movements to adjust for the figures' movements, keeping them onscreen or centered.

rhetorical form   A type of filmic organization in which the parts create and support an argument.

rhythm   The perceived rate and regularity of sounds, series of shots, and movements within the shots. Rhythmic factors include beat (or pulse), accent (or stress), and tempo (or pace).

rotoscope   A machine that projects live-action motion picture frames one by one onto a drawing pad so that an animator can trace the figures in each frame. The aim is to achieve more realistic movement in an animated film.

scene   A segment in a narrative film that takes place in one time and space or that uses crosscutting to show two or more simultaneous actions.

screen direction   The right-left relationships in a scene, set up in an establishing shot and determined by the position of characters and objects in the frame, by the directions of movement, and by the characters' eyelines. *Continuity editing* will attempt to keep screen direction consistent between shots. See also *axis of action, eyeline match, 180° system.*

segmentation   The process of dividing a film into parts for analysis.

sequence   Term commonly used for a moderately large segment of film, involving one complete stretch of action. In a narrative film, often equivalent to a *scene.*

shallow focus   A restricted *depth of field*, which keeps only one plane in sharp focus; the opposite of *deep focus.*

shallow space   Staging the action in relatively few planes of depth; the opposite of *deep space.*

shot   1. In shooting, one uninterrupted run of the camera to expose a series of frames. Also called a *take.* 2. In the finished film, one uninterrupted image, whether or not there is mobile framing.

shot/reverse shot   Two or more shots edited together that alternate characters, typically in a conversation situation. In *continuity editing*, characters in one framing usually look left, in the other framing, right. Over-the-shoulder framings are common in shot/reverse-shot editing.

side lighting   Lighting coming from one side of a person or an object, usually in order to create a sense of volume, to bring out surface tensions, or to fill in areas left shadowed by light from another source.

simultaneous sound Diegetic sound that is represented as occurring at the same time in the story as the image it accompanies.

size diminution A cue for suggesting represented depth in the image by showing objects that are farther away as smaller than foreground objects.

soft lighting Illumination that avoids harsh bright and dark areas, creating a gradual transition from highlights to shadows.

sound bridge 1. At the beginning of one scene, the sound from the previous scene carries over briefly before the sound from the new scene begins. 2. At the end of one scene, the sound from the next scene is heard, leading into that scene.

sound over Any sound that is not represented as coming from the space and time of the images on the screen. This includes both nondiegetic sounds and nonsimultaneous diegetic sound. See also *nondiegetic sound, nonsimultaneous sound*.

sound perspective The sense of a sound's position in space, yielded by volume, timbre, pitch, and, in stereophonic reproduction systems, binaural information.

space Most minimally, any film displays a two-dimensional graphic space, the flat composition of the image. In films that depict recognizable objects, figures, and locales, a three-dimensional space is represented as well. At any moment, three-dimensional space may be directly depicted, as onscreen space, or suggested, as *offscreen space*. In narrative film, we can also distinguish among story space, the locale of the totality of the action (whether shown or not), and plot space, the locales visibly and audibly represented in the scenes.

special effects A general term for various photographic manipulations that create fictitious spatial relations in the shot, such as *superimposition, matte shots*, and *rear projection*.

story In a narrative film, all the events that we see and hear, plus all those that we infer or assume to have occurred, arranged in their presumed causal relations, chronological order, duration, frequency, and spatial locations. Opposed to *plot*, which is the film's actual presentation of events in the story. See also *duration, ellipsis, frequency, order, space, viewing time*.

storyboard A tool used in planning film production, consisting of comic-strip-like drawings of individual shots or phases of shots with descriptions written below each drawing.

style The repeated and salient uses of film techniques characteristic of a single film or a group of films (for example, a filmmaker's work or a national movement).

superimposition The exposure of more than one image on the same film strip or in the same shot.

synchronous sound Sound that is matched temporally with the movements occurring in the images, as when dialogue corresponds to lip movements.

take In filmmaking, the shot produced by one uninterrupted run of the camera. One shot in the final film may be chosen from among several takes of the same action.

technique Any aspect of the film medium that can be chosen and manipulated in making a film.

telephoto lens A lens of long focal length that affects a scene's perspective by enlarging distant planes and making them seem close to the foreground planes. In 35mm filming, a lens of 75mm length or more. See also *normal lens, wide-angle lens*.

three-point lighting A common arrangement using three directions of light on a scene; from behind the subjects (*backlighting*), from one bright source (*key light*), and from a less bright source balancing the key light (*fill light*).

tilt A camera movement with the camera body swiveling upward or downward on a stationary support. It produces a mobile framing that scans the space vertically.

top lighting Lighting coming from above a person or an object, usually in order to outline the upper areas of the figure or to separate it more clearly from the background.

tracking shot A mobile framing that travels through space forward, backward, or laterally. See also *crane shot, pan*, and *tilt*.

typage A performance technique of Soviet Montage cinema. The actor's appearance and behavior are presented as typical of a social class or other group.

underlighting Illumination from a point below the figures in the scene.

unity The degree to which a film's parts relate systematically to each other and provide motivations for all the elements included.

variation In film form, the return of an element with notable changes.

viewing time The length of time it takes to watch a film when it is projected at the appropriate speed.

whip pan An extremely fast movement of the camera from side to side, which briefly causes the image to blur into a set of indistinct horizontal streaks. Often an imperceptible cut will join two whip pans to create a trick transition between scenes.

wide-angle lens A lens of short focal length that affects a scene's perspective by distorting straight lines near the edges of the frame and by exaggerating the distance between foreground and background planes. In 35mm filming, a wide-angle lens is 35mm or less. See also *normal lens, telephoto lens*.

wipe A transition between shots in which a line passes across the screen, eliminating one shot as it goes and replacing it with the next one.

zoom lens A lens with a focal length that can be changed during a shot. A shift toward the *telephoto* range enlarges the image and flattens its planes together, giving an impression of magnifying the scene's space, while a shift toward the *wide-angle* range does the opposite.

Grateful acknowledgement is made for use of the following:

Figure 1.14-1.15 Wisconsin Center for Film and Theater Research; **1.18** Courtesy Scott Sklenar, Rocky Gersbach, and Matt Rockwell of Star Cinema, Fitchburg, Wisconsin; **1.28-1.29** The Museum of Modern Art Film Stills Archive; **1.32** Wisconsin Center for Film and Theater Research; **1.43** Courtesy Keith Stern, McKellan.com; **1.46** Wisconsin Center for Film and Theater Research; **4.130** Courtesy of Norman McLaren with permission of the National Film Board of Canada; **5.35** Courtesy Ernie Gehr; **5.192-5.194** Courtesy Michael Snow; **6.38-6.39** Courtesy of Bruce Conner; **10.54-10.55** Courtesy J. J. Murphy; **10.73** The Museum of Modern Art Film Stills Archive; **10.77-10.90** Courtesy Bruce Conner; **10.93** Courtesy Norman McLaren with permission of the National Film Board of Canada; **11.43-11.61** *Tokyo Story* directed by Yasujiro Ozu, 1953 © 1953 Shochiku, Co., Ltd.; **12.1** George Eastman House; **12.35** The Museum of Modern Art Film Stills Archive; **12.36-12.37** Wisconsin Center for Film and Theater Research.

INDEX